The Making of Indigeneity, Curriculum History, and the Limits of Diversity

Conceptually rich and grounded in cutting-edge research, this book addresses the often-overlooked roles and implications of diversity and indigeneity in curriculum. Taking a multidisciplinary approach to the development of teacher education in Guatemala, López provides a historical and transnational understanding of how "indigenous" has been negotiated as a subject/object of scientific inquiry in education. Moving beyond the generally accepted "commonsense" markers of diversity such as race, gender, and ethnicity, López focuses on the often-ignored histories behind the development of these markers and the crucial implications these histories have in education—in Guatemala and beyond—today.

Ligia (Licho) López López is a researcher at the Melbourne Graduate School of Education-University of Melbourne, Australia.

Routledge Research in Educational Equality and Diversity

Books in the series include:

Youth & Inequality in Education
Global Actions in Youth Work
Dana Fusco and Michael Heathfield

Social Justice and Transformative Learning
Culture and Identity in the United States and South Africa
Edited by Saundra M. Tomlinson-Clarke and Darren L. Clarke

Race and Colorism in Education
Edited by Carla R. Monroe

Facilitating Educational Success for Migrant Farmworker Students in the U.S.
Edited by Patricia A. Pérez and Maria Estela Zarate

The Media War on Black Male Youth in Urban Education
Darius Prier

Educational Policy Goes to School
Case Studies on the Limitations and Possibilities of Educational Innovation
Edited by Gilberto Conchas and Michael Gottfried

The Making of Indigeneity, Curriculum History, and the Limits of Diversity
Ligia (Licho) López López

An Asset-Based Approach to the Education of Latinos
Understanding Gaps and Advances
Eugene E. Garcia and Mehmet Dali Öztürk

Whiteness, Pedagogy, and Youth in America
Critical Whiteness Studies in the Classroom
Samuel Jaye Tanner

The Making of Indigeneity, Curriculum History, and the Limits of Diversity

Ligia (Licho) López López

Routledge
Taylor & Francis Group
NEW YORK AND LONDON

First published 2018
by Routledge
711 Third Avenue, New York, NY 10017

and by Routledge
2 Park Square, Milton Park, Abingdon, Oxon, OX14 4RN

Routledge is an imprint of the Taylor & Francis Group, an informa business

© 2018 Taylor & Francis

The right of Ligia (Licho) López López to be identified as author of this work has been asserted by her in accordance with sections 77 and 78 of the Copyright, Designs and Patents Act 1988.

All rights reserved. No part of this book may be reprinted or reproduced or utilised in any form or by any electronic, mechanical, or other means, now known or hereafter invented, including photocopying and recording, or in any information storage or retrieval system, without permission in writing from the publishers.

Trademark notice: Product or corporate names may be trademarks or registered trademarks, and are used only for identification and explanation without intent to infringe.

Library of Congress Cataloguing-in-Publication Data
A catalog record for this book has been requested

ISBN: 978-1-138-22848-1 (hbk)
ISBN: 978-1-315-39242-4 (ebk)

Typeset in Sabon
by Apex CoVantage, LLC

Printed and bound by CPI Group (UK) Ltd, Croydon, CR0 4YY

Contents

Foreword by Edgar Esquit	xvii
List of Figures	xxi
List of Appendices	xxiii
Preface	xxv
Acknowledgements	xxix

0 Zero = Nothing = Everything: Recasting the "Indigenous" Subject in the Making 1

1 "The Indian Problem": Contouring the Retina and the Indian and Pre- and Post-War Educational and Social Policies Pro Diversity 33

2 Language Heritage(s) and the Role of "Indigenous" and "Non-Indigenous" Missionaries and Experts in Curricular Foundations 57

3 Anthropological Borders and the Performance of Diversity in Teacher Preparation Classrooms 95

4 Authoritarian Regimes in Reform and Fractal Curricular Possibilities in Protests 137

5 No Closure 167

Appendices 179
Index 225

Nab'ey taq tzij

Re wuj k'o pa qaq'a' wakami, nutzijoj chi chupam ri ruch'obïk, rusolik ri k'aslem nib'an, nisamajix Iximulew, xemestäx kan k'ïy b'anob'äl, nib'ïx chi ri achi'a' chuqa' ri ixoqi' yeb'ano' re samaj re', re ch'ob'onïk re', nikimestaj k'ïy chuxtäq k'iq'axan ri ojer kan. Ri k'ayewal man kanta ja ri nimestäx ri b'anatajnäq pe' ri ojer tzij wawe' Iximulew; chuqa' ni b'ïx chi ri mestanïk män känta ja ri' man ni natäx ta' ri ruxe'el ronojel ri k'ayewal xek'ulun ojer wawe Iximulew. Ri mestanïk, ri k'ayewal, ni b'ïx, noqa toq niqamestaj chi ri qasamajib'al, chi ri q'ijub'äl niqokisaj richin niqach'ob' rij ri k'aslem, k'o re toq ruximon ri', rik'in ri k'ayewal niqajo niqatur. Ruma ri' re ixöq xb'ano' re wuj re' nub'ij chiqe chi, ruk'amon wi niqaya ruq'ij ri samaj, ri ch'ob'onik b'anompe chi rij ri ojer k'aslem, po chuqa' -nub'ij- janila k'atzinel chi ni qanik'oj ri qasamajib'al. K'o chi niqatz'ët ri ruq'ajarik, k'o chi niqetamaj achike e nuk'uyun kan, akuchi' petenäq wi ri q'ijub'äl xkokisaj toq xb'ïx kan, ja samajib'äl re'. Ruma ri' k'o chi ni qa tz'ët üzt wi ri jalajöj q'ijub'äl niqokisaj yojruto' richin niqatowaj el ri k'ayewal qachajin, o chuqa xa man niqana ta toq k'ate' yeqanim ri qawinaq chupam ri poqonal.

Re wuj re' nutzijoj rij ri samaj kib'anon pe' ri achi'a' achi'el ri Daniel Brinton, Alberto Valdeavellano, Miguel Ángel Asturias, Antonio Goubad Carrera, Joaquin Noval, o xa ri Ramón González. Po man ruma ta ri', ri tzijonïk nib'an chupam re wuj re' manjun ta ruximon ri' rik'in ri samäj, ri ch'ob'onïk niqab'än röj wakami pa jalajöj taq jay, pa jalajöj taq tinamït. Ri samaj, ri ch'ob'onïk, qachapon richin niqasöl rij ri k'aslem; ri winaqi kichapon samaj richin nikïl rub'eyal ri kitijoxïk ri ak'uala', chub'lan ri yesamäj chi rij ri runuk'ik ri k'aslem pa Iximulew, rojonel ri q'ijub'äl niqab'än wakami, ruximon ri' rik'in ri samäj kib'anon kan la achi'a' xeqanataj qa nab'ey. Re wuj re' nuq'alajrisaj chi qawäch chi röj, chupam ri qasamäj k'ïy mul re, man xa xe ta niqanataj, man xa xe ta niqatzijoj rij ri rub'eyal ri kik'aslem ri winaqi'; chupam re wuj re' ni b'ïx chi röj rumak ri qa samäj k'o re toq yeqanim pa k'ayewal ri winaqi'. Ni b'ïx chi k'o re toq yeqato' ri winaqi', po k'o mul re toq ruma ri qaq'ijub'al, ri rub'eyal yoj ch'ob'on, xa yeqaxim riwinaqi' chupam ri k'ayewal, chupam ri poqonal.

Chupam re samaj re, ri Ligia López nu söl chiqawäch ri jalajöj tzijonïk b'anon pe' chi rij ri kik'aslem ri qawinaq wawe' Iximulew. Nu k'üt chi qawäch chi chupam ri ru k'isb'äl wo'o' k'al juna' q'axnäq kan k'ix samaj, k'ïy ch'ob'onïk xb'an chi rij ri ki k'aslem ri maya' winaqi' pan Iximulew. Re ixöq re' nu tzijoj chi qe' achike rub'eyal toq ri jalajöj ch'ob'onela', xkib'än re samäj, achike rub'eyal toq xkinuk' ri kitzij, achike kojqan chupa ri kina'ojib'al. Rija' nu b'ij chi ri samäj b'anon pe', nuk'un pe', achi'el jun b'ey, achi'el jun samajib'äl nokusäx richin yenuk', richin yetaqchi'ix ri winaqi', rije' xa choj yetojtob'ëx, achi'el taq chuxtäq ri nib'an xa b'a achike samaj chi kij. Rije' yeokisäx achi'el winaqi' echapon, eximon chupam ri samaj, chupam poqonal. Ri ixöq xtzib'an re wuj re', nub'ij chi ri rurayib'al rija' ja ri nretamaj ¿achike rub'anikil toq yenük' ri q'ijub'äl, achike rub'eyal toq nib'ïx, ja b'anob'äl re' tojqäx, ja re' ütz, re jun chik re' k'o ta rejqalen, k'o ta rik'atz; nrajo' nretamaj achike ruma toq ja rub'eyal ri xuk'waj ri ch'ob'onïk? Ri Ligia López nub'ij chi ri rusamaj man richin ta nutzeqelb'ej jun chi ke chi q'ijub'äl, jun chi ke ri tzijonem o xa winäq, nu b'ij chi nurayij rija' ja ri' nrïl ri rub'eyal ri samäj b'anon pe' chi kij ri qawinaq. Rija' nrajo' nretamaj achike ru b'eyal toq ri kiq'ijub'al, ri ki tzij ri ch'ob'onela', chi kij ri maya' winäq, janila ya'on ru q'ij. Achike ruma toq re q'ijub'äl re' k'a k'o na rejqalem, k'a k'o na retal chi rij ri ki k'aslem ri qawinaq.

Chupam re wuj re' ni qa tz'ët chi ri ch'ob'onïk b'anon pe chi rij ri kik'aslen ri qawinaq, chi rij ri kitijoxik ri alab'o', ri xtani', ri ak'wala', nuk'un chupam ri ojer q'ijunïk, ri xch'o chi rij ri ruq'ij ri kik'aslem ri qawinaq. Wakami chuqa' ju'ul chupa ri q'ijunïk nub'ij chi k'o chi niya' kiq'ij ri jalajöj taq tinamït, taq b'anob'äl ek'o wawe' Iximulew, ke ri' xa chuqa' chijun re ruwach'ulew. Re ka'i' rub'eyal q'ijunïk re', kitunub'an ki', junam ki xeel, ruma xa e nuk'un pe chupam ri kiq'ijub'al ri juley winaqi' echapayon ri Iximulew. K'o chiniqab'ij wawe' chi re q'ijub'ul re', nuya' ruq'ij ri jalajöj kib'anikil ri tinamït po man nuya ta' ruq'ij ri kirayib'al ri qawinaq, chi ja ta rije', chi kiwäch qa nikinük', nikik'waj ri kik'asalem. Re ch'ob'onela' re' nikib'ij chi qe chi röj oj maya' winaqi', chi roj oj ajpayu', chi roj oj meb'a, ruma ri' nib'ix chiqe' k'o chi niqajäl ri qab'anikil, ri qaq'ijub'äl richin keri' niqaqäxaj jun utziläj k'aslem. Ronojel re q'ijub'äl re', nïm rejqalem chi kiwäch ri ajpopi' wawe' Iximulew, chi kiwäch jujun, o xa k'ïy ch'ob'onela', po chuqa' niqa chi kiwäch jalajöj tijonela' ye samäj pa taq samajay. Re q'ijub'äl re', chuqa' ja xapon pa kiwi' chi konojel ri winäqi' wawe' Iximulew. Ruma ri' ch'ob'onela', chub'lan ri winaqi kichapon runuk'ik ri rub'eyal richin yetijöx ri xtani' kik'in ri alab'o' nikitij kiq'ij richin ni kinük' ri samäj chupam re q'ijub'äl re'. Rije' man yechame ta', rije' kichapon ri toqtob'enïk, ki chapon runik'oxik ri rub'eyal ri kiq'ijub'al, rikib'anob'al ri qawinaq. Ri nikajo' rije' ja ta ri nikïl ri rub'eyal ri qajalik röj maya' winaqi'.

Ri Ligia López nutzijoj rij ronojel re k'ayewal re'. Chi nu söl chiqawäch ri ruq'ijub'al, nrokisaj ri tzij (s)objets. Ri rusolik re tzij re', nub'ij rija', ja toq ri qawinaq yeyax pa jun tojtob'enïk, k'a ri' kan eqal eqal nikanöx rub'eyal richin nijal ri kib'anikil. K'ïy ch'ob'onela', nikib'än ri kisamaj rik'in ronojel ki k'u'x, rije nikajo' yekito', nikiya' ruq'ij ri kib'anob'al ri qawinaq. Po k'o mul re' ri kiq'ijub'al kejqan pe' janila k'ayewal ru k'ampe' pa kiwi' ri winaqi'. Re tzij (s)objets ja re nrokisaj ri Ligia López richin nu söl chiqawäch ri ruq'ajarik, ri ru nuk'ik nib'an chi rij ri kik'aslem ri qawinaq. Toq nib'an ri toqtob'enïk, ri ch'ob'onel nunük', nutzijoj achike rub'anikil ri chuxtäq, la xa ri kik'aslem ri winaqi' echapon kinik'oxik. Ni tz'ët chi' epetenäq wi, achike ru b'eyal toq xkib'os ki', achike rub'eyal toq xe chojmirisatäj, achike ruma' xjech'ejo' ri kik'aslen. Ja k'a re' toq ri ch'ob'onela' nikitzijoj, nikib'ij kan, ja re' kib'anikil re winaqi' re', ja re' kalaxik, ja re' ruq'ajarik ri ki k'aslem. Toq niqab'än re samaj re', roj ch'ob'onela' k'o re toq yeqato' ri winaqi', po k'o mul re toq yeqaya' pa k'ayewal.

¿Achike k'a ni b'e'el, achike k'a rejqalen ronojel re tzij re' chupam ri qasamaj röj ch'ob'onela', roj tijoxela'? Toq xinsik'ij re ruwuj ri Ligia López, k'a ja ri' xo qa pa nu jolom ri k'ayewal xutikirib'a' wawe' Iximulew, chi rukojol ri juna' 1946–1948, ri ch'ob'onel John Charles Cutler. Rija xeruya pa toqtob'enïk k'ïy winaqi e itzelan, achi'el ri achia' e tz'apäl pa che', winaqi taq emoxi', alab'o' ajpokob', chub'lan jalajöj taq ixoqi'. Rije', man xb'ix ta chi ke', man xk'utüx ta chi ke, man la ütz la, man la manäq la, toq xya' pa kich'akul jun itzel yab'il. Toq xk'ulwachitäj ronojel re', ri ch'ob'onela' xkib'ij chi ronojel ri samaj nikib'än, ronojel ri toqtob'enïk kichapon rik'in ri kich'akul ri ixoqi', ri achi'a', xa janila rejqalem chupam ri qak'aslem chi qonojel ri winaqi' chwäch re ruwach'ulew, xecha'. Toq chupam ri juna' 2010 xnab'ëx wawe' Iximulew re jun k'ayewal re', k'ïy winaqi', k'ïy ch'ob'onela' xe ch'ojin, xpe koyowal, rije' nikib'ij chi re jun samäj re' janila k'ayewal xuk'üm pe' pan Iximulew, re xa jun kamïk nqa chi qij qonojel ri winaqi' öj k'o chwäch re ruwach'ulew, xecha' rije'. Xb'ïx chi ri ch'ob'onela' xeb'ano re k'ayewal re' man jun kik'ix, manjun utziläj ki q'ijub'al, ruma xa rije' xkitz'uk tzij chi kiwäch ri winaqi' xekitz'ila'.

Wakami ninb'ij qa rïn chi, k'o rejqalen niqatzijoj rij ronojel re k'ayewal re', chi k'o etamab'äl nuya' kan chi qawäch. Toq niqab'enik'oj pe achike k'a ri xk'ulwachitäj ri kela' kan, ri juna' xeq'ax yan kan, niqatzët chi ri samäj ri', kan ru ximon wi ri' rik'in ri samäj qachapon roj wakami', toq niqab'anala' taq toqtob'enïk chi rij ri ki k'aslem ri qawinaq, toq niqajo niqatoqtob'ej achike ru b'eyal niqanuk' ri ki k'aslem ri ak'wala', ri alab'o', ri xtani' e k'o pa tijob'äl. Qitzij na wi chi röj, ri yojsamaj reke', ri niqach'öb rij ri k'aslem, man kan ta ki niqaju' ri yab'il pa kich'akul ri winaqi'. Qitzij na wi chi man ke ta ri yojsamäj röj, po chuqa' q'aläj wi chi toq niqach'öb achike tzij ni qokisaj, achike rub'eyal ni qatzijoj ri k'aslem, achike ruq'ajarik niqaya' ri kib'anob'al ri winaqi', toq niqab'än ronojel re', chuqa' k'o re' toq yeqaya' pa k'ayewal ri qawinaq. Röj chuqa' niqachäp, niqasaluj ri kik'aslem ri winaqi'.

Chi rukojol ronojel re tzij re', k'atzinel niqab'ij chi röj ch'obonela', kan ya'on wi qejqalem, ya'on ruq'ij ri qasamaj, rik'in jub'a' man junam ta ri qaq'ij ya'on chiqa jujunal po yojtikïr yoj samäj, ni nimäx ri qatzij. Ri winaqi yeqaya' pa toqtob'enik rije k'o re toq choj ye qakusaj, man niqaya' ta kiq'ij, man niya'öx ta kejqalem. Ri Ixöq xtz'ib'an re wuj niqatzjijoj rij, xu söl ronojel re k'ayewal re', ruma ri' nu b'ij chiqe chi toq rija' xujek' rij, toq rija xunik'oj ri kisamaj kib'anon pe' wawe' Iximulew ri jalajöj taq ch'ob'onela', chi rukol ri wok'al juna k'a ri ti q'ax kan, rija' janila k'ayewal xu tz'ët chi kipam ri samäj ri', nu b'ij chi ri ch'ob'onïk b'anon pe' k'o re' toq yekolon, po k'o mul re' toq yemakun. Ruma ri' rija' nub'ij chi qe röj, ri ch'ob'onela' qachapon samäj wakami, chi tiqatzu qi' chupam ri kisamaj ri ojer taq ch'ob'onela' wawe' Iximulew, ruma xa junam k'ayewal qachapon wakami. Rija nub'ij chi tiqelesaj qa na'oj chikij ri samaj xeb'an ri ojer kan, ti qa tzu' jeb'ël wi ri rub'eyal niqab'än che ri qasamaj wakami, wi ri rub'anikil niqatzijoj ri kik'aslem ri winaqi' pa ruchojmilal, o xa nqoyoj rik'ayewal pa kiwi', pa kik'aslem ri qawinaq. Rija' yojrunim, nub'ij chi qe chi tiqatz'eta' jeb'ël achike ri qachapon rub'anikil, ri qachapon ruch'ob'ik.

Chupam ri ruk'isb'äl wo'o' k'al q'axnäq kan, xb'ïx chi ri ch'ob'onïk, chi ri kitijoxik ri ak'wala', ri xtani', ri alab'o', tikirel nujäl ri kik'aslem, tikirel yojruto' chupam ri k'ayewal qachajin; kan ke wi ri ru b'anikil, man k'o ta' junchik rub'eyal xb'ix chi qe'. Ruma ri' wäkami kan b'anon che re' chi ke ri rub'anikil, chi man jun chike ta, chi k'o chi niqab'än ri samaj, k'o chi niqab'än ronojel ri k'atzinel chi nichojmir ri kik'aslem ri alab'o', ri xtani', ri ixoqi', konojel ri qawinaq. Po chuqa' xb'ïx chi qe' chi ronojel re' samäj niqab'än pa rub'i ri tinamït Iximulew niqaya' wi'. Nib'ix chi k'atzinel, ruma xa ri qawinaq kan k'ayew kib'anon, chi man pa ruchojmil ta kik'wan ri kik'aslem. Nib'ix chi ri rayil, ri poqonal kichajin tikirel nik'is wi rije' nikitzeqelb'ej ri qitzij rub'eyal ri k'aslem. Ruma ri' nib'ïx k'o chi nikojqaj ri k'aslem nib'an, ri nuk'un pe juk'an ya, juk'an ulew. Chi kikojol k'a ronojel re tzij re', wakami nib'ix chi wawe' Iximulew k'o chi niya'x kiq'ij ri jalajoj kib'anikil ri winaqi', ri molaj, chub'lan ri jalajöj taq tinamït junan qak'wan qi. Toq nitzijox ronojel re b'anobal re', chuqa nib'ix chi qe' chi ri qawinaq kichapon rusachik ri ojer b'anob'al, ri ojer k'aslem (achi'el ri kich'ab'al), ruma ri' -ni b'ïx chi qe'- k'o chi nqetamaj jun chik mul ri qach'ab'al, k'o chi nqetamaj yojok qitzij aj mayib'. Po chuqa nib'ïx, niq'ijux, chi ri qawinaq k'o chi niketamaj yek'ase' chupam ri amaq Iximulew, chi män ruma ta' ri jalajoj qab'anikil, män ruma ta ri' xtiqayuj, xtiqasach ri rub'eyal, ri rub'anikil ru k'amon pe, ri amaq Iximulew.

Kan kewi re' rub'anikil, kan kewi re' rub'eyal ri ch'ob'onik b'anom pe', ruma ri' ri ixoq xnuk'u re wuj re' nub'ij chi qe', yojrupixab'aj, yojrutäqchij chi tiqaya' ru q'ij ri samaj b'anompe', chi tiqaya' chuqa ruq'ij ri samäj qa chapon roj wakami. Po chi kikojol ronojel re tzij re', chuqa nub'ij chi qe', chi tiqajaqa' ütz ri pa qawa', chi ke ri' niqatz'ët jeb'ël ri reqalem, chub'lan ri ruq'ajarik qayo'on ri qasamäj. Nu b'ij chi qe', ütz, kix samäj, män kix pae kan chi ri', man ti torij el ri samäj ichapom pe' chirij ri kik'aslen ri maya' winäqi', po chuqa' nub'ij, ti nik'oj ütz ri samaj ichapon, ti kamluj, tiq'ijuj ütz, chi ke ri' yix tikir nitzet ri k'ayewal, ri poqonal ruk'amon pe', reqan pe ri ch'ob'onik ichapon. Nu b'ij, ti tz'eta ütz ri samaj ruma k'ib'a' jachik rix xkixkamlun, xtitemej, ri k'ayewal kiyo'on ri b'eyoma', ri kaxlani', ri aj pokob', ri nimalaj ajpopi' pa kiwi ri maya' winaqi'. Re rusamaj ri Ligia López nu q'alajrisaj kan chi qa wa' chi k'o janila samaj, janila k'ayewal xti qatz'ët, xtiqil chupa' ri b'ey qachapon, richin nyox ru q'ij ri jalajöj b'anob'al, q'ijub'äl, rayb'äl, wawe' Iximulew, po chuqa juley chik tinamït. Chupam re wuj re', Ligia López nutzijoj chiqe achike' rub'eyal rub'anon pe' ri qak'aslem, ri kitijoxik ri ak'wala' wawe' Iximulew. Pa ru k'isb'äl ru xaq re wuj, pa ruk'isb'äl taq tzij, ri ixoq nuq'alajrisaj chi qa wa' chi re samäj xu tz'ib'aj ruk'wan ri' rik'in ronojel ri ch'ob'onik b'anon kan ri ojer. Rija' nub'ij chi re samaj re' kan man k'isel ta', po achi'el jun ixoq nib'ano' pach'un tzij, ri Ligia López k'o chi nuya' kan ruchi ri rutzij, k'o chi nichame', k'iy k'a tzij re' man xeb'ix ta', man xetzijox ta'. Ruma k'a ri' wakami toq re samaj re' k'o pa qaq'a', tiqatojtob'ej yojtzijon rik'in re ixoq re', tiqa ch'ob'o' ri ru tzij, tiqa tzu k'a' achike' ri nub'ij, achike' nrewaj, achike' b'anob'al nutemej, achike' k'ayewal ru chajin. Pa qaq'a' k'o wi rutzijoxik ri reqalem re samaj re', pa qaq'a' ko wi' ru b'ixik achike' ru k'amompe' pa kikaslem ri qawinaq, wu nikajin, wu nitoo'n, achike' rub'eyal nutzijoj rij ri jalajöj kik'aslem ri qawinaq, ri ajiximulew, ri ch'ob'onela', ri tijonela' chub'lan ri tijoxela'. Chupam ronojel re tzijonen re' k'atzinel chi ni qanim qi' roj, k'o chi niqatzijoj rij ri qasamaj, ri qach'ob'onik. Ruma' k'a ri' chikonojel ta k'a ri samäj, ri ch'ob'onik xkeb'os pe', jun kere', jun kela', xtikil ta kik'ojlib'al (chi na' wi'). Re ixoq xtzib'an re wuj re' yoj ru nim k'a' chi niqa q'ijuj, niqachik'aj jun chik ru b'eyal ri samäj, ri ch'ob'ïk, ma ri' chi nuk'isb'ej ri rusamäj, rija' nu b'än kan jun k'isb'el k'utunik, rija nrajo nretamaj ¿achike k'a b'ey xtiqa jäq, achike k'a b'ey xtiqa chäp wakami'?

Edgar Esquit
San Carlos nimatijob'äl chi Iximulew

Prólogo

En este libro se apunta que tanto en las ciencias sociales como en las de educación que se practican en Guatemala se sufre de amnesia histórica, sin embargo, se advierte que esta pérdida de memoria no está vinculada exactamente al olvido de los hechos del pasado y su impacto en los procesos sociales que se viven en la actualidad. En cambio, se considera que la distracción se encuentra en el hecho de que no nos damos cuenta que, ciertas herramientas prácticas, ideas y deseos a partir de los cuales trabajamos, son portadores o mantienen legados que muchas veces reproducen los sistemas de dominación que queremos contradecir. En este sentido, se nos invita a valorar los trabajos académicos y políticos desarrollados hasta este momento, pero, también se nos incita a dudar de nuestras propias herramientas de indagación y acción, así como de los planteamientos teóricos y políticos que buscaron y buscan la estabilidad.

De acuerdo a esta argumentación, aunque este trabajo alude a la actividad de investigación o los discursos de personajes específicos como Daniel Brinton, Alberto Valdeavellano, Miguel Ángel Asturias, Antonio Goubad Carrera, Joaquin Noval o Ramón González, la discusión que se realiza nos incumbe a todos. Es decir, a los hombres y mujeres que nos dedicamos a la investigación, al trabajo en educación y a los que de alguna manera intervenimos en la definición de políticas públicas, desde diferentes lugares y en distintos momentos. Esta indagación, nos muestra la capacidad que tenemos de modelar imágenes, palabras, políticas, leyes y pensamientos a través de los cuales terminamos gestionando la identidad e incluso la vida de personas que al ser sometidas a nuestros marcos y herramientas de trabajo pasan a formar parte del espacio útil que nos requiere la política, la ciencia y la nación.

En este escrito Ligia López nos presenta su indagación sobre los diferentes modos en que *lo indígena* ha sido discutido en Guatemala, a lo largo del siglo XX, es decir, a través del trabajo o los escritos de antropólogos, historiadores, sociólogos o educadores. Pero aún más, nos muestra cómo los pensamientos generados en estos procesos tienen un lugar importante en la reproducción de teorías, políticas, pedagogías, metodologías y estrategias que sirven para modelar la vida de esos mismos seres que han sido o siguen siendo manipulados como materiales de un laboratorio o como cuerpos conducidos y usados en un régimen colonial. En este sentido, plantea que su propósito es reconocer cómo se construyen las fronteras o se delimitan las ideas, las cosas o las personas y de qué manera son colocados dentro de un orden que posibilita el acercamiento hacia ellos. Plantea que su trabajo no está hecho con el afán de vincularse o avalar alguna de estas discusiones sino más bien su interés central es localizar los patrimonios de la teoría sobre lo indígena y explicar cómo estos, en la práctica, siguen influyendo sobre las vidas de esos seres definidos como indígenas, atrasados, rurales, discriminados u oprimidos.

Se puede observar que los dos momentos sobresalientes en esta relación entre teorización y el trabajo por llevar a la práctica la educación de los indígenas, se ubican en el tiempo del indigenismo y del multiculturalismo e interculturalismo. Ellos forman parte del proyecto general liberal y neoliberal que se ha producido en el siglo XX así, la creación de lo indígena está vinculado a la reproducción de las ideas sobre progreso y desarrollo que se han establecido en esta centuria. Es notable que las dos perspectivas, cada una en su momento, tuvieron y tienen un lugar privilegiado en el pensamiento y acción de funcionarios, académicos, políticos e incluso tienen un lugar en las mentes de la población en general quienes aprueban, de una u otra forma, las ideas y las acciones que se ejecutan desde ellas en educación. De esta forma, podemos ver que tanto en el momento del indigenismo como el actual tiempo del interculturalismo, los investigadores desplegaron gran parte de sus energías usando los modelos propuestos y los que ellos inventaron para analizar la vida indígena, con el propósito de crear conocimiento útil para tratar a los indígenas y a los estudiantes.

Esto sería lo mismo en las palabras de la autora cuando afirma que los indígenas se vuelven (s)objects de investigación con el fin de buscar los mecanismos para controlarlos, ayudarlos, para cambiarlos, admirarlos o emularlos. Cuando las disciplinas académicas intentan formular conocimientos producen (s)objects mediante procesos complejos que permiten la observación y manipulación de ideas, cosas y personas. Además, a través de la actividad indagatoria se intenta decir cuáles son los atributos del material investigado y al mismo tiempo se busca su regularidad. A través de este proceso se va reduciendo y fijando lo indígena, considerándose como algo claramente definido y por eso manipulable. Como es claro todo ello sucede a partir de condiciones específicas y usando un instrumental minuciosamente construido. No obstante, esas fijaciones son difíciles de sostener porque el movimiento de las personas o la transformación de las cosas y las ideas son constantes, así se establecen otras relaciones que al final provocan nuevas investigaciones, fijaciones e intervenciones.

¿Qué significa todo esto en nuestra actividad como investigadores sociales o como educadores? Mientras leía este escrito, varias veces vino a mi mente el caso de los experimentos que John Charles Cutler dirigió en Guatemala entre los años de 1946 y 1948. Como sabemos, en ese entonces, seres humanos definidos como anormales o bajo el control de las instituciones guatemaltecas (reos, pacientes psiquiátricos, soldados y prostitutas) fueron inoculados directamente con sífilis, sin su aprobación. En su tiempo, esta actividad fue justificada afirmándose que hombres y mujeres eran sacrificados en bien de la humanidad o de las naciones. Cuando este hecho fue conocido en Guatemala, en el año 2010, muchos intelectuales se indignaron y consideraron el suceso como un crimen contra la humanidad. La mayor parte de las discusiones sobre este caso estuvieron centradas en el problema ético y el de salud de las personas que fueron engañadas y sometidas al realizarse estos ensayos.

No es exagerado traer a la discusión este caso porque los experimentos médicos que manipulan la vida de seres humanos, de forma legal o ilegal, pueden servirnos para ver reflejado nuestro trabajo en las ciencias sociales y en las de educación. Al compararlas es posible observar las complejas y múltiples implicaciones de nuestra actividad indagatoria con la gente en diferentes lugares. Aunque los científicos sociales y educadores no inyectamos sustancias peligrosas en los cuerpos de personas, nosotros también estamos involucrados en la manipulación de la vida de seres humanos a través de nuestros conceptos, marcos analíticos, conclusiones y acciones en las aulas y en las comunidades. Como sabemos nuestra posición en los contextos sociales, en los que desarrollamos nuestro trabajo siempre es privilegiado frente a nuestros sujetos-objetos de estudio que, persistentemente, son colocados en un lugar subalterno. La autora de este libro nos invita no solamente a ver de manera rápida los espejos (los trabajos de los antropólogos, educadores, burócratas que trabajaron la educación de los indígenas en el siglo XX) sino, a detenernos para observar nuestras propias imágenes en ellas y ver con detalle nuestro reflejo. A través de esta acción podremos analizar con precisión las formas en que procedemos, las consecuencias de nuestras conclusiones y los resultados de las acciones que desarrollamos en la práctica indagatoria y educativa.

A lo largo del siglo XX ha sido normal pensar que desde la ciencia y la actividad educativa se podría resolver el *problema indígena* los *derechos de los pueblos indígenas* o la *diversidad cultural en el Estado y nación guatemalteca*. En este sentido, ha sido normal la manipulación de la vida de los jóvenes, las mujeres, los indígenas, de los campesinos o de la gente que vive en las regiones rurales teniendo en mente el bien de la nación. De una u otra manera, se piensa que estas personas y lugares al ser *subdesarrollados*, *atrasados*, o estar lejos de las ciudades, necesariamente, deben ser llevados a la centralidad del mundo urbano moderno guatemalteco o mundial. A partir de las nuevas teorías sobre multiculturalismo e interculturalismo, también se ha normalizado la idea de que los indígenas deben ser instruidos en su propia cultura porque están perdiendo idiomas, trajes, tradiciones o religión. Se considera que, sin perder su cultura, les corresponde aprender a vivir en la nación y el Estado, es decir, sin cuestionarlas o disputarlas desde esas otras formas de existir que han sido históricas, lo que es lo mismo, deben aprender a *vivir la diversidad en la unidad*.

En nuestro tiempo ha sido normal trabajar o indagar desde estas perspectivas, pero, frente a ello, la autora de este escrito nos invita a desarrollar un doble movimiento de afirmación y crítica. Uno que no nos lleve al quietismo o a desechar nuestro propio trabajo y la experiencia en la indagación sobre la vida social y otro que nos permita visualizar y combatir la reproducción de los sistemas de dominación en nuestras indagaciones, metodologías, conclusiones y nociones generales sobre la vida social. Es aquí en donde se inscriben o deben ser registradas, tanto la producción de nuevos conocimientos desde lugares hegemónicos, como las universidades de Estados Unidos o de Guatemala, cada cual en su contexto. Así como aquellos otros sistemas de producción de conocimientos que existen en diversas partes del planeta y que, aún si son negados, están allí generando mundos y formas de vida. Este trabajo nos advierte que los esfuerzos hacia la pluralidad también necesitan ser reflexionados.

A través de este libro Ligia López nos entrega una historia sobre los indígenas y sobre la educación en Guatemala. Para decirnos que su trabajo también está inscrito en la misma historia que nos narra, al final del texto la autora afirma que el trabajo no está terminado. Ahora que este trabajo está en nuestras manos procuraremos conversar con ella, a partir de los argumentos que nos presenta, los que esconde entre líneas, sus complicidades, las brechas que ha abierto y tomando en cuenta las fronteras que ella misma y su contexto se han impuesto. A los lectores nos incumbe hablar, sobre las implicaciones de su trabajo, es decir, sobre cómo éste toca las vidas de los humanos y las comunidades que de manera compleja, acaba representando en este escrito ya sean indígenas, guatemaltecos, académicos, maestros o estudiantes. En este proceso también se sumarán nuestras propias indagaciones y acciones que como fractales tendrán un lugar (cualquiera sea éste) y contribuirán a darle forma tan diversa a la vida, en lugares determinados e indeterminados. A estas acciones y a muchas otras aún no imaginadas, son a las que nos anima la última pregunta de la autora, ¿y ahora qué sigue?

Edgar Esquit
Universidad de San Carlos de Guatemala

Foreword

This book points out that both the social sciences and education, as they are practiced in Guatemala, suffer from historical amnesia. At the same time, it warns us that this historical amnesia is not directly linked to forgetting the past and its impact on social processes as they are lived in the present. In turn, it points out, the distraction resides in the fact that we do not realize that certain practical tools and desires from which we work, carry, or maintain legacies oftentimes reproduce the systems of domination that we aim to contradict. In this sense, we are invited to evaluate the works of academics and politicians developed up to now. Moreover, we are urged to question our own tools and actions of inquiry as well as our theoretical and political approaches that have sought and still seek stability.

Regarding that discussion, although the book refers to the specific work of figures such as Daniel Brinton, Alberto Valdeavellano, Miguel Ángel Asturias, Antonio Goubad Carrera, Joaquin Noval, and Ramón González, the discussion in the text concerns every one of us. That is, the men and women like us who are dedicated to research and educational work and who in one way or another intervene in defining public policy from multiple places and moments. The inquiry in this book shows us the capacity we have to shape images, words, policies, laws, and thoughts, through which we end up negotiating identity and even the lives of people who, when subjected to our frames and work tools, become part of the useful space that politics, science, and the nation demand.

In this manuscript, Ligia López presents to us an inquiry on the multiple modes in which *lo indígena* (indigeneity) has been discussed in Guatemala, during the twentieth century through the writings and works of anthropologists, historians, sociologists, and educators. More specifically, it shows us how the styles of thought generated through their work have a crucial place in the reproduction of theories, policies, pedagogies, methodologies, and strategies and in shaping the lives of the very beings that have been and continue to be manipulated like materials in a laboratory or as bodies exploited by a colonial regime. In that sense, the purpose of the text is to recognize and question how borders are constructed and ideas, things, and people are defined and the ways in which they are situated in a system that allows them to be studied.

The author argues that her work is not meant to join or endorse these discussions, but rather that her central interest is to locate the heritages of theories about *lo indígena* and explain how these, in practice, continue to influence the lives of those defined as indigenous, underdeveloped, rural, disadvantaged, and oppressed.

We can observe the two salient moments in this relationship between theorization and the work to be done regarding educational policies for Indigenous Peoples: first, during the time of the Indigenism movement, and second during the current periods characterized by multiculturalism and interculturalism. They are both part of the general liberal and neoliberal project produced in the twentieth century. Therefore, the making up of what is *indigenous* is linked to the production of ideas of progress and development established during this century. We can note that both perspectives, each in their own moment, have and continue to have a privileged place in the thinking and actions of government officials, academics, and politicians and even in the minds of the general population who approve, in one way or another, of the ideas and actions that are executed in education.

In this sense, we can notice that during the Indigenist movement and the current moment of interculturalism, researchers have devoted much of their energy to using existing models and the ones they have invented to analyze Indigenous Peoples' lives, with the goal of creating practical knowledge to deal with Indigenous Peoples and students.

In the author's words, this is when she affirms that Indigenous Peoples become research (s)objects for the purposes of finding mechanisms to control, help, change, admire, and emulate them. When academic disciplines try to formulate knowledges, they produce (s)objects through complex processes that allow the observation and manipulation of ideas, things, and people. Additionally, the attributes of the object of study are defined through inquiry and, simultaneously, the object is normalized. Through this process, that which is indigenous is being fixed and reduced. It is changing into something clearly defined and therefore readily available for manipulation.

Evidently, this takes place under specific conditions and employing meticulously constructed tools. However, these fixtures are difficult to uphold because the movement of people and the transformation of things and ideas is constant. In this way, other relationships are established, which then produce new research, fixtures, and interventions.

What does all this mean in our activities as social researchers or educators? While I was reading this manuscript, the experiments directed by John Charles Cutler in Guatemala between 1946 and 1948 came to my mind on several occasions. As it is known, during these times, human beings defined as abnormal or under the control of Guatemalan institutions (prisoners, psychiatric patients, soldiers, and prostitutes) were injected with syphilis without their consent. At the time, this activity was justified by affirming that these men and women were sacrificed for the sake of the good of humanity and the nations. In 2010, when this situation came to light in Guatemala, many intellectuals were outraged and considered it a crime against humanity. The great majority of the discussions revolved around ethical problems and health of the people who were deceived and subjected to these experiments.

It is not an exaggeration to bring this case to this discussion because medical experiments that manipulated the lives of human beings, legally and illegally, can be useful for reflection on our work in the social sciences and in education. When comparing them, it is possible to notice the multiple and complex implications of our inquiry with people in multiple places. Even though as social scientists and educators we do not inject dangerous substances into people's bodies, we are also implicated in the manipulation of lives of human beings through our concepts, analytical frames, conclusions, and actions in classrooms and communities. As we know, our position in social contexts in which we do our work is always a privileged one in relation to our subjects-objects of study, who are constantly placed in a subaltern space. The author of this book invites us not only to quickly gaze on the mirrors (the studies of anthropologists, educators, and bureaucrats that have worked on the education of Indigenous Peoples in the twentieth-century), but also to pause and observe our own images and the details in the reflections. In this way we will analyze more precisely the ways in which we act, the consequences of our conclusions, and the results of the actions we carry out in inquiry and educational practice.

During the twentieth century it has been common to think that science and educational activities could resolve the *indigenous problem*, the problem of *the rights of Indigenous Peoples*, or *cultural diversity in the Guatemalan state and nation*. In that sense, it has been common to manipulate the lives of young people, women, peasants, Indigenous Peoples, and those who live in rural regions for the best interests of the nation. In one way or another, it is believed that these people and places, by being *underdeveloped, behind*, or far from the cities, must necessarily be brought to the center of the urban and modern Guatemalan world. In addition, springing from the new theories on multiculturalism and interculturalism, the notion that Indigenous Peoples ought to be educated in their own culture has been normalized because it is assumed that they are losing their languages, costumes, traditions, and religion. It is considered that, without losing their culture, they ought to learn to live in the nation and the state without challenging or disputing the nation and the state from those other historical ways of being. In other words, Indigenous Peoples ought to learn to *live in unity in diversity*.

In our times, it has been common to work or inquire through these intercultural and multicultural perspectives. However, the author of this book invites us to operationalize a multifaceted approach of affirmation and critique. One reason for this is so that it does not drive us to stillness or make us abandon our own work and inquiry into social life. Another reason is so that it allows us to visualize and fight the reproduction of systems of domination in our inquiries, methodologies, conclusions, and general notions about social life. It is here where the production of new knowledges from hegemonic locations and the universities in the United States and Guatemala are inscribed and registered, each from within its own context. There are other systems of knowledge production in diverse parts of the world which, despite being denied, do exist, generating new worlds and forms of life. This manuscript warns us that the efforts toward plurality are also in need of reflection.

Through this book, Ligia López gives us a history of Indigenous Peoples and education in Guatemala. To indicate that the work is also inscribed in the story it narrates, at the end of the text, the author affirms that her work is not concluded. Now that this book is in our hands, we will have a conversation with her from the arguments she proposes, the ones hidden between the lines, their complicities, the cracks it has opened, and the consideration of the frontiers presented by herself and her context. It is our responsibility as readers to discuss the implications of this work, on how it touches the lives of people and communities—which are represented in a complex manner in these writings, be they Indigenous People, Guatemalan citizens, academics, teachers, and/or students. We must add to this discussion our own inquiries and actions, which, as fractals, must have a place—whatever this might be—and contribute to shape life in its diversity, in both intended and unintended places. To these actions and to many others yet imagined is what the author encourages with her last question: so, what follows?

Edgar Esquit
Universidad de San Carlos de Guatemala

Figures

0.1 "Remains of a kid who died of hunger while hiding in the mountains with part of his or her family in 1983." Nebaj, Quiché, Guatemala, 2000   2
0.2 Zoomorfo. Quiriguá, Izabal, Guatemala   7
0.3 "*Tipos Indígenas*" (Indigenous Kinds)   9
0.4 "We do not want soldiers in our communities, what we want is teachers, notebooks and pencils, and no armament"   12
1.1 "Kaqchiquel Region—Chimaltenango or San Juan Sacatepéquez"   34
1.2 "Portrait in a First Communion"   37
1.3 "Ladino Boy"   39
2.1 SIL, IIN, and President—Dr. Juan José Arévalo Bermejo   64
2.2 "Indian Girls at the festival of Minerva." San Miguel Chicaj, near Rabinal, Baja Verapaz   68
2.3 *El Normalista* Teacher education journal cover. Issues 7 and 9, year VI, 1951, Guatemala   76
2.4 Map of literacy percentages in the Republic of Guatemala. 1950 census   78
3.1 Second-grade textbook (*Módulos de Aprendizaje*) used in a "rural" town   119
3.2 Trans. Objectives. Help better [as in get beyond, or get past oneself] our communities. Continue studying   120
4.1 Fractal art—Fulani textile   139
5.1 Untitled   174
5.2 "*Juego de Niños*"   177
6.1 Century Normal School   181
7.1 *Jóvenes* Institute   185
8.1 Rural Bilingual Intercultural Normal School   189

Appendices

Appendix 1   Guatemalan University   179
Appendix 2   Century Normal School   181
Appendix 3   *Jóvenes* Institute   185
Appendix 4   Rural Bilingual Intercultural Normal School   189
Appendix 5   Chapter 0 Spanish Excerpts   193
Appendix 6   Chapter 1 Spanish Excerpts   197
Appendix 7   Chapter 2 Spanish Excerpts   203
Appendix 8   Chapter 3 Spanish Excerpts   209
Appendix 9   Survey to Classify the *Indígena*   215
Appendix 10   Chapter 4 Spanish Excerpts   217
Appendix 11   Linguistics Program Guatemalan University and *Jóvenes* Institute Spanish Excerpts   223

Preface

"No, *You* Be Prepared to Tell Us *Your Historia*"

This preface carries the sense of trust and suspicion I encountered throughout this inquiry. I invite the readers to meet the pages that follow with the same sense of trust and suspicion. The prelude is explicitly a response to the request of a pre-service teacher in Ixcán, Guatemala. Juana was in her second year of the early childhood teacher preparation program at Rural Bilingual Intercultural Normal School (see Appendix 4). With one of her friends, Juana approached me suspiciously, with some hesitation, trust, a forward question, and an invitation: "We do not have a history class, but why don't you come by our classroom?" During the friendly exchange I agreed to stop by and jokingly asked them to be prepared to "tell me *historias*," to which Juana responded emphatically, "No, *you* be prepared to tell us *your historia*." Following is my response to what I suspect Juana, her friend, and many people who asked similar questions were looking for. Suspicious that as a reader what you are expecting from these first pages is a biographical sketch to pin down my "identities" so the value of this inquiry can be determined, I trust that you are looking for something different that will enable you to locate this book within the particular set of concerns that animate it.

Response

Seeking understanding about diversity and the survival of a people who, despite centuries of oppression, marginalization, and genocide, continue to resist and to a certain extent thrive, I came to Guatemala. Arguably I could have stayed in the United States or gone to, for example, Europe, Australia, Congo, or Bolivia. Guatemala mattered because it has been fabricated as one of the most linguistically diverse areas in Latin America and the world. My interest in diversity, and specifically in language and culture, has deep roots in my longer history, a history we have been forced to forget. We have also been forced to forget our "indigenous ways of being." For four generations, my family has assimilated into other ways of being nonindigenous Zenúes in the Caribbean coast of Colombia. This is a bold statement to make considering there is little to no recognition of that cultural legacy. Being indigenous was, although in different ways now, a state of rejection and negation. Pejorative expressions such as "Don't be so Indian!" "The Indian thinks five days after his death" (referring to lack of intelligence), "The Indian doesn't age," "the Indian is good to make *jolón*, and the black is good to carry it,"[1] were often part of everyday humor and quotidian life. I know similar expressions exist in other contexts in the Americas, Australia, and perhaps elsewhere where particular people are made "other" or "diverse." These racist expressions have forced us to repress memories and cultural legacies, and paradoxically they have maintained a link, even if via despicable language, to our indigenous legacy. This book draws from that link to trouble even the multiple assumptions in this seemingly coherent biographical narrative.

With the question of diversity in mind, an intellectual curiosity into the complexity of the politicocultural dynamics of Guatemala, and a preoccupation with language as a site of dehumanization from the fifteenth century, I began inquiring into language maintenance, the role of educational policies, and sociocultural practices. I was driven to understand the ways in which indigenous peoples kept struggling for their cultural and linguistic survival, especially after a thirty-six-year war, including the horrific scorched earth campaigns to exterminate indigenous peoples. Central in this inquiry was the nation-state as an ordering entity in language matters in education. In my history of assimilation, as would be the case for many people socialized in the twentieth century, in the era of human rights and citizenship, the state is almost always indispensable in any kind of political inquiry. This initial examination did not just draw from this socialization of state-centeredness, but was driven by it. In my trip to Guatemala in 2010 I began to ask what kind of Guatemalan society was envisioned through current language policies, programs, and practices. I was aware of the official discourses of bilingual and intercultural education from the 1980s but more so from the mid-1990s. In connection to Mayan sociocultural practices I asked how language policies, programs, and practices related to current Mayan communities who may not be actively participating in their discursive construction. Thinking in a vertical order and critically, the state was at the top and indigenous peoples were at the bottom. Recognizing in practice that the relationship between the state and the people was more complicated than that and that Mayan people have always been actors despite dominant histories, I asked why parents were invested in Mayan schools for their children and how their reasons were translated into sociocultural practices in the home, how the parents chose which language to communicate in with their children, and how they facilitated their children's literacy development in the home.

Enthusiastic about the positive response the research received and the openness with which most participants welcomed these questions, I was off to a good start. While talking to people in the ministry of education, living with Mayan families and conversing with Mayan leaders, I began to be suspicious about "my own" questions. The questions were instrumental in tapping into matters of discrimination, the struggle for widening the scope of what counts as ways of existing, and the aspirations for inclusiveness and diversity announced in educational policies that were often contradicted by people's quotidian *historias*. However, I began to realize that my questions were impractical and insufficient to account for diversity, which instead of a matter of fact was becoming for me a matter of concern. Matters of facts, in Latour's analytics,[2] are *there*, "whether we like them or not!" They hold an indisputable presence. It is not that they in themselves are indisputable, but what is indisputable is that they are there. Matters of concern are what happen to matters of fact when you zoom out of them so they are no longer just there! Though they are still there, they look suspicious, are suspended, and are historically interpreted so that they appear to look different, revealing the unnatural and taken-for-granted containers in which they are ordered.

Tropical storm Agatha precipitated that inquiry shift from matters of fact to concern. The storm touched ground in late May 2010 as I was transcribing interviews and analyzing field notes. I paused the research to work at a nearby shelter. In attempting to interact with the people, asking all the wrong questions, and overwhelmed by the natural and historic devastation, I decided the course of the research had to take a turn. I realized that the initial set of topics and questions carried assumptions far too harmful and unsustainable for the kind of inquiry I sought to pursue. I argue that this kind of inquiry is currently necessary if education is to become other than the recapitulation of colonization. Colonization also has to be constantly subjected to interrogation. If I was going to tackle the question of plurality, the assumptions that sustain the political discourse of diversity had to be questioned in the first place. Discourses of diversity encompassing notions of bilingualism, multilingualism, multiculturalism, *Mayanización*, and so on are possible within particular ways of reasoning people and difference, and within particular histories. In my initial questions, language, literacy, culture, and nation were assumed as undisputed and indisputable facts. Education and the notion of reform underlying the policies, programs, practices, and revitalization efforts were also left unjustifiably unquestioned, as is often the case in common salvific educational and social science research agendas. With the urge toward action in education to correct historical and social wrongs, to include people historically marginalized, and to counter colonial and assimilationist practices, solutions are offered and research agendas are crafted at the surface level.

One of the things I have encountered despite efforts to recuperate historical memory in Guatemala is that the social sciences and education suffer from historical amnesia. Amnesia here does not mean to forget difficult pasts and to pretend they left no legacy in the present,[3] but to forget that some of the practices, ideas, and desires we hold so dear and without which we ostensibly cannot do politically engaged work have histories with legacies in the present, often implicated in the very same things they have aimed to reject. I noticed that in the frenzy for action there is apathy to trouble idealized recent political pasts and a desire to hold on to the political tools that have been the product of the struggle for justice. Throughout the inquiry that ensued from the shift I mentioned before, I have recognized and continue to recognize and trust these struggles because their victories are important. At the same time I have remained utterly suspicious of the various tactics of stabilization that strive to contain the uncontainable, to order and to discipline, which continue to abject people. Gestures to historicize *lo indígena*, employing and challenging conventional and insufficient ways of doing social science research in education, borrowing from literatures outside of education to enable a second look at education, diversity, and justice, is how I channel my suspicion for what we often assume to be benevolent in education, including education itself.

References

Latour, Bruno. *What Is the Style of Matters of Concern?* Amsterdam: Uitgeverij Van Gorcum, 2005.

Lydon, Jane. *Calling the Shots: Aboriginal Photographies*. Camberra: Aboriginal Studies Press, 2014.

Notes

1 Wasp's nest. In this context a basket or baskets put on each side of a donkey to transport agricultural goods.
2 Bruno Latour, *What Is the Style of Matters of Concern?* (Amsterdam: Uitgeverij Van Gorcum, 2005).
3 Jane Lydon, *Calling the Shots: Aboriginal Photographies* (Camberra: Aboriginal Studies Press, 2014).

Acknowledgements

Because there is more to bones than making soup, and there is more to pictures than providing evidence, I salute and thank the spirit of the many children and grown-ups in Guatemala who died in an atrocious war for progress. Their death and life trails have led me back to regain some of the sensibilities kidnapped by the pathetic Colombian war in which I was born and raised. To the many children, mothers and fathers, strangers, and friends in Guatemala who taught this book difficult lessons, thank you. I have learned, and continue to learn, a great deal from them. The enthusiasm and unwavering support that the questions in this book received and the gracious response to my request for entering spaces, places, and lives are unmatched. I would like to thank the students, student teachers, school leaders, principals, secretaries, indigenous leaders, and state officials who appear in this work under pseudonyms. Without their commitment to education, the spirit of debate would have not found its way to these pages.

This book is a continuation of my doctoral dissertation. Immense thanks go to Tom Popkewitz, who more than an advisor, has been a friend and a champion of difficult questions often dismissed or intentionally ignored in a field too nice to wrestle with difficult knowledge. Bernadette Baker deserves special thanks for inviting me to think with literatures from multiple corners of the globe to question what I had taken for granted in education. I am forever indebted to her for being a great source of inspiration to do the work. I thank Steve Stern for being an endless source of wisdom on Latin America, for his mentorship, and kindness in moments of great anxiety. Engaging with atrocities is painful and unsettling even when conducting research. This book and my work owe so much to Edgar Esquit for offering profound insights, rigorous critique, and unwavering support from the beginning. Guatemala has in him one of the most committed historians of all times, and I have been fortunate enough to learn from him.

In Guatemala there are a great many people who shaped this book in countless ways and who deserve special thanks: Magda Aju for her friendship and unbreakable commitment to education and justice; Doña Elizabeth Sam's, Angela Sop's, and Gilberta's family in Chokiak, Zunil, and Patzún, for imagining their children's education otherwise; Lilian Pablo Cruz who though no longer with us, continues to inspire us to struggle and serve, and Lilian's family Doña Nico and Don Cecilio, Dani, Madelyn, Jhoselin, Myrna, Glendi, Hugo, Eli, Sonia, Arely, and Nico for their nourishment and guidance, and stories of migration, the war, and Ixcán; Genaro Fabian for being the lead to the complex galaxies of Ixcán, and Miguel Ugalde for his migration work and connection to the northern border; Gustavo Palma Murga at AVANCSO for some initial insights on educational reform in Guatemala, Bienvenido Argueta for discussions on the histories of Guatemalan education, Julio Pinto Soria for offering important insights on the trajectories of the social sciences and history in Guatemala, Luis Antonio Rodríguez Torselli for his personal introduction to *indigenismo*, and for introducing me to his father Francisco (Paco) Rodríguez Rouanet; Paco, in his mid-nineties, took the time to answer my questions and patiently walked me through his history as one of the precursors of the Indigenist Institute; Richard Adams for similar conversations about the history of anthropology in Guatemala; Virginia Tacam Batz for generously sharing her history and work with teachers on interculturalism and bilingualism; Josué Quiacaín for fervent discussions and for introducing me to localized complexities of religion, language, culture, ethnicity, and indigeneity; Héctor Concohá and Arnoldo Caposeco at the Center for Interethnic Studies San Carlos University deserve special thanks for the enriching historical conversations when they thought them irrelevant to educational research; Cata Lorenzo and Josh McLeod for their company during difficult times in the capital; Justo Magzul, his partner Christina, and her extended family for their hospitality during my stay in Patzún; Catarina Garcia and Wielman Cifuentes at CNEM and the Rogoberta Menchu Tum Foundation for their insights on Mayan leadership in Education, Luis Enrique López at GIZ for some preliminary and crucial conversations about language education and interculturalism, and Justo Magzul at USAID for his insights in the histories of bilingualism and assessment; Daniel Vicente, Yenifer Estrada, Alfonso Rafael, and Higinio Marcelo for continuing the conversations that started years ago now through the photo exhibit *Mira*.

The inquiry in this book emerged in Madison Wisconsin, one of the most politically and intellectually vibrant spaces. The list is far too long. Special thanks go to the many friends, colleagues, and support staff who wrestled with me; read portions of the work in Madison, in conferences, and across the globe; and simply offered their kindness when it was most needed: Yasin Tunç, John Ivens, Ayşegül Mester, Stefan Betergson, Martin Harling, Catherina Schreiber, Ji-Hye Kim, Alberto Ortiz, Julie Gibbings, Min Yu, Ernesto Treviño, Elisa Zweir, Alissa Blair, Anneliese Cannon, Belen Hernando Llorens, Daniel Friedrich, Manali Sheth, Julia Koza, Torrey Kulow, Ru Dawley-Carr, Sophia Rodriguez, Jason Salisbury, Monica Torres, Michael Thomas, Rohany Nayan, Pallavi Chhobra-Dhokarh, Chachi Chiu,

Jorge F. Rodriguez, Elham Milani, Anisha Vittee, Ingrid Bolivar, Christopher Morrison, Alex Allweiss, Jim Jupp, Kate Turner, Laissa M. Rodríguez, Natalie Belisle, and Bicho Azevedo.

Navigating paper and image archives as well as local literatures was made possible by a number of esteemed colleagues. I thank Thelma Porres and Anaís García at CIRMA for their invaluable support in making archives available even when I was away from Guatemala. The staff at the General Archive of Central America (AGCA) deserve special thanks for their gracious support during multiple trips up and down stairs of folios. The librarians at the Ministry of Culture, Ministry of Education, the César Brañas Library, Sergio Robles at the National Library, and the collection of periodicals, the PRODESSA library, and the USAC library, AVANCSO, the Geography and History Academy, and Julio Alfredo Díaz Caballeros and the Mariano Gálvez School of Linguistics' small library, all deserve special thanks for their patience and eagerness to contribute. The University of Wisconsin-Madison Memorial Library, Interlibrary Loan, and Todd Michelson-Ambelang also deserve a great deal of gratitude. The synergies at various programs, centers, and departments at the University of Wisconsin-Madison offered multiple orientations that affirmed the commitment to and suspicion for education written in these pages: Curriculum and Instruction, Educational Policy Studies, History, Geography, Dance, Law, Gender and Women's Studies, English, Art History Program, History of Science, Anthropology, Philosophy, and LACIS.

I acknowledge the financial support from the Theodora Herfurth Kubly Research Fellowship, the International Studies Graduate Student Field Research Award, and Tinker and NAVE awards, as well as other small grants at the University of Wisconsin-Madison. The McKenzie fellowship at the University of Melbourne has supported me in the final writing stages of the book.

Last but not least, my village—parents and siblings—deserve all the credit for the completion of this book. Despite the language barriers, they are all eager to read it, to finally understand what took me to Guatemala so many times besides the fact that it has also become home. Mamá Francia's spirit moves through these pages along with her stories of humiliation, abuse, dignity, and resourcefulness that continue to remind me to always hand out service. Lucas' humor lightens life, and Lalita has gracefully and lovingly borne the burden of reading multiple iterations of this and other texts, untangled difficult sentences, and nourished me and this book through difficult moments of intensity. I thank them the most.

Earlier versions of a few chapters were published elsewhere. A shorter version of Chapter 2 was published in *Knowledge Cultures* under the title "Language, Science, and a Mission: Another Look at Pluralism." Chapter 1 was published under the title "The Problem: Historicizing the Guatemalan Projection and Protection of the 'Indian' " and appeared in *The "Reason" of*

Schooling Historicizing Curriculum Studies, Pedagogy, and Teacher Education edited by Tom Popkewitz. A section of Chapter 4, published under the title "Fractal Education Inquiry," will appear in *Educational Temporalities: Local, National, and Global Perspectives* edited by Hannah Tavares and Jie Qi to be published by Sense Publishers.

ⓖ* 0 Zero = Nothing = Everything
Recasting the "Indigenous" Subject in the Making

Instead of a geopolitical map, as seems customary in research of this kind, I begin this book with signposts. They are meant to map the cartographies of the inquiry and serve as a compass to locate the intellectual efforts in this book. The statements that follow serve as a means to trace the (con)texts in which this book moves, revealing the contours of education—especially that which is meant to serve "diversity."

"Cómo Es En Indio" "How Is an Indian"(?)

Signpost Statement 1

They have been tortured and disappeared.[1] Indigenes. Different. Communists. The last decades of the twentieth century also marked bloody times for them. Numbers of them, "Indian"-looking people,[2] were dropped in *fosas* (pits excavated to bury those killed during the armed conflict en masse) to be later unearthed by forensic teams in Nebaj in the Ixil region, Rabinal, Ixcán, and other places.[3] Many escaped the reach of the army, and some have joined the "indigenous" people's struggle.[4] With boots, *tortillas*, and determination, they told stories of themselves.[5] These stories were left to be collected and told. Jonathan "Jonás" Moller photographs their bones that are not just bones. For a week in July 2011, a collection of his photographs was part of a "memory exhibit" inside the Presidential Palace in Guatemala City, the same palace that was built by General Jorge Ubico during his thirteen-year dictatorship (1931–1944).

The photograph of "Remains of a kid . . ." is, for me, a vivid event. The image brought tears to my eyes when I saw it for the first time and wrinkles my senses every time. The colors in the tissues and my imaginary reconstruction of a young flesh takes me back again and again to the many pairs of small eyes I have met on the *camionetas* (buses) in Guatemala City, on the way to Quiché and Patzún; babies on their mother's backs, by the sides of dirt roads in Chokiak, walking Antigua's central park while their mothers sell woven goods, playing on the pavement of San Juan Sacatepéquez while their parents and neighbors protest the cement factory and the army

2 *Zero = Nothing = Everything*

Figure 0.1 "Remains of a kid who died of hunger while hiding in the mountains with part of his or her family in 1983." Nebaj, Quiché, Guatemala, 2000. (Photo courtesy of the Jonathan Moller Collection, CIRMA. Caption by Jonathan "Jonás" Moller)

garrison. It is also the epistemologic death and the ends of avenues of being in education that compels my efforts in this research. Epistemologic death refers to the ever-shrinking spaces that in and through education limit the imagination, not in the aporetic ways or the fertile ends that Jacques Derrida wrote about.[6] This book is less about the naturalized and "neutralized" spaces of education and more about their harmfulness.

The Guatemalan Armed Conflict is a highly contested site of meanings, emotions, and passions. This event has been experienced as a moment of intensity in the lives of peoples in what has come to be known today as Guatemala.[7] The war and the "post-"war (after the signing of the Peace Accords in 1996) marked a time of abundant production of social and educational policies that serve as an important point of reference in educational reforms, including the one for teacher education proposed in 2012 and implemented in 2013.

In 1961 Jorge Luis Arriola reported on anthropological activities carried out by the *Instituto Indigenista* to "define the Indian."[8] Before going to the field, a group of "Indians" are trained as anthropologists by Chicago graduate Antonio Goubaud Carrera. Their initial mission is to go out into "the field" and survey the people in the rural areas:

Signpost Statement 2

[T]hree quarters of the people that completed the survey consider that customs are the essential characteristic [to differentiate what is indigenous]. This criterion is based, like we said, on the persistence of cultural patterns (house, dress, tongue [/language], bilingualism, with indigenous phonetics predominance, kind of food, furniture, technological limitations in various professional activities, belief in magic, civic-religious organization, etcetera).

"The cultural characteristic referred to by the term 'custom'," says Goubaud Carrera, who died too soon for anthropology and continental indigenism, and who initiated this kind of work in Guatemala, "received 86% votes in the entire country, followed by speaking an indigenous language in the home, 84%; ethnic group (physical appearance) is of least importance amongst them, with 67% votes."

This survey proves what almost all of us know in relation to the possibilities that the indigenous person has to change *status*, passing into the non-indigenous group through the social mobility process, which could be faster if the attitude toward him was more appropriate in terms of creating the possibilities for integration in the various scenarios of his life, so that individual and group *ladinización* can be accelerated,[9] which would lead to important benefits for the country.[10]

The following statement was made possible in part by the cultural and linguistic discourses made available during the 1950s and 1960s. More fundamental was the "Mayan efflorescence" of the 1980s and the "*Mayanización*" project from the 1990s, in combination with the proliferation of policies before and after the signing of the Peace Accords of 1996.[11] On the mission of the *Instituto Indígena Santiago*, as a teacher preparation school, Oscar Azmitia wrote:

Signpost Statement 3

The pedagogic experience at Instituto Indígena Santiago is framed in the question of how to educate within cultures. To achieve this, it was necessary to strengthen the cultural foundations through teaching native languages, studying the Mayan alphabet, recuperating historical memory and research as a means for students to acquire instruments of analysis of their own identity, revaluing their habits and traditional beliefs and feeling proud of being indigenous.[12]

Almost a century earlier, the first Guatemalan Nobel Laureate Miguel Ángel Asturias, preoccupied with the "Indian problem"—of "abandonment, misery, and illnesses"—advocated for "a change."[13] In his thesis to obtain his

4   Zero = Nothing = Everything

law degree, Asturias defines the subject of his social inquiry: the "Indian" problem.

Signpost Statement 4

> The highest intellectual levels [the Indian] can reach are difficult to score; but it is known that he has slow comprehension and is stubborn. [He] speaks Spanish phonetically disrupting the vocabulary, repeating the same words with a regretful syntax. Psychologically [he] has attitudes to be a lawyer, politician, military and farmer. His ability to imitate is also notable (which is a quality of inferior races) thanks to this ability, [he] is skilled to work in architecture and drawing, but is incapable of creating.
>
> The Indian should be educated with the goal of changing him from slave to a free man; from selfish man into a useful man to his fellow man; from being coarse in life to a man apt and intelligent. To transform the Indian social environment based on education is what common sense recommends. Make him think. Make him feel. Make him act.[14]

Asturias offers this succinct definition of an "Indian" as part of his research findings; it serves as the complement to the question/statement *Cómo es un indio* in his thesis and also serves as the title of this section. I borrow this statement/question to draw attention to Asturias, not to agree or disagree with him or his work or to reinforce his statement's stereotypes and epistemic violence to which many scholars have already pointed. In fact, my purpose is far from that. The gesture here is to highlight the various modes in which what is "indigenous" has been discussed since the turn of the twentieth century and to put into motion an analysis from the educational sciences that revisit its heritages when seeking to serve the "less privileged," "discriminated," and "oppressed," all of which are specific phrases taken from common discourses around "indigenous" matters.

* * *

"What are these statements, most of which seemingly removed from education, doing in a book *about* education?" You may be wondering. The statements include several modes within which "difference" and "what is indigenous/indigeneity as difference" have been constituted in recent history. Both of these are fundamental in formulating curriculum meant to serve multiplicity. These modes, in interaction with the educational (in its practical, discursive, and theoretical sense), produce educational performance, its planning, imaginaries, and possibilities.

In the statements noted earlier, the languages that follow the phrase "what an Indian is" are contentious and, in most cases, ambivalent. The meanings assigned to what gets constituted as "indigenous"/*lo indígena* or who is understood as "Indian/indigenous/*indígena*" are conditioned by the politicocultural and historical circumstances of the times in which the statements were generated.[15] Moreover, these meanings also have epistemological, ontological, and theological heritages.

This book aims to trace these heritages in theory and practice.[16] The statements are constructed from the various disciplines of the visual arts, history, anthropology, sociology, and law. All of these have dialogued with education historically and have been fundamental in shaping the contours of curriculum, particularly as it pertains to *lo indígena*.

Even though the contexts of enunciation of the statements are "Mesoamerica," they are inscribed in transnational flows of thought traceable to "North America," "Europe," and "South America." Many of the curriculum dynamics in Guatemala—and by implication how "difference" is negotiated—have been in close interaction with other (con)texts. To call this a Guatemalan case study would be to remain loyal to stability and a logic of origins, and thus to the insufficiency of engaging with the dynamism of meanings. Not any kinds of meanings, but the ones (i.e., time, difference, identity, and politics) that dent people's "existence" in "repressive times," "war times," "democratic times," "development times," "intercultural and/or multicultural times."[17] This is thus an historical case about the particular configurations of meanings in the making of anthropological borders that have implications, applications, and direct effects in curriculum.

As for temporalities, the statements span from the 1920s to the "present" (2012). However, all of them make, in some way, reference to a heritage or vision outside of this bracket, making the temporal demarcation of "before" and "after" the 1920s fuzzy.[18] This suggests two things. First, this is where the analysis will be undertaken, particularly in moments of intensity in the history of indigenous making via the social and educational sciences. Second, it suggests the impossibility of discounting the "before" the 1920s and the "after" 2012. Planning society, the future, and people requires paying attention to statements pointing to "the future," commonly understood as what lies ahead of us, and the past, which in Guatemala is commonly linked to colonialism(s). Despite the linearity I am employing to write about temporalities here, my hope is that through the complex analytics in the book I engage with the palimpsestic quality of the past (or the present, or the future, or time) in doing curriculum. I do this by thinking of time as *fractal* and adopting *eventalizing* in doing historically oriented research. These are discussed at length later in the chapter.

Within the temporalities suggested here, one may notice how border dynamics that produce and constitute *lo indígena* and "indigenous" kinds play out through the collaboration of a number of institutions (i.e., *Instituto Indigenista*, teacher education schools), their experts (i.e., anthropologists), and their knowledges (i.e., statistics), their interaction with the people to be classified (i.e., those with slow comprehension, with different customs, with cultural identity) and classifications (i.e., "Ladino," "Indian," "Maya").[19] This book explores these border-making dynamics of *lo indígena* by means made available through the social sciences and their close interaction with educational concerns, which in turn shape what has come to matter in education and *how*.

Education has multiple teaching and schooling environments. I have chosen teacher education as the entry point in my inquiry. Teacher education carries the traditional assumption that teachers matter in schooling, the making of curriculum, and the making of history. Making history in this research means the making of "indigenous" kinds through schooling. Thus the archives that primarily inform this book are from teacher education contexts. Teacher education in general and in relationship to "indigenous" discourses in Guatemala emerges in the late nineteenth and early twentieth centuries and is constituted along with the anthropological, the pedagogic sciences, and religious knowledges. Additionally, in current debates on educational improvement in Guatemala, (where *lo indígena*, though not explicitly stated, is dutifully at the center of the task for improvement), teacher preparation always appears as a necessary technology.

The Noticeable (s)Object of Inquiry and Their Making-Up[20]

The templates of the so-called modern social sciences/humanities, dynamically constituted with what is known today as "indigenous" peoples (or its cognates "Indian" and "Maya"), announce the possibility of *lo indígena*, or what is "indigenous" as a (s)object.[21] These disciplines shape how knowledge is produced and who produces it.[22] More interestingly, however, are which particular (s)objects and their constructions produce such knowledge and what effects this process generates. In this book the effects refer to the making of curriculum, the ordering of schooling, and the planning of people's "presents" and "futures." In a similar vein to Ian Hacking's historical ontology, my concern is with *lo indígena* as a (s)object or its effects, which is more noticeable when it becomes a (s)object of scientific inquiry.[23]

The turn of the twentieth century serves as a point of salience when analyzing the discourses circulating in the social sciences and humanities in the nation's capital that narrate *lo indígena* in Guatemala (and in some cases Mesoamerica). I now turn to the analytical compass that orients this inquiry, first to scientific (s)objects and then to the making-up.

Scientific (s)Objects

Lorraine Daston in the introduction to *Biographies of Scientific Objects* differentiates between *objects of quotidian experience* and *scientific objects*. The former are those that need not be investigated; "they possess the self-evidence of a slap on the face. These are solid, obvious, sharply outlined, in-the-way things of quotidian experience [. . . i.e.,] the walls that obstruct . . . the projectile that hits."[24] Scientific objects are, for constructionists, "inventions, forged in specific historical contexts and molded by local circumstances. Those circumstances may be intellectual or institutional, cultural or

Figure 0.2 Zoomorfo. Quiriguá, Izabal, Guatemala. (Photo courtesy of the Valedavellano Collection, Academia de Geografía e Historia de Guatemala, 1861–1928.)

philosophical, but they are firmly attached to a particular time and place."[25] *Lo indígena* and the notions, practices, and feelings now associated with it (all of which are not unitary or universal) were *real* (in the Deleuzian sense of a series of ideas—for example, the understanding that time is infinite)[26] and *actual* things (Mayan glyphs carved in stones in the image in Figure 0.2 or stories painted on pottery) before and after they became a scientific object.[27] In other words, dynamics of "indigeneity," or as Aura Cumes and Santiago Bastos put it, the group and its cultural elements, were present, at least for some people, before *lo indígena* becomes a phenomenon of scientific inquiry.[28] As in the earlier signposts, this happens, for example, through the sociological work of Miguel Ángel Asturias from the 1920s, the anthropological initiatives of the *Instituto Indigenista* from the 1950s, and through the political/cultural efforts of the *Mayanización* movement from the 1970s.[29]

Nonetheless, the coalescence of those (now referred to as) elements that define *lo indígena* into domains of scientific inquiry, where they can be observed and manipulated,

> alters them in significant ways: phenomena that were heretofore scattered (as in the case of monsters and figured stones) amalgamate into

a coherent category; criteria of inclusion and exclusion grow sharper (as in the case of identity); new forms of representation stabilize regularities (as in the case of mortality tables); intense investigation renders evanescent phenomena more visible and rich in implications (as in the case of dreams).[30]

The implications can be the "theoretical ramifications and empirical surprises, which cohere, at least for a time, as an ontological entity."[31] I understand ontological as a way of being, for instance "Maya," which could be a way of being a person, a thing such as a Mayan language class, an idea such as bilingualism, or an institution such as a boarding school exclusively for Mayan youth.

The consideration of "indigeneity" as a scientific object is particularly relevant in post/colonial contexts such as Guatemala where languages of the social sciences have been employed, for better or for worse, in the struggle of marginalized peoples to re/configure spaces of participation within what they consider dominant "Eurocentric" cosmologies. An example of this is the creation and maintenance of the *Vicedespacho Bilingüe Intercultural* (the Bilingual Intercultural Vice-Ministry) (see Chapter 1) as a separate division within the Ministry of Education—which as an "indigenous" space was unimaginable before. From it, policies, materials, and curricula are created in an attempt to attend to the diversity of the nation through the administration of bilingual intercultural schools, including those that prepare teachers to teach bilingual curricula.

Considering that a) *lo indígena* becomes an object of scientific inquiry from existing dynamics and prior to its becoming in the surface of scientific and political engagement, and considering that b) it happens in specific historical contexts under particular conditions, and c) through various instruments afforded by so-called modern technologies such as experts and classifications, I use *salience, emergence,* and *making-up* as approaches to its historicity. These approaches are helpful in describing the moments in which *lo indígena* becomes a point of intensity that leads to its noticeability. Thus, these approaches will be helpful in tracing where *lo indígena* attains its heightened ontological status when producing results, implications, applications, and manipulations in its connections to educational matters.

Making-up (s)Objects and Kinds of People

We think of many kinds of people as objects of scientific inquiry. Sometimes to control them, as prostitutes; sometimes to help them, as potential suicides. Sometimes to organize and help, but at the same time to keep ourselves safe, as the poor or the homeless. Sometimes to change for their own good and the good of the public, as with the obese. Sometimes to admire, to understand, to encourage, and perhaps even to emulate, as (sometimes) with genius.[32]

Figure 0.3 "*Tipos Indígenas*" (Indigenous Kinds). Guatemala in 1943. Graphic album. Jorge Ubico Admin. (Photo courtesy of the Academia de Geografía e Historia de Guatemala.)

To explore the principles that order how the *indígena* "(s)object" emerges or is produced, I use Ian Hacking's five-aspect dynamic framework of analysis (classifications, people, institutions, knowledge, experts) for making-up objects, things, kinds of people. I employ this framework as it allows the examination of phenomena as a matter of course rather than as fixity. This denial of fixity is particularly relevant considering the tendency to reduce *lo indígena* in educational texts to a fixed entity for curriculum planning and policy design purposes, as well as the way in which it is discussed and performed in particular classrooms. The framework's five aspects are compatible with schooling as a site of making in the most literal sense. This can reveal what has been possible and impossible to imagine, think, and enact in education's ordering and actualization.

Hacking's five-aspect dynamic framework refers to the belief that "there are no reasons to suppose that we shall ever tell two identical stories of two different instances of making up people."[33] The stories of *lo indígena*, which articulate how an "Indian" is as defined in the statements provided earlier, vary according to their conditions of production: sensitivities and preoccupations, the area of inquiry which generated them, the nature of the genre, and who wrote it and under what historical conditions. The influence of "indigenous" peoples and the objects themselves on the stories and their producers is important. This framework is dynamic because it recognizes that the properties that define the object are fluid:

> They are moving targets because our investigations interact with the targets themselves, and change them. And since they are changed, they are not quite the same kind of people as before. The target has moved. That is the looping effect. Sometimes our sciences create kinds of people that in a certain sense did not exist before. That is making up people.[34]

Aura Cumes and Santiago Bastos' influential work coincides with Hacking's in that they argue that being "Maya," or considering oneself "Maya," was a new way of being.

> We are talking about one or various processes that take shape in a new phenomenon, the introduction in the life of Maya people of a discourse that did not exist before: of considering oneself Maya and through that reclaim equality with pride and rights.[35]

Considering oneself "Maya" comes via the "Maya" themselves as a possible classification of a kind of person, which emerges politically in the 1980s and 1990s. Classification is one of the five elements in Hacking's interactive network of making-up people. "Communist" is another classification used with more intensity in the 1970s to the 1990s and relates to the image of "remains of a kid who died of hunger . . ." (Signpost Statement 1 earlier). A classification of people in Asturia's statement (statement four earlier) is "Indian." "Indian" has a much longer history that dates back to the first years of Spanish colonization and becomes more salient in Guatemala's liberal period and through the sciences from the 1920s onwards.

Classification requires people, things, and ideas to be classified, which is another element of the framework. "Maya" is claimed by individuals as a way of being (Signpost Statement 3), and is also used to organize objects found in the region archaeologically defined as "Mesoamerica." The "communist" category was attached to those who "illegally" militated against the Guatemalan state. According to Miguel Ángel Asturias (Signpost Statement 4), people who had slow comprehension, were stubborn, spoke Spanish disrupting the conventional vocabulary, or who had an ability to imitate but were incapable of creating were "Indians."

Making-up people, things, and ideas involves the participation of institutions. The *Instituto Indigenista* (Signpost Statement 2) from 1945 studied *"el problema indígena"* (the indigenous problem) and "autochthonous cultures and the inclusion of the indigene to the national culture."[36] In the process they defined what "an Indian" was, as well as their "autochthonous cultures": "Indian" practices, languages, and objects. The *Instituto Indígena Santiago* (Signpost Statement 3), as an educational and religious institution, has the mission of "revaluing *indígena* students' habits and traditional beliefs and feeling proud of being indigenous."

Institutions interact with the expert knowledges that they produce. In the case of the *Instituto Indigenista*, this expert knowledge is anthropological, archaeological, demographic, statistical, and linguistic. That is also the case for the *Instituto Indígena Santiago* in addition to the more explicitly pedagogical, sociological, and religious knowledges it produced. In the case of Signpost Statement 1, it is the army and the expert knowledge of guerrilla warfare that produces people as communists and turns them into the bones that photographic and forensic knowledges document.

Expert knowledge is produced by the dynamic process of the four elements noted earlier, as well as by individual experts: anthropologists, archaeologists, linguists, ethnographers, statisticians, pedagogues, classroom instructors, clergy and religious leaders, military commanders, and soldiers. These experts are at the same time themselves constituted in the process of making up people and ordering the (s)object of their inquiry or "action." The framework thus remains dynamic even before any attempts to position experts as a constant. The dynamism of the framework also refers to the ongoing production of these elements as people are being made up.

Each of the elements in the framework themselves could be studied as objects of scientific inquiry; they are not ahistorical. Although the biographies of these elements are not a primary concern in this book, I will make reference to their salience when relevant to my analysis of the *indígena* (s)object making. The remainder of the chapter is dedicated to the book's methodological organization.

Event-alizing *lo Indígena*

> The eternal truth of the event is grasped only if the event is also inscribed in the flesh. But each time we must double this painful actualization by a counter-actualization, which limits, moves, and transfigures it.[37]

> [Eventalization] means making visible a singularity at places where there is a temptation to invoke a historical constant, an immediate anthropological trait or an obviousness that imposes itself uniformly on all.[38]

The focus on "how" in this book—on the ways in which *lo indígena* as difference is reasoned and the languages through which it is simultaneously

Figure 0.4 "We do not want soldiers in our communities, what we want is teachers, notebooks and pencils, and no armament." Picture taken in San Juan Sacatepéquez in a protest 07/01/12. (Photo credit El José Subuyuj)

constructed and expressed—requires a substantial discussion of the style of inquiry used in the book to research the making of *lo indígena*.

The primary concern in this book is "reality" as a making: reality is a process constituted in series of ideas and through actual things. In this sense reality is an event, or rather, as I am proposing here the event-aliz*ing* of reality.[39] The particular notion of event I employ derives primarily from the works of Gilles Deleuze.[40] For Deleuze, events are happenings, verbs, and processes, rather than things, nouns, and substances.[41] They are produced in chaos, which would be "the sum of all possible perceptions being infinitesimal."[42] In this sense, I understand *lo indígena* as an event. What is "indigenous" in Guatemala slides, for example, from legitimizing but essentialized postulates of ancestral exceptionalism to delegitimizing, pro-globalism agendas that seek to create a more scientific, orderly, and "advanced" citizenry. *Lo indígena* is a happening that gets discussed, theorized, deployed, and lived in multiple directions that are contested whether or not such contestations are visible. An example from the public space is the massacre of K'iche' indigenous leaders on October 4 2012, in Alaska, Totonicapán.[43] These K'iche' leaders, accompanied by dozens of supporters, protested multiple repressive measures that would negatively affect small, prominently indigenous villages, including a proposal for teacher education reform (see Chapter 4). This protest was just one of several in recent years, including the one in San Juan Sacatepéquez (see the image earlier) in July 2012. An example of the contestation of "indigenous" is the Rigoberta Menchú controversy concerning her legitimacy as an *indígena* "Maya" and a presidential candidate in 2011.[44] From inside a teacher-education classroom, one additional example is the pushback of indigenous student teachers when their literacy teacher asserted that "everyone in the room [was] *mestizo*"; her students disagreed, asking her to explain what she meant.

To expand on the event as a style of thinking and doing historically orientated research, James Williams offers a helpful depiction of event in the Deleuzean sense.[45]

> For Deleuze, an event is a real process in different kinds of realm—virtual and actual—that together constitute a complete reality. An event is therefore something that runs through real series of ideas and through actual things. It runs through them not in terms of break-like changes in actual and ideal relations, but in terms of changes in degrees of intensity,[46] in their relations carried by the movement of placeless occupants along empty places in different series, for instance when a question runs along a series of different possible answers illuminating them differently when each in turn is seen as the right one. The empty places determine a lack in actual series and an excess in virtual ones. Intensity can be seen as a wave-like effect running through both series as they interact.[47]

Lo indígena is a reality made: a real process, in the Deleuzian sense. It runs through a real series of ideas—for instance through development, interculturalism, migration, and actual things such as a body dressed in *corte* and *güipil*; stories printed in a school textbook; the vacation homework (to draw the Mayan pyramids in Northern Guatemala) assigned to students in a boarding school in Guatemala City to complete when they return to their hometowns.[48] *Lo indígena* can be experienced in degrees of intensity, in actual and virtual relations, for instance, in the making of intercultural education policies in a massive education reform movement, in what animates the professionalization reform of teacher education, or as it gets naturalized and standardized in Mayan languages.

The components, or defining conditions of an event in my interpretation of Deleuze, are extensions (one element stretching over others), intensities (of a value and degree in extensions), and prehensions (the eye is prehension of light, and living beings prehend water, soil, carbon, salts).[49] These components manifest through emotion, evaluation, and conscience, which are in motion via self-enjoyment of prehensions' own becoming, and finally eternal objects, including qualities, figures, and things in flux, which are constantly gaining and losing molecules and which remain over the succession of moments.

Archives and Statements

These four elements served as guides in the selection and analysis of data. The exemplar statements (data if you will) that are offered throughout the book relate to moments of intensity when the construction of what is "indigenous" becomes prehensible or more noticeable in memory (the memory knots),[50] in the production of texts that leave a trace, and the discourses that serve as resources to build particular arguments. Michel Foucault defines a statement as a "function that cuts across a domain of structures and possible unities and which reveals them with concrete contents in time and space."[51] Though a statement-event cannot be rendered in space and time because it occurs throughout actual and virtual series at different degrees of intensity,[52] it can still be referenced because traces can be found in the actions of subjects, and their classification, in the creation of institutions, in the fabrication of expert knowledges and experts, and in changes in intensities of a sensation around the statement-event.[53]

The exemplar statements in this book are documents borrowed from archives. These archives are alphabet-oriented texts, that is documents written in a-b-c, printed on paper commonly used today in the so-called "Western(ized) world," stored in boxes and files in institutions, organizations, and libraries. The archive that informs this inquiry is also visual and includes photographs boxed or displayed in institutions, printed images on paper, on announcements, and circulating on the Internet, and photographs of events that happened in the coarse of this research. Photographs are an intentional feature of the book. Images have been crucial in the visual construction of the social, in how difference and kinds of people have been produced and are inserted in discourses of diversity. Several of the images dusted from the archive and now presented here have survived to meet the historical inquiry in this book.[54] They raise questions and trouble the ways in which difference gets visually fabricated and implicated in current ways of doing education. Archival documentation also comprises my conversations and exchanges (in interviews, classroom observations, protests) in teacher education schools and university classrooms; in public events of a social, cultural, and political nature; in the streets, conference rooms, and public offices.

This archival documentation is (or was) not just there, ready to be collected as solid or virtual impassive objects merely occupying so-called public space. The exemplars are eternal objects influx that both inform the research questions and are not hardened data closed to further rereading, interpretation, challenges, and questions. They were and still are eventful statements gaining and losing molecules, becoming dustier, more faded, gaining and losing strength, a fresh creation in each new encounter. I am suggesting that the use of the exemplars and the archive in this study is not a claim to a source of "truth," or a positivistic knowledge of history,[55] as was the case in the nineteenth century, when "German idealistic notions were placed in the archive to claim the positivist knowledge of history that could compete with the emerging sciences."[56] Rather, the archive of statements informs this inquiry as traces that offer a referent of "points of connection or meditations of complex movements of thought and cultural practices," which gestures toward a historicizing of the role of the educational in the making-up of "indigenous" peoples that often goes unnoticed.[57]

Noticing requires paying attention to the archive of things—said, remembered, photographed, and written—that are grouped together in distinct figures, composed together in accordance with multiple relations, maintained or blurred in accordance with specific regularities. This determines that they do not withdraw at the same pace in time, but shine, as it were, like stars—some that seem close to us are shining brightly from afar, whereas others that are in fact close to us are already growing pale.[58]

Fields of Play

Both archives and teacher preparation classrooms are the fields of play in this inquiry.[59] In a teacher preparation classroom the curriculum is oriented to preparing teachers for working in primary education classrooms, regardless of whether the aspiration of the students during the program are a direct indication of what occurs upon completing their program of study.

The primary classroom observation sites were located in four different teacher preparation schools before the teacher education reform (pre-service primary education teacher education reform) implementation in 2012. The schools were carefully selected according to their trajectories and relationships to "indigenous" matters, whether explicitly or implicitly suggested. Following the ever-elusive binaries of the urban/rural, male/female, new/traditional, public/private, the schools were selected intentionally to qualify how the educational discussion may be happening within diverse schooling environments in Guatemala. They were also selected according to their curricular history and orientation toward bilingualism and interculturality, or whether they were experiencing the linguistically oriented curriculum phenomena in recent years, or whether they referred back to the indigenist discourses emerging in the 1940s and 1950s.

Each of these four research sites—Guatemalan University, Century Normal School, *Jóvenes* Institute, and Rural Bilingual Intercultural Normal School—are described in the appendices. Exemplars from all four sites are threaded throughout the chapters; thus the chapters are not dedicated to particular schools, and neither is there a particular chapter dedicated to teacher education. The entire book takes teacher preparation as the gateway into the main inquiry of "indigenous" making. In the appendices, descriptions of the research sites add relevant details of the contexts to serve as an accompaniment to the chapters, each of which follows its own analytical spiral style.

Spending intense periods of time in school and university classrooms and in Guatemala in general opened up possibilities for noticing how what is "indigenous" comes to the surface in the everyday, in how it is performed, narrated, and contested. The everyday here is the historical in every moment. The informal conversations in school and archive corridors, in protests, festivals, state and private offices, households, city streets, village paths, markets, and buses add rich texture to the archives in the motion of everyday making and beyond the confines of documents classified in archive boxes and files.

Platicas, or informal interviews with teacher educators, former teachers and policy makers, students, parents, education officials, activists, archivists, historians, "Maya" and "non-Maya," Guatemalan scholars, and community organizers informed this inquiry not only in its content, but also in opening up new avenues for the research design. Eventalizing was forged in those *platicas*.

Considering the little funding available for cataloging mountains of documents, including images, Guatemala is not the easiest place for conducting historical research, much less studies of the recent "past" or education-related research. Documents are located in multiple archival "hubs" in Guatemala, Guatemala City, and other locations. While locating and navigating archives in Guatemala posed a challenge, the research participants were crucial in my accessing relevant sources. The research participants also, in important ways, influenced the theoretical compass that orients my curriculum work as these pages were written.

Eventalizing *lo indígena* as a (s)object of scientific inquiry, which I study here in relation to education, focuses on knowledges, experts, institutions, and classifications at various moments of intensity in Guatemala's history since the turn of the twentieth century. The four chapters that follow engage with (1) photographic and legislative, (2) linguistic and pedagogic, and (3) anthropological knowledges that make intelligible current teacher education curriculum performance, and (4) teacher education reform.

In Chapter 1 I examine the intensity of educational policies in the making-up of "indigenous" peoples, as an attempt to interrogate the emergent logic of "the Indian problem" salient in the late 1800s and early 1900s in Guatemala. The examination begins with a visual analysis of photographs, their making, the photographers, the photography studio, and the photographed whose portraits, like many others, circulated and gave problematic contours to the retina just as the logic of "the Indian problem" was becoming salient. I argue that this logic of *problēma*—a task to be accomplished and a duty to be completed—operates in making up *lo indígena* through the educational sciences and schooling. I point to how this logic is manifested through the opening and closure of the borders of *lo indígena* in the most celebrated and progressive policies and initiatives before and since the Accords for a Firm and Durable Peace. I demonstrate that the terms that define the "Indian" as a problem have shifted in the course of the late nineteenth, twentieth, and early twenty-first centuries. The analysis of these terms reveals that the celebrated progressive struggle for uplifting the "Indian" and integrating him into the present and the nation leaves the problematic logic unquestioned.

In the "indigenous" event, language(s) has been central. Chapter 2 traces the heritages of language and how they became pivotal to curriculum, teacher education, and "indigenous" making. In exploring the moments of intensity in the emergence of language as central in "indigenous" making, I focus on 1) colonial linguistics, 2) Protestant missions, and 3) pedagogies of illiteracy. The chapter meanders through shifts in discourses and performances of exclusion and inclusion of "indigenous" peoples in relationship to language and in educational contexts. I delineate how religious, linguistic, and sociolinguistic experts; expert knowledges; and institutions, acting through classifications, generated languages and ways to reason what is "indigenous" that make possible particular curricular configurations in teacher education classrooms today. Through classroom observations, interviews, and teacher education journals I gesture to the continuities of phono-centric and logo-centric logics that order what can be done and imagined in educational spaces inhabited and meant to serve "indigenous" peoples. The analytics addressed in the chapter through the three main sections do not follow a symmetrical, chronological, or neatly patterned order from past to present or present to past. Rather, in order to respect the temporal complexities that this book is committed to, the analytics flow through interconnections of discourses that travel in and out and cut across the three sections.

18 Zero = Nothing = Everything

Whereas Chapter 1 engages with linguistics, linguistic activities, and production in relation to and with education, Chapter 3 takes up anthropology, its experts, institutions, and the production of what is "indigenous," which runs through a real series of ideas and actual things. Linguistic and anthropological institutions worked together closely and developed ways of reasoning that produced ways of ordering curriculum in the making of what is "indigenous" through teacher education. The analytics of moments of intensity in anthropological thinking and the production of *lo indígena* are triggered by curriculum events in teacher education classrooms today. Such moments of intensity are noticeable through the wavelike effect running through 1) multiculturalism, 2) interculturality, and 3) evolutionism coming in and out of the major cultural accounts and theorizing of the *Instituto Indigenista* (Indigenist Institute) from the 1940s onwards. More than the shift of terms in indigenist production, one of the central arguments in the chapter is the unquestioned developmentalist logic installed in defining what is "indigenous" as a moving target and its ordering through contemporary educational aspirations.

In Chapter 4 I trace the multiple impulses in attempting to "reform" teacher education throughout the twentieth and twenty-first centuries. I examine more overtly the pedagogical knowledges in conversation with linguistic and anthropological knowledges. Given the intense mobilization that the government-mandated 2012 "professionalization reform of teacher education" generated, I focus on the educational aspirations inscribed in the written curriculum distributed to schools. I also read the proposals presented by "indigenous" groups as an alternative to the government mandate. Considering the analysis in the previous chapters, I suggest that teacher and teacher education, through more sophisticated languages and series of ideas of pertinent education for "indigenous" peoples, are far from being newly reconstituted via the proposed re-formations. Taking the reform as a real series of ideas, and the schools that are part of this study as actual things, suggests what has been possible and impossible to imagine and aspire in education—through teacher education—by being aware of multiplicity. In the twenty-first century *lo indígena* is a task to be accomplished, a duty to be fulfilled, an eternal (s)object constantly changing in terms how it is externalized, its inclusions, and exclusions, and which remains the same over the succession of moments in the styles in which it is reasoned.

Lastly, Chapter 5 is less a conclusion or a resolution and more a space to offer implications for educational aspirations meant to serve multiplicity. Charting the twentieth-century historical trajectories of *lo indígena* through teacher preparation reveals the limit points of making up (s)objects as a way to design teaching, curriculum, and the future of the youth. Charting and recognizing these limit points is a productive space for releasing the imagination from what is (dis)allowed in education. The chapter is formed in three beginnings with a spoken word poem, four monologues, and *Mira.*, which is a teacher preparation encounter that releases the educational imagination, not beyond, but beside, any past, present, and future re-form.

Notes

* This drawing of the shell hand, one of the three forms of "zero" found in "Maya" inscriptions on stones, was possible because of the science of archeology, a nineteenth century invention. Paradoxically, this book points to the limitations of scientific reasoning in the planning and making of people through education, particularly in its capacity to engage with diversity. And this is the first example of the paradoxes this book embodies: the necessity and limitations of social science thought and methodologies to politically engage with multiplicity. I use this glyph as the title of the introduction to honor other forms of what we (in the scholarly community) call written communication, recognizing, again, that the reading of this stone carving is a fabrication. I intend to begin educating the eye of the reader to more complex means of reading the pages that follow, and the intellectual-political project suggested in them. Zero for the "Maya," as some have read it, means *el todo* [everything]. More conventionally zero means nothing. This section is both everything that may be involved in this book, and nothing of what the reader may expect or make of it.

    If this is a tension, it captures the nature of doing educational research meant to serve disadvantaged "kinds." I thank Iyaxel Cojtí Ren for conversations about "Maya" Cholq'ij calendrics and epistemology (06/24/2012). The sketch is by David Stuart in David Stuart, "The Calligraphic Zero," Maya Decipherment, accessed August 2, 2012, http://decipherment.wordpress.com/2012/06/15/the-calligraphic-zero/.

1   Between 1960 and 1996 Guatemala experienced one of its cruelest and most violent periods as quantified by the 200,000 people who were assassinated and/or disappeared and the many who fled their homes and the country. Most of these people lived in rural communities and were thus "*campesinos*" and "*indígenas.*" For extensive documentation on the Guatemalan Armed Conflict, see the report of Proyecto Interdiocesano de Recuperación de la Memoria Histórica (Guatemala), *Guatemala, nunca más: Informe* (Guatemala: ODHAG, 1998); Victoria Sanford, *Buried Secrets: Truth and Human Rights in Guatemala* (New York: Palgrave Macmillan, 2003); Ricardo Falla, *Masacres de la selva: Ixcán, Guatemala, 1975–1982* (Guatemala: Editorial Universitaria, 1992); Gustavo Porras Castejón, *Las huellas de Guatemala*, 2nd edition (Guatemala: F&G Editores, 2009). For testimonial accounts see Rigoberta Menchú and Elisabeth Burgos-Debray, *Me llamo Rigoberta Menchú y así me nació la conciencia* (México: Siglo Veintiuno Editores, 1985); Victor Montejo, *Testimony: Death of a Guatemalan Village* (Willimantic: Curbstone Press; Distributed by Talman Co., 1987); Museo Comunitario Rabinal Achi (Rabinal, *Oj k'aslik/ Estamos vivos: Recuperación de la memoria histórica de Rabinal, 1944–1996.* Rabinal, Baja Verapaz, Guatemala: Museo Comunitario Rabinal Achi, 2003); Santiago Otero Diez et al., *Testigos del morral sagrado: En homenaje a los catequistas sobrevivientes que han trabajado con dedicación, aun arriesgando la propia vida, por la construccion del reino de dios* (Guatemala: ODHAG, 2011); José Flores, *El Verde Púrpura / José Flores* (Guatemala: Fenix, 1986); See also Alison Crosby, M. Brinton Lykes and Brisna Caxaj, "Carrying a Heavy Load: Mayan Women's Understandings of Reparation in the Aftermath of Genocide," *Journal of Genocide Research* 18, no. 2–3 (July 2, 2016): 265–83. For audio-visual materials see, for example, "When We Were Young There Was a War," accessed January 24, 2017, www.centralamericanstories.com/; and the work of Jonathan Moller

20   *Zero = Nothing = Everything*

in Jonathan Moller, *Our Culture Is Our Resistance: Repression, Refuge, and Healing in Guatemala* (New York: Power House Books, 2004) (which is also a travelling exhibition of 44 black and white images), as well as Moller, *Refugees Even After Death: A Quest for Truth Justice and Reconciliation* (40 color images), and Moller, *Rescatando nuestra memoria/Rescuing our Memory* (Guatemala: F&G Editores, 2009). See also, Jean-Marie Simon, *Guatemala: Eterna primavera, eterna tiranía* (Guatemala: Fundación Soros Guatemala/CIRMA/Centro Cultural de España/Estudio A2, 2010); Pamela Yates, *When the Mountains Tremble*, DVD (United States: Skylight Pictures, 1983); Bob Foss et al., *Pumaens Datter*, DVD (Sweden: Domino Film & TV-Produktion: Distribution Statens Filmcentral, 1995); Patricia Flynn et al., *Discovering Dominga*, DVD (Berkeley: Berkeley Media, 2002). See also Ejército de Guatemala, "Operación Sofía" (National Security Archive, 1982), www.gwu.edu/~nsarchiv/NSAEBB/NSAEBB297/index2.htm.

2 The quotations around "Indian," "Indigenous," "*Indígena*," "Maya," "Ladino," and other populations invite an interrogation into their making up of kinds of people as historically constituted.

3 See especially Victoria Sanford, *Buried Secrets*; and Falla, *Masacres de la selva*.

4 See Rosalinda Hernández Alarcón, *Memorias rebeldes contra el olvido/Paasantzila txumb'al ti' sotzeb' al k'u'l* (Guatemala: Cuerda/Plataforma Agraria/AVANCSO, 2008); and Arturo Arias, "Letter from Guatemala: Indigenous Women on Civil War," *PMLA* 124, no. 5 (October 2009): 1874–77, doi:10.1632/pmla.2009.124.5.1874; Porras Castejón, *Las huellas de Guatemala*. Specifically on the "Maya" movement see, for example, Edward Fischer and McKenna Brown, *Maya Cultural Activism in Guatemala* (Austin: University of Texas Press, 1996); Victor Montejo, "The Multiplicity of Mayan Voices: Mayan Leadership and the Politics of Self-Representation," in *Indigenous Movements, Self-Representation, and the State in Latin America*, eds. Jean E. Jackson and Kay B. Warren (Austin: University of Texas Press, 2002); Arias Arturo, "The Maya Movement, Postcolonialism and Cultural Agency," in *Coloniality at Large: Latin America and the Postcolonial Debate*, eds. Mabel Moraña, Enrique Dussel, and Carlos Jáuregui (Durham: Duke University Press, 2008), 519–38. On "Pan-Maya" activism see, for example, Kay B. Warren, *Indigenous Movements and Their Critics: Pan-Maya Activism in Guatemala* (Princeton: Princeton University Press, 1998); Edgar Esquit, "Nationalist Contradictions: Pan-Mayanism, Representation of the Past and the Reproduction of Inequalities in Guatemala," in *Decolonizing Histories: Collaboration, Knowledge and Language in the Americas*, ed. Florencia E. Mallon (Durham: Duke University Press, 2012), 167–92. And for some foundations on the movement see Carlos Guzmán Böckler and Jean-Loup Herbert, *Guatemala: Una interpretación histórico-social* (Guatemala: Cholsamaj, 1995).

5 *Tortillas* are corncakes, in this context, made by "indigenous" women. During the time of the war, combatants (especially those who were from the local villages) lived on a few tortillas a day provided by women in the villages through which they passed.

6 Jacques Derrida, *Aporias* (Stanford: Stanford University Press, 1993).

7 "Moment of intensity" refers to the wave-like effect of excesses in affect and emotions, which leave a trace of actual and virtual series. These moments of intensity are crucial in the interaction and constitution of *lo indígena* and the sense of making people. Throughout the book I use this in relation to *lo indígena* as an event, as will be described later. Gilles Deleuze, *The Logic of Sense, European Perspectives* (New York: Columbia University Press, 1990); Gilles Deleuze, *The Fold: Leibniz and the Baroque* (London:

Continuum International Publishing Group,1988); and James Williams, "'If Not Here, Then Where?' On the Location and Individuation of Events in Badiou and Deleuze," *Deleuze Studies* 3, no. 1 (2009): 97–123.

8   Jorge Luis Arriola was long preoccupied with the integration of "indigenous" peoples into the Guatemalan state through *indigenismo*, especially as it pertained to education. He was a fundamental figure in the *Seminario de Integración Social Guatemalteca*. The *Seminario* included a group of American and Guatemalan anthropologists (including Richard Adams, Manning Nash, and Sol Tax) who believed that the process of transculturation would enable the majority of *indígenas* to achieve complete economic, political, and citizenship integration into the Guatemalan state. Among other roles, Arriola was the minister of education in 1944 and director of the *Instituto Indígena Nacional* from 1955 to 1963, but was, above all, a pedagogue who gave conferences on childhood (*infancia*), humanism, and culture. For more on Arriola, see Chapter 3.

The *Instituto indigenista* was founded August 28, 1945, in Guatemala. Guatemala was one of several Latin American countries participating in the Inter-American Indigenous Congress in Michoacán, Mexico, in 1940. From this congress, an Inter-American Institute was founded and with it a National Indigenist [*indigenista*] Institute in countries participating in the congress (Bolivia, Ecuador, Guatemala, Mexico, Peru). The purpose of such institutes was to study "*el problema indígena*" [the indigenous problem] or "indigenismo" in Guatemala. Its goal was "to study autochthonous cultures and the *incorporación* [inclusion] of the indigene to the national culture." Francisco Rodríguez Rouanet, "Algunos datos biográficos y la participación del lic. Antonio Goubaud Carrera en la creación y primeros trabajos del Instituto Indigenista Nacional" (Lecture given at the Academia de Geografía e Historia, Guatemala City, 2002); Francisco Rodríguez Rouanet, *El indígena guatemalteco: Su cultura tradicional, complejos problemas y posibles soluciones* (Guatemala: Cómite de Arte y Cultura del Banco de Guatemala, 1990). For extensive research on *Indigenismo* and the Institute, see Dennis F. Casey, "Indigenismo, the Guatemalan Experience" (Ph.D. Dissertation, History, University of Kansas, 1979); Jorge Ramón González-Ponciano, "De la patria del criollo a la patria del shumo: Whiteness and the Criminalization of the Dark Plebeian in Modern Guatemala" (Ph.D. Dissertation, Anthropology, University of Texas-Austin, 2005), esp. chap. 2.

9   Richard Adams, in his survey of the culture of *Ladinos* in Guatemala, describes *ladinización* as individual and group processes. "Individual ladinization involves a process of social mobilization and the learning of new personal habits by the individual in question. That means that an individual has come out of a cast or social class and that, through a change of habits and other associations, has entered another one. Group ladinization, in which an entire community abandons gradually 'indigenous' customs, does not imply social mobility, but is in essence a transcultural process, through which a social group gradually becomes more 'Ladino' and less 'indigenous'; that means it is a process though which norms and social organization change." Richard Adams, *Encuesta sobre la cultura de los ladinos en Guatemala*, 2nd edition (Guatemala: Centro Editorial "Jose Pineda Ibarra," 1964), 53–54. Italics added. For the Spanish original see Appendix 5, item 1.

10 Jorge Luis Arriola, "En torno a la integración social en Guatemala," *Guatemala Indígena* 1, no. 1 (1961): 12. The fragments in this statement were published in *Guatemala Indígena*, one of the three publications by the Instituto Indigenista Nacional (the other two were *Boletín del Instituto Indigenista Nacional* and *Publicaciones Especiales del Instituto Indigenista Nacional*). *Guatemala Indígena* was published between 1961 and 1983, and it included three sections

22   Zero = Nothing = Everything

specializing in (a) studies on "Indian" groups and solving the "Indian problem," (b) precursors of ethnographic studies in Guatemala from the XVI to the XIX, and (c) folkloric expressions. María Teresa de Jesús Mosquera Saravia, *Índice general de la revista Guatemala indígena* (Guatemala: Universidad de San Carlos de Guatemala, 1995). For the Spanish original see Appendix 5, item 2. Unless otherwise credited, the English translations are my own.

11 For Charlie Hale, "Maya efflorescence" is the "Maya" collective rights movement that grew in part from the crusade for civil rights and in part for the defensive struggle for survival in the shadow of a repressive state. Charles R. Hale, *Más que un indio/More Than An Indian: Racial Ambivalence and Neoliberal Multiculturalism in Guatemala* (Santa Fe: School of American Research Press, 2006). Beside the struggle for rights, for Santiago Bastos and Aura Cumes and their team of colleagues in the voluminous *Mayanización* project, *Mayanización* means a "new formulation, articulation and appropriation of the Maya World" from a multicultural paradigm and "the process self-identifying as Mayas." It implies the importance and presence of "Mayas" in decision-making roles and as activists. Santiago Bastos and Aura Cumes, *Mayanización y vida cotidiana: La ideología multicultural en la sociedad Guatemalteca*, 3 vols. (Guatemala: Cholsamaj Fundación, 2007).

12 "Instituto Santiago," accessed October 12, 2011, www.lasallesantiago.edu.gt/. For the Spanish original see Appendix 5, item 3. The institute, founded in 1949 by the Catholic Church, is a boarding school that serves "indigenous" youth mostly from rural Guatemala and prepares them to become teachers in their "communities of origin." In the opening speech, Monseñor Mariano Rosell Arellano (then archbishop of Guatemala) explains the need for the institute: "Given the conditions of exploitation of the life and conscience of the Indian, [. . . it is necessary] to form seeds of apostles of the *indígena* race . . . so that from childhood, formed integrally, which means Christianly, tomorrow he would be the new essence of the exploited race of yesterday and abandoned today, so that he would be the free race of tomorrow, free of fear, free of ancestral holes, free from racial humiliations, free from ignorance." This statement appears in pages one and two of the written speech made available to Dr. Emma Chirix via one of the Indigenist Institutes funded by Rosell Arellano. I thank Dr. Chirix for making the speech available to me. For the Spanish original see Appendix 5, item 4. For more general information by Azmitia on the La Salle mission in Guatemala and the Institute, see Oscar Azmitia, *El Instituto Indígena Santiago, una alternativa de educación media rural: Sistematización de la experiencia* (Guatemala: PRODESSA, 1993), and Berkley Center for Religion, Peace, and World Affairs: Georgetown University, "A Discussion with Oscar Azmitia of the Universidad de la Salle, Costa Rica (Spanish)," accessed December 8, 2012, http://berkleycenter.georgetown.edu/interviews/a-discussion-with-oscar-azmitia-of-the-universidad-de-la-salle-costa-rica-spanish.

13 Miguel Ángel Asturias, *Sociología guatemalteca: El problema social del indio*, ed. Julio César Pinto Soria (Guatemala: Editorial Universitaria, Universidad de San Carlos de Guatemala, 2007).

14 Miguel Ángel Asturias, "El problema social del indio" (B.A. Theses Licenciatura en Derecho, Universidad de San Carlos de Guatemala, 1923), 25, 45. For the Spanish original see Appendix 5, item 5.

15 "*Indian*/indigenous/*indígena*" belong with each other semantically; however, there are discursive differences between them. In contemporary usage, "Indian," for instance, is perhaps most understood as a pejorative used to signal inferiority and dehumanize (but not always; sometimes *indígena* carries the same meaning). *Indígena*, more widely used in the latter decades of the twentieth century, is associated with revitalizing efforts connected to larger international

"indigenous" peoples' struggles since the conquest(s) (Inga Clendinnen, *Ambivalent Conquests: Maya and Spaniard in Yucatan, 1517–1570*, 2nd edition. Cambridge: Cambridge University Press, 2003). *Indígena*, however, is still a colonial category for some, and, just like "Indian," of little use, in postcolonial efforts. "Maya" or "Mayense" (which do not encompass "Xinca" and "Garifuna"), however, are more acceptable ways of naming and identifying that which has been historically fabricated "Indian" or "*Indígena*." Even this assertion, that "Indian" and "Maya" may share some meaning, is a contested terrain. For more on the struggles of "indigenous" people, see Karen Engle, *The Elusive Promise of Indigenous Development: Rights, Culture, Strategy* (Durham: Duke University Press Books, 2010. On the struggles of "indigenous" peoples and de-colonial projects see, for example, Florencia E. Mallon, ed., *Decolonizing Native Histories: Collaboration, Knowledge, and Language in the Americas* (Durham: Duke University Press Books, 2011), and for chapters on "Mayas" in particular, see Jan Rus and Diane L. Rus, "The Taller Tzotzil of Chiapas, Mexico: A Native Language Publishing Project, 1985–2002," 144–74; and Edgar Esquit, "Nationalist Contradictions: Pan-Mayanism, Representations of the Past, and the Reproduction of Inequalities of Guatemala," 196–218. See also Warren, *Indigenous Movements and Their Critics*; Jan Rus, "The 'Comunidad Revolucionaria Institucional': The Subversion of Native Government in Highland Chiapas, 1936–1968," in *Everyday Forms of State Formation: Revolution and the Negotiation of Rule in Modern Mexico*, eds. Gilbert Michael Joseph and Daniel Nuget (Durham: Duke University Press, 1994), 265–300; Jean E. Jackson, *Indigenous Movements, Self-Representation, and the State in Latin America*, ed. Kay B. Warren (Austin: University of Texas Press, 2002), and for a chapter on Mayan voices and leadership see, especially Victor Montejo "The Multiplicity of Mayan Voices: Mayan Leadership and the Politics of Self-Representation," 123–48. See also, Richard Adams, "Strategies of Ethnic Survival in Central America," in *Nation States and Indians in Latin America*, eds. Greg Urban and Joel Scherzer (Austin: University of Texas Press, 1991), 181–206; and Richard Adams, "A Report on the Political Status of the Guatemala Maya," in *Indigenous Peoples and Democracy in Latin America*, ed. Donna Lee Van Cott (New York: St. Martin's Press, 1994), 155–86. For some additional details on the context of the struggles, see, for example, Arturo Taracena Arriola, *Invención criolla, sueño ladino, pesadilla indígena: Los Altos de Guatemala, de región a Estado, 1740–1871* (Guatemala: Centro de Investigaciones Regionales de Mesoamérica (CIRMA), 1999); Marta Casaús Arzú, *Guatemala: linaje y racismo* (Guatemala: Facultad Latinoamericana de Ciencias Sociales, 1995). Throughout the book I employ the Spanish *lo indígena* to encompass people, material, and virtual items that include discourses, ideas, practices, and beliefs and also for textual purposes; I do so in full recognition of the complexities inherent in the term.

16 The division between theory and practice here is fictive. I use both terms to inform the education reader of whose heritages I am referring to. The heritages of this division itself are not a central task of this book.

17 Existence here means present and presence. Existence here means neither present nor presence. In this apophatic use of existence I want to highlight that the present does not refer only to itself, and therefore is not the ultimate horizon of curriculum engagement in this book. I am not privileging the present (in the exclusion of "indigenous" peoples in Guatemala). I recognize it as respectfully as I recognize people's pasts (which is not always the absence of presence), pasts that inform the scholarly and political actions of the "Maya" on a day-to-day basis. Present and past may not be at all separate. Likewise, existence may very well mean alternatives to different kinds of times and futures. For an

examination of presence and present see Guzmán Böckler and Herbert, *Guatemala: Una interpretación histórico-social*.

18 Here the work of Kathleen Davis on periodization is instructive in raising one's awareness of the Judeo-Christian heritages of temporal divisions that moderate, divide, and regulate the ways in which one engages with "history" (AD, BC, medieval/modern, contemporaneity, twentieth century, 1920s, and so on). With much hesitation I define the periodization of the book from the 1920s to 2012; at the same time I pay attention to how texts are (dis)organized in neat and not-so-neat bundles of discourses that cross-fertilize, with concepts and notions that slide and therefore blur any attempt at defining clear lines of rupture of meanings. Periodization is, as Davis explains, a "complex process of conceptualizing categories, which are posited as homogeneous and retroactively validated by the designation of a period divide" and are not a "mere back-description that divides history into segments, but . . . a fundamental political technique—a way to moderate, divide, and regulate—always rendering its services *now*." Kathleen Davis, *Periodization and Sovereignty: How Ideas of Feudalism and Secularization Govern the Politics of Time* (Philadelphia: University of Pennsylvania Press, 2008), 3, 5.

19 Ian Hacking, *Rewriting the Soul: Multiple Personality and the Sciences of Memory* (Princeton: Princeton University Press, 1998); Ian Hacking, "Inaugural Lecture: Chair of Philosophy and History of Scientific Concepts at the Collège De France," *Economy and Society* 31 (2001): 1–14; Ian Hacking, "Kinds of People: Moving Targets" (The Tenth British Academy Lecture, London, 2006).

20 The textual play in (s)object here suggests a sensitivity to the distinctions made (from the eighteenth but more so in the nineteenth century) between "object" and "subject," which are linked to the discussions in the history of science as elucidated by Lorraine J. Daston and Peter Galison, *Objectivity* (New York: Zone Books, 2010). In contexts such as the long struggle for "indigenous" peoples' self-determination and positioning as subjects within the broader discourse of rights, the linguistic difference—between being an object as the recipient of action from a more powerful subject, and vice versa—matters. The analytical work I launched here recognizes that such difference matters politically. The latent preoccupation in this book, however, is beyond any subject–object dichotomy which, in itself is colonial to a certain extent, "posited that objects of study did not produce knowledge in their own right." Sonia E. Alvarez, Arturo Arias, and Charles R. Hale, "Re-visioning Latin American Studies," *Cultural Anthropology* 26, no. 2 (2011): 228. The preoccupation lies indeed with how something/someone—a (s)object—gets constituted and ordered through the educational. I will discuss this more at length later on in the chapter.

21 At times these disciplines (i.e., anthropology, sociology, history, and their subfields) are not rigid or stable, but are put in motion through the reflections and critiques that scholars engage in from within (such practices of reflective anthropology and the questioning of historicism), as well as with scholars from without the social sciences and humanities.

22 Alvarez, Arias, and Hale, "Re-Visioning Latin American Studies."

23 Ian Hacking, *Historical Ontology* (Cambridge: Harvard University Press, 2004).

24 Lorraine Daston, *Biographies of Scientific Objects* (Chicago: University of Chicago Press, 2000), 2.

25 Ibid., 3.

26 One of the common notions of time in Mayan cosmology is that it is infinite. Carlos López reads time in the Popol Wuj as infinite for it constructs and destroys itself, it evolves and involves, has no beginning or end, gets expanded and contracted, moves in different directions, is not a fixed point, and thus it is

in perpetual motion. To "represent" time, López uses the geometry of thee Koch curve fractal; distance seen in fragments allows the creation of larger distance. The zooming in and zooming out gives one the idea of movement. Therefore, the more fragmented reality is, the more complex it becomes, and the closer it gets to the infinite in endless motion. Carlos M. López, *Los Popol Wuj y sus epistemologías: Las diferencias, el conocimiento y los ciclos del infinito* (Quito: Abya-Yala, 1999), see esp. chaps. 1 and 2. Popol Wuj are a set of texts whose origins are located in the "Maya K´iche´ culture." Seen Luis Enrique Sam Colop, *Popol Wuj/Popol Vuh* (Guatemala: F&G Editores, 2011); and Adrián Inés Chávez, *Pop Wuj: Libro del tiempo o de acontecimientos* (Quetzaltenango: Vile, 1981).

27 The question here is not whether *lo indígena* did (does) or did not (does not) exist before or after a set frontier, in this case the scientific inquiry of "the indigenous." This frontier "is not an absolute demarcation between what has never been there and what has always been there." Bruno Latour, "On the Partial Existence of Existing and Nonexisting Objects," in *Biographies of Scientific Objects*, ed. Lorraine Daston (Chicago: University of Chicago Press, 2000), 257. Rather, the question engages the theory of *lo indígena's* relative existence; "it is relatively real and relatively existent." Ibid.

28 Bastos and Cumes, *Mayanización y vida cotidiana*.

29 See for example Edgar Esquit Choy, "Las rutas que nos ofrecen el pasado en el presente: Activismo político, historia y pueblo maya," in *Memorias del mestizaje: Cultura política en centroamérica de 1920 al presente*, ed. Darío A Euraque, Jeffrey L Gould, and Charles R Hale (Guatemala: CIRMA, 2004), 167–92; Fischer and Brown, *Maya Cultural Activism in Guatemala*.

30 Daston, *Biographies of Scientific Objects*, 6.

31 Ibid., 5.

32 Hacking, "Kinds of People: Moving Targets," 2.

33 Ibid., 2.

34 Ibid., 2.

35 Bastos and Cumes, *Mayanización y vida cotidiana*, 21. For the Spanish original see Appendix 5, item 6.

36 Rodríguez Rouanet, "Algunos datos biográficos y la participación del lic. Antonio Goubaud Carrera en la creación y primeros trabajos del Instituto Indigenista Nacional," 2.

37 Deleuze, *The Logic of Sense*, 161.

38 Michel Foucault, "Questions of Method," in *The Foucault Effect: Studies in Governmentality*, eds. Graham Burchell, Colin Gordon, and Peter Miller (Chicago: Chicago University Press, 1991), 76.

39 The italicized suffix -ing in event-aliz*ing* stresses the action and movement orientation of the event.

40 Deleuze, *The Logic of Sense*. See also François Zourabichvili and Kieran Aarons, *Deleuze, a Philosophy of the Event: Together with the Vocabulary of Deleuze* (Edinburgh: Edinburgh University Press, 2012). For other literatures on "event" see, for example, Fernand Braudel, *The Mediterranean and the Mediterranean World in the Age of Philip II: Vol. 1* (Berkeley: University of California Press, 1995); François Dosse, *New History in France: The Triumph of the Annales* (Chicago: University of Illinois Press, 1994); and Stuart Clark, "The Annales Historians," in *The Return of Grand Theory in the Human Sciences*, ed. Quentin Skinner (Cambridge: Cambridge University Press, 1985), 175–98.

41 For a provocative discussion of this element of Deleuze's argument, see Steven Shaviro, *Without Criteria: Kant, Whitehead, Deleuze, and Aesthetics* (Cambridge: The MIT Press, 2012).

42 Deleuze, *The Fold: Leibniz and the Baroque*, 77.

43 For accounts of these events, see, for example, "Indigenas sufren masacre militar en tiempos de paz," *El Potosi*, accessed November 24, 2012, www.elpotosi.net/2012/1006/31.php; "Guatemala: Cuestiones de fondo detrás de la masacre de Alaska," *America Latina en Movimiento*, accessed October 30, 2012, http://alainet.org/active/58769&lang=es; "Totonicapán: La historia de la última masacre en Guatemala," *Centro de Investigación Periodística*, November 23, 2012, http://ciperchile.cl/2012/10/11/totonicapan-la-historia-de-la-ultima-masacre-en-guatemala/; "Diplomáticos y Funcionarios Cuestionan uso del Ejercito en Desalojo," *El Periódico*, accessed October 15, 2012, www.elperiodico.com.gt/es/20121009/pais/218993; "Indigenous Protesters Killed in Totonicapan, Guatemala," *NISGUA*, accessed October 30, 2012, http://nisgua.blogspot.de/2012/10/indigenous-protesters-killed-in.html.
44 On the Rigoberta Menchú controversy, see Menchú and Burgos-Debray, *Me llamo Rigoberta Menchú y así me nació la conciencia*; David Stoll, *Rigoberta Menchu and the Story of All Poor Guatemalans*, expanded edition (Boulder: Westview Press, 2007); Arturo Arias, ed., *The Rigoberta Menchú Controversy*, 1st edition (Minneapolis: University of Minnesota Press, 2001); Diane M. Nelson, *Reckoning: The Ends of War in Guatemala*, 1st edition (Durham: Duke University Press Books, 2009), esp. chap. 4, "Indian Giver or Nobel Savage? Rigoberta Menchú Tum's Stoll/en Past"; Greg Grandin, "It Was Heaven That They Burned," *The Nation*, September 8, 2010, www.thenation.com/print/article/154582/it-was-heaven-they-burned; "Debate over I, Rigoberta Menchú Continues . . . David Stoll's Response," *Middlebury Blogs Network*, accessed December 10, 2010, http://blogs.middlebury.edu/rigoberta/.
45 Williams, "If Not Here, Then Where? On the Location and Individuation of Events in Badiou and Deleuze."
46 Degrees of intensity announce that this inquiry is not anchored in "breaks" and continuities and discontinuities of meaning as an approach to history; though that is indeed a productive way of doing historical analysis, it is insufficient for ("post")colonial contexts like Guatemala. I seek to account for what is "indigenous" as an event with changes in degrees of intensity of meaning, demonstrated when they become more noticeable, rather than on when a "new" idea or a "new" construction emerges. I am interested in complex dynamics of emergences of meanings, their extensions, relations, and how they are used to mobilize certain educational agendas.
47 Williams, "If Not Here, Then Where? On the Location and Individuation of Events in Badiou and Deleuze," 105. Italics added.
48 *Corte* and *güipil* are the skirt and blouse that make the colorful woven dresses that "Mayan women" wear.
49 Deleuze, *The Fold: Leibniz and the Baroque*.
50 "Memory knots are sites of society, place, and time so bothersome, insistent, or conflictive that they move human beings, at least temporarily, beyond the *homo habitus* [. . . they] are sites where the social body screams. . . . They refer to sites of humanity, sites in time, and sites of physical matter or geography. Special human groups and leaders, specific events and dates and specific physical sites all seem to stir up, collect, and concentrate memories." Steve J. Stern, *Remembering Pinochet's Chile: On the Eve of London 1998 (Latin America Otherwise)* (Durham: Duke University Press Books, 2006), 121.
51 Michel Foucault, *The Archaeology of Knowledge* (New York: Pantheon Books, 1972), 87.
52 Deleuze, *The Fold: Leibniz and the Baroque*.
53 Williams, "If Not Here, Then Where? On the Location and Individuation of Events in Badiou and Deleuze."
54 Georges Didi-Huberman, "L'image brûle," in *Penser par les images: Autour des travaux de Georges Didi-Huberman* (Lormont: Cécile Defaut, 2006), 11–52.

See also, Inés Dussel, "Historicizing the Material and Visual Culture of Schooling: Reflections on the Use of Objects, Images and Technologies as Sources in the History of Education," in *Critical Methodologies for Researching Teaching and Learning*, eds. Christina Siry and Catherina Schreiber (Amsterdam: Sense Publishers, in print).
55 By positivistic I mean the "unity of science and scientific inquiry" as the *sine qua non* of living, engaging, and inquiring into life and cosmologies. Knowledge produced in positivistic frames dwell in essentialisms and flatten life, reducing it to a "core" under the surveillance of the Apollonian eye, which, as Denis Cosgrove puts it, is the divine and mastering view from a single perspective. Denis Cosgrove, *Apollo's Eye: A Cartographic Genealogy of the Earth in the Western Imagination* (Baltimore: The Johns Hopkins University Press, 2003).
56 Thomas Popkewitz, "Styles of Reason and the Historical Object: (Re)visioning The History of Education," in *(Re)visioning The History of Education: Transnational Perspectives On the Questions, Methods and Knowledge*, ed. Thomas S. Popkewitz (New York: Palgrave, 2013), 7.
57 Ibid., 12.
58 Foucault, *The Archaeology of Knowledge*, 129.
59 *Archivo General de* Centro América (AGCA), *Hemeroteca del* AGCA, *Centro de Investigaciones Regionales de Mesoamérica* (CIRMA), *Biblioteca Nacional, Hemeroteca Nacional, Biblioteca* César Brañas, *Biblioteca del Ministerio de* Educación, *Centro de Documentación del Ministerio de Cultura Nacional, Biblioteca Universidad San Carlos de Guatemala, Biblioteca Universidad del Valle, Biblioteca del Programa de Lingüística Universidad Mariano Gálvez, Centro de Documentación de* PRODESSA, and the libraries and small archives of the specific schools where I observed classes.

References

Adams, Richard. *Encuesta sobre la cultura de los ladinos en Guatemala*. 2nd edition. Guatemala: Centro Editorial "Jose Pineda Ibarra," 1964.

———. "A Report on the Political Status of the Guatemala Maya." In *Indigenous Peoples and Democracy in Latin America*, edited by Donna Lee Van Cott, 155–86. New York: St. Martin's Press, 1994.

———. "Strategies of Ethnic Survival in Central America." In *Nation States and Indians in Latin America*, edited by Greg Urban and Joel Scherzer, 181–206. Austin: University of Texas Press, 1991.

Alvarez, Sonia E., Arturo Arias, and Charles R. Hale. "Re-Visioning Latin American Studies." *Cultural Anthropology* 26, no. 2 (2011): 225–46.

Arias, Arturo. "Letter from Guatemala: Indigenous Women on Civil War." *PMLA* 124, no. 5 (October 2009): 1874–77.

———. "The Maya Movement, Postcolonialism and Cultural Agency." In *Coloniality at Large: Latin America and the Postcolonial Debate*, edited by Mabel Moraña, Enrique Dussel, and Carlos Jáuregui, 517–39. Durham: Duke University Press, 2008.

———, ed. *The Rigoberta Menchú Controversy*. 1st edition. Minneapolis: University of Minnesota Press, 2001.

Arriola, Jorge Luis. "En torno a la integración social en Guatemala." *Guatemala Indígena* 1, no. 1 (1961): 7–30.

Arzú, Marta Casaús. *Guatemala: linaje y racismo*. Guatemala: Facultad Latinoamericana de Ciencias Sociales, 1995.

Asturias, Miguel Ángel. "El problema social del indio." B.A. Thesis Licenciatura en Derecho, Universidad de San Carlos de Guatemala, 1923.

———. *Sociología Guatemalteca: El problema social del indio.* Edited by Julio César Pinto Soria. Guatemala: Editorial Universitaria, Universidad de San Carlos de Guatemala, 2007.

Azmitia, Oscar. *El Instituto indígena Santiago, Una alternativa de educación media rural: Sistematización de la experiencia.* Guatemala: PRODESSA, 1993.

Bastos, Santiago, and Aura Cumes. *Mayanización y vida cotidiana: La ideología multicultural en la sociedad Guatemalteca.* 3 vols. Guatemala: Cholsamaj Fundación, 2007.

Braudel, Fernand. *The Mediterranean and the Mediterranean World in the Age of Philip II.* Vol 1. Berkeley: University of California Press, 1995.

Casey, Dennis F. "Indigenismo, the Guatemalan Experience." Ph.D. Dissertation, History, University of Kansas, 1979.

Chávez, Adrián Inés. *Pop Wuj: Libro del tiempo o de acontecimientos.* Quetzaltenango: Vile, 1981.

Clark, Stuart. "The Annales Historians." In *The Return of Grand Theory in the Human Sciences*, edited by Quentin Skinner, 175–98. Cambridge: Cambridge University Press, 1985.

Clendinnen, Inga. *Ambivalent Conquests: Maya and Spaniard in Yucatan, 1517–1570.* 2nd edition. Cambridge: Cambridge University Press, 2003.

Cosgrove, Denis. *Apollo's Eye: A Cartographic Genealogy of the Earth in the Western Imagination.* Baltimore: The Johns Hopkins University Press, 2003.

Crosby, Alison, M. Brinton Lykes, and Brisna Caxaj. "Carrying a Heavy Load: Mayan Women's Understandings of Reparation in the Aftermath of Genocide." *Journal of Genocide Research* 18, no. 2–3 (July 2, 2016): 265–83. doi:10.1080/1 4623528.2016.1186952.

Daston, Lorraine. *Biographies of Scientific Objects.* Chicago: University of Chicago Press, 2000.

Daston, Lorraine J., and Peter Galison. *Objectivity.* New York: Zone Books, 2010.

Davis, Kathleen. *Periodization and Sovereignty: How Ideas of Feudalism and Secularization Govern the Politics of Time.* Philadelphia: University of Pennsylvania Press, 2008.

Deleuze, Gilles. *The Fold: Leibniz and the Baroque.* London: Continuum International Publishing Group, 1988.

———. *The Logic of Sense: European Perspectives.* New York: Columbia University Press, 1969.

Derrida, Jacques. *Aporias.* Stanford: Stanford University Press, 1993.

Didi-Huberman, Georges. "L'image brûle." In *Penser par les images: Autour des travaux de Georges Didi-Huberman*, edited by Laurent Zimmerman, Georges Didi-Huberman, Araund Rykner, Karine Wikelvoss, Estelle Jacoby, Martine Créac'h, and Muriel Pic, 11–52. Lormont: Cécile Defaut, 2006.

Dosse, François. *New History in France: The Triumph of the Annales.* Chicago: University of Illinois Press, 1994.

Dussel, Inés. "Historicizing the Material and Visual Culture of Schooling: Reflections on the Use of Objects, Images and Technologies as Sources in the History of Education." In *Critical Methodologies for Researching Teaching and Learning*, edited by Christina Siry and Catherina Schreiber. Amsterdam: Sense Publishers, in print.

Ejército de Guatemala. "Operación Sofía." *National Security Archive*, 1982. www.gwu.edu/~nsarchiv/NSAEBB/NSAEBB297/index2.htm.

Engle, Karen. *The Elusive Promise of Indigenous Development: Rights, Culture, Strategy*. Durham: Duke University Press Books, 2010.
Esquit Choy, Edgar. "Las rutas que nos ofrecen el pasado en el presente: Activismo político, historia y pueblo maya." In *Memorias del mestizaje: Cultura política en centroamérica de 1920 al presente*, edited by Darío A. Euraque, Jeffrey L. Gould, and Charles R. Hale, 167–92. Guatemala: CIRMA, 2004.

———. "Nationalist Contradictions: Pan-Mayanism, Representation of the Past and the Reproduction of Inequalities in Guatemala." In *Decolonizing Histories: Collaboration, Knowledge and Language in the Americas*, edited by Florencia E. Mallon, 167–92. Durham: Duke University Press, 2012.

Falla, Ricardo. *Masacres de la selva: Ixcán, Guatemala, 1975–1982*. Guatemala: Editorial Universitaria, 1992.

Fischer, Edward, and McKenna Brown. *Maya Cultural Activism in Guatemala*. Austin: University of Texas Press, 1996.

Flores, José. *El Verde Púrpura / José Flores*. Guatemala: Fenix, 1986.

Flynn, Patricia, Mary Jo McConahay, Denese Becker, Berkeley Media, Jaguar House Films, Independent Television Service, and KQED-TV (Television station : San Francisco, California). *Discovering Dominga*. DVD. Berkeley: Berkeley Media, 2002.

Foss, Bob, Åsa Faringer, Ulf Hultberg, Monica Zak, and Dirk Brüel. *Pumaens datter / la hija del puma*. DVD. Sweden: Domino Film & TV-Produktion: Distribution Statens Filmcentral, 1995.

Foucault, Michel. *The Archaeology of Knowledge*. New York: Pantheon Books, 1972.

———. "Questions of Method." In *The Foucault Effect: Studies in Governmentality*, edited by Graham Burchell, Colin Gordon, and Peter Miller, 73–87. Chicago: Chicago University Press, 1991.

González-Ponciano, Jorge Ramón. "De la patria del criollo a la patria del shumo: Whiteness and the Criminalization of the Dark Plebeian in Modern Guatemala." Ph.D. Dissertation, Anthropology, University of Texas-Austin, 2005.

Grandin, Greg. "It Was Heaven That They Burned." *The Nation*, September 8, 2010. http://www.thenation.com/print/article/154582/it-was-heaven-they-burned.

"Guatemala: Cuestiones de fondo detrás de la masacre de Alaska." *America Latina en Movimiento*, October 30, 2012. http://alainet.org/active/58769&lang=es.

Guzmán Böckler, Carlos, and Jean-Loup Herbert. *Guatemala: Una interpretación histórico-social*. Guatemala: Cholsamaj, 1995.

Hacking, Ian. *Historical Ontology*. Cambridge: Harvard University Press, 2004.

———. "Inaugural Lecture: Chair of Philosophy and History of Scientific Concepts at the Collège de France." *Economy and Society* 31 (2001): 1–14.

———. "Kinds of People: Moving Targets." The Tenth British Academy Lecture, London, 2006.

———. *Rewriting the Soul: Multiple Personality and the Sciences of Memory*. Princeton: Princeton University Press, 1998.

Hale, Charles R. *Más que un indio / More Than an Indian: Racial Ambivalence and Neoliberal Multiculturalism in Guatemala*. Santa Fe: School of American Research Press, 2006.

Hernández Alarcón, Rosalinda. "Indigenas sufren masacre militar en tiempos de paz." *El Potosi*. Accessed November 24, 2012. www.elpotosi.net/2012/1006/31.php.

———. *Memorias rebeldes contra el olvido = Paasantzila txumb'al ti' sotzeb' al k'u'l*. Guatemala: Cuerda/Plataforma Agraria/AVANCSO, 2008.
Jackson, Jean E. *Indigenous Movements, Self-Representation, and the State in Latin America*. Edited by Kay B. Warren. Austin: University of Texas Press, 2002.
Latour, Bruno. "On the Partial Existence of Existing and Nonexisting Objects." In *Biographies of Scientific Objects*, edited by Lorraine Daston, 247–69. Chicago: University of Chicago Press, 2000.
López, Carlos M. *Los Popol Wuj y sus epistemologías: Las diferencias, el conocimiento y los ciclos del infinito*. Quito: Abya-Yala, 1999.
Mallon, Florencia E., ed. *Decolonizing Native Histories: Collaboration, Knowledge, and Language in the Americas*. Translated by Gladys McCormick. Durham: Duke University Press, 2011.
Menchú, Rigoberta, and Elisabeth Burgos-Debray. *Me llamo Rigoberta Menchú y así me nació la conciencia*. México: Siglo Veintiuno Editores, 1985.
Moller, Jonathan. *Our Culture Is Our Resistance: Repression, Refuge, and Healing in Guatemala*. New York: PowerHouse Books, 2004.
———. *Rescatando nuestra memoria / Rescuing Our Memory*. Guatemala: F&G Editores, 2009.
Montejo, Victor. "The Multiplicity of Mayan Voices: Mayan Leadership and the Politics of Self-Representation." In *Indigenous Movements, Self-Representation, and the State in Latin America*, edited by Jean E. Jackson and Kay B. Warren, 123-48. Austin: University of Texas Press, 2002.
———. *Testimony: Death of a Guatemalan Village*. Willimantic: Curbstone Press, 1987.
Mosquera Saravia, and María Teresa de Jesús. *Índice general de la revista Guatemala indígena*. Guatemala: Universidad de San Carlos de Guatemala, 1995.
Museo Comunitario Rabinal Achi (Rabinal, Guatemala). *Oj k'aslik/Estamos vivos: Recuperación de la memoria histórica de Rabinal, 1944–1996*. Rabinal, Baja Verapaz, Guatemala: Museo Comunitario Rabinal Achi, 2003.
Nelson, Diane M. *Reckoning: The Ends of War in Guatemala*. Durham: Duke University Press Books, 2009.
Otero Diez, Santiago, Marcelino López Balan, Marcelino Cano Saucedo, Angel Ovidio Velázquez Castellanos, and Tiburcio Hernández Utuy. *Testigos del morral sagrado: En homenaje a los catequistas sobrevivientes que han trabajado con dedicación, aun arriesgando la propia vida, por la construcción del reino de Dios*. Guatemala: ODHAG, 2011.
Popkewitz, Thomas. "Styles of Reason and the Historical Object: (Re)visioning The History of Education." In *(Re)visioning The History of Education: Transnational Perspectives on the Questions, Methods and Knowledge*, edited by Thomas S. Popkewitz, 1–26. New York: Palgrave, 2013.
Porras Castejón, Gustavo. *Las huellas de Guatemala*. 2nd edition. Guatemala: F&G Editores, 2009.
———. *Las Huellas de Guatemala*. Guatemala: F&G Editores, 2009.
Proyecto Interdiocesano de Recuperación de la Memoria Histórica (Guatemala). *Guatemala, nunca más: Informe*. Guatemala: ODHAG, 1998.
Rodríguez Rouanet, Francisco. "Algunos datos biográficos y la participación del lic: Antonio Goubaud Carrera en la creación y primeros trabajos del Instituto Indigenista Nacional." Lecture given at the Academia de Geografía e Historia, Guatemala City, 2002.

———. *El indígena guatemalteco: Su cultura tradicional, complejos problemas y posibles soluciones*. Guatemala: Cómite de Arte y Cultura del Banco de Guatemala, 1990.

Rus, Jan. "The 'Comunidad Revolucionaria Institucional': The Subversion of Native Government in Highland Chiapas, 1936–1968." In *Everyday Forms of State Formation: Revolution and the Negotiation of Rule in Modern Mexico*, edited by Gilbert Michael Joseph and Daniel Nuget, 265–300. Durham: Duke University Press, 1994.

Sam Colop, Luis Enrique. *Popol Wuj / popol vuh*. Guatemala: F&G Editores, 2011.

Sanford, Victoria. *Buried Secrets: Truth and Human Rights in Guatemala*. New York: Palgrave Macmillan, 2003.

Shaviro, Steven. *Without Criteria: Kant, Whitehead, Deleuze, and Aesthetics*. Cambridge: The MIT Press, 2012.

Simon, Jean-Marie. *Guatemala: Eterna Primavera, Eterna Tiranía*. Guatemala: Fundación Soros Guatemala/CIRMA/Centro Cultural de España/Estudio A2, 2010.

Stern, Steve J. *Remembering Pinochet's Chile: On the Eve of London 1998 (Latin America Otherwise)*. Durham: Duke University Press Books, 2006.

Stoll, David. *Rigoberta Menchu and the Story of All Poor Guatemalans: Expanded Edition New Foreword by Elizabeth Burgos*. Expanded edition. Boulder: Westview Press, 2007.

Stuart, David. "The Calligraphic Zero." *Maya Decipherment*. Accessed August 2, 2012. http://decipherment.wordpress.com/2012/06/15/the-calligraphic-zero/.

Taracena Arriola, Arturo. *Invención criolla, sueño ladino, pesadilla indígena: Los Altos de Guatemala, de región a Estado, 1740–1871*. Guatemala: F&G Editores, 2011.

———. "Totonicapán: La historia de la última masacre en Guatemala." *Centro de Investigación Periodística*, November 23, 2012. http://ciperchile.cl/2012/10/11/totonicapan-la-historia-de-la-ultima-masacre-en-guatemala/.

Warren, Kay B. *Indigenous Movements and Their Critics: Pan-Maya Activism in Guatemala*. Princeton: Princeton University Press, 1998.

Williams, James. "If Not Here, Then Where? On the Location and Individuation of Events in Badiou and Deleuze." *Deleuze Studies* 1, no. 1 (2009): 97–123.

Yates, Pamela. *When the Mountains Tremble*. DVD. United States: Skylight Pictures, 1983.

Zourabichvili, François, and Kieran Aarons. *Deleuze, a Philosophy of the Event: Together with the Vocabulary of Deleuze*. Edinburgh: Edinburgh University Press, 2012.

1 "The Indian Problem"
Contouring the Retina and the Indian and Pre- and Post-War Educational and Social Policies Pro Diversity

This chapter is an intertwined analysis of educational policy documents and visuality. Following Deborah Poole's line of inquiry, I meditate here on the role images have played and continue to play in the making-up of "indigenous kinds" and how such roles relate to policies concerned with "indigenous" matters.[2] The chapter begins with an analysis of images in order to engage with the reasoning of the problem. My analytics of the moments of intensity in "indigenous" making point to the emergence and prominence of the problematic "Indian" as a project of both projection and protection. The "Indian problem" as a way to continue making up what is "indigenous" as an educational (s)object has been in circulation from around the end of the nineteenth century and into the twentieth and twenty-first centuries. Although the language of the "Indian" as a problem may no longer be explicitly employed in contemporary political-educational discourses, the style of reasoning that makes it possible is ever present. This "problem" reasoning permeates even the most progressive policies, laws, and accords employed to justify respect for diversity in the name of equity and equality.

Policies in Guatemala are understood in various educational spaces as the base upon which a better education for "indigenous" peoples is to be built. A few may argue that policies have little educational impact as they are "theoretical," and therefore far removed from what actually happens in "practice" on the ground, in schools. However, they do often serve as a warrant to put forth arguments for advancing the project of a more intercultural, peaceful, and just education that benefits "indigenous" peoples and the Guatemalan nation. They are also an accessible archive of the languages and imaginations that are at stake in the priorities for sculpting education in particular ways. The specific educational policy documents I have selected are not only relevant in matters of "indigenous" making, but are also key reference signposts for teacher educators, education advocates, activists, public officials, and lay people that I came in contact with. Some of them have been directly or indirectly involved in the drafting of the documents.

34 *"The Indian Problem"*

Figure 1.1 "Kaqchiquel Region—Chimaltenango or San Juan Sacatepéquez."[1] (Photo courtesy of the Valdeavellano Collection, Academia de Geografía e Historia de Guatemala). Original caption on the back of the picture.

This chapter takes up Jacques Derrida's analytics of *problēma* as projection and protection. The task is to question the reasoning of the "Indian" as a protection of all that has gone wrong in Guatemalan "modern" history and as a projection of the desirable aspirations anchored in the same violent systems of reason that were at the inception of the "Indian-Other" in the first place. Historicizing "the problem" is possible through an examination of Guatemalan archives from the turn of the twentieth century. This archive includes photographs, policy documents, interviews, and classroom observations. The chapter follows a spiral style. In taking a point and retuning to it in a fractal fashion, it aims to show the layers of complex dynamics of border drawing that projects and ostensibly plans the future of "indigenous" youth.

The Subject-ivity of Photographs and Gestures of "Modern" Configurations

Arguably, Alberto G. Valdeavellano's (1861–1928) and Tomás Zanotti's (1898–1950) photography circulated widely. Their portraits gave contours to the retina in the making of *lo indígena*.[3] Valdeavellano was Guatemalan, a fact that breaths pride into the development of Guatemalan photography.[4] His father was from Santa María in the Iberian Peninsula and his mother from Guatemala. The work in Guatemala (and Latin America) of daguerreotypists such as the Belgian Leon de Pontelle and the German Emil Herbruger paved the technological, aesthetic, and sociological way for Valdeavellano and other photographers of his generation.[5] Valdeavellano's quiet introduction of images in the late nineteenth to early twentieth centuries visually spoke for what is called rural Guatemala today. He traveled the country extensively, documenting "rural" and "urban" life. His voluminous body of work also visually documents what is known today as pre-Hispanic Guatemala: monuments and archaeological sites such as the image of the zoomorfo in Quiriguá in the introductory chapter is one of many of his archeological photography projects. These visual re-presentations traveled as postcards, through and out of the Guatemalan borders at the same time that they participated in the constitution of such borders.

The photographing of the "Indian" and the "rural," among other things (and other binaries, perhaps), highlighted the "Indian's" anthropological distance from the "non-Indian." This distance is the temporal relation created by anthropological activities to define the world of the savage, the primitive, an Other. This world is a temporal state, a stage, and a condition—of "backwardness," "underdevelopment," and "mental death." Anthropological distance is marked by temporal sequences enshrined in evolutionist time, where the "Indian" lives in another time, an undesirable past: a past of misery inflicted by colonization, as opposed to a victorious past of pre-Hispanic Mayan intellectual production.[6] This distance served as the framework upon which the project of nation was mounted as exemplified in the words of Batres Jáuregui and Asturias later.

The image of the "Indian" child, barefoot and scruffily dressed, came to epitomize what the nation needed to surpass if it were to progress and modernize. While working with Mayan youth and teachers in the photo archive at the Center for Mesoamerican Research (CIRMA) in 2016, a young man noted that the people featured in one of Valdeavellano's photos were not *indígena* because they were not dirty and were wearing shoes. "That's not

36 "The Indian Problem"

how it was," he explained. Valdeavellano's photographs have traveled to museums, made their way to personal collections, and relate to Miguel Ángel Asturias' literary production. In Asturias, the "Indian" is innocent, dirty, barefoot, rural, in need, and a problem.[7]

> How far does this difference go? The Indian represents a past civilization and the mestizo, or *ladino* as we call him, a civilization that is to come. The Indian comprises the majority of our population, lost his strength in the time of slavery to which he was subjected, he is not interested in anything... he represents the mental, moral, and material poverty of the country: he is humble, dirty, dresses differently and suffers without batting an eye. The ladino makes up the third part, lives in a distinct historical moment, with desires of ambition and romanticism, aspires, wishes, and is, in the end, the living part of the Guatemalan nation. What a brave nation that has two-thirds of its population dead to intelligent life![8]

It is important to underline that Miguel Ángel Asturias has been very influential in the field of education. Among other things, he founded and directed the *Universidad del Popular* in 1922, an institution whose aim was to "eradicate" illiteracy. Asturia's literary work is widely respected especially when it comes to its value for national pride. He received the first Nobel Prize for Guatemala in 1967 (the second one is Rigoberta Menchú in 1992). His books *Hombres de Maíz*, *Mulata de Tal*, and others can be found in teacher preparation schools today and are read by Mayan youth, for instance those who attend the *Jóvenes* Institute (see Appendix 3), who come to Guatemala City to receive an education and are expected to return to their communities to teach in elementary schools where most of the children are considered "indigenous."[9]

Whereas Valdeavellano photographed "Indians" in rural life, Zanotti photographed "Maya-K'iches'" from Quetzaltenango and its surroundings in a studio. This is the most prominent theme of the Zanotti collection housed in the CIRMA. Zanotti was born in Mexico to an Italian father and a Mexican mother and came to Guatemala in 1898. There appears to be a popular sentiment that Zanotti's portraits—in contrast to nineteenth-century European imperialistic practices such as anthropology and travel writing—give the viewer a sense of dignified "Maya-K'iche'" "men, women and children," who "looking at the camera project a lovely, dignified sense of self."[10] According to Greg Grandin, it was the "Maya-K'iches'" themselves who "sought and consumed the images shot by Zanotti."[11] To enter the photography studio and consume photography in this way would speak of the market freedom of the "Mayas" to choose and participate in a local practice previously consecrated to the few.

Portrait in a First Communion is a rich entanglement of elements that invite the participant viewer to venture into questions of religiosity and a

Figure 1.2 "Portrait in a First Communion." (Photo courtesy of the Tomás Zanotti Collection, CIRMA).

vision of modernity.[12] The First Communion is an occasion to be commemorated in Roman Catholic cultures. It is a life cycle event that arguably serves as a checkpoint in the progressive development of one's own Christianity and for the enactment of civil control by Catholic cultures.[13] The choice of props and the use of Victorian furniture imbues the images with a sense of elegance, sophistication, and stability. These Victorian references also suggest the influence of social Darwinism, notably the practices of observation and of classification, which are important relations to photography of this

38 "The Indian Problem"

kind, especially in terms of their role in making up people and "Indigenous" kinds.

The pearl necklace, the rosary, the veil, the candle, and the Renaissance-like painting of St. Peter and Jesus in the background all relate to a particular material and visual sophistication via "Europe," summoned here as a construct, a temporal and spatial location of aspiration. They are discursive elements of integration, transition, enlightenment, and modernization in which the "Indian" is allowed to participate via her presence both in the photographic studio and in schools.[14] The bare feet are a question, a statement of comfort or, perhaps, resistance.[15]

The textures of religion and science are the backdrop of educational texts emerging at the time Zanotti (and Valdeavellano) were shooting. This backdrop is an intertwining of (true) science not in opposition to Christianity, where the choice is not between social Darwinism or Christianity, but for a choice for liberal ideology, for the advancement of the nation, abandoning dogmas and addressing social problems by "thinking and acting in a scientific and modern way and, at the same time in a Christian way."[16] In *Los indios, su historia y su civilización*, Batres Jáuregui writes:

> In September 1797, [the Economic Society of Friends of the Country] offer[ed] a gold medal and meritorious membership to whoever wrote the best essay on the following subject: "Demonstrate solidly and clearly the advantages that would result for the State if all Indians and ladinos of this kingdom put on shoes and dressed in Spanish styles, and they experienced for themselves the physical, moral and political benefits; proposing the most smooth, simple and practicable means to reduce them to the use of these things, without violence, coercion or mandate"
>
> ... one of the most important social problems was about, as you can see, no other than to propose the means to make the aboriginal class and the other large portion of the less privileged social class, to enter civil life and partake of its benefits.
>
> Let's just say it straight. Primary and educational practical instruction is what we need for those masses of struggling Indians that constitute a real hindrance for the development of the country.[17]

The sober portrait of *Ladino Boy*, with clean suit, tie, and shoes, invites the retina to the focus on the *mappaemundi* and the alphabetical text in print, books, and literacy.[18] This distinct logocentric and phonocentric globe making,[19] privileges reading the printed text as the practice *par excellence* for development. Literacy of the kind suggested in this image secures Guatemala a prominent and historical second place in illiteracy rates in Latin America.[20] The book in connection to the globe inserts this young reader in a three-dimensional world projection philosophically and mathematically located in the "West,"[21] which is separate from the rest.[22] The world that he

Figure 1.3 "Ladino Boy." (Photo courtesy of the Tomás Zanotti Collection, CIRMA). Caption on the back of the picture.

points to makes him a Guatemalan citizen at the beginning of the twentieth century and, in the twenty-first century, a "global" and "cosmopolitan" citizen. The notion of cosmopolitanism here is one that, as Thomas Popkewitz asserts, organizes difference at the "divide of those who are enlightened and civilized and those who do not have those qualities—the backward, the savage, and the barbarian of the nineteenth century."[23] Sitting outside the global, with the globe at his fingertips, framed in an Olympian perspective, "the world becomes an abstract form held in the mind, hand and eye of a sovereign, imperial intelligence," of a Guatemalan citizen who is no longer a problem of the otherworldly sphere inhabited by *lo indígena*.[24] This split of the thisworldly and otherworldly, understood as verifiable via science (mathematical) and literacy (Judeo-Christian), is fundamental for the unquestioned grounds on which intercultural and inclusive educational projects are designed and instructed via pro-diversity educational policies.[25]

El Problema del Indio and "Indian" Making

The logic of "*el problema del indio*" in Guatemala (and the other places in the Americas and the Pacific) has historically emerged and traveled around "urban" corners, inside government cubicles, and up and down floors in the ivory tower, staging the "Indio" in the past, premodern, and thus a problem for development. The act of naming and pointing to "el Indio" is an orientalist philosophical performance of the kind that Edward Said alluded to, which makes an Other and talks about it as if it had acquired reality or is reality.[26] This discourse also enables the language of diversity that permeates public and educational policies and how they are discussed in bilingual education classrooms today. Consider this statement from a "Maya-Kaqchikel" teacher educator in a Bilingual-Intercultural Education Class for in-service and pre-service teachers at Guatemalan University[27]:

> When we speak of the multilingual, multiethnic, we are talking about a concrete matter, if we say that Guatemala is multilingual, why? Because there are 25 languages, right? It is not an ideological matter, it is a reality, we can go and count, we can survey, we can keep an account of how many people there are by language.[28]

Employing the same philosophical tools that create the reality of the Other (and of diversity), other possibilities inscribed within the same reality of the Other emerge, for example, "savage,"[29] "Xinca,"[30] "Mayan,"[31] "guerrilla,"[32] and unlawful.[33] "*El problema del indio*" is enunciated from the perspective of an "us–them" relation in which the "us" side is the point of departure, the here, from where no questions are asked. It is done that way because presumably it cannot be done otherwise.[34] The here is the "us" that defines the template against which the "Indian" is inserted as a "reality." In this template, the "Indian" as reality becomes a project, a task, a kind of division that allows for protection in case of danger, a *problēma*. At the same time, the "Indian," "them," becomes the problem for "us" in "our" reality. *Problēma*, as Derrida explains, is a Greek word that can signify projection or protection. As projection, *problēma* is "that which one poses or throws in front of oneself, either as a projection of a project or as a task to accomplish."[35] As protection, *problēma* is "a substitute, a prosthesis, that we put forth in order to represent, replace, shelter, or dissimulate ourselves, or as to hide something unavowable."[36]

In what follows, I highlight how this *problēma*tic mode of thinking is salient in the planning of education through educational policies and laws related to education. Let me begin by stating that "modern," formal, and public education, through educational legislation, has persistently been tasked with the resolution of the "Indian problem." Solving the "Indian" problem was a form of critical intellectual and political engagement of the first decades of the twentieth century with resonances in legislation later on in the century, and which can be traced in twenty-first century discourses of multiculturalism and inclusion—the new recognizable forms of critical and intellectual political engagement.

In the 1962 National Education Organic Law, the *Instituto Indigenista Nacional* (IIN) was a "technical" division which existed within the structure of the Ministry of Education. As a technical division (as was the case with the Institute of Anthropology, Ethnology, and History, and the National Education Technical Council), the IIN was charged with carrying out tasks, planning, and advising education on concrete matters related to "indigenous" peoples. One of the functions the IIN had was "to propose to the ministry of Public Education the necessary recommendations that it considers appropriate for the *solution of the Indian problems in the country* (Article 306, e)" (emphasis added). These solutions were to be informed by the anthropological knowledge gathered from the extensive fieldwork the IIN conducted in most rural areas of Guatemala. Ultimately the IIN's activities were to "lead to accelerating the process of landinization and contribute to the culturization of the indigenous communities (Article 305)."

The National Education Organic Law engages with "indigenous" matters more openly than in previous iterations.[37] The law is important in highlighting one of the noticeable moments when the "Indian" problem becomes more salient as a legal matter and thus relevant to educational demands. The law constitutes an important part of the linguistic and philosophical heritages that fund the educational preoccupations with working on the "Indian subject," a task to be accomplished for the advancement of the Guatemalan nation, which since 1996, signifies a "peaceful nation."

Policies and "Post"-War Problem Solving

Perhaps the most influential text in the educational legislation and reform of recent years is the Accords for a Firm and Durable Peace signed in 1996. The accords serve as a strong marker in public spaces to support arguments for a "better" education for "indigenous" youth. The document is used as a starting point for the analysis of current policies and serves to authorize particular claims for a future national project, at least those that concern public education, especially vis-à-vis bilingual and intercultural education that in many cases point to "indigenous themes" and diversity. The text is and is not about education.

The accords serve as a projection of the peace project that arguably concludes a painful historical time, never to be repeated. The document aims to mark a passage from the painful past into a peaceful present that can serve as a foundation for future political action, an invitation for educational reform. The first lines draw a *problēmatic* closure around the times of atrocities and throw in front of the nation the illusion of a durable peace. The document rhetorically serves as protection or shelter against the dangers that wars represent, wars derived from the "agrarian problem and rural development" and no longer the "Indian problem" but a "situation" of the "majority of the population that live in rural environments." The accords state that:

> The state and organized sectors of society should join forces for the solution of the *agrarian problem and rural development* which are fundamental to respond to *the situation of the majority of the population that lives in rural environments*, and which is the most affected by poverty, inequity and the weakness of state institutions.[38]

In Batres Jáuregui's words, "population . . . in rural environments" translates into "the aboriginal class and the other large portion of the less privileged social class,"[39] and which in Asturias' words means "the majority of our population . . . two thirds dead for intelligent life!"[40]

The document suggests that peace comes through the absolutist paths of "economic growth," "solving the agrarian problem," and "rural development" toward a generalized "common good" of the "entire or majority of the population" and for "national unity."

> Firm and durable peace should be cemented in socioeconomic participatory development oriented toward *common good*, which should respond to the necessities of the *entire population*. Such development requires social justice as one of the pillars of *national unity* and solidarity and of sustainable *economic growth* as conditions to respond to the social demands of the population.[41]

The suggestion here emerges from two "modern" notions: a *homogeneous* conception of materiality (embedded in "national unity") and *straight linear time* (suggested in development of the rural). This suggestion in the accord is also borne out of a struggle for a nonexistent uniformity. This homogenizing logic, perhaps not pertaining to economics but rather in relationship to ways of being and knowing, is precisely one of the triggers for (armed) conflicts in Guatemala (the plural here is intentional). Finally, the suggestion in the Peace Accords also emerges in covert discriminating and alienating relations within a "participative development" framework inside government offices as demonstrated by Claudia Dary's study in *Trabajando desde adentro*.[42] Government offices in the Ministry of Education are indeed designated to "perfect a democratic system without exclusion" by looking after the education of "indigenous" peoples.[43]

The accords invite a gaze over "rural environments" that, by default, also creates the non-rural. Here the gesture within linear time and a stagist frame is probably a transition from the rural or not-yet-modern stage to the nonrural or modern. Recall how, in Asturia's work, the evolutionist time inserted the "Indian" in the stage of "a past civilization," and the "Ladino" in the stage of a "civilization that is to come." The terms of *what* is to move from stage/point A to stage/point B are diverse and complex and do not remain the same over the course of the twentieth century or in what is discussed during the second decade of the twenty-first. However, the evolutionist and developmental aspirations still prevail. Education, through "official programs," is charged with the duty to widely disseminate the accords.

The project of the Peace Accords is announced and takes shape in other laws such as the Educational Advancement Against Discrimination Law (EAADL) of 2002, the National Languages Law, and the Accord for the Creation of the Vice-Ministry of Bilingual Intercultural Education. All of these engage with the dynamics of anthropological border drawing through education that relates to salient moments of "indigenous" making. The EAADL puts forth the formation of a "new citizen" who can be made through certain "knowledge," "attitudes," and "values." These are described in curricula that have emanated from these policies such as the National Base Curriculum (CNB), and refer to, for example, scientific and linguistic knowledge, intercultural attitudes, and moral values.

The CNB is the largest curriculum reform in Guatemala since the Peace Accords. Some of the notions the CNB officializes are precisely interculturality in the curriculum and pro-diversity moral values. The CNB also extends the century-long concern for scientific education and the preoccupation with linguistics in that it "promotes an education of excellence, adequate for the advancement of science and technology." The preoccupation with the linguistic is a suggested shift in orientation toward the identity of "indigenous" peoples, their self-determination, and respect for the diverse nation, which also counters assimilationist linguistic orientations such as *Castellanización* from the 1920s onwards.

Although elaborate notions of interculturality were present in the making in Zanotti's photography from 1900, the elements that enable the image captured in *Portrait of a First Communion* relate to the "new citizen" suggested in the lines of the 2006 CNB. According to Greg Grandin, Zanotti opened a conversation between the commercial photography lens of a foreigner and the "Maya-K'iches" seeking his services. Recall that the image includes elements of "indigeneity," religiosity, and linguistic and scientific knowledge, all of which were central to educational discourses in Manuel Estrada Cabrera's administration (1898–1920). Inspired by Minerva, the Roman goddess of wisdom, the arts, school, commerce, and war, the *Minervalias* were "festivals of instruction" during Estrada Cabrera's twenty-two-year dictatorship. As very popular spaces for educating the populace in ways to think about and implement education, the festivals were successful in orienting the compass of education to the North, to science, and to the notions of progress I have discussed so far. *Minervalias* were celebrations of science, "progresses of human reason," and language. Poems of "Homeric" qualities were recited in this event that took place at the end of the academic year in Minerva temples scattered throughout the nation. Minerva albums, printed at the time of the event, were voluminous texts that included messages and letters written in English, French, and Spanish by "enlightened" people from other countries to commemorate the festival and the ideals it represented. It also included images of portraits of "advanced" people, poems by students, and, of course, "the sublime words of the benefactor of the Patria." This is an instantiation of the developmental time and comparative reason embedded in the notion of progress. In a speech given at one of the festivals and reprinted in a Minerva album, Estrada Cabrera said, "Oh! Sublime Minerva Temple . . . always remain as eternal/enduring as the science of which you are an emblem. And you, oh noble Guatemalan nation, venerate in your Minerva Temple the love for study and progress."[44]

The linguistic knowledge advocated within this discourse of progress is known in today's policies as L2, the national language or Spanish, and L3 foreign languages (i.e., English, French, or German). The stress on learning an L3 (to use twenty-first-century language policy terminology) at the turn of the twentieth century is founded on "interculturalism" and "modernity," concepts that are also key in Guatemala's twenty-first-century educational agenda. This hope for interculturalism and modernity at the turn of the twentieth century is better expressed in an excerpt from Felipe Estrada Paniagua's commissioned speech given at the Minerva Temple in 1907:

> Yes, Gentleman, the civilizations of the Old world and the vigor of the far Orient already in our two seas and via the railroad that joins us, converge to the heart of Guatemala to cure it of the anemia of more than three centuries of atavism, and the intake of oxygenated and new blood make it throb with the heartbeat of interculturalism and the modern sentiment.[45]

The interculturalism sentiment announced here is arguably different from how it has been constructed in more recent policies, because it engages not only with the global, which in this excerpt refers to the "West" (Europe and the United States), but also the "multiplicity" of groups that live within the Guatemalan national borders, which needless to say, were defined by "Western" knowledges and practices such as anthropology and sociology. This is the acknowledgement made in the Accord of the Identity and Rights of Indigenous Peoples (AIRIP, 1995) discussed later.

Like the Peace Accords, the AIRIP relies on the educational system as the "most important" technology in its operationalization. The document makes explicit the "linguistic [and ethno-] diversity" of the nation in a way that was not available for most of the first half of the twentieth century. The document, with the political and academic discourses that made its existence possible, arguably can and has been able to open participatory spaces for the "Maya," "Garífuna," and "Xinca" "indigenous" groups that have been historically excluded from "the unity of the Guatemalan nation."

> The identity of the *Mayan* peoples is recognized as well as the *identities* of the *Garífuna* and *Xinca* peoples within the *unity of the Guatemalan nation*, and the government is committed to promoting a reform to the Political Constitution to this end before the Congress of the Republic.[46]

The accord arguably crystallizes the historical struggles for "indigenous" participation.[47] It does so by defining and patrolling the conceptual border of "indigenous" identity ("Maya," "Garífuna," and "Xinca") demanding a reform of the constitution, which would open the anthropological borders of the territories, languages, and cultures of the Guatemalan nation. "Indigenous" identity is put forth as a prosthesis in order to represent a kind of *problēma*, as protection of people, and to represent what is not "indigenous." *Indígena* shelters both "us" and "them" under an appeal for unity that can hide things that are unavowable, and perhaps unspeakable, but that respond to a sense of duty. The appeal for unity reinscribes a means of Othering that continues to fabricate differences.

In the AIRIP, for instance, Garífuna remains within anthropological demarcations; the anthropological reasoning here classifies and orders "people," their "identity," and their "values," but "Garífuna" is also mobilized to open the conceptual and anthropological demarcation of Guatemala as a "nonindigenous nation." These border-crossing and border-opening dynamics can challenge the limits guarded by traditions in which education was conceivable only through Spanish-medium instruction and only within the "dominant" culture. The ethical duty that policies carry aims to patrol some borders while opening others.

By demanding to "integrate the educational conceptions of the Mayas and of the other ninety-indigenous groups, in the philosophical, scientific, artistic, pedagogic, historical, linguistic and socio-political components [of the educational system], as a source of integral educational reform" as in article 1c, the AIRIP continues century-long efforts toward "indigenous" making. However, against the backdrop of "indigenous revival and revitalization" of the 1980s, the terms of such making have shifted to "recognizing and strengthening indigenous cultural identity, Mayan values and educational systems" as stated in Article 1 on educational reform.

The policies I have discussed thus far are in fact "fragile" and "hardly ever implemented"; "we are going from bad to worse." These arguments can be heard from classroom teachers to bilingual and intercultural education officials to parents. Their main point is that material resources and budget allocations are insufficient to implement this educational reform. Hardly ever are questions posed on *lo indígena*, and the systems of reason through which it emerged, and the ways in which it serves as a protection of all that has gone wrong in Guatemalan "modern" history and as a projection of the desirable aspirations anchored in the same violent systems of reason that have been at the inception of the "indigenous" as an Other in the first place. Leaving the foundations unquestioned that *problēma*tically keep *lo indígena* under closure may no longer be a viable "solution."

> The philosophy of Bilingual and Intercultural Education is based on *the coexistence of various cultures and languages* in the country, oriented towards strengthening *unity in diversity* of the Guatemalan nation.

Develop a stable social bilingualism for the Maya-speaking student population and a harmonious coexistence amongst peoples and cultures.[48]

The Direction of Bilingual and Intercultural Education (DIGEBI Accord No. 726–95) is understood as the most concrete iteration of the efforts to physically open up an "indigenous" space within the Ministry of Education. As an office within the buildings of the Ministry of Education, the DIGEBI aims to redraw borders with a dotted line that allows for the "coexistence of various cultures and languages," otherwise known as interculturality, while following the transnational folklore of "unity in diversity." This universalized desire suggests a porousness of the anthropological borders of the "Maya," "Xinca," and "Garífuna" cultures enunciated in the texts I have already discussed. Paradoxically, there is a solid line of closure of the same borders in "develop[ing] a *stable* social bilingualism for the *Mayan speaking student population*." A "harmonious life" is to be achieved through that unifying slogan that disciplines the "indigenous" peoples to live "harmoniously" as opposed to in a warlike (counter)insurgent reality and in a "backward state of exploitation, or mental death."

Article 11 of the DIGEBI Accord states that "the Regional and Departmental Directors and the leader-technicians of the DIGEBI must recognize, respect and promote *the culture of the place*." There is a sense of decentralization in delegating, through legal means, responsibilities to the regions to imperatively respond to the "culture of the place." This decentralization is in tension with the notion of the "coexistence of various cultures" in Article 3. The "culture of the place" draws a territorial and geographic boundary that reduces the possibilities to responsibly and substantively recognize the "multilinguistic," "pluricultural," and unstable dynamics of "culture/s," especially given that the DIGEBI is responding to "post-"war internal and transnational migratory populations that challenge stable sociospatial configurations. This is the case of the multilingual region Ixcán, for instance, where small villages, whose inhabitants have migrated from several geographic locations in the Guatemalan territory, use multiple languages. Another instance is the case of Guatemala City. "The culture of the place" invites a spatial distancing under the shadow of the temporal, which creates a divide and a projected difference, a reinstated Otherness, a kind of arborescent relationship.[49]

Imbued with a duty to respond to the "culture" and "multi-ethnicity themes" in the nation, the Vice-Ministry of Bilingual Education (Government Accord 626-2003) is embraced as a celebrated space of "indigenous" participation within the state apparatus. However, more recently concern has been voiced about the lack of substantial educational change, suggesting disenchantment with the project. Nonetheless, it is highly regarded as a marker of the success of "indigenous" struggles in education, breaching the rigid walls of a hostile Guatemalan state. Its specific duty, as Article 1D states, is to work toward the "development of indigenous peoples, based on their own languages and cultures." Underdevelopment is an undesirable condition. The locale of enunciation for this duty seems to be "us," which is anything other than the underdeveloped, distant, perhaps peripheral rural villages. The development project is thus dutifully indebted to "them," "their own languages and cultures." We continue to see the repeated themes in these policy documents: the stagist reasoning, the anthropological distance, the border demarcations between us and them. Both the DIGEBI Accord and the Vice-Ministry of Bilingual and Intercultural Education demarcate, open, and relocate boundaries and make them porous, and are boundaries in themselves, both open and closed.

So far I have been referring to the duty and the project of policies as a task to accomplish, a duty that has a debt to pay back to those who have been *problēma*tized historically, who have suffered the most dehumanizing atrocities of necropolitical decision making, a duty within *problēma*tic closure.[50] There is a constant problem posing. The creation of DIGEBI is the deployment of a program, a technical application of a rule or a norm "to protect the decision of responsibility by knowledge, by some technical assurance, or by the certainty of being right, of being on the side of science, of consciousness, or of reason."[51] None of these, Derrida warns us, should ever be abandoned, "but as such, are only the guardrail of a responsibility to whose calling they remain radically heterogeneous."[52] In other words, we must continue to interrogate the duties, debts, norms, rules, and problems in terms of their definitions, determinations, and heterogeneity, especially when they are presented as solutions or as supportive of particular educational agendas.

A final document in this analysis, which also leads us into the next chapter, is the National Languages Law Decree Number 19-2003. This law is another text that is commonly referenced by teacher educators and other educationists aware of critical politics in Guatemala. Language has been an important construct for "indigenous" making. The law specifies that "the official language in Guatemala is Spanish" and that "the state recognizes, promotes and respects the languages of the Mayas, Garífuna and Xinka peoples."[53] This highlights the borderline redrawn between the colonial language—Spanish—and others: "Mayas, Garífuna, and Xinka." The former is "official" and the latter "recognized, promoted, and respected." What both kinds of descriptors suggest is not clear. What seems clear, however, is their separation. The gesture is toward the historical separation in a linear line of historical development. This separation stages Spanish as a *language* and the others as *lenguas* (tongues) in need of "advancement" and "development" to become languages. Phonocentric linguistic reasoning, and logics of separability and enumerability (see Chapter 2) make possible the naming of "Xinka," "Garífuna," and "Maya," as well as counting the various Mayan languages (twenty-two in total, including Kaqchikel, Ixil, Poqomam, and Tz'utujil),[54] thus turning them into manageable units

48   *"The Indian Problem"*

readily available to be inserted into grids such as policies, laws, and accords like the ones analyzed in this chapter.

As a language, Spanish is at the center, and "Mayas," "Garífuna," and "Xinka," as *lenguas*, continue to be a project of "indigenous" making; a project that, in turn and through the struggles that made this language law possible, is meant to challenge such center.

> *Identity*. The Mayans, Garífuna and Xinka languages are essential elements in national identity; their acknowledgment, respect, advancement, development and usage in the public and private spheres is oriented towards national unity in diversity and are meant to strengthen interculturalism between co-nationals.[55]

The law is also enshrined in stagist ("advancement," "development"), essentializing ("languages"), and totalizing ("national unity") theories. Languages suggest an instrumental developmentalizing task for the peoples affiliated to "Mayan," "Xinca" or "Garífuna." They and their languages are essential and matter as long as they can be inserted in the project of "national unity." The motion toward national unity here suggests a pre-stage of nationhood and a desirable one that can come about if that which is *not national* passes through the stage of becoming a "co-national." Like in other texts analyzed in this chapter, the Languages Law continues to make anthropological borders (language and languages communities, "Mayas," "Garífuna," and "Xinca") official.

> *Usage*. In the Guatemalan territory Mayas, Garífuna and Xinka languages can be used in the *languages communities in which they correspond*, in all their forms, without restrictions in the public or private space, in educational, academic, social, economic, political and cultural activities.[56]

Finally, "Maya, Garífuna, and Xinka languages can be used in the communities" where "they correspond," suggesting their acceptance in certain places (for example the villages where they are spoken) and not in others (for instance Guatemala City, and other urban centers). This is a similar spatializing and linguistic-territorializing logic to that which we have seen in previous excerpts.

The National Languages Law, as well as the other policies discussed, are popularly known as battles won by the "indigenous" peoples after several years of struggle to open up the anthropological borders of the Guatemalan state. Although the passing of this law is at times celebrated for the feelings of presence—and inclusion—that it affords for "indigenous" peoples and advocates, it is paradoxically necessary and insufficient, as both Derrida and Dipesh Chakrabarty warn us, to break through the problematic and/or *problēmatic* heritages from which it emerges.[57]

In Conclusion

Images do not simply reflect or express a subject, but also constitute it. The photographs that introduced the chapter "function as clues in terms of the specific theoretical schemes that orient 'the historian's effort to shape an intelligible and usable past.'"[58] They also serve as clues for specific schemes that suggest a reading of how the "Indian problem" has been philosophically defined. Such terms that define the "Indian" as a social, political, and even ontological problem have shifted in the course of the late nineteenth, twentieth, and beginning of the twenty-first centuries. The crafting of the policies demonstrates the complex dynamics of border drawing, of locating centers, temporalizations, and spatializations. Educational aspirations have been installed in a *problēma*tic logic where *lo indígena* is perpetually problematized, posed as a problem to be solved, as a task to be accomplished in order to produce a more just education system, as a project to protect the nation and the self (both "us" and "them") from their own past and from more atrocities.

Historicizing a past that is intelligible and usable is crucial for engaging with questions—generated from within education—that help us understand why things don't change. Why does Guatemalan education not move forward? Why do "indigenous" peoples not progress if we have educational and other policies in place that are to serve precisely the "indigenous" peoples' cause? The thesis, assumptions, logics, and history behind these very questions are hardly ever held in abeyance, even when a desire for openings is faced with closures.

Notes

1. This caption can be found on the back of the photograph and it is believed to be handwritten by historian Luis Muñoz, who owned the collection from which this photograph is taken.
2. Deborah Poole, *Vision, Race, and Modernity: A Visual Economy of the Andean World* (Princeton, N.J.: Princeton University Press, 1997).
3. W. J. T. Mitchell argues that "we live in a culture of images, a society of the spectacle, a world of semblances and simulacra," where such images are "a complex interplay between visuality, apparatus, institutions, discourses, bodies, and frugality." W. J. T Mitchell, *Picture Theory: Essays on Verbal and Visual Representation*, New edition (Chicago: University of Chicago Press, 1995), 5, 16. In such a culture of images, Nicholas Mirzoeff states, we are visual subjects, "agents of sight (regardless of our capacity to see) and as the objects of certain discourses of visuality." Nicholas Mirzoeff, *Watching Babylon: The War in Iraq and Global Visual Culture* (New York: Routledge, 2005), 3. We are also "educated in particular regimes of appearance, as Inés Dussel would warn us, and instructed by ways in which one should look and what is to be made of the visual encounter." Inés Dussel, "Teachers' Visual Culture and the Works of Global Imagination" (presented at the IVSA, Buenos Aires, 2008), and Inés Dussel, "School Uniforms and the Disciplining of Appearances: Towards a Comparative History of Regulation of Bodies in Early Modern France, Argentina, and The United States" (Ph.D. Dissertation, Curriculum and Instruction, University

of Wisconsin—Madison, 2001). For more on the visuality of classroom and schooling specifically see Ian Grosvenor, ed., *Silences and Images: The Social History of the Classroom* (New York: Peter Lang AG, 1999); and Ian Grosvenor, "From the 'Eye of History' to 'a Second Gaze': The Visual Archive and the Marginalized in the History of Education," *History of Education*, no. 36 (2007): 607–22; and for some initial efforts on visuality and images in Guatemalan museums, see Marta Elena Casaús Arzú, "Museo nacional y museos privados en Guatemala: Patrimonio y patrimonialización: Un siglo de intentos y frustraciones," *Revista de Indias* 72, no. 254 (2012): 93–130.

4 See, for example, Luis Luján Muñoz, *Los indígenas de Guatemala vistos por el fotógrafo Alberto G. Valdeavellano (1861–1928)* (Guatemala: INGUAT/Academia de Geografía e Historia, 1987); and Claudia Graciela López Cuat, "Análisis semiótico del mensaje estético de la fotografía artística del guatemalteco Alan Benchoam" (B.A. Thesis Licenciatura en Ciencias de la Comunicación, Universidad de San Carlos de Guatemala, 2005), esp. chp. 1.

5 Peter Palmquist and Thomas Kailbourn, *Pioneer Photographers of the Far West: A Biographical Dictionary, 1840–1865* (Stanford: Stanford University Press, 2002).

6 Johannes Fabian, *Time and the Other: How Anthropology Makes Its Object* (New York: Columbia University Press, 1983); W.J. T Mitchell, "World Pictures: Globalization and Visual Culture," in *Globalization and Contemporary Art*, ed. Jonathan Harris (Malden: Wiley-Blackwell, 2011), 267.

7 Miguel Ángel Asturias, "El problema social del indio" (B.A. Thesis Licenciatura en Derecho, Universidad de San Carlos de Guatemala, 1923). For an English translation of the thesis, see Miguel Ángel Asturias, *Guatemalan Sociology: The Social Problem of the Indian*, trans. Maureen Ahern (Tempe: Arizona State University, Center for Latin American Studies, 1977).

8 Ibid., 12. For the Spanish original see Appendix 6, item 1 (emphasis added).

9 For critical perspectives on Asturias's work *vis-à-vis* "indigenous" matters, see, for example, Julio Cesar Pinto Soria's introduction to Miguel Ángel Asturias, *Sociología guatemalteca: El problema social del indio*, ed. Julio César Pinto Soria (Guatemala: Editorial Universitaria, Universidad de San Carlos de Guatemala, 2007); and Preble-Niemi Oralia, ed., *Cien años de magia: Ensayos críticos sobre la obra de Miguel Ángel Asturias* (Guatemala: F&G Editores, 2006).

10 Margarett Lock, "A Strong Silent Gaze, No Matter What," *The New York Times*, January 20, 2000.

11 Greg Grandin, "Can the Subaltern Be Seen? Photography and the Affects of Nationalism," *Hispanic American Review* 84, no. 1 (2004): 86.

12 There is, of course, more to this image and the following one (*Portrait of a Ladino Boy*) than the elements I reflect upon here, for instance, questions on gender, complicated or suspended by sexuality, the speed at which "men" assimilated (?) to "Western" dress in relationship to "women." The contemporary argument often goes that "men" wear more "Western" clothing than women do (the towns around Lake Atitlan are an exception, where both "men" and "women" still wear "Mayan" clothing), that "women" have held on to their *traje* (dress) longer than "men," and this opposition generates a multitude of speculations as to why. "Women" have resisted longer? "Women" are slower at modernizing? "Men" leave their village to work and assimilate to the demands of the market? "Men" are leading modernity? And so on.

13 "The Catholic Church and its separation from the Mexican State dwells on the loss of privileges during the colonial period: the tithe, civil control over the population through the 'sacred sacraments' and its censuses, mainly baptisms, communions, and anointing of the sick and the dead. They provide a spectrum by ages, and current civil condition. There is also education, which is exclusive

to the Catholic Church during the same period. [The Church] even controls the immigration of foreigners into the country, prohibiting permanent residence in the national territory to foreigners whose country of origin is not Catholic." For the Spanish original see Appendix 6, item 2. Jorge Isauro Rionda, "Los conflictos gobierno-iglesia," *El Heraldo*, August 28, 2012. See also, Severo Martínez Peláez, *La patria del criollo: Ensayo de interpretación de la realidad colonial guatemalteca* (Guatemala: Editorial Universitaria, 1970); and Carlos Guzmán Böckler and Jean-Loup Herbert, *Guatemala: Una interpretación histórico-social* (Guatemala: Cholsamaj, 1995).

14 See, for example, Bienvenido Argueta's research on the modernization project in Guatemala via schools for "indigenous" peoples and pedagogy between 1885 and 1899. Bienvenido Argueta Hernández, *El nacimiento del racismo en el discurso pedagógico* (Guatemala: PACE-GIZ, 2011); and Bienvenido Argueta Hernández, "La pedagogía del doctor Darío González," *Revista Educación*, no. 7 (2011): 27–58. See also Emma Delfina Chirix García, *Cuerpos, poderes y políticas : Mujeres Mayas en un internado católico/Ch'akulal, chuq'aib'il chuqa b'anobäl : Mayab' ixoqi' chi ru pam Jun kaxlan tz'apatäl Tijonik /*, Primera edición (Guatemala: Ediciones Maya' Na'jo, 2013).

15 I thank the curating team of the photo exhibit *Mira. Aun no es historia* for their comments and critical appreciation of Valdeavellano's collection at CIRMA.

16 Daniel Tröhler, *Languages of Education: Protestant Legacies, National Identities, and Global Aspirations* (New York: Routledge, 2011), 106.

17 Antonio Batres Jáuregui, *Los indios, su historia y su civilización* (Guatemala: Tipografía la Unión, 1894), 168, 188. For the Spanish original see Appendix 6, item 3.

18 According to Batres Jáuregui, in 1799 the *Sociedad Economica de Guatemala* (Guatemalan Economic Society) held contests to generate substantial theses or propositions on *"regenerar el país"* (regenerate the country). According to a *"memoria impresa"* (printed memoire) written by Fr. Antonio Muro of the *"orden Betlemitico"* (Bethlehemite Order), part of this project to regenerate the nation was to "try to persuade the utility and means so that the Indians and Ladinos dress and use footwear the Spanish way." Ibid., 170. For the Spanish original see Appendix 6, item 4.

19 Phonocentrism is for Derrida where "voice and being, voice and the meaning of being, and voice and the ideality of meaning" are in absolute proximity. Logocentrism is "the determination of being of the entity as present." Jacques Derrida, *Margins of Philosophy* (Chicago: University of Chicago Press, 1982), 12. See also Nelson Goodman, *Ways of Worldmaking* (Indianapolis: Hackett, 1978). This presence that Derrida refers to comes about first in speech (or the first-order representation of meaning) produced by the thinking subject and second in writing as the representation of speech (the second-form representation of meaning). Lynn Mario Menezes de Souza, "Entering a Culture Quietly: Writing and Cultural Survival in Indigenous Education in Brazil," in *Disinventing and Reconstituting Languages*, eds. Alastair Makoni and Sinfree Pennycook (New York: Multilingial Matters, 2007), 135–69.

20 Of course, this has not been established using evaluation measurements such as the Organisation for Economic Co-operation and Development's (OECD) Program for International Student Assessment (PISA). As of 2016 Guatemala is not a PISA participant and is far from "making it" as a "global" and "knowledgeable economy"—although it is also not necessarily the case that it should continue to aspire to be one. The aspirations driving PISA are interesting to examine in order to understand how dialogue and competition between national education systems are set up within and from "European" modes of ordering. For a critical reading of PISA and the reasoning behind international ranking

52 "The Indian Problem"

practices via standardized assessments of reading, mathematics, and science, see, for example, Miguel A. Pereyra, Hans-Georg Kotthoff, and Robert Cowen, eds., *PISA Under Examination: Changing Knowledge, Changing Tests, and Changing Schools* (Rotterdam: Sense Publishers, 2011). And for a more historical overview, see Johanna Kallo, "OECD Education Policy: A Comparative and Historical Study Focusing on the Thematic Reviews of Tertiary Education" (Jyväskylä Finnish Educational Research Association, 2009).
21 The *mappaemundi* in this image is a method of map projection. Its heritage goes back to dominant types of maps before the Renaissance (T-O maps and others). These kinds of maps, John P. Snyder argues, initially had bases that were philosophical rather than mathematical. But "the attraction towards scientifically sound map projection was prompted by various factors. Fundamental was the desire for knowledge itself, whether philosophical or scientific. Many of those contributing to the advancement of map construction, and specifically map projections, were renowned philosophers or ordinary clergymen. . . . The study of projections is now frequently termed mathematical cartography, but the development of appropriate mathematics was often contemporary with the development of map projections both during and after the Renaissance." John P. Snyder, *Flattening the Earth: Two Thousand Years of Map Projections* (Chicago: University of Chicago Press, 1997), 3.
22 Edward Said, *Orientalism* (New York: Vintage Books, 1979).
23 Thomas S. Popkewitz, *Cosmopolitanism and the Age of School Reform: Science, Education, and Making Society by Making the Child*, 1st edition (New York: Routledge, 2007), 4.
24 Mitchell, "World Pictures: Globalization and Visual Culture."
25 Bernadette Baker, "Provincializing Curriculum? On the Preparation of Subjectivity for Globality," *Curriculum Inquiry* 40, no. 2 (2010): 83–111.
26 Said, *Orientalism*.
27 See Appendix 1.
28 Classroom observation (Bilingual-Intercultural Education Class), August 18, 2012. For the Spanish original see Appendix 6, item 5.
29 "It is known that the first civilized men who came to these regions were captained by Votán, the mysterious and extraordinary character who disembarked in Tabasco, Mexico, from the northern regions. To establish his civilizing system, he had to dominate the savage Mexicans and later founded a powerful empire named Xibalba or Xibalbay, whose capital was Nachan or Na-Chan." For the Spanish original see Appendix 6, item 6. Manuel Estrada Cabrera, *El libro azul de Guatemala* (Guatemala, 1915), 37.
30 "According to Juarros is *Sinca; xorti*, according to the small ethnographic map that was published in Paris, with the 'Letter from the Republic of Guatemala,' compiled by Juan Gavarrete. The 17th of October 1884, Daniel G. Briton presented before the American Philosophical Society the following, translated into English: The name is said in different ways *Xinca, Xinka* and *Sinca*. The first one is correct, in which the initial x is the same as the soft English *sh*, as in *show*." For the Spanish original see Appendix 6, item 7. Marco Vinicio Mejía Dávila, "El Xinca histórico: Una investigación bibliográfica," *Winak: Boletín intercultural* 4, no. 1 (1988): 4.
31 "The identity of the Mayan peoples is recognized . . . Maya values and educational systems and other indigenous peoples." *Acuerdo sobre Identidad y Derechos de los Pueblos Indígenas* (Accord of the Identity and Rights of Indigenous Peoples) (1995).
32 "The Indian problem. Who can tell us what to do about it? They are ignorant. They are dirty. They don't even speak Spanish. We made some mistakes, but

"The Indian Problem" 53

we had to terminate the guerrilla." From a 1994 interview with a high-ranking official responsible for dozens of massacres in Ixcán in 1982. Victoria Sanford, *Buried Secrets: Truth and Human Rights in Guatemala* (New York: Palgrave Macmillan, 2003), 201.

33 See the image of special police forces surrounding the Normal Institute for Women Belén occupied by pre-service teacher education students peacefully protesting the creation and implementation of a teacher education reform in 2012. The caption of the photograph reads "Un contingente de las Fuerzas Especiales se apostó alrededor del Instituto Normal para Señoritas Belén, en la zona 1, desde ayer por la tarde [A Contingent of Special Forces has Guarded Belén Normal Institute for Girls in Zone 1 since Yesterday Afternoon]." "Mineduc Solicita Orden de Desalojo," *Prensa Libre*, June 21, 2012.
34 Jacques Derrida, *Aporias* (Stanford: Stanford University Press, 1993).
35 Ibid., 11.
36 Ibid., 11.
37 For an account of Guatemalan educational laws from 1831 to 1991 see Bienvenido Argueta Hernández, "Una perspectiva histórica de las leyes de educación en Guatemala y los desafíos actuales para una nueva ley de educación nacional," in *Memoria X encuentro nacional de investigadores educativos de Guatemala: Legislación e investigación educativa* (Guatemala: Universidad Rafael Landivar, 2006), 7–75.
38 *Acuerdo de Paz Firme y Duradera*, 1996 (emphasis added). For the Spanish original see Appendix 6, item 8.
39 Batres Jáuregui, *Los indios, su historia y su civilización*, 168.
40 Asturias, "El problema social del indio," 12.
41 *Acuerdo de Paz Firme y Duradera*, 1996 (emphasis added). For the Spanish original see Appendix 6, item 9.
42 Claudia Dary, *Trabajando desde adentro: De activistas a funcionarios: Los mayas frente a los desafíos de la multiculturalización del estado (2000–2010)* (Guatemala: Instituto de Estudios Interétnicos, Universidad de San Carlos de Guatemala, 2011).
43 *Acuerdo de Paz Firme y Duradera*, 1996.
44 *La Hora*, January 24, 1977. For the Spanish original see Appendix 6, item 10. For more on Minervalias see Jorge Luján Muñoz, "Un ejemplo de uso de la tradición clásica en Guatemala: Las 'minervalias' establecidas por el presidente Manuel Estrada Cabrera," *Revista de la Universidad del Valle de Guatemala* 2 (1992): 25–33; Catherine Rendón, *Minerva y la palma: El enigma de don Manuel Estrada Cabrera* (Guatemala: Artemis Edinter, 2000); Catherine Rendón, "Temples of Tribute and Illusion," *Americas* 54, no. 4 (2002): 16–23; Maynor Carrera Mejía, "Las fiestas de Minerva en Guatemala, 1899–1919: El ansia de progreso y de civilización de los liberales," *Portal Historia Centroamericana*, (2009): 1–13.
45 Speech given at the Minerva Temple on the name of the government by Felipe Estrada Paniagua at the Fiestas Escolares, 1907. Guatemala. (Taracena Arriola Collection, 495), CIRMA. For the Spanish original see Appendix 6, item 11.
46 *Acuerdo sobre Identidad y Derechos de los Pueblos Indígenas*, 1995 (emphasis added). For the Spanish original see Appendix 6, item 12.
47 On the peace process and the Accords see, for example, Rachel Sieder, ed., *Guatemala after the Peace Accords* (London: Institute for the Study of the Americas, 1999); Susanne Jonas, *Of Centaurs and Doves: Guatemala's Peace Process* (Boulder: Westview Press, 2000); FLACSO (Organization), *Guatemala, historia reciente (1954–1996)*, ed. Virgilio Álvarez A. (Guatemala: Editorial de Ciencias Sociales, 2012).

54 *"The Indian Problem"*

48 *Dirección General de Educación Bilingüe Intercultural (DIGEBI) Acuerdo Gubernativo* No. 726-95 (emphasis added). For the Spanish original see Appendix 6, item 13.
49 Gilles Deleuze and Felix Guattari, *A Thousand Plateaus: Capitalism and Schizophrenia*, trans. Brian Massumi, 1st edition (Minneapolis: University of Minnesota Press, 1987).
50 Achille Mbembé, "Necropolitics," *Public Culture*, no. 15 (2003): 11–40.
51 Derrida, *Aporias*, 19.
52 Ibid., 19.
53 *Ley de Idiomas Nacionales, Decreto Número* 19-2003 (emphasis added). For the Spanish original see Appendix 6, item 14.
54 This is the complete list of Mayan languages according to the Mayan Languages Academy in 2012: Poqomchi', Achi', Q'eqchi', Ch'orti', Kaqchikel, Poqomam, Sipakapense, Tz'utujil, Mam, Ixil, Sakapulteka, Uspanteka, Awakateka, Chalchiteka, Akateka, Chuj, Jakalteka, Q'anjob'al, Tektiteka, K'iche', Itza', Mopan. See http://almg.org.gt/
55 *Ley de Idiomas Nacionales, Decreto Número* 19-2003 (emphasis added). For the Spanish original see Appendix 6, item 15.
56 *Ley de Idiomas Nacionales, Decreto Número* 19-2003 (emphasis added). For the Spanish original see Appendix 6, item 16.
57 Dipesh Chakrabarty, *Provincializing Europe: Postcolonial Thought and Historical Difference* (Princeton: Princeton University Press, 2000).
58 Fernando Coronil, "Seeing History," *Hispanic American Review* 84, no. 1 (2004): 4.

References

Argueta Hernández, Bienvenido. *El nacimiento del racismo en el discurso pedagógico*. Guatemala: PACE-GIZ, 2011.
———. "La pedagogía del doctor Darío González." *Revista Educación*, no. 7 (2011): 27–58.
———. "Una perspectiva histórica de las leyes de educación en Guatemala y los desafíos actuales para una nueva ley de educación nacional." In *Memoria X encuentro nacional de investigadores educativos de Guatemala: Legislación e investigación educativa*, 7–75. Guatemala: Universidad Rafael Landivar, 2006.
Asturias, Miguel Ángel. "El problema social del indio." B.A. Thesis Licenciatura en Derecho, Universidad de San Carlos de Guatemala, 1923.
———. *Guatemalan Sociology: The Social Problem of the Indian*. Translated by Maureen Ahern. Tempe: Arizona State University, Center for Latin American Studies, 1977.
———. *Sociología guatemalteca: El problema social del indio*. Edited by Julio César Pinto Soria. Guatemala: Editorial Universitaria, Universidad de San Carlos de Guatemala, 2007.
Baker, Bernadette. "Provincializing Curriculum? On the Preparation of Subjectivity for Globality." *Curriculum Inquiry* 40, no. 2 (2010): 83–111.
Batres Jáuregui, Antonio. *Los indios, su historia y su civilización*. Guatemala: Tipografía la Unión, 1894.
Carrera Mejía, Maynor. "Las fiestas de Minerva en Guatemala, 1899–1919: El ansia de progreso y de civilización de los liberales." *Portal Historia Centroamericana* (2009): 1–13.
Casaús Arzú, Marta Elena. "Museo nacional y museos privados en Guatemala: Patrimonio y patrimonialización: Un siglo de intentos y frustraciones." *Revista de Indias* 72, no. 254 (2012): 93–130.

Chakrabarty, Dipesh. *Provincializing Europe: Postcolonial Thought and Historical Difference*. Princeton: Princeton University Press, 2000.

Chirix García, Emma Delfina. *Cuerpos, poderes y políticas: mujeres mayas en un internado Católico/Ch'akulal, chuq'aib'il chuqa b'anobäl : Mayab' ixoqi' chi ru pam jun kaxlan tz'apatäl tijonik*. Guatemala: Ediciones Maya' Na'jo, 2013.

Coronil, Fernando. "Seeing History." *Hispanic American Review* 84, no. 1 (2004): 1–4.

Dary, Claudia. *Trabajando desde adentro: De activistas a funcionarios: Los mayas frente a los desafíos de la multiculturalización del estado (2000–2010)*. Guatemala: Instituto de Estudios Interétnicos, Universidad de San Carlos de Guatemala, 2011.

Deleuze, Gilles, and Felix Guattari. *A Thousand Plateaus: Capitalism and Schizophrenia*. Translated by Brian Massumi. Minneapolis: University of Minnesota Press, 1987.

Derrida, Jacques. *Aporias*. Stanford: Stanford University Press, 1993.

———. *Margins of Philosophy*. Chicago: University of Chicago Press, 1982.

Dussel, Inés. "School Uniforms and the Disciplining of Appearances: Towards a Comparative History of Regulation of Bodies in Early Modern France, Argentina, and the United States." Ph.D. Dissertation, Curriculum and Instruction, University of Wisconsin–Madison, 2001.

———. "Education and the production of global imaginaries: A reflection on teachers' visual culture", *Yearbook of the National Society for the Study of Education*, 108(2), 2009, Volume on Globalization and the Study of Education edited by T.S. Pokewitz and F. Rizvi, pp. 89–110

Estrada Cabrera, Manuel. *El libro azul de Guatemala*. Guatemala, 1915.

FLACSO (Organization). *Guatemala, historia reciente (1954–1996)*. Edited by Virgilio Álvarez Aragón. Guatemala: Editorial de Ciencias Sociales, 2012.

Goodman, Nelson. *Ways of Worldmaking*. Indianapolis: Hackett, 1978.

Grandin, Greg. "Can the Subaltern Be Seen? Photography and the Affects of Nationalism." *Hispanic American Review* 84, no. 1 (2004): 83–111.

Grosvenor, Ian. "From the 'Eye of History' to 'a Second Gaze': The Visual Archive and the Marginalized in the History of Education." *History of Education*, no. 36 (2007): 607–22.

———, ed. *Silences and Images: The Social History of the Classroom*. New York: Peter Lang AG, 1999.

Guzmán Böckler, Carlos, and Jean-Loup Herbert. *Guatemala: Una interpretación histórico-social*. Guatemala: Cholsamaj, 1995.

Jonas, Susanne. *Of Centaurs and Doves: Guatemala's Peace Process*. Boulder: Westview Press, 2000.

Kallo, Johanna. *OECD Education Policy: A Comparative and Historical Study Focusing on the Thematic Reviews of Tertiary Education*. Jyväskylä: Finnish Educational Research Association, 2009.

Lock, Margarett. "A Strong Silent Gaze, No Matter What." *The New York Times*, January 20, 2000.

López Cuat, Claudia Graciela. "Análisis semiótico del mensaje estético de la fotografía artística del guatemalteco Alan Benchoam." B,A. Thesis Licenciatura en Ciencias de la Comunicación, Universidad de San Carlos de Guatemala, 2005.

Luján Muñoz, Jorge. "Un ejemplo de uso de la tradición clásica en Guatemala: Las 'minervalias' establecidas por el presidente Manuel Estrada Cabrera." *Revista de la Universidad del Valle de Guatemala* 2 (1992): 25–33.

Luján Muñoz, Luis. *Los indígenas de Guatemala vistos por el fotógrafo Alberto G. Valdeavellano (1861–1928)*. Guatemala: INGUAT/Academia de Geografía e Historia, 1987.

Martínez Peláez, Severo. *La patria del criollo: Ensayo de interpretación de la realidad colonial guatemalteca*. Guatemala: Editorial Universitaria, 1970.

Mbembé, Achille. "Necropolitics." *Public Culture*, no. 15 (2003): 11–40.

Mejía Dávila, Marco Vinicio. "El Xinca histórico: Una investigación bibliográfica." *Winak: Boletín Intercultural* 4, no. 1 (1988): 3–64.

Menezes de Souza, Lynn Mario. "Entering a Culture Quietly: Writing and Cultural Survival in Indigenous Education in Brazil." In *Disinventing and Reconstituting Languages*, edited by Alastair Makoni and Sinfree Pennycook, 135–69. New York: Multilingial Matters, 2007.

Mirzoeff, Nicholas. *Watching Babylon: The War in Iraq and Global Visual Culture*. New York: Routledge, 2005.

Mitchell, W. J. T. *Picture Theory: Essays on Verbal and Visual Representation*. Chicago: University of Chicago Press, 1995.

———. "World Pictures: Globalization and Visual Culture." In *Globalization and Contemporary Art*, edited by Jonathan Harris, 135–69. Malden: Wiley-Blackwell, 2011.

Oralia, Preble-Niemi, ed. *Cien años de magia: Ensayos críticos sobre la obra de Miguel Ángel Asturias*. Guatemala: F&G Editores, 2006.

Palmquist, Peter, and Thomas Kailbourn. *Pioneer Photographers of the Far West: A Biographical Dictionary, 1840–1865*. Stanford: Stanford University Press, 2002.

Pereyra, Miguel A., Hans-Georg Kotthoff, and Robert Cowen, eds. *PISA Under Examination: Changing Knowledge, Changing Tests, and Changing Schools*. Rotterdam: Sense Publishers, 2011.

Poole, Deborah. *Vision, Race, and Modernity: A Visual Economy of the Andean World*. Princeton, N.J.: Princeton University Press, 1997.

Popkewitz, Thomas S. *Cosmopolitanism and the Age of School Reform: Science, Education, and Making Society by Making the Child*. New York: Routledge, 2007.

Porras Castejón, Gustavo. *Las Huellas de Guatemala*. Guatemala: F&G Editores, 2009.

Rendón, Catherine. *Minerva y la palma: El enigma de don Manuel Estrada Cabrera*. Guatemala: Artemis Edinter, 2000.

———. "Temples of Tribute and Illusion." *Americas* 54, no. 4 (2002): 16–23.

Rionda, Jorge Isauro. "Los conflictos gobierno-iglesia." *El Heraldo*, August 28, 2012.

Said, Edward. *Orientalism*. New York: Vintage Books, 1979.

Sanford, Victoria. *Buried Secrets: Truth and Human Rights in Guatemala*. New York: Palgrave Macmillan, 2003.

Sieder, Rachel, ed. *Guatemala After the Peace Accords*. London: Institute for the Study of the Americas, 1999.

Snyder, John P. *Flattening the Earth: Two Thousand Years of Map Projections*. Chicago: University of Chicago Press, 1997.

Tröhler, Daniel. *Languages of Education: Protestant Legacies, National Identities, and Global Aspirations*. New York: Routledge, 2011.

2 Language Heritage(s) and the Role of "Indigenous" and "Non-Indigenous" Missionaries and Experts in Curricular Foundations

Signpost One

During an informal interview in 2010, Lidia, a prominent "indigenous" and education leader in Guatemala, narrated a childhood memory in a classroom from some time in the early 1960s.[1]

> I have more of a village vision, more of conviction, more of support for the boys and girls, because I understand the struggle. I *lived* that discrimination in school. Just recently when I was in a small school in Huehuetenango on Thursday, I was telling the teachers that I lived that painful life in school. In one of the most painful punishments that I have endured in my life, my third grade teacher put me on a shelf, like on a bookshelf because I did not speak Castilian. It was punishment for not saying "*buenos días*." She left me there in front of all the Castilian-speaking kids, *Ladinos, Mestizos*. That puts a mark on you. But it is not about vengeance, it is about willingness to work for kids not to suffer.[2]

Lidia's experience of this punishment and discrimination is a moment of intensity (repeated by various research participants in interviews and anecdotes that teachers told their student teachers during classroom observations), in which the languages are constructs used to define an "indigenous" (s)object. The early 1960s saw intense activities that aimed to anthropologically define, linguistically order, and educationally shape *lo indígena* in times of inclusion by assimilation. In that memory (one Lidia has continued to experience even as a professional woman in a leading position), she was made "indigenous" via exclusion and ridicule of what is not desirable in the classroom: a "Mam-language speaker" incapable of even uttering a greeting in the official, colonial language. This pedagogical event emerged from the assumed matter-of-fact nature of language as a meta-construct, invented via scientific means, in combination with particular religious beliefs, which operates in ordering, sorting, and ranking kinds or species.

Signpost Two

The year is 2012, fifteen years after the signing of the Accords for Firm and Durable Peace in 1996, which ended thirty-six years of armed conflict in Guatemala, a case difficult to summarize here as the terms of the conflict and its outcomes continue to be highly contested. Nevertheless, one of the obvious outcomes of the Accords was the National Base Curriculum (CNB), the largest curricular reform in recent history. The CNB is often narrated as a triumph of the "indigenous" people's struggle for plurality in education. The CNB incorporates the teaching of "indigenous languages" in the area of communication and language L2 or L1 toward multi-culturalism and inter-culturalism.

Angela teaches Kaqchikel (linguistically classified as one of twenty-two Maya languages in Guatemala), her "mother tongue" as she calls it, which is also the "first language" of some of her students. She begins her pre-service teachers' class with a greeting in Kaqchikel followed by a song.

Q'ejolonik B'ix

¿Ütz' iwach ixtani? [How are you, misses?]
Ütz iwach [How are you?]
Ütz' matyox [Fine, thank you]
¿Ütz' iwach ri ate' atata? [How are your mother and your father?]
Ütz' matyox [Fine, thank you]

Ri tz'ib'äl

Rïn ko' jun nutz'ib'ab'äl [I have a pencil]
Nitz'ib'än, nitz'ibän [That writes, writes]
Nitz'ib'äj ajilab'al [writes numbers]
Nitz'ib'äj rub'i nute' [writes the name of my mother]
Rïn 'ko jun nutz'ib'ab'äl [I have a pencil]
Nitz'ib'än, nitz'ibän [That writes, writes][3]

Next week is exams week. Angela goes on to give the students the "themes" that they will be tested on in the exam: the vegetables, the rodents, and the fruits. Before proceeding to check and grade the students' notebooks to ensure they are keeping good notes and are up to date with their work (a customary assessment practice for most teachers in this and other schools), Angela presents a request for the students. "Please girls, I am asking you, write in your notebooks . . . [so that] when the supervising teacher [during student teaching] asks you, can you teach the kids Kaqchikel?"[4] Surprised by the student's negative response, she continues:

How come? Yes! That's why I need you to keep your notebooks, you have material there. You can teach them the numbers, the parts of the body in Kaqchikel, the songs that we know . . . Don't make me look bad. And not only me, also the school, because "in Century Normal School they are not teaching them well." . . . Let me anticipate that I need for us to work a lot on didactic materials. You will have to make an album with drawings or whatever as teachers you consider you can teach the kids in Kaqchikel . . . You are being educated to be teachers and you are creative. You are going to invent games on how to teach the kids the Kaqchikel vocabulary, so in this unit, please, I am going to need lots of creativity . . . The Kaqchikel vocabulary is infinite. I have a booklet . . . In this unit, I can give you more vocabulary so you can copy it, make your own binders, and choose from there."[5]

Angela devotes the rest of this class time and the next two weeks to checking students' notebooks one by one. Her last instruction for the day is for students to make a cover for the next unit in their notebooks, "a drawing related to Kaqchikel. You can choose a *nahual*. You already have the chart with the *nahuales*."[6]

The shift from condemning the use of "indigenous" languages within a classroom greeting in the 1960s (signpost one) to an "indigenous" teacher in *corte* and *güipil* opening the class with a greeting in an "indigenous" language in 2012 (signpost two) is understood as a crucial turn. The two signposts signal curriculum performance that in distinct and yet similar ways exemplifies language, which as an object of scientific inquiry, serves as a marker of difference in the re/making of "indigenous" as a kind of people. In processes of "indigenous" identification, language serves as a strategy of stabilization and has become so taken for granted that it is worth examining for curricular purposes in this chapter.

This chapter is a historical examination into language heritages—or the heritages of language—that is the activities, tactics, and modes of reasoning difference that privilege language in both the making of "indigenous" (s)objects and in setting the horizon of enactment for curriculum and educational aspirations.

Whereas the previous chapter focused on law as a field of expert knowledge, the focus of this chapter is linguistics intertwined with religion: the role of its experts and expert knowledges in the making of *lo indígena*. The analysis I offer takes a sidestep in order to interrogate what permits language to be a main category to order what is (im)possible to think and do in curriculum that addresses diversity. Language (e.g., Kaqchikel, Spanish, etc.) will be treated as a historical, cultural, and political category upon which difference is demarcated and the frontiers of multiplicity are delimited.

The analysis draws from journals primarily intended for teacher education. Journals are produced via expert activities and are an example of the tactics and modes of reasoning circulating at particular historical moments in the "indigenous" event. The journals document the activities generated from academia, the government, and the church. As printed material that exists within a logocentric heritage, the journals are a privileged and respected source of and for education, or rather, the education of those who could have access to them. I put these journals in dialogue with the dynamics of a teacher education classroom in order to interrogate the performative effects of language heritages in curriculum and "indigenous" making.[7] Studying classrooms as a site for tracing educational matters in their performativity is hardly a familiar educational and policy research practice in Guatemala. Interestingly, the makers of policy and curriculum (which are ostensibly practical and empirical) hardly ever examine their effects, and even less the effects of the heritages upon which they are predicated, *in* schools and classrooms.

The chapter is divided into five sections, each dedicated to the heritages that inform the centrality of language as it becomes salient in moments of intensity since the turn of the twentieth century. The first section locates the centrality of language within broader colonial practices and engages with the invention of language within the context of coloniality from which "indigenous" kinds emerge. In the second section, a mission's activities, desires, and aspirations are addressed in an effort to understand how a religion–science tactic emerges and is enacted in the making of "indigenous" kinds. The third section takes up comparative linguistics, which invents and orders languages by reproducing representation via "Europe." Comparative linguistics enacts a strategy of stabilization inscribed in gestures of language revitalization in education. The fourth interrogates arboreal or root–tree principles from which an assumed whole, as the origin of identities, delimits multiplicity. The presumed unity of origin, too, authorizes the revitalization project. Finally, the last section engages with the perseverance of logo- and phono-centrism in defining the "Indian" since at least the late eighteenth century and in ordering teacher education practices in the twenty-first century.

Before beginning the first section, it is important to note that the "colonial period" is far outside the archival examination of this book. Therefore, the first section does not include primary sources or engage in close analysis of how language as a colonial invention was exercised in Guatemala particularly during that period. The subsequent sections are more specifically dedicated to that kind of analysis and particularly for the twentieth and twenty-first centuries. The task of the first section is to draw attention to the logics that serve as foundation for the heritages of language in contemporary curriculum.

Language Invention and Coloniality in "Indigenous" Salience

The existence of the Kaqchikel course offered through the curriculum *Área de Comunicación y Lenguaje L2* (or *L1*) (Language and Communication Subject) in Guatemala's 2003 National Base Curriculum (CNB as it is commonly known in Spanish) is, in recent history, the outcome of "indigenous" struggles for a multi-intercultural curriculum. This celebrated outcome is made possible in the heritage of language itself as an invention, the invention of languages as separate and enumerable entities, and linguistic territorialization.[8] For example, Kaqchikel as well as German, Xhosa, Mam, French, Latin, Popti, Sanskrit, Swahili, Chinese, and the meta-construct of "language" are an invention reasoned through notions of separability and enumerability (e.g., there are twenty-two Mayan languages, South Africa has seven languages, and there are "7,102 living languages in the world"),[9] and territorialization (i.e., in Guatemala, for example, Sacatépequez, Chimaltenago, Guatemala, Baja Verapaz, Sololá, and Suchitepéquez, are Kaqchikel territories). Before engaging with this set of language heritages, I will briefly locate them within the colonial practices from which they emerged.

The making and increasing privileging of language ("indigenous" or not) in education owe a great deal to colonial encounters,[10] encounters that stem from "European" practices of describing, sorting, bounding, enumerating, experimenting with (what were becoming European) ideas about language, and writing about the alien languages "Europeans" encountered.[11] The invention of language (and later its study as an object of scientific inquiry) was part of the impulse to pursue colonial interests: sometimes to "facilitate barter, movement, and assimilation through conversion,"[12] to "garner honors and rewards from the Spanish Monarch or to entice investors for future ventures."[13] Sometimes they were to admire and organize, as "tribes" and "ethnicities." Sometimes to evangelize, for people's good, and to protect ourselves. Sometimes to understand, and sometimes to invade, in plantation and extractive economies in the nineteenth century. Sometimes to write linguistic descriptions whose effects, within a metaphysics of presence, could reach far in time and space. Sometimes to develop "empirically accurate, isomorphic mappings of artificial written symbols onto speech sounds" in order "to fix them to familiar orthographic conventions."[14] Sometimes in the twentieth century "to preserve tribes from chaos" aided by phonemics.[15] Sometimes for the good of humankind, and in this century, human rights.

The *invention of language* refers to the identification, delimitation, mapping, and description, for example, in "grammars" and dictionaries (see for example Daniel G. Brinton's 1884 Kaqchikel Grammar, and Harry McArthur's 1959 Xinca vocabulary list in *Lenguas de Guatemala*),[16] of people's complex engagement with their "life-worlds" and the creative projections of their "world views" via an ideology of essences. The invention of language does not analytically underlie the origins of "languages," because, as Sinfree Makoni and Alistair Pennycook explain, "languages pre-existed the naming."[17] This also relates to Bruno Latour's theory of relative existence, as I have described in the introductory chapter, where the question is not whether language did or did not exist before or after colonial practices and aspirations. The colonial is, in fact, not an "absolute demarcation between what has never been there and what has always been there."[18] The invention of language analytically also underlies—in its colonial linguistic heritage, beyond language being relatively real and relatively existent—how naming, simultaneously with other modes of reasoning, practices, and faith, called into being what today we refer to as languages and which has real implications in people's lives. Examples of these are Lidia's discriminatory experience and Angela's preoccupation that her student teachers accept the challenge of educating their future students in the Kaqchikel language, thus extending what she understands to be her cultural and linguistic legacy.

Along with the invention of languages, as Makoni and Pennycook argue, came the notion of languages as *separate* and *enumerable* entities. This arithmetic logic of ordering complex milieus is part of a broader project of governmentality.[19] This logic is "Eurocentric" in nature and passion, as Edward Said put it, in observing, coding, and attempting to grapple with everything that is non-European, "the orient," "the rest," the alien, the bewildering diversity.[20] Separating and counting languages works with what Joseph Errington describes as "assumptions about a given naturalness of monoglot conditions," which European explorers employed to regulate and balkanize the "problematic babel like conditions" of the overwhelming linguistic diversity they eventually (and confusedly) recognized.[21]

In the charting of territory,[22] in the colonial, Christian, evangelical, and later scientific projects, languages have been linked to geographical space— what Makoni and Pennycook and Errington call *linguistic territorialization*.[23] That is "the capacity of linguistics to concretize and normalize the territorial logic of power exercised" over sub-Saharan Africa, Southeast Asia, and parts of Latin America, for instance, by English, French, Belgian, Dutch, and Spanish colonial authorities.[24] The territorial logic of power, Errington explains, was a reproduction of European modes of territoriality to control people and their relationships within a geographic area "which assumed bounded linguistic *cum* cultural homogeneity among national citizenries within sovereign European states."[25]

Guatemala is an instance of how this logic was translated in the twentieth century to determine the geographic limits of "indigenous" languages through common survey practices. According to Jorge Ramón González-Ponciano in 1938,[26] a survey of "indigenous" languages was conducted throughout the country employing twenty-four words in Spanish and their translation in "indigenous" languages.[27] The data generated from this and other surveys conducted in 1946 by the Indigenist Institute (see Chapter 3) were used to more precisely delimit the borders of "indigenous" languages. Though the borders constantly change, the linguistic territorializing logic that produces them, alongside separability and enumerability, also produces effects in education.

Complaints in various regions of the country emerge because, unlike Angela who is a Kaqchikel speaker in a Kaqchikel-speaking region, teachers are assigned and given government contracts to teach in areas where they do not speak the language spoken in the community or any other Mayan language. This practice is understood to be counterproductive to the bilingual/multilingual education agendas supported by advocates of "indigenous" language education pro-diversity and inclusion. In "multilingual regions" of the country, such as Ixcán, policies like the Indigenous Languages Law that stipulate the provision of services, like public education, in the languages of the specific regions become irrelevant in classrooms populated with students from multiple "linguistic communities" (see Appendix 4). Although demands for teachers who speak the languages of the communities they serve and for services to be rendered in the local languages may be valid under a linguistic territorialization logic, little attention is drawn to how that same logic may also disallow participation and promote exclusion within the impulse to include. Disputes over belongingness (those who belong and those who don't), discourses of minorities vs. a majority, and order of arrival (we were here first, they came after), though profoundly harmful, are left intact when language territoriality, as well as separability and enumerability (a set of language heritages), are undisputed. That languages *are*, and *are countable*, and *are different* from one another is necessary and at the same time insufficient to engage with the set of concerns that are in and surround the question of diversity and inclusion.

While remaining aware of this necessity and insufficiency for educational purposes, it is worth meditating on what curricula could be carved out in the ambivalent, contingent, strange, and familiar scenarios of, for example, teachers who "don't speak the languages of the communities" *and* those who do. What classroom (and community) events could be invented, given the current conditions, to turn "harmful" historical legacies inside out? What educational debates, exchanges, and interactions could be generated at all educational levels in denaturalizing language/s as determinants of who we are, who we should become, and where we belong? The centrality of "language/s" not only in determining ontology, but also in orienting education, and aspirations for inclusion and justice continue to be salient in more recent moments of intensity in the twentieth century.

The Conversion Mission: The Religion–Science Tactic in the Making of a Kind

The pluralism paradigm that sponsors the multicultural/intercultural curricula that aspire to repair historical wrongs owes a great deal to twentieth-century, Christo-centric linguistics and Biblio-centric Protestant activities. The intense missionary heritage through which language becomes central can be traced in various evental moments of "indigenous" making. That mission heritage is still present in schools. Presence not only refers to the physical presence at the time this research was conducted, of Protestant missionaries in classrooms (as in the Guatemalan University), or Catholic school buildings (as in the *Jóvenes* Institute) where "indigenous" youth are educated to become teachers, but also in the classroom materials produced

64 *Language Heritage(s)*

Figure 2.1 SIL, IIN, and President—Dr. Juan José Arévalo Bermejo. "From left to right. R. R. Gregory, Secretary of the American Biblical Society[;] [Lic. Antonio Goubaud Carrera, Director of the National Indigenist Institute] [;] Mrs. Nora de Burgess—Translator of the New Testament to the Quiché dialect[;] Guatemalan President—Dr. Juan José Arévalo Bermejo[;] Ignacio Xec—Quiché translator[;] Rosendo Peñaloza—Mam translator, Rev. H. Deidley Peck—Translator of the New Testament to the Mam dialect[;] Rev. H. Stanley Wick—Missionary in Quiché[;] Miss Ignacia Xoc—Quiché teacher in Quetzaltenango. Picture taken March 22, 1948. National Palace, Guatemala." (Caption handwritten on the back of the photograph by Antonio Goubaud Carrera. Photo courtesy of the Juan José Arévalo Collection, CIRMA.)

by missionary work, which are consumed by teacher educators and student teachers. The Summer Institute of Linguistics (SIL), evangelical at its inception, is no longer operating officially in Guatemala as it was in the 1960s and 1970s, but its teachings and the ideas the missionaries espoused are ever present in education oriented toward "indigenous" peoples. Protestant aspirations intertwined with Catholic (primarily Jesuit and La Salle) social justice agendas inform much of the language-related curricula in teacher education classrooms today.

This section will focus on moments of intensity around the SIL and "indigenous" making via Protestant linguistics. The animating efforts of this section are not to draw boundaries between Catholic and Protestant missions, nor to address the specificities of their intervention, but rather to begin understanding how a religion–science tactic emerges and enacts the making of "indigenous" kinds.

Guatemala, Mayan peasants, and Kaqchikel peoples are the cradle of the joint American fundamentalist Protestant-linguistic project of what later became the dual identity of the SIL and the Wycliffe Bible Translators (WBT). At the end of the twentieth century, the WBT was one of the world's largest missionary organizations, and the SIL was its scientific incarnation.[28] The founder of the mission, William Cameron Townsend, son of a Presbyterian minister, came on his first mission to Guatemala in 1917, where he stayed until 1932. The mission entailed "evangelization of the world" in order to "pave the way for the second coming of Jesus Christ."[29] His mission among Mayan peasants was connected to what he called the "'oppression' of the Maya and saw [how] it extended to the treatment meted out by the "Ladino" (non-"Indian") to "Indian" converts."[30] Townsend "dedicated himself to building Mayan churches in vernacular rather than Spanish, by working with Mayan evangelists, translating the New Testament into Kakchiquel Maya, and experimenting with bilingual education."[31] Speaking at a summer institute, Townsend told the WBT:

> For the Cakchiquels I had established five schools. I had established a hospital. I had established a printing program, a bit of agriculture, and a Bible institute. And I had translated the New Testament. I had always wanted a rounded-out program. That is what I dreamed of for the Cakchiquels.[32]

The history of the "indigenous struggle" discourse vis-à-vis education and languages alongside scientific claims emerges among Townsend's initial aspirations for the Kaqchikeles, as well as alongside negotiations and compromises of the Protestant mission to penetrate "native" communities. After linguistics and survival training, the American translators (and later linguists) participated in moving *lo indígena* into a domain of scientific inquiry in which it could be observed and manipulated.[33] Via training and field assignments, the becoming-scientists/experts collected ethnographic and ethnolinguistic data "to obtain knowledge of the culture as well as the language of the group."[34] Through the field missions, selected informants, and in the laboratory-like conditions of the SIL headquarters in Guatemala City, the knowledge produced in biblical translations, dictionaries, grammars, linguistic maps, textbooks, tests, etc., became empirical reality by rendering cultures, languages, and later modes of ontological identification.[35] Crucial to this rendering process was the "people in the communities who mastered the language of each of them" because "foreigners could not do all of that work without the tight collaboration [with people in the communities]."[36] The people in the communities, in Ian Hacking's analytics,[37] are the people to be categorized, the moving target whose anthropological borders continue to be delineated in the recalcitrant impulse to stabilize and render transparent, enumerable, and separable by scientific means. This religion-science horizon of enactment consolidated in this moment of intensity is made possible in the strategic move to separate science from religion in the missionary identity.[38]

This separation comes about just as the existence of the Protestant conversion mission was threatened in the 1930s. At this time, Mexican social movements' politics of anti-American and anti-ecclesiastic resistance and Townsend's religious supporters' rejection of Mexican president Lázaro Cárdenas, a "Bolshevik" and follower of "satanic Marxism," triggered the strategic move to separate the mission into two entities. In 1942 the WBT and the SIL were incorporated in the United States as two separate entities. The WBT incorporated the religious side of Bible translation, maintaining relations with religious groups, raising money, and recruiting personnel at home in the United States. The SIL continued to export the mission abroad as scientific and linguistic initiatives that fit into local government's efforts to grasp the socioeconomic realities of "indigenous" communities.[39] Through the SIL Townsend earned contracts with governments in Latin America. Claiming to be nonsectarian, and with President Cárdenas' blessing, Townsend was welcomed by Mexican indigenists, and eventually the SIL was officially incorporated through the Indigenist Institute in Guatemala and under the reformist presidency of Juan José Arévalo (1945–1951) (see group image earlier). During and after the "democratic spring" of the Arévalo and then the Jacobo Árbenz (1951–1954) administrations, the SIL, its linguists, and its anthropologists were crucial in the integrationist experiment mobilized by the Seminary of Social Integration and its commitment to alphabetization and castilianization of "indigenous" peoples.[40] After the democratic spring, the linguistic-scientific-educational mission became focused on countering communism.[41]

Other than a reference to the "holy scriptures," justified by the moral imperatives for development and improvement via literacy and the printed text, the SIL's goals were nonecclesiastical and reflected its scientific tenor: 1) to linguistically and culturally research the autochthonous groups in the country and publish the findings; 2) to translate sections of the Holy Scriptures to support the development of written literature; 3) to collaborate with public and private literacy and bilingual education programs; 4) to serve the basic necessities of communities where members of the SIL are based; and 5) to train suitable people, both beginning readers and advanced students, on linguistic concepts, anthropology, bilingual education, and translation.[42] Rather than what in recent years has been referred to as "linguicide,"[43] Townsend and other SIL members were interested in using the "indigenous" language because "Christianity should reinforce the culture rather than undermine it."[44] This approach favored "indigenous" church building.

Employing principles of bilingual education, "experimental projects" on alphabetization were conducted, for instance, by American field workers, linguists, and Guatemalan classroom teachers in the late 1950s and early 1960s in rural areas of Alta Verapaz and the Ixil region.[45] The booklets produced were field tested for their effectiveness in accelerating Spanish language literacy among "indigenous" children, and later contributed towards the production of similar materials for other regions.[46] However, the design of these materials relied on earlier studies, which, under the expertise of linguists-anthropologists such as Norman McQuown and Mark Hanna Watkins,[47] established the "fundamental phonemes" and a "generalized dialect" for each of the nation's main "tongues."[48]

These are just a few instances of how science, through linguistics, performatively acted to delimit the frontiers of a kind of people, and their subsequent division into countable subgroups was made upon these frontiers. *Lo indígena* was being defined and refined through processes of observation, experimentation, and verification of ("indigenous") languages. At the same moment, the impulse to convert (castilianize) the newly reconstituted *indígena* into that which was not (Spanish speaking, European-like) created a looping effect of perpetual "Indians" as a kind of people to be made in relationship to that which "they were not." These religion–science tactics seemed to be twofold: the making-up of people in their own terms (dialects, fundamental phonemes) and in relationship to that which they should become (literate, suitable people, with comprehension) generated a template on which educational aspirations are ordered today.

Indigenous Emergence Through Comparativism, Representation, and Language Revitalization

Lidia's painful experience in Signpost One took place as linguistic research and missionary expeditions produced knowledge upon which her processes of identification depend as an "indigenous" child in need of conversion. The conversions from "indigenous" tongues to the Spanish language, from *the oppressed Bible-less* to *print and Bible-literate converts*, and from *noncivilized* to *civilized* all relies on late nineteenth-century pedagogic civilizational tactics via the positioning of Castilian as a "first rank" language and the underlying heritages of comparative philology. This section is dedicated to another language heritage: comparativism.[50] This heritage reproduces and is made possible by representational modes of reasoning that underlie language revitalization activities.

Fundamental to the comparative philology enterprise was the invention of language families or language groups via grammatical elements in which both "indigenous tongues/vernaculars" and the "Spanish/Castilian language" can be located.[51] The driving passion of comparative philology experts was, as Tomoko Masuzawa noted:

> the exaltation of a particular grammatical apparatus: *inflection* . . . Inflection was construed as a syntactical structure resulting naturally

68 *Language Heritage(s)*

Figure 2.2 "Indian Girls at the festival of Minerva." San Miguel Chicaj, near Rabinal, Baja Verapaz. Photographer: Gustav Eisen. Date: 1902 (Caption in original. Photo courtesy of the Gustav Eisen Collection, CIRMA).[49]

and directly from the innermost spiritual urge of a people (*Volk*), and as such it was said to attest to the creativity and the *spirit of freedom* intrinsic to the disposition of those who originated this linguistic form.[52]

Inflection, or "*flexia*," is what Friedrich von Schlegel (1772–1829), the German philology visionary and son of a Lutheran pastor, called the grammatical technique where words are "comprised of roots and additional elements marking number, tense, gender, etc."[53] *Flexia* defines the *family of Indo-European (Aryan) languages* (a family of Greek, Latin, Teutonic, Slavonic, and most modern European languages and "organic" languages such as Sanskrit and Persian).[54] These languages were considered *active* in responding to external forces, unlike the other families, which without internal coherence had no capacity to survive over time. As a modern European language that is derived from Latin, Spanish and those who use Spanish were therefore active and creative, with a spirit of freedom and strength that activates the representational politics under which the "indigenous" making project has been mobilized.[55]

Freedom and creativity were the tenets of Antonio Batres Jáuregui's quest for the solution of the "Indian problem" and Miguel Ángel Asturia's "Indian" sociology (see Chapter 1), as well as Townsend's liberation linguistics, Blanca Estela Acevedo's pedagogy, and Pablo's teacher education curriculum (see later).[56]

These tenets of freedom and creativity surfaced during a history class in a teacher preparation program in 2012. In the context of a discussion about Spanish colonialism or the "invasion," Pablo, a pre-service teacher from "the highlands," asserted that one of the "positive aspects" of the conquest, next to "the costumes," "the horses," and "the arms that were inherited," was the "language that the Spanish brought and which we kept." "One of the negative aspects of the conquest," he concluded, was "that many lost their lives." Edgar, another pre-service teacher, challenged these positive aspects, contending that although there was a positive side to what his classmate was saying, "[the Spanish] changed all the modernity that the Mayas had, and the organization they had."[57] For Blanca Estela Acevedo, in an article published in *El Normalista* teacher education journal in 1945,

> The Spanish brought us a magnificent present: the language, a pure language, abundant, expressive, better than the existing [indigenous] languages; a language that is constantly elevated by poets and those of us [Spanish users] who enjoy its beauty and harmony.[58]

According to the great majority of nineteenth-century philologists, the *Semitic languages family* (Arabic, Hebrew, etc.), when compared to the Indo-European (Aryan) languages, was "imperfect and inchoate in inflectional capability."[59] Amerindian and colonially separated, linguistically enumerated, grammatically described, and politically and educationally termed "indigenous" languages today are part of a *family of innumerable languages*. These languages were unrelated. Their syntactical structures were the furthest removed from inflection. "Their form of signification was believed to have developed in reverse order to that of the Aryan languages" given that they contain primitive grammatical elements called "affixa" and follow a process of "incipient agglutination" of root words, rather than word endings growing naturally from internal word roots as was the case with Aryan languages.[60] This inflection syntactical structure explained the "purity" of Aryan languages, the "impurity" of Semitic and *other* languages, and by implication the ordering of those who used and were associated with them.

These nineteenth-century comparativist tactics were invented in Germany and deployed to define a people and a nation. This process required an Other, the weaker, a species bound to disappear in a social Darwinian world reserved for the fit and full of vitality. Later in the twentieth century, and in the name of the nation, Guatemala sought the purification of the "Indian race," its advancement, and alphabetization of "Indians'" in order to release them from their backwardness, systematizing their languages, grammatically describing them through familiar (Indo-European) linguistic terms, making the languages official, and making them part of the curriculum to rescue and revitalize the culture and a people.

In education, the civilizing agenda inscribed in the pedagogic project outlined in the first Central American Pedagogic Congress of 1893 followed this philological comparative logic and scientific typological distinction. The "indigene" who used an imperfect language emerged as needing to be migrated to the "first rank" Castilian language. The urge for him not to have another language than Spanish would be a development in his becoming a different—better and purer—race. This would also solve the problem of language development in reverse order and "Indian" backwardness as defined sociologically in the 1920s and anthropologically in the 1940s (see Chapter 3).

These structural comparative linguistics and scientific activities, in combination with the Catholic and Protestant discourses of liberation, social justice, and revitalization for "indigenous" peoples, served as heritages for the sociolinguistic "expert" activities of the 1980s. The project of linguistic revitalization, defined in political and educational terms, became more salient in the 1980, in the context of the most intense years of the armed conflict and as a response to the noticeable discourses of the "dying fate" of "indigenous" languages over time. Later I offer an account of how institutions and experts, within the heritages described earlier, emerged and participated in expanding the task of language revitalization and in the process remake *lo indígena*.

Neville Stiles, as editor of *Winak*, writes in the December 1985 issue that:

> For the first time in Guatemala, from February 1986, the university [Mariano Gálvez] will begin the professional training of national linguists that can contribute to the *solution of linguistic-educational problems* in the country and additionally carry out the necessary sociolinguistic research for the profound knowledge of the autochthonous tongues and cultures of Guatemala.[61]

By the mid-1980s several institutions in Guatemala that specialized in Mayan linguistics formed. One of these "expert" institutions was the Linguistics School at Mariano Gálvez University, which opened in 1966. The school's goal was to educate linguists who could "solve the problems derived from multilingualism."[62] Another "expert" institution dedicated to language planning was the Jesuit university Rafael Landivar founded in 1961 and its Linguistics Institute. This institute coordinated and carried out studies in support of language policies in the state and the "growth" and "modernization of Guatemalan languages."[63] The Center for Mesoamerican Research (CIRMA), founded in 1978 by American scholars, was broadly concerned with research in the social sciences. In the mid-1980s one of its "visions" in the area of linguistics was publishing a series of "grammars" about Mayan languages in Spanish. The intention was to begin with the work already done by "foreigners" and to continue with the grammars written by Mayan-language speakers.[64] In collaboration with the SIL (closely connected to Mariano Gálvez University) and the Francisco Marroquín Linguistic Project (related to Rafael Landívar University), CIRMA hosted the eighth Maya linguistics workshop in 1985. A number of now-renowned experts (including Judith Maxwell, Norman McQuow, Wesley Collins, and Nora England) participated in the congress, many of them affiliated with the SIL. The overarching aims of the meeting were framed as the promotion of an "intercultural dialogue" as the country had just passed through one of the highest moments of intensity in the history of the armed conflict. There was an implicit recognition of the hostility toward "indigenous" peoples and languages historically. The activities of these experts and their expert institutions are noticeable in the journals (*Winak* is one example) intended to educate teachers in language education and to capture their teaching practices.[65]

Winak, as SIL's linguist Wesley M. Collins described in 1986, was a journal for *promotores* (roughly "bilingual teachers") who aided "indigenous" children's learning by using the children's mother tongue for instructional purposes. *Promotores* also taught "illiterate adults" and worked for the "development of the community." The journal was also for *PRONEBI* professionals who were dedicated to bilingual/intercultural education.[66] Additionally *Winak* served cultural leaders at the Summer Institute of Linguistics who were engaged in the making of literature and working in health-related projects, community development, literacy, and biblical translation. *Winak* was also dedicated to students of seminars and biblical institutes who worked among "indigenous" people.[67] Some of the materials reproduced in the journal in order to inform the *promotores*, professionals, cultural leaders, and students were sociolinguistic studies on the "changes" and "evolution" of "indigenous" languages to facilitate "the making of mother tongue texts within the Bilingual education project."[68]

The research activities of surveying communities—collecting data, comparing language evolution, and textual production toward growth, development, and solving linguistic-educational problems while aiming for linguistic revitalization in the preparation of educators—operated within comparative heritages. If the aspiration was no longer to convert "indigenous" peoples via the Spanish language into "first rank" Beings, the desire was nonetheless an "indigenous" ontology possible via linguistics; having linguistic consciousness reconstituted one as an "indigenous" subject that is worth of existence and striving for the existence of others via education.

We will now return to contemporary educational situations, to a "Maya" morphology class in 2012 that focused on allomorphy and that was taught by a Bible translator and former SIL member in a sociolinguistics master's program founded in the mid-1980s.[69] The instructor celebrated how "balanced" the Mayan languages are and, at the same moment, insisted that the students "go to the [Mayan] languages and find the morphological rule . . . because it's there. Find it!"[70] The impulse to elevate the status of the languages through its examination in a university classroom continued to fabricate the language borderlines via comparative linguistics enacting a strategy of stabilization via "Europe"–science–religion. The students and Mayan professionals working for education, the state, nongovernmental organizations (NGOs), and the Mayan Languages Academy engaged in the exercise, which ensued in an animated debate on how the rule does not necessarily apply, considering the nuances of specific Mayan languages and their multiple variations.

Angela's pedagogy in the Kaqchikel class had a similar preoccupation with language and cultural loss and revitalization. Her attempts to persuade the pre-service teachers to agree to teach Kaqchikel through its limitless vocabulary by appealing to the students' creativity were pedagogical and political acts within current curricular configurations. The "indigenous" language education and policies that produced them were not only predicated on comparative tactics, but also employed structural-functional logics that drive the lexicon-oriented (quantitative) curricular content, assessment, and aspirations for these future teachers' practices in elementary education classrooms. These same practices—as teacher preparation materials, curricula, and policy—were often informed by Anglo-language education models and their variations such as English as a second language, English as a foreign language, and (American) bilingual education. With them comes a certain set of restrictive priorities on the conceptualization of meaning and of Being that presuppose and reinforce comparative configurations indicative of a specific era of subject formation in societies of representation.

Arboreal Principles of Origin and Possible Identities

Within the revitalization mode of reasoning, and in order to counter the "indigenous" annihilation politics to which she has been a direct witness, Mariela, self-identified as Maya-Ixil, taught her students a lesson on diversity and the origins of "indigenous" peoples. This lesson emerged from the familial or arboreal language heritages that this section is dedicated to. The arboreal heritage uses what Gilles Deleuze referred to as

> the Tree or Root as an image, [which] endlessly develops the law of the One that becomes two, then the two that becomes four. . . . Binary logics is the spiritual reality of the root-tree. Even a discipline as "advanced" as linguistics retains the root-tree as its fundamental image, and thus remains wedded to classical reflection [. . .]. This is as much to say that this system of thought has never reached an understanding of multiplicity: in order to arrive at two following a spiritual method it must assume a strong principal unity.[71]

Language Heritage(s) 73

This language tree, the fundamental image of linguistics, was available in Mariela's Indigenous Language L1 class, which addressed "the diversity of languages in Guatemala" through a story entitled *"The beginning . . ."* of Mayan languages.[72] Enabled by the religion–science tactics, the story drew from two seemingly distinct sources. First, "according to Nora England" (an influential American linguist once affiliated with the SIL), Mariela began to explain, "there was only one language. The ancient language was the proto Maya. Nab'ee Maya Tzij, . . . the grandmother, or the grandfather of the languages, the proto Maya." While writing it down on the board and requesting emphatically that the students take notes, she continued, "there was only one language for the Maya but little by little they were separating themselves and from that proto Maya derived all other languages, Mam, the Q'anjobal language, the Ixil language, the K'iche' language."[73] This principal unity, the one becoming two, and then many more separate, countable languages, in Mariela's words, confirmed the truth of an origin that is mediated by linguistic-scientific knowledges.

Recounting this story of the dispersal of peoples from the root, the proto-Maya spreading throughout the Mesoamerican territory in search of fertile land to guarantee their subsistence, made the lesson culturally relevant to the Ixcán region, where the school is located, as it directly related to Mariela's, her students', and their families' recent internal and transnational migration histories.[74] Considering Guatemala's strong Christian heritages, could this lesson also be made possible by biblical stories, the book of Genesis in particular, and the dispersal of the sons of Noah (Ham [Hamites], Shem [Semites], and Japhet [Aryans])? If so what kind of implications does this have for our understanding of subject formation and the possible scope for Mariela's and other teacher educators' critical curricula to destabilize histories?

For her second source, Mariela turned to local history, which was also mediated by "European" intervention and scientific activities: linguistics, anthropology, and archaeology.[75] Mariela passionately explains that "according to what Maya writers have left written, . . . the forefathers, . . . what comes up in the Popol Wuj, also in the Chilam Balam, and the Annals of the Kaqchiqueles, . . . all of that explains the origins of the Maya people."[76] Citing Mayan classical texts, like the Popol Wuj, emphasized a history that is locally re-produced—the glorious existence of the magnificent Mayan civilization that Mariela had come to inherit and was proud to share with her "indigenous" students. Mariela assured her student teachers that

> the Mayas are not the cause of backwardness in Guatemala, without development. [It's not true that] they oppose development . . . No, because if one were to study properly one can realize that the Mayas knew what Europeans and other peoples had not discovered.[77]

This was a common lesson in uncommon critical spaces such as Mariela's "rural" teacher preparation school. Mariela's appeal to the classical

Mayan texts, and the Popol Wuj in particular, was a gesture toward survival by reaffirming her existence as Maya-Ixil via the empirically provable, material, tangible, alphabetical, and written text. The Popol Wuj, although still a site of contestation in "scientific circles," produces rather straightforward quotidian politics. Without hesitation, Mariela relied on the Popol Wuj, cognizant of the power the texts hold when it is almost a sacrilege to question "the sacred Bible of the Maya" (as the Popol Wuj is often referred to) and the enormous respect paid to the Bible in a society that is increasingly Christian and arguably Protestant. For Manuel Estrada Cabrera, the quintessential populist governor concerned with letters and sciences and the salvation of the "Indian," the "Popol Vuh" was

> incomplete and over-abundant with vivid imaginations, purely tropical in character. Like the Bible of the Hebrews, the *Popol Vuh* also tells the creation of the world and mentions a supreme creator who produces and makes the beings . . . As a whole, this book gives proof of some intelligence and culture, at least if one considers the age of barbarism and prejudice in which they lived.[78]

Identities and the limits of diversity, or what Deleuze calls never reaching an understanding of multiplicity, are thus unquestionably mediated, from left to right, via a common origin Bible-centric tale. Importantly, Mariela strategically employs the very same tale that, at other moments, has been violently deployed to threaten her existence. In a rich country like Guatemala, where the fertile land is owned by a small "Ladino" bourgeoisie, these systems—of reasoning, education, and ordering everyday actions in schools—tend to elude the struggle for a different state of living affairs.

The diversity of language, as the lesson to be learned, assumes a single-origin, root–tree, and biblical narrative as the single story delimiting the frontiers of multiplicity, based on the divisibility and enumerability of a presumed whole. The invention of the boundary lines by way of linguistics created units of "indigenous" languages as though all were part of the same whole. As with modern map making, drawing lines to describe and separate languages was "the encoding of desire, the building of nations and ethnicities as political entities whose boundaries define 'identity.' "[79] Inscribed in both the act of border drawing and in the whole from which "all" originate, is the binary logics of the root–tree, which is deployed to determine who people are and can be, where and how educational policy is to be built, and how curricular resources are to be distributed. The strong principal unit that orders this logic disallows the necessary risk of conceiving of a multiplicity besides stabilization and the subordination of other worlds.[80] The struggle for survival and the revitalization of Being in necropolitical trajectories begs the question of whether stabilizing the infinite possibilities of living in one's body and in relationship to others is indispensable for such struggle.[81] Or could there be other ways yet to come in which education, however defined, would mean to draw courageously and seriously from the complex, paradoxical, and contentious palimpsestic histories that produce the struggle for survival in the first place?

What is important to highlight here, as I, too, borrow from the experts and their debates, is the need for a vigilant scrutiny of the heritages that make education possible today. This includes even the controversial, tender, and most cherished items, ideas, and actions that have been mobilized in Guatemala's painful history toward "indigenous" revindication in education. Though these sensibilities must be recognized within the discourse/performance of survival and revitalization in a country with strong colonial and genocidal histories, education, at the service of "indigenous" peoples, could benefit from debates that deterritorialize its "missionary" and "scientific" foundations.

Analfabetismo and Phono-/Logo-centrism

Returning to Angela's Kaqchikel communication and language L2 or L1 lesson, the centrality of literacy, particularly of writing, in the opening pencil song (Ri tz'ib'äl), in insisting on students taking notes, and in the amount of class time devoted to checking students' notebooks bares the historical preoccupation with what in these times is justified as correcting a historical wrong: alphabetizing the "Indian" child. These pedagogic tactics uphold the word, speech, and writing as the primary repositories of meaning and truth. The tactics are founded in what Jacques Derrida calls phonocentrism and logocentrism. This is the last heritage of language I address in the chapter. Phonocentrism is where "voice and being, voice and the meaning of being, and voice and the ideality of meaning" are in absolute proximity.[82] Logocentrism is "the determination of being of the entity as present."[83] This presence comes about first in speech (first-order representation of meaning) produced by the thinking subject and second in writing as representation of speech (second-form representation of meaning).[84]

The celestial image of a benevolent being from heaven, handing down the "A-B-C," paper, a book, "education," and "teaching" is a gesture of intervention and in making-up people. This image tells the twentieth-century story of the alphabetizing project, which was first the castilianization of the "Indian," not-yet-but-to-become Guatemalan. The *analfabeto* hands of an illiterate crowd submerged in absence are promised ascendance to a presence possible, as the image suggests, via the centrality of the logos.[85] This privileging of the speech and writing overdetermines what constitutes Being and engaging with the world, the making of possible new worlds, or even the absence of world in its representational instantiation and how questions of life or death were to be resolved in atrocious war times ("backward illiterate Indians are the enemies of the nation").[86]

"Illiteracy as a problem and literacy as a solution" has been a crucial preoccupation from the turn of the twentieth century, generating various

76 *Language Heritage(s)*

Figure 2.3 El Normalista. Teacher education journal cover. Issues 7 and 9, year VI, 1951, Guatemala.

moments of intensity in "indigenous" re/making.[87] The "Indian" has been at the center of defining this problem. The language of the problem/solution borrowed from liberalism is installed onto the "Indian" as the project (see Chapter 1) of protection and projection of the nation-state. Rather than focusing on the various literacy campaigns carried out throughout the twentieth and twenty-first centuries, let us consider instead how demographic activities together with logocentric principles chart the cartographic space of the Guatemalan territory, the space upon which those literacy campaigns and social policies have been formulated, and that current international interventions are predicated.

Illiteracy, announced as a cultural problem, was characterized by the Guatemalan Ministry of Education in 1980 as being "concentrated in the northwestern region of the country . . . and more often affects the indigenous Guatemalan than the non-indigenous, more women than men, more the rural that the urban population."[88] The northwestern region of the country—Huehuetenango, Quiché, Quetzaltenango, Sololá, Totonicapán departments (circled on the map)—has been fabricated in twentieth-century history as densely populated with "indigenous" peoples.[89]

Demographic practices of census taking and the statistical ordering of gathered data have been crucial in such fabrication. In the censuses between 1880 and 2002, people in the Guatemalan territory were sorted according to whether they knew how to read and write.[90] The demographic information gathered was matched to the map of where the most "indigenous" peoples (also defined by other markers) lived, thus adding one more scientific marker of difference in making the "Indian"/"*indígena*."[91] From 1964 to the 2002 census, a literate person was defined as "someone who could read and write a simple paragraph in any language." An illiterate person is therefore someone who "a) cannot read nor write a simple paragraph, b) only knows how to read, c) only knows how to sign and or write his name, d) at another time knew how to read or write but has forgotten." The "paragraph" as a conceptual unit that logocentrically and phonocentrically orders the alphabetical logic of meaning making and presence aids the production of "illiterate Indians." The possibilities of their becoming participants in the state are reduced to encoding and decoding alphabetical text that carries the promise of bringing the "illiterate Indians" into the present of the developing/modernizing nation.

The fabrication of numbers—drawn from census data and common statistical practices of populational reasoning—is not only employed to rank "indigenous" peoples as inferior, and to rank Guatemala as behind in regional and global comparisons. The numbers and the maps serve to justify international intervention (by the United Nations, the World Bank, the International Monetary Fund, etc.) with innovative activities and tactics that reproduce established modes of reasoning difference and (s)objects. Numbers, which are not just numbers but ways of reasoning people and order, produce tangible applications for curriculum.

To conclude, I offer examples of two moments of intensity, which, like the two signposts that introduced the chapter, contrast the different ways that activities, tactics, and modes of reasoning have centered the logos and continue making-up "indigenous" as a kind of people.

78 *Language Heritage(s)*

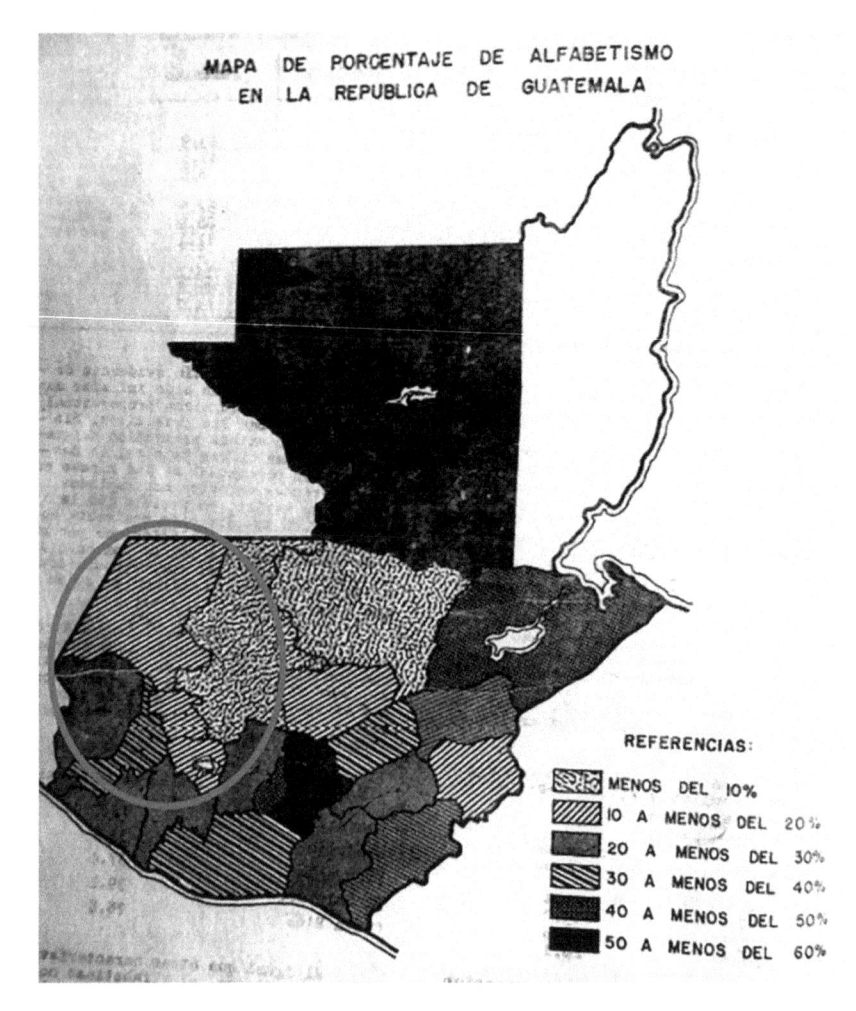

Figure 2.4 Map of literacy percentages in the Republic of Guatemala. 1950 census.

A Moment of Intensity in the 1920s

The "problem of illiteracy" became more salient in the 1920s. "Science, progress, and civilization" were part of Manuel Estrada Cabrera's legacy (1898–1920) for the 1920s, and this generated intense concern over illiteracy, which produced effects in gestures of teacher preparation. The opening article of January–June 1922 issue of *Revista Magisterio* addressed concerns that teachers' "bad methods" were sustaining a "teaching disaster," adding to the "already overwhelming illiteracy figures, with an inflated percentage of schoolers leaving obligatory instruction more ignorant than when they started."[92] In this and other issues of the *magisterio* journal, this general preoccupation with illiteracy was projected onto the "Indian"/"indigene." In order to offer a literacy solution, in an article entitled *La instrucción del indígena* (The Instruction of the Indigene), J. Refugio Valdés, director of the Nahualá's Day and Night Boys' Schools, encouraged teachers at the National Academy of Teachers in Sololá to acquire the tongues of "our aborigines."[93] Using the "native language" is the "most effective way to teach them better and make them understand until civilizing them."[94] He uses "colonial" missionaries and Francisco Marroquín as role models.

> Those missionary gentle men . . . taught writing, reading and a little more to very many indigenes using mostly the Spanish alphabet. These teachings produced good results one of which is the *kiché* author of the POPOL VUY. This *kiché* author's name is unknown; the good results were also the authors of the MEMORIAL KAKCHIKEL written here in Sololá by the gentlemen Sir. Francisco Hernández Arana SHAJILA and Sir. Francisco Díaz SHEBUTA (ej-lease "quej").[95]

Valdés was adamant that the missionary example should be followed because "it is simply the majesty of *Nature*" that the "indigenes do not abandon their native language either spontaneously nor due to obligation of the School, or in any brutal way."[96] If the "students are simply given Spanish reading and writing, they write and read mechanically, like parrots."[97] Valdés' advice for teachers was both typical and in many ways atypical. In the 1920s it was common to adopt the colonial practices of missionaries because they were perceived as "good" in educating/assimilating the "indigene." Much like Townsend, annihilating the vernacular language of the "Indian" was not Valdés' aspiration. Alphabetizing the "Indian," even without attempting to eradicate his language, was highly desirable for reading and writing (alphabetically). Yet Valdés' advice was atypical of a much larger tactic to assimilate the "indigene."

> The teacher should try to teach more Castilian in a progressive manner and in a very elementary way to castilianize the indigenous students . . . and continue these exercises until having formed LADINO CHILDREN that can interpret the true meaning of words they hear in the course of the upcoming classes.[98]

Castilianization oftentimes entailed the eradication of the "Indian's tongues."[99] Valdés was fully aware of this and made explicit his position against what today would be called linguicidal policies. Valdés stressed that this was not an acceptable practice for alphabetizing and civilizing the "indigene."

A Moment of Intensity in 2012

The terms of the solution to the illiteracy problem have changed since the 1920s through the multiple heritages addressed in the previous sections in this chapter. Nevertheless, in an actual teacher preparation class in 2012, the curricular aspirations continued to draw from the phonocentric heritage and also from census and numerical practices of populational reasoning to justify the educational intervention. The focus of the Help a Child *lectura* class for "indigenous" student teachers at *Jóvenes* Institute was exploring "what good readers and writers do."[100] The class is funded by Help a Child (a pseudonym for an organization founded by an American anthropologist and a clinical psychologist) whose goal is to "help hundreds of teachers in remote villages teach children to read more effectively," particularly in Guatemala, given that the country "has the lowest literacy rate in all of Latin America." *Jóvenes*, as described in Appendix 3, serves "indigenous" boys from the "interior" of the country, which is a synonym of rural areas. Help a Child aims to train "young indigenous men and women from remote villages, students who grew up in extreme poverty and are now studying to become teachers when they return to their communities."[101] The class' focus on good reading and writing is relevant because, as the teacher described it, "the boys, when they come from their communities, they barely know how to read or write."[102]

In an animated whole-class conversation, after the students had time to independently list four things a good reader does and after sharing their responses in groups of four, Sofia, the teacher, gathered the students' responses. Most of these responses kept the words the students named, and other times the teacher translated them in a way that could be recorded on the board (a conventional teaching practice).

The outcome of the exercise was that a good reader "analyzes," "shares what he understands" a couple of students reiterated, "asks for help," proposed the teacher, and "is competent in other languages," asserted a voice far in the back of the room, accompanied by another one that said "imagines." A good reader "enjoys," said a student, to which the teacher responded with a question "do we always enjoy reading?" The students' answers were "no," "maybe," and "it depends." The teacher extended the students' responses. "It depends on what you are reading because if I am reading an informational book that is teaching me the process of cultivating rice, would I enjoy it?"[103] The expected answer from the students was "no." The teacher continued. "No. I am informing myself. Because I do not enjoy it does not mean I am not a good reader. A good reader is that one who reads to inform her/himself, to learn."[104] Yet there are books to be enjoyed such as "novels" and "poetry," the teacher remarked. The point the teacher stressed was to be a good reader does not always require enjoyment. Enjoyment and reading an informational book on how to cultivate rice were inconceivable in this example. In the context of the rural background in which most of the students were raised, the gesture of the teacher was perhaps to make the example culturally relevant for them. However, how is one to decide what should be enjoyable to read? And what are the implications for casting as unenjoyable an informational book on an agricultural topic historically associated with the undesirable rural and pitting it against the enjoyable novel or poetry book? Is such an example reinforcing—educationally in the imaginary of these students—the development trope of the undesirable rural inhabited by *indígenas*?

Good readers, another student proposed, "look up words in the dictionary that he does not know," and the teacher said and wrote on the board "improve their vocabulary." Good readers "follow the punctuation marks," the students continued, and the teacher explained "because sometimes we read in a rush without understanding." The tendency at this point was to relate the good reading to reading aloud because good readers "like to read in public," "read aloud," and "have very good oral [expression]." After these remarks, a student concluded that good readers "modulate." Before all these characteristics were offered, Polvito, a student in the class, expressed that a good reader "*da lectura de forma escénica*" (reads in a scenic way), which the teacher translated, after some hesitation, as readers who "read with emotion making all the necessary pauses." Polvito's good readers were absorbed into the reading aloud method, or perhaps silent reading in which what counted were the punctuation marks that ensure "understanding" when the reader is not "in a rush." Polvito's good readers were reduced to alphabetical decoding and voice as first-order representation of meaning. Reading scenically was translated as reading with emotion. Reading with emotion was conveyed via the explanatory power of alphabetical text conventions and norms. The externalization of meaning via textual conventions and very good oral skills refers to the 1950s preoccupation (in the *El Normalista* article cited above) for "cultivating correct pronunciation" especially in "indigenous" peoples learning Spanish, as are these students according to several teachers in the school. Yet what was Polvito's actual proposition? What does it mean to read scenically? What could read scenically entail without taming the opacity in Polvito's proposition of the good reader strategy or reifying it within the historically available ways of determining what a good reader is and should be?

* * *

The analysis throughout the chapter has sought to open up spaces from which questions such as the ones noted earlier could be asked as a way to unearth the possibilities that have fallen away in processes of identification established via "language." Tracing the moments of intensity of "indigenous" remaking vis-à-vis language has been an attempt to destabilize the centrality of "language," to make possible educational scenarios from which one could dare to imagine what multiplicity would be like beyond thinking of oneself as, for example, "indigenous" and a "Kaqchikel/Mam/

Spanish speaker." The provocative suggestion here is to create generative spaces where we can consider what Deborah Britzman calls "the not-yet thought."[105] This provocative suggestion must not be understood as another annihilation strategy. Quite the contrary. The provocation desires a curriculum unlike the one "we" have come to know. Curriculum and education owe Polvito, his classmates, other pre-service teachers, and the students they will serve participatory spaces at the limits of the well-rehearsed language heritages analyzed throughout this chapter. Opening up these participatory spaces is a way of responding to what Aura Cumes calls "the . . . structuration of colonial life in Guatemala," that is the life of education centered on "language," and the lives of people, including student teachers, and teacher educators who not only live it but are profoundly immersed in it.[106]

Notes

1 All research participants' names are pseudonyms.
2 Interview with Lidia Quiej, May 6, 2010. For the Spanish original see Appendix 7, item 1.
3 Classroom observation (communication and language L2/L1 class), July 24, 2012. This is copied directly from the teacher's handwritten transcription. Any discrepancies with other *variantes dialectales* (dialects) or "the standardized" form of Kaqchikel should be understood as part of the diversity within which people interact with the languages they learned—in this case, the one the teacher grew up with in San Antonio Aguas Calientes. The English translation is based on the Spanish version that the teacher also provided. I thank Magdalena Aju for revising the transcription of the song in Kaqchikel.
4 Classroom observation (communication and language L2/L1 class), July 24, 2012. For the Spanish original see Appendix 7, item 2.
5 Classroom observation (communication and language L2/L1 class), July 24, 2012. For the Spanish original see Appendix 7, item 3.
6 Classroom observation (communication and language L2/L1 class), July 24, 2012. For the Spanish original see Appendix 7, item 4. In the context of this lesson, and as commonly understood in Mayan cosmovision, *nahuales* refers to the visual representations or symbols that accompany each of the twenty days of each month in the Colq'ij calendar. The names of these *nahuales* are B'atz', E, Aj, I'x, Tz'ikin, Ajmaq, No'j, Tijax, Kawoq, Ajpu, Imox, Iq', Aq'ab'al, K'at, Kan, Kame, Kej, Q'anil, Toj, and Tz'i'. For more on *nahuales* see, for example, Ajpub' Pablo García et al., *Ruxe'el Mayab' k'aslemäl = Raíz y espíritu del conocimiento maya* (Ciudad de Guatemala: Programa de Educación Intercultural Multilingüe de Centroamérica PROEIMCA, Componente Nacional Guatemala : Universidad Rafael Landívar, Instituto de Lingüística y Educación, 2009); Eduardo León Chic, *El corazón de la sabiduría del pueblo maya/Uk'u'xal ranima' ri qano'jibal* (Iximulew [Guatemala]: Fundación Centro de Documentación e Investigación Maya, 1999).
7 Judith Butler, *Gender Trouble: Feminism and the Subversion of Identity* (New York: Routledge, 2006).
8 As examples of how this notion operates in the production of territories in maps, see the linguistic maps (re)produced by the American Fredrick Jonson (1940), Thomas Sebeok, ed., *Native Languages of the Americas* (New York: Springer Science & Business Media, 2013); Norman A. McQuown, *Handbook of Middle American Indians, Volume 5: Linguistics* (Austin: University of Texas

Press, 1968); John Reed Swanton, *The Indian Tribes of North America* (Washington: Washington Genealogical Publishing Company, 1952)); the Guatemalan José Antonio Villacorta (1934), José Antonio Villacorta Calderon, Francisco Hernandez Arana, and Francisco Díaz Gebrita Quey, *Memorial de tecpán Átitlan* (Guatemala: Tipografía Nacional, 1934). For the actual map, see William Gates, *Map of the Mayance Nations and Languages Prepared for the Maya Society Quarterly*, Plate, 1936. The Americans Cyrus Thomas y John Swanton (1911), Cyrus Thomas and John Reed Swanton, *Indian Languages of Mexico and Central America and Their Geographical Distribution* (Washington: U.S. Government Printing Office, 1911)); the German Kart Sapper (1901); Carl Sapper, "Beiträge zur Ethnographie de südlichen Mittelamerika Tippenhauer, L.G.': Beiträge zur Geologie Haïtis: IV: Die Erzfundstätten von Terre-Neuve und Gonaïves," *Dr. A. Petermanns Mitteilungen aus Justus Perthes' Geographischer Anstalt* 47 (1901): 25–121. For the actual map, see, Schmidt C., *Die Verbreitung der Sprachen im Südlichen Mittelamerika ums Jahr 1899*, Plate, 1901, http://zs.thulb.unijena.de/rsc/viewer/jportal_derivate_00221942/Mitthei lungen_Perthes_129489816_1901_047_0713.tif?logicalDiv=log_jportal_derivate_00221942.); and the Swiss Otto Stoll (1884) (Otto Stoll, *Zur Ethnographie der Republik Guatemala* (Zürich: Orell Füssli, 1884)).

9 "'World,' *Ethnologue: Languages of the World*." Accessed November 6, 2013, www.ethnologue.com/world.

10 The history of the invention of language through colonial encounters has been thoroughly documented. For Latin America, see for example James Lockhart, *Nahuas and Spaniards: Postconquest Central Mexican History and Philology* (Stanford: Stanford University Press, 1991); Walter D. Mignolo, *Darker Side of the Renaissance: Literacy, Territoriality, and Colonization* (Ann Arbor: University of Michigan Press, 1995); and Elizabeth Hill Boone and Walter D. Mignolo, *Writing Without Words: Alternative Literacies in Mesoamerica and the Andes* (Durham: Duke University Press, 1994).

11 Joseph Errington, "Colonial Linguistics," *Annual Review of Anthropology* 30, no. 1 (2001): 19–39. See also Joseph Errington, *Linguistics in a Colonial World: A Story of Language, Meaning, and Power* (Malden: Wiley-Blackwell, 2007).

12 Stephen Greenblatt, *Marvelous Possessions: The Wonder of the New World*, 1st edition (Chicago: University Of Chicago Press, 1992), 104.

13 Maria M. Portuondo, "Conquistadors as Scientific Observers: Early Spanish Instructions for Travelers" (Instructions, Questions, and Directions: Learning to Observe in Early Modern Scientific Travel, Max Planck Institute, Berlin, 2012).

14 Errington, "Colonial Linguistics," 21.

15 Kenneth L. Pike, *With Heart and Mind: A Personal Synthesis of Scholarship and Devotion* (Duncanville: Adult Learning Systems, 1996).

16 Daniel G. Brinton, *A Grammar of the Cakchiquel Language of Guatemala* (Philadelphia: McCalla & Stavely, Prs., 1884); McArthur cited in Marco Vinicio Mejía Dávila, "El Xinca Histórico: Una Investigación Bibliográfica," *Winak: Boletin Intercultural* 4, no. 1 (1988): 3–64; and Marvin Keene Mayers, Julio Vielman, and Seminario de Integración Social Guatemalteca (Organization), *Lenguas de Guatemala* (Guatemala: José de Pineda Ibarra, 1966).

17 Sinfree Makoni and Alastair Pennycook, eds., *Disinventing and Reconstituting Languages* (New York: Multilingual Matters, 2007), 10.

18 Bruno Latour, "On the Partial Existence of Existing and Nonexisting Objects," in *Biographies of Scientific Objects*, ed. Lorraine Daston (Chicago: University of Chicago Press, 2000), 257.

19 Michel Foucault, "Governmentality," in *Power: The Essential Works of Michel Foucault 1954–1984*, ed. James D Faubion, vol. 3, The Essential Works of Foucault (London: Allen Lane, 2000), 201–22.

84   *Language Heritage(s)*

20 Edward Said, *Orientalism* (New York: Vintage Books, 1979).
21 Errington, "Colonial Linguistics," 23.
22 For a sample analysis of early colonial practices of observation and description of the land and people through *capitulaciones*, see for example Portuondo, "Conquistadors as Scientific Observers: Early Spanish Instructions for Travelers."
23 Sinfree Makoni and Alastair Pennycook, eds., *Disinventing and Reconstituting Languages* (New York: Multilingual Matters, 2007), and Errington, "Colonial Linguistics." However, the territorial—not as in fictive land demarcations within an administrative and legal apparatus, but in cosmologies of what is referred to as *mother earth*—is paramount for disinventing the centrality of the human, which is itself also key to the larger disinventing provocation that Makoni and Pennycook pose. And yet the logics of fixing peoples and identities to particular languages and territories are insufficient to the complexities of the common phenomena of mobility and migration. Guatemala, like many other countries, has both a long and recent history and a difficult present of highly displaced peoples, both "internally" and "internationally," and forced migration of various sorts.
24 Errington, "Colonial Linguistics," 23.
25 Ibid.
26 Other exercises of linguistic territorialization prior to this were Stoll's maps of 1884 and 1886; Cyrus Thomas and John R. Swanton, 1911; William Gates, 1920, and 1932 (see Jose Antonio Villacorta Calderon, Francisco Hernandez Arana, and Francisco Diaz Gebrita Quey, *Memorial de tecpán Átitlan* (Guatemala: Nacional, 1936)); Fredrick Jonson, 1940. Jorge Ramón González-Ponciano, "De la patria del criollo a la patria del shumo: Whiteness and the Criminalization of the Dark Plebeian in Modern Guatemala" (Ph.D. Dissertation, Anthropology, University of Texas-Austin, 2005).
27 According to González-Ponciano these translations were supplied by schoolteachers in municipalities throughout the nation. How the survey was designed and conducted is unclear. González-Ponciano, "De la patria del criollo a la patria del shumo: Whiteness and the Criminalization of the Dark Plebeian in Modern Guatemala."
28 Todd Hartch, *Missionaries of the State: The Summer Institute of Linguistics, State Formation, and Indigenous Mexico, 1935–1985* (Tuscaloosa: University Alabama Press, 2006). In 1975, "the WBT/SIL had a reported income of US $16,900.000" and was the sixth-richest Protestant missionary organization. Søren Hvalkof and Peter Aaby, *Is God an American? An Anthropological Perspective on the Missionary Work of the Summer Institute of Linguistics* (Copenhagen: International Work Group for Indigenous Affairs (IWGIA), 1981), 10. Nora England claims, citing Hvalkof and Aaby, that by 1979 the SIL/WBT had "3,700 members working with approximately 675 different languages in 29 countries, making it the largest protestant missionary society in the world with regard to members sent abroad [from the United States]." Nora England, "Is God an American? An Anthropological Perspective on the Missionary Work of the Summer Institute of Linguistics by Søren Hvalkof and Peter Aaby," *American Anthropologist* 85, no. 3 (September 1, 1983): 711. England is a respected linguist and scholar among many of the sociolinguists she trained in Guatemala. Many of these scholars work in sociolinguistics training themselves, in education-related activities such as textbook and standardized test production, teacher training, the Ministry of Education, policy, international cooperation with USAID, and the German cooperation, among other public and private engagements.
29 David Stoll, "Words Can Be Used in So Many Ways," in *Is God an American? An Anthropological Perspective on the Missionary Work of the Summer Institute of Linguistics*, eds. Søren Hvalkof and Peter Aaby (International Work Group for Indigenous Affairs (IWGIA), 1981), 25.

30 Ibid., 25.
31 Ibid.
32 William Cameron Townsend and Richard S. Pittman, *Remember All the Way* (Huntington: Wycliffe Bible Translators, 1975), 7.
33 For more on the SIL and its beginnings as Camp Wycliffe in 1935 see Stoll, "Words Can Be Used in So Many Ways" and also David Stoll, *Fishers of Men or Founders of Empire? The Wycliffe Bible Translators in Latin America* (London: Zed Press, 1982).
34 Hvalkof and Aaby, *Is God an American?*, 11.
35 Would it be possible to draw a connection here to Columbus taking Indians captive in an attempt at "intercultural communication" and Christianizing, though in the case of the SIL no physical force was employed? From Columbus' diary, as quoted in Greenblatt: "They should be good and intelligent servants for I see that they say very quickly everything that is said to them, and I believe that they would become Christians very easily, for it seemed to me that they had no religion. Our Lord pleasing, at the time of my departure I will take six of them from here to Your Highness in order that they may learn to speak. No animals did I see on this island except parrots" (*Diario*, 67–9). Greenblatt, *Marvelous Possessions*, 90. Informants were brought to the SIL's base because "better working facilities [were] available and the translation work [was] uninterrupted by outsiders or by problems of everyday village life." Hvalkof and Aaby, *Is God an American?*, 11–12.
36 David Henne, "Breve historia del Instituto Lingüístico de Verano de Centroamerica," *Winak: Boletín intercultural* 2, no. 1 (1986): 32. For the Spanish original see Appendix 7, item 5.
37 Ian Hacking, "Kinds of People: Moving Targets" (The Tenth British Academy Lecture, London, 2006); Ian Hacking, *Rewriting the Soul: Multiple Personality and the Sciences of Memory* (Princeton: Princeton University Press, 1995); Ian Hacking, "Kinds of People: Moving Targets," in *Proceedings of the British Academy 151* (British Academy Lecture, London, 2007), edited by P.J. Marshall, 285–318.
38 Bernadette M. Baker, *William James, Science of the Mind, and Anti-Imperial Discourse* (New York: Cambridge University Press, 2013).
39 González-Ponciano, "De la patria del criollo a la patria del shumo: Whiteness and the Criminalization of the Dark Plebeian in Modern Guatemala."
40 Castillianization as a tactic of people making had been in operation in emergent pedagogic discourses since the late nineteenth century. A report of a commissioned paper produced in the first Central American Pedagogic Congress in 1893 states "the indigenous that speaks Castilian, that dresses like the Europeans, we will not call him Indian, we will not differentiate him from the mixed race." For the Spanish original see Appendix 7, item 6. *Primer congreso pedagógico centroamericano: primera exposicion escolar nacional* (Guatemala: Tipografía Nacional, 1894), 182.
41 Literacy, González-Ponciano argues, served as an instrument to grasp the socioeconomic reality of "indigenous" peoples with the partnering support of entities such as the SIL and the Inter-American Cooperative Service for Education (SCIDE). Out of this literacy experiment emerged "scientific initiatives" to improve "indigenous" peoples living conditions. Though these American partnerships (both the SCIDE and the SIL) were challenged and interrupted, "North American technical personnel, linguists, and anthropologists participated in the Guatemalan educational experiment of the revolutionary governments, and integrationist initiatives in the counter revolution in 1954." The priority of integrationism was castilianization and alphabetization to "ladino-ize indigenous peoples and combat communism." González-Ponciano, "De la patria del criollo

86 *Language Heritage(s)*

a la patria del shumo: Whiteness and the Criminalization of the Dark Plebeian in Modern Guatemala," 85.

42 Henne, "Breve historia del Instituto Lingüístico de Verano de Centroamerica." For Spanish original see appendix 7, item 7.

43 See Tove Skutnabb-Kangas, *Linguistic Genocide in Education, or Worldwide Diversity and Human Rights?* (Mahwah: L. Erlbaum Associates, 2000), and Amir Hassanpour, "The Politics of A-Political Linguistics: Linguistics and Linguicide," in *Rights to Language: Equity, Power, and Education*, ed. Robert Phillipson (Mahawah: L. Erlbaum Associates, 2000), 33–40.

44 Stoll, "Words Can Be Used in So Many Ways," 33.

45 Jaime Bucaro, *Historial de IIN 1945–1956: Instituto Indigenista de Guatemala: Informe de sus trabajos y actividades* (Guatemala, n.d.).

46 González-Ponciano, "De la patria del criollo a la patria del shumo: Whiteness and the Criminalization of the Dark Plebeian in Modern Guatemala."

47 According to Denis Casey, Watkins traveled throughout the department of Alta Verapaz, Chimaltenango, and Sacatepéquez for two weeks, with several others doing detailed "field work" in Patzún, Chimaltenango. "The investigation involved lengthy considerations of the *morphology, syntax,* and *phonetics* of the language." The outcome was an alphabet using Spanish-language sounds for the Kaqchikel language. Later at the request of the Maryknoll missionaries and more field work in Huehuetenango, Watkins also developed alphabets in the Mam and Q'anjob'al languages based on vowels and consonants. These linguistic anthropological developments served as the basis for literacy training in public schools in 1948 and the fabrication of booklets (*cartillas*). These didactic materials would be "used later by staff members at the *Instituto Indigenista* for teaching Spanish speaking Guatemalans the native languages." Dennis F. Casey, "Indigenismo, the Guatemalan Experience" (Ph.D. Dissertation, History, University of Kansas, 1979), 281–282.

48 Bucaro, *Historial de IIN 1945–1956: Instituto Indigenista de Guatemala: informe de sus trabajos y actividades*, 10–11.

49 For more on the *Minervalias*, see, for example, Jorge Luján Muñoz, "Un ejemplo de uso de la tradición clásica en Guatemala: Las 'minervalias' establecidas por el presidente Manuel Estrada Cabrera," *Revista de la Universidad del Valle de Guatemala* 2 (1992): 25–33; Catherine Rendón, *Minerva y la palma: El enigma de don Manuel Estrada Cabrera* (Guatemala: Artemis Edinter, 2000); Maynor Carrera Mejía, "Las fiestas de Minerva en Guatemala, 1899–1919: El ansia de progreso y de civilización de los liberales," *Portal Historia Centroamericana*, (2009): 1–13.

50 "Trabajos de las comisiones de ponencia: tema I. dictamen," 181.

51 In a chapter entitled "Philology's Evolutions," Joseph Errington discusses the emergence of this "'very German science,' as Germans are grappling with the political and cultural crises [of identity] brought on by Prussia's defeat" (Errington, *Linguistics in a Colonial World*, 72). Philology visionaries and writers such as Johann Herder, Friedrich and August von Schlegel, Wilhelm von Humboldt, Franz Bopp, and Jakob Grimm studied linguistic diversity in the search for an origin of peoples and languages, and partly through the making of language families, developed linguistic evolutionary theories that were put to the service of Germany to confirm its own superiority as part of "The West." Germans, according to Schlegel, were to "recognize their language and literature's organic vitality if they were not to risk . . . disappearing altogether from the list of independent nations" (Errington, *Linguistics in a Colonial World*, 74). Philologists "made the past into a resource for nationalist ideologies in an industrializing Europe" (Ibid., 71). In Guatemala, Spanish officialdom and language diversity drawn from a "Maya' past as told by missionaries, linguists, and archaeologists

shape national ideologies, as evidenced in the educational policies of a "globalizing" and "developing" Guatemala. Ibid.
52 Tomoko Masuzawa, *The Invention of World Religions: Or, How European Universalism Was Preserved in the Language of Pluralism* (Chicago: University of Chicago Press, 2005), 24 (emphasis added).
53 Errington, *Linguistics in a Colonial World*, 73.
54 Ibid.
55 Here I draw from Martin Heidegger's discussion of representation. Martin Heidegger, *The Question Concerning Technology and Other Essays* (New York: Garland Publishing, 1977).
56 Antonio Batres Jáuregui, *Los indios, su historia y su civilización* (Guatemala: Tipografía la Unión, 1894); Miguel Ángel Asturias, "El problema social del indio" (B.A. Theses Licenciatura en Derecho, Universidad de San Carlos de Guatemala, 1923); Townsend and Pittman, *Remember All the Way*; Blanca Estela Acevedo, "Fundación de la ciudad de Santiago de los Caballeros de Guatemala," *El Normalista*, (1945): 47–50.
57 Classroom observation (history class), August 13, 2012. For the Spanish original see Appendix 7, item 8.
58 Ibid., 50. For the Spanish original see Appendix 7, item 9.
59 Masuzawa, *The Invention of World Religions*, 25.
60 Ibid., 25.
61 Neville Stiles, "Nota del Editor," *Winak: Boletín intercultural* 1, no. 3 (1985), 1 (emphasis added). For the Spanish original see Appendix 7, item 10.
62 Neville Stiles, "La Escuela de lingüística de la Universidad 'Mariano Gálvez' de Guatemala," *Winak: Boletín intercultural* no. 2 (1986), 113.
63 Guillermina Herrera Peña, "Instituto de lingüística, de la Universidad 'Rafael Landívar,'" *Winak: Boletín Intercultural* 2, no. 2 (1986), 123.
64 Stiles, "La Escuela de lingüística de la Universidad Mariano Gálvez' de Guatemala," *Winak: Boletín Intercultural* 2, no. 2 (1986): 112–21; Guillermina Herrera Peña, "Instituto de lingüística, de la Universidad 'Rafael Landívar,'" *Winak: Boletín Intercultural* 2, no. 2 (1986): 121–24; Stephen R. Elliott, "CIRMA y la lingüística," *Winak: Boletín Intercultural* 2, no. 2 (1986): 124–29.
65 *Winak*'s publications ranged from morphology, phonology, jokes, coverage of linguistic, and sociolinguistic changes to surveys, linguistic historical comparisons, language standardization, to classroom material design, "Maya" writers, human/linguistic rights, bilingual intercultural education, and few articles with a slightly more "political" orientation in the 2000s. The contributors were primarily experts affiliated with the SIL, the Jesuit education mission, and emerging "Maya" scholars, many of whom were educated outside of Guatemala.
66 PRONEBI stands for Bilingual Education National Program. It started in 400 rural communities in Guatemala (with four main "indigenous" languages "Quiché, Cakchiquel, Mam, Kekchí") in January 1986. The program was financed by the United States Agency for International Development (USAID). In 1986 it had planned to develop four main tasks related to the production of 1) school dictionaries, 2) grammars for professional use, 3) a manual of anthropological and sociolinguistic aspects of the four main linguistic areas mentioned earlier, and 4) a historicocultural analysis of the same languages. The purpose of this manual, Julia Richards and Michael Richards stated, was to "train [*adiestrar*] the teaching personnel of the Ministry of Education so they can conduct studies independently at the community and regional level." Julia Richards and Michael Richards, "Plan de trabajo para el componente antropológico y lingüístico de la consultoría de asistencia técnica del programa nacional de educación bilingüe en Guatemala," *Winak: Boletín intercultural* 2, no. 2 (1986): 107.

88 Language Heritage(s)

67 Wesley M. Collins, "Introducción a Winak: El Boletín Intercultural," *Winak: Boletín Intercultural* 1, no. 1 (1985): 8–9.
68 Andrés Cuz Mucú, "Estudio sociolinguistico area Kekchi 1982," *Winak: Boletín intercultural* 1, no. 2 (1985): 15.
69 Allomorphy is the alternation of two or more forms in a morphological or lexical unit. The concept occurs when a unit of meaning can vary in sound without changing meaning. The past tense for regular verbs in English is—*ed* which can be pronounced /əd/, /ɪd/, /t/, /d/.
70 Classroom observation (sociolinguistics class), July 21, 2012. For the Spanish original see Appendix 7, item 11.
71 Gilles Deleuze and Felix Guattari, *A Thousand Plateaus: Capitalism and Schizophrenia*, trans. Brian Massumi, 1st ed. (Minneapolis: University of Minnesota Press, 1987), 5.
72 The story was photocopied from a book produced by the Santiago Development Project, a Catholic initiative of the La Salle brotherhood inspired by the "liberation faith." The project aims to "transform the cruel reality" of disposed peoples in Guatemala.
73 Classroom observation (language and literature in L1), April 19, 2013. For the Spanish original see Appendix 7, item 12.
74 For an account of Ixcán's history, see, for example Catholic Church and Diocese of Santa Cruz del Quiché, *Padre Guillermo Woods* (Guatemala: Diócesis del Quiché, 2000); Santiago Otero Diez et al., *Testigos del morral sagrado: En homenaje a los catequistas sobrevivientes que han trabajado con dedicación, aun arriesgando la propia vida, por la construcción del reino de Dios* (Guatemala: ODHAG, 2011).
75 Drawing from "Maya texts" is made possible through the mediation of the work of eighteenth-century Spanish friars such as the Dominican Fray Francisco Ximénez in the case of the Popol Wuj and to some extend the work of nineteenth-century "European" Americanists such as the "Austrian" Carl Scherzer (Carl Scherzer and Francisco Ximénez, *Las historias del origen de los indios de esta provincia de Guatemala: Exactamente según el texto español del manuscrito original que se halla en la biblioteca de la Universidad de Guatemala, publicado por la primera vez* (Viena: Carlos Gerold é Hijo, 1857)), and the French Étienne Charles Brasseur de Bourbourg (Étienne Charles Brasseur de Bourbourg, *Popol Vuh: le livre sacré et les mythes de l'Antiquité américaine, avec les livres héroïques et historiques des Quichés: Ouvrage original des indigènes du Guatémala* (Paris: A. Bertrand; Trübner, 1861)), as well as the "Guatemalan" Juan Gavarrete. In the late nineteenth- and twentieth-century controversies over the origins of the texts, Ximénez appears as the copyist and translator of the texts, as well as recipient of the manuscript (Carlos M. López, "Nuevos aportes para la autenticidad del Popol Wuj," *Revista Iberoamericana* 75, no. 226 (2009): 125–51.). As Carlos López explains, Ximénez's work was framed in "colonial supremacy" and tries to prove, among other things, that the "natives" were descendants of the Israeli tribe Cam, linking them to the hegemonic history of the Bible, and making the natives "deviant" and far from "the Truth" (Ibid., 127). The Popol Wuj has also been made available through the intervention of Maya's intellectuals such as Adrián Inés Chávez (Adrián Inés Chávez, *Pop Wuj: Libro del tiempo o de acontecimientos* (Quetzaltenango: Vile, 1981); Adrián Inés Chávez, *Pop Wuj: Libro del tiempo; poema mito-histórico Kí-chè* (Buenos Aires: Ediciones del Sol, 1994)), and Enrique Sam Colop (Luis Enrique Sam Colop, *Popol Wuj/Popol Vuh* (Guatemala: F&G Editores, 2011); Luis Enrique Sam Colop, *Popol wuj: Versión poética kíche'* (Quetzaltenango: PEMBI-GTZ; Cholsamaj, 1999)). The production of these two respected "Maya" scholars was mediated by the means made available via the "European" and "American" academe, but also in their resilience and commitment to the struggle for better conditions for "indigenous"

Language Heritage(s)   89

peoples. Adrián Inés Chávez translated the Popol Wuj in 1981. Chávez's first writings were made possible "not by the material affordances of the Guatemalan state but by the support of Germany in donating the first typewriter he used," notes Raxeche' Demetrio Rodriguez Guarán in a session entitled "Promoting the bibliographic production of indigenous languages" (Personal communication, July 18, 2012.). Enrique Sam Colop wrote a poetic version of the Popol Wuj in 1991. Colop was first a lawyer from Rafael Landivar, the Jesuit University, and later obtained a PhD in English from the State University of New York at Buffalo under Dennis Tedlock; Nora England served on his doctoral committee. Colop's poetic version of the Popol Wuj gained popularity for shifting the trajectory from prose to poetics or a combination of both in order to, as Matthias Abram from the Bilingual and Intercultural Education Project states in the book's introduction, offer "a key to opening the text and making accessible its mystic and profound poetics" (Ibid., 12).

76 Classroom observation (language and literature in L1), April 19, 2013. For the Spanish original see Appendix 7, item 13.
77 Classroom observation (language and literature in L1), April 19, 2013. For the Spanish original see Appendix 7, item 14.
78 Manuel Estrada Cabrera, *El libro azul de Guatemala* (Guatemala, 1915), 43. For the Spanish original see Appendix 7, item 15.
79 Bernadette Baker, "Empiricism, Perception, Vision: A Nomadology of Tactics in Social Scientific Thought," in *Intersectionality and Urban Education: Identities, Policies, Spaces & Power*, ed. Carl Grant and Elisabeth Zwier (Charlotte: Information Age Publishing, 2014), 55.
80 Boaventura de Sousa Santos, *Epistemologies of the South: Justice Against Epistemicide* (Boulder: Paradigm Publishers, 2014).
81 Achille Mbembé, "Necropolitics," *Public Culture*, no. 15 (2003): 11–40.
82 Jacques Derrida, *Of Grammatology*, trans. Gayatri Chakravorty Spivak (Baltimore: The Johns Hopkins University Press, 1998).
83 Ibid.
84 Lynn Mario Menezes de Souza, "Entering a Culture Quietly: Writing and Cultural Survival in Indigenous Education in Brazil," in *Disinventing and Reconstituting Languages*, eds. Alastair Makoni and Sinfree Pennycook (New York: Multilingial Matters, 2007), 135–69.
85 *Analfabeto* literally means without alphabet. Throughout this section I will be referring to *alfabetización*, as it appears in most archives, which is the process of alphabetizing. It can loosely be translated into English as *literacy* and *analfabetismo* as *illiteracy*.
86 This refers strictly to the encoding of alphabetical text considered coherent according to widely accepted linguistic rules.
87 Luis Antonio Méndez, *Educación en Guatemala 1954–1982* (Guatemala: Piedra Santa, 1984).
88 *Versión Preliminar del Plan Nacional de Alfabetización 1980–1984. Ministerio de Educación, Guatemala, 1980.* Cited in Luis Antonio Ménendez, *Educación en Guatemala 1954–1982* (Guatemala: Piedra Santa, 1984), 9. For the Spanish original see Appendix 7, item 16.
89 In the 1950 census, within the framework of Census of the Americas Committee, the United States Census Bureau and the Inter-American Institute of Statistics "sent experts" to conduct trainings on population census and run experiments that aimed to perfect the practice of census taking. This was done in collaboration with the technicians from the local Guatemalan division of statistics. "Sexto censo de población 1950" (Guatemala: Dirección General de Estadística, 1950).
90 The given category was "*alfabetismo*," which fell under the larger category of "education." "Instruction" was used instead of "education" before 1950.

90 *Language Heritage(s)*

91 "*Analfabetismo*," "*indígena*," "rural," and "*calzado*" are categories that are in close proximity when presented in the census data gathered over a century. *Calzado* roughly translates as "wears shoes." The category of "calzado" implied finding out whether people wore "*caites,*" an open-toe shoe, described as a pre-Hispanic shoe style and worn by some "indigenous" peoples in Mesoamerica. Although the categories mentioned above are presented in separate locations in the census book reports, they overlap in making what have become "indigenous" Beings upon which intervention is believed to be required.
92 Los Redactores, "Dos Palabras," *Magisterio: Revista de Instrucción Primaria* 1, no. 1, 2, 3, 4, 5, and 6 (1922): 5.
93 Valdés, "La instrucción del indígena," 33.
94 Ibid., 33.
95 Ibid., 34. For the Spanish original see Appendix 7, item 17.
96 Ibid., 33.
97 Ibid.
98 Abelardo A. Rodas, "Los Indios," *Magisterio: Revista de Instrucción Primaria* 1, no. 1, 2, 3, 4, 5, and 6 (1922), 41. For the Spanish original see Appendix 7, item 18.
99 Valdés, "La instrucción del indígena," 35.
100 Classroom observation (Help a Child *lectura* class), May 18, 2012.
101 "Reading for Life Overview," *Help a Child*, accessed June 29, 2013, http://child-aid.org/our-program/reading-for-life-overview/#sthash.vKSxTUqJ.dpuf
102 Informal interview with Sofia, the teacher, May 18, 2012.
103 Classroom observation (Help a Child *lectura* class), May 18, 2012. For the Spanish original see Appendix 7, item 19.
104 Classroom observation (Help a Child *lectura* class), May 18, 2012. For the Spanish original see Appendix 7, item 20.
105 Deborah P. Britzman, *Lost Subjects, Contested Objects: Toward a Psychoanalytic Inquiry of Learning* (Albany: State University of New York Press, 1998).
106 "Mujeres indígenas y racionalidad criolla en Guatemala," Television, *Kotzijon: Una mirada critica sobre Guatemala* (Guatemala City: TV Maya, May 30, 2013), www.youtube.com/watch?v=5bAie-7PlGg.

References

Acevedo, Blanca Estela. "Fundación de la ciudad de Santiago de los Caballeros de Guatemala." *El Normalista* (1945): 47–50.

Asturias, Miguel Ángel. "El problema social del indio." B.A. Theses Licenciatura en Derecho, Universidad de San Carlos de Guatemala, 1923.

Baker, Bernadette. "Empiricism, Perception, Vision: A Nomadology of Tactics in Social Scientific Thought." In *Intersectionality and Urban Education: Identities, Policies, Spaces & Power*, edited by Carl Grant and Elisabeth Zwier, 29–64. Charlotte: Information Age Publishing, 2014.

———. *William James, Science of the Mind, and Anti-Imperial Discourse*. New York: Cambridge University Press, 2013.

Batres Jáuregui, Antonio. *Los indios, su historia y su civilización*. Guatemala: Tipografía la Unión, 1894.

Boone, Elizabeth Hill, and Walter D. Mignolo. *Writing Without Words: Alternative Literacies in Mesoamerica and the Andes*. Durham: Duke University Press, 1994.

Brasseur de Bourbourg, Étienne Charles. *Popol Vuh: le livre sacré et les mythes de l'Antiquité américaine, avec les livres héroïques et historiques des Quichés: Ouvrage original des indigènes du Guatémala*. Paris: A. Bertrand; London: Trübner, 1861.

Brinton, Daniel G. *A Grammar of the Cakchiquel Language of Guatemala*. Philadelphia: McCalla & Stavely, Prs., 1884.
Britzman, Deborah P. *Lost Subjects, Contested Objects: Toward a Psychoanalytic Inquiry of Learning*. Albany: State University of New York Press, 1998.
Bucaro, Jaime. *Historial de IIN 1945–1956: Instituto Indigenista de Guatemala: Informe de sus trabajos y actividades*. Guatemala, n.d.
Butler, Judith. *Gender Trouble: Feminism and the Subversion of Identity*. New York: Routledge, 2006.
C., Schmidt. *Die Verbreitung der Sprachen im Südlichen Mittelamerika ums Jahr 1899*. Plate, 1901. http://zs.thulb.uni-jena.de/rsc/viewer/jportal_derivate_0022 1942/Mittheilungen_Perthes_129489816_1901_047_0713.tif?logicalDiv=log_ jportal_derivate_00221942.
Carrera Mejía, Maynor. "Las fiestas de Minerva en Guatemala, 1899–1919: El ansia de progreso y de civilización de los liberales." *Portal Historia Centroamericana* (2009): 1–13.
Casey, Dennis F. "Indigenismo, the Guatemalan Experience." Ph.D. Dissertation, History, University of Kansas, 1979.
Catholic Church, and Diocese of Santa Cruz del Quiché. *Padre Guillermo Woods*. Guatemala: Diócesis del Quiché, 2000.
Chávez, Adrián Inés. *Pop Wuj: Libro del tiempo o de acontecimientos*. Quetzaltenango: Vile, 1981.
———. *Pop Wuj: Libro del tiempo; poema mito-histórico Kí-chè*. Buenos Aires: Ediciones del Sol, 1994.
Collins, Wesley M. "Introducción a Winak: El Boletín Intercultural." *Winak: Boletín Intercultural* 1, no. 1 (1985): 7–12.
Cuz Mucú, Andrés. "Estudio Sociolinguistico Area Kekchi 1982." *Winak: Boletín Intercultural* 1, no. 2 (1985): 15–28.
Deleuze, Gilles, and Felix Guattari. *A Thousand Plateaus: Capitalism and Schizophrenia*. Translated by Brian Massumi. Minneapolis: University of Minnesota Press, 1987.
Derrida, Jacques. *Of Grammatology*. Translated by Gayatri Chakravorty Spivak. Baltimore: The Johns Hopkins University Press, 1998.
Elliott, Stephen R. "CIRMA y la lingüística." *Winak: Boletín Intercultural* 2, no. 2 (1986): 124–29.
England, Nora. "Is God an American? An Anthropological Perspective on the Missionary Work of the Summer Institute of Linguistics by Søren Hvalkof and Peter Aaby." *American Anthropologist* 85, no. 3 (September 1, 1983): 711–13.
Errington, Joseph. "Colonial Linguistics." *Annual Review of Anthropology* 30, no. 1 (2001): 19–39.
———. *Linguistics in a Colonial World: A Story of Language, Meaning, and Power*. Malden: Wiley-Blackwell, 2007.
Estrada Cabrera, Manuel. *El libro azul de Guatemala*. Guatemala, 1915.
Foucault, Michel. "Governmentality." In *Power: The Essential Works of Michel Foucault 1954–1984*, edited by James D. Faubion, vol. 3, 201–22. London: Allen Lane, 2000.
García, Ajpub' Pablo, Germán Curruchiche Otzoy, Simeón Taquirá, Programa de Educación Intercultural Multilingüe de Centro América, Componente Nacional Guatemala, Universidad Rafael Landívar, and Instituto de Lingüística y Educación. *Ruxe'el Mayab' k'aslemäl = Raíz y espíritu del conocimiento maya*. Ciudad de Guatemala: Programa de Educación Intercultural Multilingüe de Centroamérica

PROEIMCA, Componente Nacional Guatemala: Universidad Rafael Landívar, Instituto de Lingüística y Educación, 2009.
Gates, William. *Map of the Mayance Nations and Languages Prepared for the Maya Society Quarterly*. Plate, 1936.
González-Ponciano, Jorge Ramón. "De la patria del criollo a la patria del shumo: Whiteness and the Criminalization of the Dark Plebeian in Modern Guatemala." Ph.D. Dissertation, Anthropology, University of Texas-Austin, 2005.
Greenblatt, Stephen. *Marvelous Possessions: The Wonder of the New World*. Chicago: University of Chicago Press, 1992.
Hacking, Ian. "Kinds of People: Moving Targets." The Tenth British Academy Lecture, London, 2006.
———. "Kinds of People: Moving Targets." *Proceedings of the British Academy* 151 (London 2007): 285–318.
———. *Rewriting the Soul: Multiple Personality and the Sciences of Memory*. Princeton: Princeton University Press, 1995.
Hartch, Todd. *Missionaries of the State: The Summer Institute of Linguistics, State Formation, and Indigenous Mexico, 1935–1985*. Tuscaloosa: University Alabama Press, 2006.
Hassanpour, Amir. "The Politics of A-Political Linguistics: Linguistics and Linguicide." In *Rights to Language: Equity, Power, and Education*, edited by Robert Phillipson, 33–40. Mahawah: L. Erlbaum Associates, 2000.
Heidegger, Martin. *The Question Concerning Technology and Other Essays*. New York: Garland Publishing, 1977.
Henne, David. "Breve historia del Instituto Lingüístico de Verano de Centroamerica." *Winak: Boletín Intercultural* 2, no. 1 (1986): 30–35.
Herrera Peña, Guillermina. "Instituto de lingüística, de la Universidad 'Rafael Landívar.'" *Winak: Boletín Intercultural* 2, no. 2 (1986): 121–24.
Hvalkof, Søren, and Peter Aaby. *Is God an American? An Anthropological Perspective on the Missionary Work of the Summer Institute of Linguistics*. Copenhagen: International Work Group for Indigenous Affairs, 1981.
Latour, Bruno. "On the Partial Existence of Existing and Nonexisting Objects." In *Biographies of Scientific Objects*, edited by Lorraine Daston, 247–69. Chicago: University of Chicago Press, 2000.
León Chic, Eduardo. *El corazón de la sabiduría del pueblo maya = Uk'u'xal ranima' ri qano'jibal*. Iximulew (Guatemala): Fundación Centro de Documentación e Investigación Maya, 1999.
Lockhart, James. *Nahuas and Spaniards: Postconquest Central Mexican History and Philology*. Stanford: Stanford University Press, 1991.
López, Carlos M. "Nuevos aportes para la autenticidad del Popol Wuj." *Revista Iberoamericana* 75, no. 226 (2009): 125–51.
Los Redactores. "Dos palabras." *Magisterio: Revista de Instrucción Primaria* 1, no. 1,2,3,4,5, and 6 (1922): 5–6.
Luján Muñoz, Jorge. "Un ejemplo de uso de la tradición clásica en Guatemala: Las 'minervalias' establecidas por el presidente Manuel Estrada Cabrera." *Revista de la Universidad del Valle de Guatemala* 2 (1992): 25–33.
Makoni, Sinfree, and Alastair Pennycook, eds. *Disinventing and Reconstituting Languages*. New York: Multilingual Matters, 2007.
Masuzawa, Tomoko. *The Invention of World Religions: Or, How European Universalism Was Preserved in the Language of Pluralism*. Chicago: University of Chicago Press, 2005.

Mayers, Marvin Keene, Julio Vielman, and Seminario de Integración Social Guatemalteca (Organization). *Lenguas de Guatemala.* Guatemalade: José de Pineda Ibarra, 1966.
Mbembé, Achille. "Necropolitics." *Public Culture,* no. 15 (2003): 11–40.
McQuown, Norman A. *Handbook of Middle American Indians, Volume 5: Linguistics.* Austin: University of Texas Press, 1968.
Mejía Dávila, Marco Vinicio. "El Xinca histórico: Una investigación bibliográfica." *Winak: Boletín Intercultural* 4, no. 1 (1988): 3–64.
Méndez, Luis Antonio. *Educación en Guatemala 1954–1982.* Guatemala: Piedra Santa, 1984.
Menezes de Souza, Lynn Mario. "Entering a Culture Quietly: Writing and Cultural Survival in Indigenous Education in Brazil." In *Disinventing and Reconstituting Languages,* edited by Alastair Makoni and Sinfree Pennycook, 135–69. New York: Multilingial Matters, 2007.
Mignolo, Walter D. *Darker Side of the Renaissance: Literacy, Territoriality, and Colonization.* Ann Arbor: University of Michigan Press, 1995.
"Mujeres indígenas y racionalidad criolla en Guatemala." Video. *Kotzijon: Una mirada critica sobre Guatemala.* Guatemala City: TV Maya, May 30, 2013. www.youtube.com/watch?v=5bAie-7PlGg.
Otero Diez, Santiago, Marcelino López Balan, Marcelino Cano Saucedo, Angel Ovidio Velázquez Castellanos, and Tiburcio Hernández Utuy. *Testigos del morral sagrado: En homenaje a los catequistas sobrevivientes que han trabajado con dedicación, aun arriesgando la propia vida, por la construcción del reino de Dios.* Guatemala: ODHAG, 2011.
Pike, Kenneth L. *With Heart and Mind: A Personal Synthesis of Scholarship and Devotion.* Duncanville: Adult Learning Systems, 1996.
Portuondo, Maria M. "Conquistadors as Scientific Observers: Early Spanish Instructions for Travelers." Instructions, Questions, and Directions: Learning to Observe in Early Modern Scientific Travel, Max Planck Institute, Berlin, 2012.
Primer congreso pedagógico centroamericano: primera exposicion escolar nacional. Guatemala: Tipografía Nacional, 1894.
Rendón, Catherine. *Minerva y la palma: El enigma de don Manuel Estrada Cabrera.* Guatemala: Artemis Edinter, 2000.
Richards, Julia, and Michael Richards. "Plan de trabajo para el componente antropológico y lingüístico de la consultoría de asistencia técnica del programa nacional de educación bilingüe en Guatemala." *Winak: Boletín Intercultural* 2, no. 2 (1986): 104–12.
Rodas, Abelardo A. "Los indios." *Magisterio: Revista de Instrucción Primaria* 1, no. 1,2,3,4,5, and 6 (1922): 41.
Said, Edward. *Orientalism.* New York: Vintage Books, 1979.
Sam Colop, Luis Enrique. *Popol Wuj / Popol Vuh.* Guatemala: F&G Editores, 2011.
———. *Popol wuj: Versión poética kíche'.* Quetzaltenango: PEMBI-GTZ; Guatemala: Cholsamaj, 1999.
Sapper, Carl. "Beiträge zur Ethnographie de südlichen Mittelamerika Tippenhauer, L.G.': Beiträge zur Geologie Haïtis: IV: Die Erzfundstätten von Terre-Neuve und Gonaïves." *Dr. A. Petermanns Mitteilungen aus Justus Perthes' Geographischer Anstalt* 47 (1901): 25–121.
Scherzer, Carl, and Francisco Ximénez. *Las historias del origen de los indios de esta provincia de Guatemala: Exactamente según el texto español del manuscrito*

original que se halla en la biblioteca de la Universidad de Guatemala, publicado por la primera vez. Viena: Carlos Gerold é Hijo, 1857.

Sebeok, Thomas, ed. *Native Languages of the Americas*. New York: Springer Science & Business Media, 2013.

Sexto censo de población 1950. Guatemala: Dirección General de Estadística, 1950.

Skutnabb-Kangas, Tove. *Linguistic Genocide in Education, or Worldwide Diversity and Human Rights?* Mahwah: L. Erlbaum Associates, 2000.

Sousa Santos, Boaventura de. *Epistemologies of the South: Justice Against Epistemicide*. Boulder: Paradigm Publishers, 2014.

Stiles, Neville. "La Escuela de lingüística de la Universidad 'Mariano Gálvez' de Guatemala." *Winak: Boletín Intercultural* 2, no. 2 (1986): 112–21.

———. "Nota del Editor." *Winak: Boletín Intercultural* 1, no. 3 (1985): 1–4.

Stoll, David. *Fishers of Men or Founders of Empire? The Wycliffe Bible Translators in Latin America*. London: Zed Press, 1982.

———. "Words Can Be Used in So Many Ways." In *Is God an American? An Anthropological Perspective on the Missionary Work of the Summer Institute of Linguistics*, edited by Søren Hvalkof and Peter Aaby, 23–39. Copenhagen: International Work Group for Indigenous Affairs, 1981.

Stoll, Otto. *Zur Ethnographie der Republik Guatemala*. Zürich: Orell Füssli, 1884.

Swanton, John Reed. *The Indian Tribes of North America*. Washington: Genealogical Publishing Company, 1952.

Thomas, Cyrus, and John Reed Swanton. *Indian Languages of Mexico and Central America and Their Geographical Distribution*. Washington: U.S. Government Printing Office, 1911.

Townsend, William Cameron, and Richard S. Pittman. *Remember All the Way*. Huntington Beach: Wycliffe Bible Translators, 1975.

"Trabajos de las comisiones de ponencia: tema I. dictamen." In *Primer congreso pedagógico centroamericano: Primera exposicion escolar nacional*, 177–88. Guatemala: Tipografía Nacional, 1894.

Valdés, J. Refugio. "La instrucción del indígena." *Magisterio: Revista de Instrucción Primaria* 1, no. 1,2,3,4,5, and 6 (1922): 33–36.

Villacorta Calderon, Jose Antonio, Francisco Hernandez Arana, and Francisco Diaz Gebrita Quey. *Memorial de tecpán Átitlan*. Guatemala: Tipografía Nacional, 1934.

● ● ● 3 **Anthropological Borders and the Performance of Diversity in Teacher Preparation Classrooms**

> We as future teachers should teach children new knowledge that we learn here so that they change the mentality that they have in the communities, mostly in rural communities where the mentality of children is not well developed. Therefore, when one receives new knowledge . . . one should apply it and teach it to the children so that they turn out intelligent and creative and well developed.[1]

This chapter engages with the making of *lo indígena* in education through "anthropology, its experts, institutions,"[2] categories, and the people who are to be made. Anthropological institutions developed ways of reasoning that produced ways of ordering curriculum in the making of teacher education and what is "indigenous" and teacher education. Triggered by curriculum events in contemporary teacher education classrooms, the analysis in this chapter stems from two moments of intensity in particular: indigenism and cultural pluralism. The analysis begins and is threaded through with data from field notes and audio recordings of activities in teacher preparation classrooms, which I transformed into a play script.

Four acts in the script serve as triggers in the four sections of the chapter. The sections point to 1) *indigenismo* discourses in scientifically making-up *lo indígena* and their performativity in relation to teacher education;[3] 2) cultural pluralism and the revival of developmental narratives that recognize multiple kinds of peoples; and 3) and the spatialized notion of time that underlies anthropological border demarcations of what is "indigenous" in both *indigenismo* and cultural pluralism; with 4) implications for an interculturalist educational agenda in which spatialized time re-inscribes the migration/conversion template and where what is "indigenous" continues to be reasoned.

Choosing to employ conventional anthropological means or methods (focus groups, observations, field notes, and audio recording) to orient the chapter is a deliberate attempt to raise concerns about anthropological border demarcations, while also "talking back" to the same methodological means and styles of reasoning that make up the "content" of this analysis.

The chapter engages with and challenges particular anthropological styles of thought, expert knowledges, and particular experts/anthropologists. Here, "particular" does not mean the opposite of "general" or "generalized" (or "some anthropologists" as opposed to "all anthropologists"). This oppositional association can lead dangerously to a stabilizing Christian dynamic—of some being absolved and others found sinful or guilty—when instead the desire is for instability and motion. The "talking back" in the chapter is a challenge to the means through which the making-up of what is "indigenous" has been emerging. This means rule over and disallow not only the complex progressive possibilities that are already well rehearsed, but also those far from being imagined. Talking back is a motion to imagine otherwise.

Borders, as suggested in the title of this chapter, refer to anthropological demarcations that separate cultures, languages, territories, and countries. These demarcations, Jacques Derrida notes, are overdetermined by conceptual demarcations.[4] In other words, determining concepts or terms in turn makes possible the definition of anthropological lines of separation. In the context of this book, the conceptual demarcations are determined via scientific practices (or practices based on claims to a scientific methodology) mobilized via a series of particular aspirations reasoned within spatialized notions of time. In this chapter, the specific conceptual demarcations are negotiated by anthropologists, anthropological knowledges, and institutions in collaboration with the Guatemalan government, as well as other "experts," their expert institutions, and expert knowledges.[5]

Conceptual demarcations tend to rigorously position two concepts, or the concepts of two essences, in opposition. An illustrative example is found against the backdrop of conspicuous indigenist thought in 1920s Guatemala. The writings of Miguel Ángel Asturias set two essences in opposition: a lack of creativity and the ability to relate socially in the process of becoming a citizen.[6] One of these ontological essences is assigned to the "Indian" (lacking creativity) and the other is assigned to the "non-Indian" (social being, citizen). In the making of scientific (s)objects of inquiry through anthropological thought and activities, conceptual demarcations like this one pave the way for separation by spatializing time in what gets constituted as "Indian" and "non-Indian" culture.[7]

The spatialization of time in anthropological discourse (a discourse that is also performative) refers to the affirmation of difference as distance, according to anthropologist and critic Johannes Fabian.[8] Fabian argues that it was upon a temporal and thoroughly spatialized time template that anthropology and anthropological activities sought to construct relations with their object of study: the Other, or in this case, the "Indian." This template was formed under the paradigm of evolutionism and was made possible by developments in the eighteenth and nineteenth centuries. Fabian maintains that discursive devices that make up the foundations of modern anthropology are recognizable in decisive developments that characterize the Age of the Enlightenment—particularly the secularization of Judeo-Christian time by generalizing and universalizing it and travel as a science, among others. These developments and foundations play out in constituting the "indigenous" (s)object during indigenist and pluralist times, as we will see later.

At the prominent Indigenist Institute particular anthropologists and anthropological knowledges devised important conceptual demarcations when scientifically classifying peoples—the "indigenous" peoples who were their main preoccupation—that were also students and teachers in rural and semi-urban Guatemala. The reasoning behind such anthropological demarcations continues to order current classroom events such as the one presented in the first act of the play script.

The Presidenta and the India

ACT . (RE)SEARCH

	A sunlit early afternoon in the future. *Researcher in her "present" arrives in the four-walled classroom:* LIGIA *Bare interior.* *Lights up on center back, in a semicircle, on the floor,* STUDENT TEACHERS *sit. Bursts of laughter.*
STUDENT PLAYING CONGRESSWOMAN:	(*standing. Walking desperately front center. At wits' end.*) What are we going to do now? Who's going to be our candidate? Where are we going to find another Lorena to be our candidate? I have an idea! (*leaves.*) *Pause. Attempting no interruption, researcher walks towards the role-played scene. Stands next to* SOCIAL STUDIES TEACHER. *Scene changes to an interior garden. Gleefully,* SOCIAL STUDIES TEACHER *looks around and admires the colorful colonial setting where the scene is set. A classroom scene outside this classroom, on the patio. Outside, but inside.*
SOCIAL STUDIES/ PEDAGOGY TEACHER:	(*comes to stage front. Addressing the spectators, school principal, other teachers, the ministry of education, parents. Rows of faces fading far back into the dark, anthropologists, activists, presidents, military officials, missionaries.*) This is the last of five skits; and it's long overdue. The niñas [girls] acted one, the Xinca, two, Garífuna, three, Ladino, and four, the Maya, pueblos [peoples] of Guatemala. Today's performance puts the four pueblos together for the first time. (*walks backwards without noticeable gesture.*)
STUDENT INDIA MARÍA:	(*in school uniform. Stands up, walks diagonally to side of stage.*) We were inspired by the India María.[9] (*addressing* LIGIA) Have you watched it? She's a TV character and a movie character, she's gracious, and da mucha risa [is very funny]. (*exits stage giggling.*)

This play script is made possible by the creativity displayed by the students in tweaking the events in the story of *La presidenta municipal* (*The Municipal President*) and in performing it to both entertain and achieve the curricular goals.[10] The skit that the students performed, and the one upon which this play script is based, was embedded in a Social Studies lesson at Century Normal School. The student teachers were asked to act out each of the four *pueblos* (peoples) in Guatemala ("Xinca," "Garífuna," "Maya," "Ladino"). Each group of students was asked to perform a different *pueblo*. Over a period of several weeks various groups were asked to perform their skits. The group of students that staged *La presidenta municipal* was the last one and had the mandate of performing the four *pueblos* together. The 1975 movie *La presidenta municipal* was an assertive choice of popular culture for engaging their peers, and also their teacher. The dramatic performance did indeed grant the actors an extended applause in appreciation of their efforts. Drama and role play were common curricular tools in the classes I observed at Century Normal School. Less common, however, were curricular connections to particular forms of popular culture whose heritage lie at the intersection of indigenismo and "indigenous" emergence.

La presidenta municipal is a Mexican film production. Similar to most films produced by Puerto Rican native Fernando Cortés during the 1970s, *La presidenta* is a mixture of sharp humor, politics, and cultural discourse. Emerging in the context of four decades of indigenist institutionalization, and many more of indigenist thought, reaching the highest moments of intensity in the 1940s to 1960s in Mexico and throughout the Americas, *La presidenta* characterizes the impulses of the 1970s vis-à-vis indigenous concerns. These impulses aimed not only to assign agency to the "Indian," but also to see her political participation in official spaces. The main character, María Nicolasa Cruz, commonly known as *La India María* in television in recent years, endures racial discrimination, segregation, and corruption. María's intuitive and perceptive capabilities, coupled with experience, assertiveness, and courage serve her well in the public office she had mistakenly inherited. With hilarious exploits, mocking the government, cultural norms, and the status quo, María overcomes challenging situations riddled with "cultural" discrimination and what Étienne Balibar calls "cultural racism" in the Mexico of the 1970s (in the movie) and the Guatemala of 2012 (in the skit staged by the students).[11] *La India María* and her movies continue to entertain little ones and adults alike in Guatemalan homes and throughout Latin America.

In its interconnection to Mexico, this classroom event reflects the conversation that Guatemala has had with its neighbor in recent history: thinking about, planning, devising, and implementing *indigenismo* and Indian assimilation policies.[12] Before engaging with the embedded suggestion of "indigenous emergence" in the movie and the skit, as well as other pedagogical complexities, I turn to a noticeable moment of intensity of indigenous making in the twentieth-century history of "indigenous" making: *indigenismo*.[13]

I enter this classroom event, not uninvited, to "conduct an observation," employing anthropological means/methods to conduct research and document events. Unlike anthropologists and linguists from the 1940s whose duty, I claim, was the intense scientific making of what is indigenous, my task is to arrive at the intersection of where the anthropological and curriculum meet in a social studies lesson. My inquiry retains the "how" of making-up people and the effects it produces in the educational imagination.

Indigenismo

Indigenismo as a series of ideas can be noticed in the wave-like effect that is the caricaturization in the students' performance of "the India," in the employment of the culturalist discourse and, in the background, the preoccupation with research and scientific practice as a means to address the "Indian problem." Jorge Luis Arriola, prominent politician, indigenist, and educator, opens the first pages of the 1961 *Guatemala Indígena* journal on "scientificity" and "rigor."[14] He states:

> that [the *Guatemala Indígena* journal] would embody the living educational space of indigenism to improve the knowledge of the world vision of the Indian, their civic-religious, social, and economic organization, their folkloric art, etcetera, analyzed with scientific rigor, far from halting or sentimental outbreaks, and for the planning of new and reasonable solutions to the Indian problem, not always understood by governments.[15]

This statement captures a central preoccupation of *indigenismo*,[16] the Indigenist Institute, indigenists, and indigenists' anthropological aspirations: to find new and reasonable solutions to the "Indian problem" (see Chapter 1). "New and reasonable solutions," to use the revolutionary rhetoric of the time,[17] refers not only to countering the deliberate neglect of "indigenous" peoples by prior military governments (e.g., the government of Gen. Jorge Ubico [1931–1944]) in their denial of an Indian problem,[18] in the face of rampant "indigenous" exploitation and impoverishment. *New* refers to forms of knowledge and methodologies made available through the pedagogic, psychological, and anthropological sciences under which a group of young intellectuals were operating, many of whom were revolutionaries, members of the 1920s generation, and educated in the United States or Europe.[19] *Reason*able solutions did not only refer to, as Guillermo Bonfil Batalla would describe it, a series of measures that would make de-Indian-ization less brutal.[20] Reasonable also made reference to modernist ideas for studying, understanding, and acting on the "Other" through social scientific means,[21] with a deliberate claim for the reason of that "Other." The aspiration projected here employs typological time in which the *indígena* is expected to abandon her location of irrationality, to become, for instance, in the educational realm, a Castilian speaker, alphabetically literate (see Chapter 2), aware of her condition of ignorance, and articulate in understanding and practicing modern ways of performing her life (wearing shoes, practicing hygiene). According to Arriola in the *Guatemala Indígena* journal, reasonableness comes via the scientific practice of accountability and precision, in how the *indígena* was defined through anthropological practices specifically in the mid-1940s, and continued to be defined at the time of his writing in the early 1960s. Arriola shared the impetus that animated these new and reasonable solutions with his indigenist predecessor Antonio Goubaud Carrera.[22]

Similar to Arriola, Goubaud Carrera served as director of the National Indigenist Institute (IIN) and also had a strong influence in making-up *lo indígena* as a (s)object of scientific inquiry with noticeable effects in curriculum today. Explaining what sets apart the *indigenismo* moment of the "indigenous" event, Goubaud Carrera describes Bartolomé de las Casas' concern with protection of the "Indians," the nineteenth century's preoccupation as an intellectual interest in the "Indian," and the twentieth-century *indigenismo* as a "scholarly interest" in *how* the "Indians" might relate to Western culture and Western civilization.[23]

In 1946, applying the basis of indigenist policies to scientific study,[24] Goubaud Carrera presented the results of a "study" carried out with "the objective methods of the social sciences."[25] The study was a survey of the population to determine the criteria that define the "indigenous" ethnic group. It was conducted partly with the aspiration of "clarifying" and demarcating these criteria. Goubaud Carrera suggested that *the existing multiplicity of criteria was a problem*. The origin of this variety or diversity, he explained, was the fact that "the indigenous population in American countries is in *transition* since it came into direct and indirect contact with other populations in the world."[26] The impulse to survey in order to tame the diversity that resulted from this transition draws from particular notions of demographic change, reasoned through physical notions of time separating pre-Hispanic times from colonial times.

Goubaud Carrera's explanation follows the lead of his mentor: Robert Redfield's anthropological motivations and models for the investigation of contemporary and complex culture,[27] the relationships between "urban" and "folk" culture, and the transition from "primitive man" to "civilized man."[28] The aspirations of these transitions are inserted in intervals of typological time, templates within which relations and differences are constructed. Redfield's continuum from folk to urban allowed the placing of rural "Maya" towns in the space of the "folk" and the more "civilized and occidentalized" ones in the urban space where most people were "*mestizos*" or "Ladinos."[29] Redfield's pioneering anthropology—which, among other things, focused on understanding the connection between urban and rural people within the same society—was influential to Guatemalan *indigenismo* and in configuring the making of difference that served as a template for aspiring to convert/migrate the "Indian."[30] Beyond understanding this process of transition from folk to urban, Goubaud Carrera, unlike his mentor, had the practical task of reducing the characteristics by which an "Indian" could be defined. This way, in accordance with the revolutionary and constitutional changes of the time, it was easier to ensure that the "Indian" would "enjoy liberty, culture, economic well-being, and social justice,"[31] similarly to the "non-Indian." Embedded in this constitutional aspiration was Redfield's and his students' defense for the *change and modernity*—liberty, culture, well-being—associated with urban and "non-Indian" or "Ladino" cultures, whereas *immobility and tradition* were associated with "indigenous" cultures. Thus, liberty, culture, economic-well-being, and social justice—modernity—would come to "indigenous" cultures through a process of ladinization.[32] *Converting* the situation of the "Indian" *and* the "Indian" himself or herself was Goubaud Carrera's and *indigenismo's* commitment.

For Goubaud Carrera, surveying the population was necessary given that Guatemala did not have "precise" criteria to define the "indigenous" group as determined by an existing institution dedicated to "indigenous" peoples, as was the case in the United States. This was the task of the newly opened Guatemalan IIN. Surveying the population was also necessary given the fact that censuses had been conducted based on "general opinion" and the "prevalent criteria" were not necessarily held by "public opinion" (mainly a "Ladino" public). The larger aspiration in surveying the population was, however, to influence future population censuses in the country. Under the moral call for the "well-being of humanity in the future,"[33] and, considering human relations, Goubaud Carrera believed that defining ethnic groups had a true functional meaning.

1,248 surveys were sent to urban and rural schools in sixteen departmental jurisdictions in the country where there was "an indigenous population. The great majority of the people who were surveyed belong to the Ladino (non-indigenous) population."[34] From the standpoint of what Redfield would refer to as social anthropology,[35] Goubaud Carrera justified the items included in the survey titled "IN THIS MUNICIPALITY A PERSON IS INDIGENOUS:"[36] with the following reason:

> If we try to study the sociological characteristics that determine a human group, we realize that there are sufficient bases of support to conduct an analysis of such characteristics. When a person or a group of people enter into a social relationship with another person or group of people, there are *palpable characteristics* that influence both of them in their treatment of one another. Some of these outstanding differences are: (1) clothing; (2) the language; (3) the habits, customs or conduct; and of course, perhaps more importantly (4) the person's physical appearance: the size and body shape, the skin color, the hair and the eyes, and any other detail of the physical aspect.[37]

Of the five questions that the survey included, four were taken directly from these four "palpable characteristics": clothing, language, customs, and race. These characteristics are based on a visual paradigm of "Western" culture and an ocularcentric logic that determines presence and existence.[38] The fifth characteristic asked about "indigenous" last names, which is "an incidental aspect" influencing social relationships. As Goubaud Carrera would have it, last names are an "abstract aspect of cultural transmission," unlike the other four. Yet, as he put it, this was one that could be "easily manageable" in the survey. Holding Goubaud Carrera's "scientific" attempts (to define the "indigenous" person) up against itself, one must question how little information he provides about *how* these five characteristics were selected.[39] He does, however, include a short explanation to stress why they matter in defining the *indígena*. Language, as a category, allows for the narrowing down of the multiplicity of criteria used to define the "*indígena*," which the survey is meant to control. The open-ended question in the customs item is important to collect "empirical data," whereas the "regular systematicity" in the responses allows for "a calculation of statistical frequency." Thus, the characteristics were defined *under* a visual paradigm and also *with* statistical reasoning in asking questions whose answers would fit the desire to systematically compile the "indigenous" populations of the Republic. Some survey data, however, such as "in this municipality there are no indigenous peoples,"[40] were discarded, because, as Goubaud Carrera explained, such data were "without meaning for this study."[41] Thus the study effectively served the purpose of creating a reduced number of criteria for defining the *indígena*.

The findings, which were still referenced over a decade later,[42] reflected the sharp discrepancies found in the "public opinion" concerning which criteria should be used to define the *indígena* out of the five narrowed-down concepts: "there are no uniform or general criteria in the country" and "the criteria differ in the various departments of the Republic."[43] Goubaud Carrera argued that this lack of uniform criteria needed to be considered in order to achieve a more precise reflection of Guatemala's demographic reality. That demographic reality is defined based on two opposing concepts: "Indian" and "Ladino." Yet a totalizing conclusion is drawn for/to the "Republic," that "the most generalized criteria are the habits and customs of the *indígena* population [86%]" followed by "speaking the autochthonous language in the home [84%],"[44] which is also the generalized criterion used to determine the *indígena*. One of the survey's conclusions, delivered in a celebratory manner, is that the survey—completed by "Ladinos"—revealed that race was not an important factor to "differentiate" "indigenous" peoples.[45] A far-fetched inference for Goubaud Carrera is that "skin or hair color have no relationship [to] either man's intelligence or to his humanity, and therefore this makes it much quicker to achieve social solidarity among the ethnic groups in the country."[46]

In 1930 Goubaud Carrera undertook studies in Kaqchikel "with the goal of developing a curriculum for this language."[47] As a becoming anthropologist and indigenist, he believed education was and continued to be central to indigenist aspirations because it would serve as the engine that would transition/migrate/convert the "Indian." Around the late 1930s, Goubaud Carrera announced that there was not yet anything "concrete or *scientific* about the world vision according to the indigenous peoples of the country, [there is] nothing yet to prepare Guatemalan teachers [to work with] the indigenous population of the country."[48] Therefore a truthful research agenda was necessary because "when we know the factors that make up their mentality, the springs that activate their emotions, then perhaps we would be able to *convert* indigenous peoples to be part of our Western culture, once research has informed us of the right way."[49] Typological time in which "indigenous" is set against "Western culture" continues to animate the social and political agenda of change and the constant remaking of *lo indígena*. Although Goubaud Carrera's central scientific motivation may have shifted, as Abigail E. Adams argues, from "the illiterate peasant in colorful costumes that was delaying the progress of the nation" to "the potential citizen,"[50] the Indigenist Institute he had pioneered maintained its aspiration to migrate/ "convert" the "Indian," albeit within different terms.[51] Let us now move our focus to the late 1950s and the work of the National Indigenist Institute (IIN) and the Summer Institute of Linguistics (SIL) in direct relation to schools, the training of teachers, and making of less "indigenous kinds" through the aspirations of migration and conversion.

In 1958 Margarita Wendell and her colleague Rubi Scott, both affiliated with the SIL, were commissioned to "help" with an "experimental" project sponsored by the IIN. Tactic, Alta Verapaz, and the *indígenas pocomchíes* were the site and the (s)object of the experiment. To implement "Tactic's Integral Improvement Plan," the alphabetization experiment's final aim was "to lead children to a real comprehension of Spanish, with an ability to read."[52] Aware that this was not immediately and completely achievable, Wendell and Scott prepared a series of booklets in the *pocomchi* language for use in schools in four villages during the academic year. After having received prior "practical lessons" in the United States,[53] doing field work in Mexico under the SIL, and a "brief and general" introduction by anthropologist and director of the IIN Juan de Dios Rosales, they set off to Tactic to "prove" that with "booklets in the *pocomchí* dialect an indigenous child could learn to read faster and actually comprehend what he read if the learning process was to start in his own language and to later orient him to Spanish."[54]

In conversations with a teacher in a school in Tzalam toward the end of the experiment, Wendell explains that the teacher expressed his preference for "these kinds of materials because they created an understanding for indigenous children."[55] What's more, Wendell continued, now the process to learn to read is made meaningful compared to a learning process that did not go beyond practice. "The teacher said: 'this method is the only one that should be taught in schools like this where all the people only speak the dialect. But it came too late. It should have been used for years.' "[56] The teacher's words (or perhaps Wendell's decision to share this particular exchange) serve not only as "proof" for Wendell, the IIN, the SIL, or any other institution involved that the experiment worked, to a certain extent, but also convinced this teacher of the effectiveness of "the method."[57] The teacher's words are also an expression of an in-service teacher education curriculum that intersects with scientific activities conducted through anthropological, linguistic, pedagogic, and sociological knowledges. During the "experimental project," the teachers were trained indirectly through visits by the director of the IIN, who encouraged them to continue with "the program." The teachers were also trained through Wendell and Scott's accompaniment and guidance in implementing the program. Through "explanatory notes" Wendell and Scott gave their last push before the "exams" were administered in order to prove the effectiveness of the booklets.

The effects on the in-service teachers of the pedagogic and linguistic mission were also noticed in the Ixil region. Reinaldo Alfaro Palacios, a rural teacher of the Nebaj municipality in the Quiché department, developed a booklet in the Ixil language to alphabetize "indigenous" peoples in this region, as Jaime Bucaro describes in a report of the activities of the IIN from 1945 to 1956.[58] Palacios submitted the booklet to the Ministry of Public Education. So that the booklet "offers a good service in the future,"[59] the IIN, commissioned by the ministry, "studied, analyzed, and corrected the pedagogical technique" that Palacios had proposed in the booklet.[60] In this way, the booklet was appropriately adapted for bilingual alphabetization in the Ixil communities. The revised booklet and technique instructed Palacios as an in-service teacher on the appropriate pedagogy to migrate/convert Ixil students into alphabetized *indígenas*.

The adaptation of the booklet for Ixiles was mediated by the IIN as an expert institution, and the SIL's linguist experts (*técnicos*), who, in conjunction with the government, were steering the alphabetization efforts that necessitated the "study" of the main languages in the country to "establish a generalized dialect for each tongue."[61] Jaime Bucaro writes that since 1946 the IIN had been working on the technical tasks and data collection phases of the project, which yielded results that were revised in collaboration with American linguists. Mark Hanna Watkins,[62] from Harvard University, worked for the "Cakchiquel zone"; Norman McQuown, from the University of Chicago, worked in the Mam language establishing "the fundamental phonemes of Quiche, Kekchi, Kanjobal, Tzutujil, and Xinca"[63]; and Margarita Wendell and Rubi Scott worked in the Q'eqchi' region in the Alta Verapaz department to "provide the fundamental phonemes and the linguistic unity of the region"[64] in order to design the "successful" alphabetization booklet described earlier.

As discussed in the previous chapter, the SIL interacted closely with *indigenismo* and the Guatemalan government to shape matters of educational concern, and such interactions educated teachers during the "field" research organized and monitored by the IIN. Although indigenous peoples did not consider language a fundamental criterion to define *lo indígena* in Goubaud Carrera's anthropological survey, through education language was and continues to be an element of "indigenous" making (see Chapter 2). During the empirical research conducted by the SIL and the IIN, defining the "fundamental phonemes," for example, served as a means to define the anthropological boundaries of Xinca, Mam, Q'eqchi' (formerly Kekchi), Kaqchikel (formerly Kaqchiquel), and other languages and peoples, as employed in the *La presidenta* classroom role play of the four *pueblos*. Doing field linguistic research with the purpose of establishing a "generalized dialect" of each "tongue,"[65] for example, performatively determines ontological entities, which simultaneously instate and justify the educational mission of alphabetizing, castilianizing, integrating, ladino-izing, modernizing, and developing during the *indigenista* moment of intensity in "indigenous" making.

The aspirations for migration/conversion—in terms of social mobility, political participation, presence and recognition through cultural difference, and even in terms of development that we see earlier (in reference to the development of the *pueblos*)—also emerge in the times of cultural pluralism and multiculturalism discussed in a later section. *Indigenismo* and multiculturalism are moments of intensity in the interconnections, continuities, and transformations in "indigenous" making. This next section addresses cultural pluralism as articulated through multiculturalism.

ACT .. MY CULTURE IS BETTER THAN YOURS

	left downstage six students play the role of MARKET VENDORS *in market. Five are sitting on the floor. Four wear long skirts. One wears a San Juan Sacatepéquez Corte [skirt] and a Santiago Atitlán güipil [blouse]. One stands in a pair of jeans and a cool T.*
STUDENT MARKET VENDOR1:	Hay tomatoes! There are tomatoes! . . .
SMV2:	Potatoes!
SMV1:	Carrots! . . .
SMV2:	Hay potatoes! . . .
SMV3:	Bananas! . . .
SMV4:	(*standing in jeans and cool T. Looks down her nose and smiles at other vendors*). Hay Apples! . . .
SMV3:	Bananas. Bananas.
SMV7 INDIA MARÍA:	(*enters stage. Arrives at market. Dressed in Cobán güipil and corte, and a hat. Wears two long braids, one on each side falling in front of her shoulders, and guaraches for footwear. Joining the selling voices.*) Chicharrones calienticos [hot fried pork].

106 Anthropological Borders

SMV3: *(quietly to other* MARKET VENDORS.*)* There comes the India.

SMV7 INDIA MARÍA: *(standing. Proudly.)* India but honest, oíste [get it!] You must respect me, oíste! I am not of your same class, oíste! My culture is way better than yours.

SMV3: *(interrupting. Standing. In long skirt).* That is yet to be seen.

SMV7 INDIA MARÍA: *(sassily.)* Move away. Chicharrones calienticos. *(sitting on floor.)* Come and get them.
Students in circle laughing noisily.

SMV5 GARÍFUNA: *(overlapping).* Get your apples, potatoes, and carrots.

SMV3: *(walking towards* INDIA MARÍA.*)* Look INDIA, the only Chicharrones worth here are mine. *(grabbing* INDIA *by arms and lifting her from floor.)* So listen, get up, and learn, oístes.
SMV2 *stands next to* SMV3. INDIA *turns around.* SMV3 *stares at her defiantly.* STUDENTS *laugh.*

SMV2 XINCA: *(in long skirt. Shyly and calmly.)* The Xinca culture is indigenous but does not descend from the Mayas. The Xincas lived off fishing and collecting salt. *(pause.)*
Marimba music begins. XINCAS *dance.* INDIA *exaggerates the moves as in a caricature.* STUDENTS *laugh heartily. Music stops.* SMV1 *and* SMV5 *come forward wearing long skirts and spaghetti-strapped tops.*

SMV7 INDIA MARÍA: *(complaining).* Oh heavenly father, now what are they going to tell me?

SMV5: *(smiling at* INDIA *reads from a piece of paper).* Garífuna culture is the result of the African and Caribbean culture. They live primarily in Izabal and the Caribbean coast. People who belong to the Garífuna culture have black skin color. *(smiles shyly.)*
Animated music and a female singing voice is played. The two GARÍFUNAS *dance to the rhythm. Moves associated with African drums.* INDIA *exaggerates the moves as in a caricature.* STUDENTS *laugh loudly.* INDIA *bends over, observes the* GARÍFUNAS' *feet as if learning the steps, takes her hat off and bows in mockery.* STUDENTS *laugh vivaciously.* SMV4 *comes forward.*

SMV7 INDIA MARÍA: *(complaining).* And now what are you going to say? God!

SMV4 LADINA: Look INDIA, the Ladina cult- (INDIA *interrupts*)

SMV7 INDIA MARÍA: *(angrily.)* I *see* because I have two eyes. *(pointing to her own eyes.* LADINA *hides her giggle.)*

SMV4 LADINA: *(explaining.)* The Mayan culture *(corrects herself)* The Ladina Culture comes from the sixteenth century (INDIA *puts both hands on waist, waves right hand before fixing her hat, in dismissal of narrative)* and is the culture as you can see . . . *(pause)* I mean *(pause)* I mean *(pause. Forgetting her script.)*

SMV7 INDIA MARÍA:	(*in an act of solidarity to help* SMV4 *remember. Complaining.*) What are you going to tell me? And what happened with my dress? (*waving her corte.*) Look.
SMV4 LADINA:	-discriminate against people as (*pause.* Pointing to INDIA MARÍA.) as (*hesitating*) as we can see here.
	(*A remastered la Gasolina song blasts into the hot afternoon air.* LADINA *and* INDIA *jam to the pop-Caribbean rhythm.* STUDENTS *laugh stormingly with* INDIAN *caricature.*)
SMV7 INDIA MARÍA:	(*still jamming*). You think you are going to teach me how to dance? (*challengingly. Bumping* LADINA's *hips with her own hips.*)
	INDIA *bends over, observes* LADINA's *feet as in dismissal and as a sign of transition within the skit. Music stops.*
SMV7 INDIA MARÍA:	Come on sister, let's give them a lesson on what real dancing looks like. (*pointing to the other women.*)
SMV6 MAYA:	The Mayan civilization lived in Central America. At that time they spoke hundreds of dialects and now only a few are left.
	The song Cuando Llora un Indio [When an Indian Cries] slowly fades in. Both güipil and corte swiftly move to the marimba rhythms. On their knees they thank the Ajaw, and lift their arms up to what we would call the South, North, East, and West. Without a word or a laugh STUDENTS *watch. Music stops.*
SMV7 INDIA MARÍA:	(*proudly.*) See my culture is much better than yours.
ALL SMVs:	(*chorus.*) The INDIA.
SMV7 INDIA MARÍA:	(*proudly.*) My culture is better than yours.

Act .. is made possible by and highlights another noticeable moment of intensity of "indigenous" making in the twentieth century: *cultural pluralism* or *multiculturalism*. The teacher educator's curricular decision to address "Guatemalan diversity" by opening up a space for performance in the classroom is made possible, arguably, by educational policies such as the Accord of the Identity and Rights of Indigenous Peoples, National Languages Law, and the National Base Curriculum propelled by indigenous movements since the 1970s and consolidated in the 1990s.[66] These movements, particularly the Mayanist movement,[67] employ and deploy the knowledges produced by cultural and social anthropologists, ethnologists, archaeologists, and epigraphers from the American (Sylvanus Morley), to the British (Eric S. Thomson and Barbara and Dennis Tedlock), to the Dutch (Ruud Van Akkeren), in order to articulate the struggle for "the right to cultural pluralism."[68] Physical notions of time in which grand ages and stages of evolutionary history (i.e., pre-classic, classic, post-classic) are marked serve to produce claims for intellectual proof of "Mayan" cultural richness.

The students twist the story line of the movie script to artfully deliver the assignment, address the national curricular mandate, respond to recent history, and make history. The actresses place the focus on Guatemalan diversity quantifiably into four *pueblos*: the "Maya," "Ladino," "Garífuna," and "Xinca." At Linguistics University, the bilingual education teacher also remarks that the four portraits of children on the cover of the Intercultural Bilingual Education manual represent the four pueblos, the four cultures, and it is important "to understand that we are a very diverse country."[69] At the noticeable moments in the emergence of pluralism/multiculturalism, *pueblo* is a *unit* that has been adopted by indigenous peoples in Guatemala, and other places in Latin America, to struggle against their historical "exclusion." *Pueblo*, as social scientist Santiago Bastos describes, is "a group with a common history that is manifested in certain cultural traits, and that involves a number of collective political rights."[70] *Pueblo* as a unity has been fundamental to articulate an agenda for the progress/development of "indigenous" *communities* (often a synonym of *pueblo*).[71]

The students' ability to display critical awareness—in pointing out how "Mayas" spoke hundreds of dialects before and in naming discrimination, performing racism, marking cultural difference, and gesturing toward class stratification—could be understood as a response to the recent histories of violence and the plea for *recognition* through multiculturalism in Guatemala. The fact that the "India" in the play demands respect and recognition of her honesty—pointing out she is no longer inferior ("I am not of your same class"), defying discriminatory expressions, daring to express the superior quality of "her culture," demonstrating assertiveness, holding an elegant demeanor, and conceiving of herself as "Maya"—may not have been possible in a teacher preparation classroom at the heart of *indigenismo* as conceived in the mid-1940s. Claiming recognition for the "Indian" problem, recognition of the nation's various languages, recognition of the necessity to improve the condition of the "Indian," as were the terms during *indigenismo*, arguably would have not created the necessary conditions for the "India" *herself* to claim recognition based on her human, cultural, linguistic, and political rights.[72]

The terms under which difference is defined in the students' play are indebted to the anthropological heritages and knowledges produced under the struggle for studying—in order to recognize and uphold—the *indígena*. From the ways in which they have been socialized, The Normal School student teachers represent the Xinca's "cultural traits" (in Bastos' language) and the "customs" (using the IIN and Goubaud Carrera's allowed categories) in their reliance on fish and not being "Maya" descendants; the *Garífunas* in their life on the Caribbean coast and their black skins; the "Ladinos" and their history from the sixteenth century and the fact that they discriminate; and "Mayas" in their *corte* and *güipil* outfits and the fact that they speak fewer languages than in the past. In particular, the characterizations of the "Ladino" and the "Maya" as pitched against each other heavily rely not only on the dichotomous relation made available in Robert Redfield's and Sol Tax's influential anthropological analytics, but also on the work of

American anthropologist Richard Adams (in defining *The Culture of Ladinos in Guatemala*, 1956), and the *Coordinadora Cakchiquel de Desarrollo Integral* (in defining the *Mayan Culture*, 1989).

Drama as a pedagogical tool suggests a progressive attempt at breaking from what is often referred to as "traditional"[73] teaching methods at the same moment that the students make history in performing the transformation from assimilationist impulses in *indigenismo* to cultural pluralism in multiculturalism. The female students offer their peers, the teacher, and myself in the audience a memorable moment of entertainment, to fill in the mantra of "diverse, pluricultural, and multiethnic Guatemala." Next I trace the emergences of pluralism/multiculturalism in their most noticeable moments of intensity.

Cultural Pluralism/Multiculturalism

In 1989 COCADI (*Coordinadora Cakchiquel de Desarrollo Integral*) compiled and published what American anthropologist Charlie Hale calls one of the first "Maya" movement books: *Cultura Maya y Políticas de Desarrollo*.[74] Its chapters express the intellectual engagements of "Mayan" intellectuals such as Demetrio Cojtí Cuxil and Luis Enrique Sam Colop, as well as Mexican anthropologists Guillermo Bonfil Batalla and Rodolfo Stavenhagen and scientists Sylvanus Morley and Eric Thompson, among others. These experts and their anthropological, or anthropology-like work—Cojtí Cuxil, self-identified as "Maya Kaqchikel," is a social communication expert educated at Louvain, Belgium,[75] and Sam Colop, self-identified as "Maya K'iche'," was a lawyer, poet, and linguist educated at SUNY-Buffalo, United States—not only render the moment of pluralism in "indigenous" making noticeable, but also actively participate in such making.

With similar aspirations embedded in the spatialized time, pro-improvement, and development of rural communities (i.e., communities considered "indigenous" and "Maya") during the indigenist moment, the book attempts to define development by offering directives for development and invokes the framework of multiculturalism to prevent further "degeneration of the Maya culture."[76]

> The necessity to improve the standard of living of rural communities in Guatemala, especially the Mayan communities, poses challenges to our creativity and spirit of service. The Non Governmental Organizations for Development, NGOs, have been making various efforts to cooperate for the development of these communities; however, each day we observe that we need to better define the orientation and the kind of development that we would like to make happen, so that our programs are concrete contributions to the development of the country. Above all, we need to consider, in our activities, the multicultural characteristics of Guatemala.[77]

110 *Anthropological Borders*

To better define the kind of development to be realized for the "Maya" *pueblo*, COCADI offers a definition in the context of the "Maya" culture, and therefore for its people:

> We understand that it is the culture that the Maya people started developing more than 10 thousand years ago in the south of what is the Mexican republic today, throughout Belize and Guatemala, in part of Honduras and El Salvador. The Mayan civilization has its roots in humanity's pre-history. The Mayan culture for several millennia has been developing in what is today Guatemala, in some epochs with great splendor . . . We are Maya, the ones that carry the culture of our forefathers—more than 4 million Guatemalans that speak a Mayan language. We protect our Mother Nature, we maintain, to a certain extent, our own technology; and additionally, we identify as Mayas (roj, qawinaq; qawinaquil qi').[78]

The anthropological demarcation of the "Maya" as a culture and territory is enabled through scientific archeological expeditions which, reasoning through physical time, locate its splendor—elements such as pyramids, glyphs, and the numbering system—in the classic and postclassic times (anthropological inventions) of the "Mayan" civilization. The effects of this reasoning in contemporary teacher education are not only noticeable in the *La India* skit at Century Normal School, but also in an indigenous language lesson at Rural Bilingual Intercultural Normal School, where Matin, a "Maya Q'anjob'al" teacher, explains:

> The numbers express the quantity or the order of things. In the Mayan languages, counting has a basis of 20 numbers, that is why it is said that it uses a *vigesimal* system . . . The use of the system by the population has generally decreased. The elders still maintain and use part of the counting system. There are also books written in the past where one can research this system.[79]

Drawing the boundary around *lo indígena* "Maya" is made possible within the preoccupation with the search for cultural origins that would enable *self-definition, recognition,* and *presence,* a preoccupation exemplified by "Mayan" intellectuals such as Rodriguez Guajan, Cojtí Cuxil, and Sam Colop.[80] Additionally, throughout the *Cultura Maya* compiled works and in the innumerable materials that are part of "Maya" studies and Mayanist production, a primary argument in the perpetual making of *lo indígena* is that "indigenous" peoples have been colonized—or invaded—by the Spanish and, in more recent history, by the "Ladinos." Mariela, a "Maya Ixil" teacher in the Introduction to Curricular Design class at Rural Bilingual Intercultural Normal School, invites the students to reflect on the fact that "in books it is said that it was a conquest, and that is

Anthropological Borders 111

a traditionalist approach, but they never managed to reflect on the fact that it was an invasion."[81]

Despite colonization, and through knowledges produced archaeologically, COCADI justified the presence of "Mayas'" by defining them as the same culture that has been developing for thousands of years in current Guatemalan territory. The claim to difference was based on the unchangeable essence of the culture despite its changes in form. Claims such as this aimed to counter the effects of ethnographic accounts of education such as that offered by Robert Redfield in 1943. Upon observation of educational dynamics, Redfield noted that "Guatemalan societies seemed relatively meager with respect to moral convictions and sacred traditions."[82] From interviews and interaction with "Indians," he concluded that "Indian societies have lost in ceremonial richness . . . moral value and their integration to local traditions."[83] However, rather than being an "expression of local tradition," Redfield's observation that the school served as an additional means of regulation for rural people is compatible with the pluralist agenda, which demands an education rooted in *pueblos*' cultures and their "own" cosmo-visions.

Pivotal in the struggle for definition, recognition, and creation of presence, has been anthropology's allied technologies, demography, and census practices. "In 1921 Guatemala was described as 65 percent indigenous,"[84] "[a]pproximately 60% [out of a total of 11 million people] is Indigenous, mostly Maya."[85] Ktintz tells his students in a history class that "80% of the Guatemalan population belongs to Maya descendants . . . even if we use current technology . . . biologically [referring to DNA] and anthropologically as well, even we do not know how to speak our languages."[86] Common statements such as these, produced and reproduced in schools, emerge in almost any space where "indigenous" matters are discussed and pluralism is defended. Censuses have employed anthropological knowledges to make what is "indigenous" in the counting and what counts in the making of lo *indígena*.

A journey through the trajectory of censuses in Guatemala from 1880 to 2002 reveals the influence that anthropological activities have had in shaping possible populations and the countable pluralism available today. In 1880, *Indígena*, under the "race and sex" categories, was the opposite of "Ladino."[87] Both markers have changed, and "the indigenous" multiplied in questions and categories during the historical moment of pluralism. In 1893 the census report included the complaint that the "*indígena* race did not move at the same pace as the white or *ladina* race."[88] Both the 1880 and 1893 reports include notes on the challenges of counting "indigenous" peoples, partly due to their resistance.

In 1921 "shoes" ("puts on shoes?") emerged as a data point, and this was also the case for "language or dialect."[89] The 1940 census began to show the wider range of diversity. Race was divided into "white or *mestiza*, Indian, black, and yellow."[90] The term "ethnic" appeared for the first time to categorize the country. As an empty signifier, ethnic was filled with the classification of people's races and mother tongues. The most important languages were listed: "Quiché, Cackchiquel, Mam, Pocomam, Quecchí"[91] and among the "others" were "Tzutuhiles, Pocomchies, and Tzuj."[92] In 1950 Goubaud Carrera's desire materialized and the IIN was directly involved in the census. The "*Indígena*"–"Ladina" binary reappeared, and in collaboration with the IIN and its linguistic classification, the "indigenous" groups were sorted into five: Quiché, Mam, Pocomam, Chol, Caribe.[93] The census item on "food" was included to see whether the tortilla-eating *indígenas* had begun the transition to include bread in their diet.[94] Following food was the question on "shoes," and the next one asked whether they used indigenous "clothing."[95] In 1964 the item on shoes was justified medically[96] and was considered again for the last time in 1973.[97]

From 1973 to 2002 the main "indigenous" question became "is he/she indigenous?"[98] Until the 1973 census, the person taking the census was to make a decision on the "indigenous" question, based, for example, on the place where the census was being taken (e.g., a remote rural village) and the answers given by the interviewee vis-à-vis wearing "indigenous" clothing, speaking an "indigenous" tongue, and the kind of shoes worn.[99] From 1994 the question was to be answered by the interviewee himself or herself directly, because the individual's right to "self identification" or "self definition" as *indígena* or otherwise within her ethnic group was to be respected.[100] Not only were "K'iche', Kaqchikel, Mam, Q'eqchí, Spanish" given as mother tongue options, but also the open-ended "other," as well as whether the interviewee spoke "another language."[101] Here "*Maya*" also appears for the first time, and next to it the question on "clothing" appears for the last time. In 2002 the question became "to which ethnic group (*pueblo*) do you belong?"[102] Unlike 1994 when only four options were given, in 2002, twenty-five possibilities were given. The choice of ethnic group was given in addition to a question on languages being spoken, emphasizing ethnic preference and self-definition overall.[103]

This trajectory through the census serves as one more statement of how what is "indigenous" has been made up through demographic knowledges, especially noticeable in the effects that these numbers and percentages produce for planning people and for mobilizing claims to pluralism for educational discourses. Seldom is the use of scientific means to fabricate difference and its inherent aspirations questioned beyond some disputes over figures and formulas.[104] The claims for recognition during the multiculturalism moment can be noticed in the multiplication of possible categories in the 2002 census, which are intended to be used to exert one's right for "self"-recognition and "self"-identification: the same self-identification logic that operates in the *mayanización* discourse.

The *mayanización y vida cotidiana* (2007) flagship project is a collection of eighteen ethnographies produced by a number of social scientists, primarily anthropologists, who extend the analytics of recognition and pluralism to account for the ways in which ethnic difference is understood in quotidian experiences. Although the goal of the project was to provide an account of pluralism (the complexity of social processes that in politics are simplified and dichotomized) on pluralist terms (taking the already available ethnic categories), in its research configurations, the project preserves and therefore reiterates the anthropological demarcations that have been conceptually defined based on opposing "essences" (i.e., "Maya"–"Ladino," "indigenous" spaces–non-"indigenous" spaces). Typological time underlies these opposing or binary essences.

The ethnographers, as in the times of the IIN, were not only Guatemalans, but also "foreign nationals" (*extranjeros*) or nationals educated abroad. To keep the ethnic classification, some are presented as "Ladinos," others as "*indígenas*" and "Mayas." As the sponsoring scientific institutions for the project, CIRMA (Center for Mesoamerican Research) and FLACSO (Latin American Faculty of Social Sciences) were not the new IIN, but the project coordinators Aura Cumes and Santiago Bastos were both aware that the project remained within the anthropological tradition whose main object of study is the "different-other," a study that is often funded by organizations invested in the multiculturalism of that other, and are often of "foreign origin" (i.e., Norway, the United States, Spain, The Netherlands).

Mayanización, as Cumes and Bastos describe it, is the local version of multiculturalism in Guatemala and refers to self-identification as "Maya," with the attendant identity and ideology that it carries among "indigenous" peoples. This multicultural notion, particularly in the conceptual centrality of the self (-identification, -development, themselves, their "own"), often emerged in the teacher preparation classrooms in my research, not surprisingly considering how widespread this discourse is, as demonstrated in the *mayanización* ethnographies. With these terms, considering oneself as "Maya," or in other words making oneself up as "Maya" within the new idiom of multiculturalism,[105] references a semantic or rather an ideological migration/conversion. Using different terms, the migration/conversion of what is "indigenous" has been a primary aspiration in both the *indigenismo* and pluralism moments of "indigenous" making. The next section discusses this aspiration and its insertion in spatialized notions of time in anthropological discourses and activities in both indigenism and pluralism times.

ACT ... FIXING HER

CONGRESSWOMAN:	(*from her armored car*) There she is. The INDIA, the new Lorena, Get her! (*bodyguards run and kidnap the INDIA*)
SMV7 INDIA MARÍA:	(*screaming.*) Oh heavenly father, do not take me. (*resisting the kidnappers.*) I have paid my taxes. I have given everything to the state.

SMVs:	(*chorus.*) Take her! *Far right. Dim lights.*
THE BOSS:	(*defiantly and graciously.*) And who is this? (STUDENTS *laugh.* INDIA *sits slumped and spreading herself out on a chair as if exhausted.* THE BOSS *walks around* INDIA *examining her.* INDIA *stands up challenging* THE BOSS' *authoritarian demeanor.*) What is this? (*disgusted lifting her braids with a long stick*) Long braids? This is not Lorena! (INDIA *attempts to escape.*)
CONGRESSWOMAN:	But we'll fix her.
SMV7 INDIA MARÍA:	(*ironically.*) Ah so cute! Right?
THE BOSS:	(*irritatedly.*) Oh no, this can't be! This is not Lorena.
SMV7 INDIA MARÍA:	(*calmly and agreeably.*) Truthfully I am not! (*stressing not.*) I am María Nicolasa to serve you and God. (*standing.* THE BOSS *grabs her arm and sits her down.*) (*defiantly.*) And if I work it is with one condition, (*telling* CONGRESSWOMAN) I am not going to bathe any feral children, I am not bathing pigs. What do you think? And-
CONGRESSWOMAN:	Who said you were going to work?
SMV7 INDIA MARÍA:	(*concerned.*) And then all this is fo' wha'?
THE BOSS:	(*derogatorily.*) Oh God! Only a miracle from God can fix this? INDIA *gets closer to her face and stares*) Ah this woman stinks! She needs a bath. MAID! Come get her, remodélela [fix her up]! (*maid drags her away. Lights out.*)
CONGRESSWOMAN:	We have to teach her manners.
THE BOSS:	Teach her how to talk properly.
CONGRESSWOMAN:	How to walk up-right.
THE BOSS:	Walk in high heels.
CONGRESSWOMAN:	In style.
SMV7 INDIA MARÍA:	(*off stage, complaining and crying loudly.*) I wanted to go back to my village.
THE BOSS:	(*reappearing on stage.*) Be quiet. Let's go. Your speech awaits. Look, (*addressing* CONGRESSWOMAN) she did not even want to change her clothes.
CONGRESSWOMAN:	(*impatiently.*) Okay, let's just go.

Discussion

Act ... highlights the points raised thus far in the chapter. The humor in the impulses of trying to "fix" the India María are an expression of the students' perceptive capabilities, used here to make the audience notice the conversion/migration aspirations embedded in the fixing, which are also historical. The aspiration for conversion performed in this act is the climax of the pedagogy of the skit. Accepting the students' educational and critical invitation to notice, this section highlights how spatialized notions of time underlie the anthropological border demarcating *lo indígena* that I have touched on throughout the chapter.

Anthropological Borders 115

Spatialized time plots the India María and her difference on a universal line of evolution where she is distant from her counterparts, the congresswoman, and her party; from the "Western," the "Ladino," to use indigenists' language. The *indígena* is acted upon arguably not on the basis of sacred time, or in a sequence of specific events centered on one savior. Rather, the *indígena* is plotted on a secular scientific scheme as the (s)object of scientific, anthropological, and political activities during indigenist and pluralist times.

Returning to the analytics of anthropological borders that drive the chapter, conceptual demarcations that overdetermine the anthropological borders of *lo indígena* are drawn, employing a spatialized notion of time that separate and distance *lo indígena* from an opposing essence. The *indígena* is located in a *stage prior*, in need of development, evolution, progress, and transition, and is located primarily at a distance from its opposite essence, which is located in the present. The abject India María,[106] is a piece of filth, waste, and dung, recognizable only as such, unidentifiable as proper, devoid of the right language, modals, and posture, vomiting on the demand for high heel shoes, and style, disturbing the essence that is the contrary of all these abject characteristics, shattering a system and a defined order that aspires to fix her. The desperate demand to develop the India María, and "indigenous" peoples since the eighteenth century, found in the aspirations of indigenism and cultural pluralism, rests on a conception of spatialized linear time. "Indigenous" peoples must be migrated along this conception to cut the distance between them and that which is not them—the right now, the demand of the market and politics starved of them, their "backwardness," but also their "glorious pasts," their "objective chronological *pre*histories," their "rituals" and "primitive mentalities," and their roles as actors and producers of "beliefs, values, and means of social life."

Notions and uses of spatialized time in Fabian's critique of anthropology, *physical time*, *mundane* and *typological*, and *intersubjective*, operate in the configurations of Guatemalan "indigenous" making that I have discussed throughout this chapter. *Physical time* serves as a parameter of sociocultural processes, is objective, natural, and not culturally relative, as it is not subject to cultural variation. It employs scientific rigor through physical methods of dating and appears in the timescales used to measure demographic changes. Additionally, it structures evolutionary, pre-historical reconstructions over vast timespans such as the periods devised in "Maya" archaeology: early preclassic, preclassic, late preclassic, classic, postclassic, and so on. The classic period serves as a reference for claims of cultural validity, uniqueness in time, and in relation to other cultures. It is the period often used to highlight "Mayan" splendor and superiority, employed in political projects for cultural recognition of the indigenous struggle that arose under the pluralist paradigm and *mayanización*. Images of elements such as a Tikal, scientifically proven to have reached its apogee during the classic period, visually demarcate the "Maya/*indígena*" in school textbooks.

116 *Anthropological Borders*

Statements in the compiled volume of COCADI in 1989, which define the "Maya" in developmental terms, also emerge within naturalized conceptions of time: "Maya" are a people whose development expands over "ten thousand years," a people whose "roots are in the prehistory of humanity," and whose "culture has been developing for many years."[107]

Beyond plotting data on temporal linear scales, anthropological activities employ *mundane* and *typological time*, that is grand-scale periodizing: devising ages and stages and imposing them on the human. Time is measured in intervals between socioculturally meaningful events. This meaningfulness is politically and philosophically oriented by a logic of representation and the Apollonian gaze that pulls life on earth into a vision of unity, determined in both indigenist and pluralist discourses by the state, science, expert institutions, and their experts.[108] Notions of *typological time* underlie qualifications in "indigenous" making such as irrational vs. rational, rural vs. urban or folk/primitive vs. urban/occidentalized, illiterate or preliterate vs. literate, "Indian" vs. "Western"/"*mestizo*"/"*Ladino*," traditional vs. modern, lacking an understanding or having mechanical understanding vs. having an understanding. The statements emerging from indigenist times presented in the first section of the chapter are driven by these typological intervals. These intervals are qualities of *stages of time* that nonetheless animate the aspiration for movement, or the conversion and transition that, as Goubaud Carrera had it, was necessary for the "*indígena*," and for the benefit of the country, as was the mantra of integrationist discourses. The country's Apollonian, divine, and mastering view determined, from a single perspective, the direction and qualities of the conversion. In the 1945 survey, the characteristics that defined the "Indian" were drawn precisely from these analytics of spatialized-temporal movement, as in the fact that "the Indian is in transition from the time he came in contact with other peoples."[109] Thus what is "indigenous" is demarcated as an effect of stagist and typological uses of time within anthropological activities.

Typological notions of time also appear in cultural pluralism times, not only in COCADI's plea for development, but also in political statements that implore "the need to improve the living conditions of rural communities."[110] This "development of communities" was for the "development of the country," which, although demanding respect for the "multicultural characteristics of Guatemala," flows in an evolutionary stream of time just as do integrationist and indigenist discourses. Qualitative development and growth, as suggested in various texts in the COCADI's compilation, improves the lives of peoples in communities, that is to say "indigenous" peoples, with "positive changes," towards "betterment," and "advancement," "where there are two kinds of people distinctly different in history, language, and culture."[111] The typological scheme does not vanish in the cultural and political struggle to live in harmony with our Mother Earth, "developing mainly the potentialities of cultures and peoples."[112] The following statements by student teachers on the potentialities of the child (the "indigenous" child) and the mission of the teacher (in this case the *indígena* teacher) are an effect of these anthropological configurations within the educational imagination of future teachers. The statements emerge within pluralism and multiculturalism, and in their main curricular proposal, interculturalism.[113]

> We who are training to be teachers, . . . we should become that image of fishers, fishers of knowledge, fishers in evangelizing many children [living] in ignorance, to take that bread of knowledge to the students.[114]
> Well, my goal after finishing 6th-grade *magisterio* is first of all to change the education that teachers are practicing, the traditional model, and then apply the new models I learned here in the new institute and apply them there in my community to improve the development of my community and the society.[115]
> Our parents did not take advantage of many things, and there are many communities that continue to not take advantage, so my purpose in teaching the kids is to change their mindset, and in some ways change their imagination, change their ways of reasoning so they become more sociable, so that they change from having that mentality of being lazy, of not doing anything to work or get something economic.[116]

These student teachers, as part of *a pueblo* ("Maya" peoples) and with agency, plan to go back to their "rural communities" to "promote the development needed and deserved by their people."[117] This falls under the aegis of spatialized, typological, and *intersubjective* conceptions of time, which provide the conditions with which student teachers' educational and political imagination can be released.

Intersubjective time refers to the "emphasis on the communicative nature of human action and interaction."[118] In this temporal discourse, culture, no longer a set of rules to be enacted, is "the way in which actors create and produce beliefs, values and other means of social life."[119] The seeming complexity available in more recent census practices, informed by anthropological thought and political activities, are a gesture within population reasoning toward the recognition of "indigenous" people's various means of conducting social life. The multiple ways in which people can "self-identify" and assert their "self-determination" are conditioned by various quotidian circumstances as illustrated in the *mayanización* anthropological work. Anthropological discourses (and performances) of "ethnic difference" and "ethnic preference" within the state apparatus and other quotidian experiences contain an impulse to document the production of action and means of social life. Although an important gesture of provocation, this task is inconceivable without a reference to chronological time, which subverts the making of difference, all over again, as distance.

ACT .... DISCRIMINATED YOU? NEVER!

MARKET VENDORS:	(*cheering.*) Lorena! Lorena! Lorena!
SMV7 INDIA MARÍA:	(*addressing* MARKET VENDORS). Look, I promise to bring you electricity, and running water, and even make drainage available. Because I will stop the injustices of justice (*authoritatively*), because it's enough. There is too much inflation. I will even make a river available to solve the water problems!
MARKET VENDORS:	Wait! That's not Lorena. That's MARÍA (*in unison repeatedly.*) That's MARÍA. (*rebelliously break through security attempting to liberate* INDIA. *Successfully all* MARKET VENDORS *and* INDIA *return to market. In a parade* MARKET VENDORS *plead for their forgiveness*).
SMV3 XINCA:	Forgive us MARÍA for discriminating against you. Forgive us.
SMV7 INDIA MARÍA:	(*standing up on a table addressing the crowd.*) Look at you now, why did you save me from those kidnappers after you had discriminated against me like that? (VENDORS *plead for forgiveness multiple times.*)
SMV3 XINCA:	We should have never discriminated against you.
SMV7 INDIA MARÍA:	I'm going to forgive you but first we are going to throw a big pachangón [party] (*waving her skirt.*) *All actors dance to a mix of garífuna, reggaeton, and marimba. All actors bow, thank the student audience, and walk back fading away from stage.* (*alone on stage.*) We should respect each other for what we are, all the cultures make Guatemala, the country of the eternal spring. We should stop discriminating against each other so that Guatemala can develop better. Thank you. STUDENTS *in the audience clap.*

In part, Act .... is the performance of the intersubjective encounter and the resolution of a struggle over the recognition of difference—multiculturalism. The act is also the enactment of interculturalism. Interculturalism animates communal living, under the principle of the right to ethnocultural differences, with an emphasis on convergences rather than differences, thus surpassing the limitations of multiculturalism as staged in act two.[120] The student teachers' plea for nondiscrimination and respect for each other's cultures have transpired cosmetically, that is visually, in the textbook production from indigenous NGOs and publishing houses, to transnational cooperation and religious orders' educational projects, to state-sponsored curricular materials.

The country with a spring of cultures, celebrated in the skit, and diverse faces,[122] colored in this second-grade interdisciplinary textbook, ruptures the visual curriculum, fabricating an important intercultural illusion. The importance of it relies upon inserting images where they were not possible

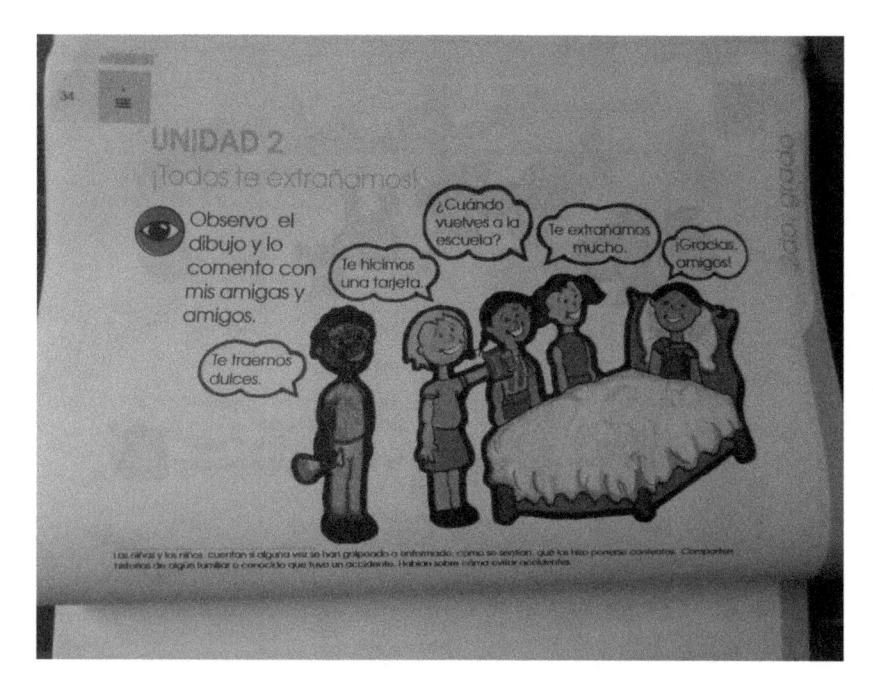

Figure 3.1 Second-grade textbook (*Módulos de Aprendizaje*) used in a "rural" town.[121]

before. This generates hope, within evolutionary reasoning, that progress has been made since, but not despite, indigenist times. The curriculum propelled by images like the one in this textbook used in a rural elementary school and the one fabricated in the student teachers' performance of "The *presidenta* and The *India*" are educational examples of various attempts to scratch the surface of history, difference, and the "indigenous" event.

Historical trajectories, analyzed from the two moments of intensity that are indigenism and cultural pluralism, in their multiple manifestations, produce ways of ordering teacher preparation curricula. This classroom display of "objectives"—a learning effect of intercultural education at a teacher preparation school, a product of indigenism—retains the conversion/migration principle historically installed on that which has been constituted as "indigenous." The desire, in the display, for "betterment" of their rural indigenous communities, and for Guatemala's "better development" in the play, remains unproblematized in the spatialized-time logic that continues to orient the compass of what is possible in the educational planning of diversity.

The larger animating risk in the chapter has been to attempt to complicate the trajectory of how difference is fabricated in the re-making of people in order to enable the discourse of diversity/plurality in education. It would be accurate to wonder whether the issue at stake in the chapter is the

Figure 3.2 Trans. Objectives. Help better [as in get beyond, or get past oneself] our communities. Continue studying.

production of the Other, and the production of the Other as different, and also the production of history as heterogeneous, *and also* suspending all of those for curriculum to take another look at "difference." By looking again, histories can be made outside the spatialization of time, or linear progressive time, as the possible template in "people-space" relations. This could be possible when education quits giving in to the taming and making of societies, and when teaching drops out of the looping effect of converting people into the next prefabricated inter-multicultural citizen in need of fixing.

Though Fabian's analytics of spatialized time has been instrumental in crafting the resistance presented in this chapter, when time is not taken for granted as linear, spatialized time encounters its limits. The spatialized-time logic requires linear time (marked as past, present, future in that order of progression) to be mobilized as a means to understand distance as difference in the stages that it produces. However, when other notions of time such as spiral, circular, queer, and fractal (see Chapter 4) are employed, other relationships, meanings, and dynamics emerge, which are unaccountable by Fabian's critique. In a conversation with Edgar Esquit (12/9/2013) while thinking about the limits of anthropology, he posed the question: where are new epistemologies—to define relations between subjects and the production of these relations—going to emerge from? The answer is far from simple. The emerging work of scholars (this may be too limited a word for their boundless force) such as Maria Jacinta Xon and Gladys Tzul Tzul are important proposals to wrestle with and at the limits of particular anthropological heritages in education.

Act .... in the play script is a gesture to what may emerge beside linear time. The act collapses differences: "all the cultures make Guatemala." Like the textbook image with all the faces, act four produces a gesture towards a performance that may be, though unaware of the histories and logics that produce the Other, becoming performative in suspending linear progressive time. The student teachers are playing with and mocking the belief that "all the cultures make Guatemala." Though the students may not be aware of the histories discussed in this book, they know that ridicule is a viable means to engage with histories of abjection. The students know that the "all the cultures make Guatemala" mantra can do little to challenge historical abjection, and the best they came up with was to invite their audience, now you, to boldly and playfully meditate on the past we think of as past, the present we think of as present and future, and the future which only fools could think is plan-able (to borrow that dear practice of education: to plan). That future is not the production of linear time, not the next stage, not the destination the "Indian" has to travel to meet modernity, not the next interval or era of its glorious history. The future, as a category of thinking, is up to what emerges in the playful act of ridicule.

Notes

1 Student teacher in focus group discussion, August 8, 2012. For the Spanish original see Appendix 8, item 1.
2 Following the intellectual compass of the book, this refers to Ian Hacking's interactive framework of making up people. In Hackings analytics, anthropology and the anthropological refer to a style of thought that includes the making of people (as "Other," as "us") by employing the particular notions of time discussed throughout the chapter. These particular notions, however, do not make up the entirety of the anthropological field. Aware that anthropology as a field has borders in itself and that such borders are porous, while cognizant of the politics and histories of anthropology, this chapter is not about anthropology per se. The preoccupation is with certain activities (e.g., defining an "indigenous" person), notions (e.g., inferiority), and aspirations (e.g., progress) with which anthropology engaged and that have been fundamental for education. Regardless of the field of study (anthropology in this case, but also in other fields such as history, sociology, law, and education), those particular activities have been mobilized and often left unproblematized. Granting or withholding political power from "indigenous" peoples by an expert, expert sets of knowledges, or an academic field has been the concern of much scholarship. The concern here is with the constant making-up of a kind of people by peoples of various identities and affiliations: expert, "indigenous," "Guatemalan," scientist, "Ladinos," foreigners, informants, rural, and NGOs.
3 In Judith Butler's analytics, performativity refers to the releasing of effects. Judith Butler, *Gender Trouble: Feminism and the Subversion of Identity* (New York: Routledge, 2006).

122   Anthropological Borders

4 Jacques Derrida, *Aporias* (Stanford: Stanford University Press, 1993).
5 Ian Hacking, *Rewriting the Soul: Multiple Personality and the Sciences of Memory* (Princeton: Princeton University Press, 1998); Ian Hacking, "Inaugural Lecture: Chair of Philosophy and History of Scientific Concepts at the Collège de France," *Economy and Society* 31 (2001): 1–1; Ian Hacking, "Kinds of People: Moving Targets" (presented at The Tenth British Academy Lecture, London, 2006). The quotes around "expert" suggest the actual making or becoming of an expert in the anthropological context of Guatemala. Though anthropological thought and performance had a trajectory by the middle of the twentieth century, in Guatemala anthropology *became about* precisely through the activities of "indigenous" making.
6 See Signpost 4 in the introductory chapter of this book. Miguel Ángel Asturias, "El problema social del indio" (B.A. Theses Licenciatura en Derecho, Universidad de San Carlos de Guatemala, 1923).
7 Whether this is *autonomous* (elements produced and reproduced by the "ethnic group"), *imposed*, *owned* (elements claimed and owned, which can therefore be produced and reproduced), or *non-owned* (claimed and used, but that cannot be produced or reproduced). Guillermo Bonfil Batalla, *México profundo: Una civilización negada* (México: Grijalbo, 1994).
8 Johannes Fabian, *Time and the Other: How Anthropology Makes Its Object* (New York: Columbia University Press, 1983), 16.
9 *La presidenta municipal*, dir. Fernando Cortés (Mexico: Estudios América and Diana Films, 1975).
10 The play script is the third iteration of the story. The first one is the *La presidenta municipal* movie, and the second one is the skit performed by student teachers in a social studies class. In the play script where the main actors are the student teachers, I am inserted as an actor, present as a spectator-researcher. Overall this is a suggestion of the role I played in all the classroom observations I conducted throughout this research. The play script also contains fractions that add to the classroom event in the reiterative moment of "indigenous" making in teacher education curriculum. Additionally, the fragments include gestures that, as the readers stage the play in their minds, lead them to notice the elements of history (and the complexities of time) available in the curricular event and in pedagogical acts. An example of this is the physical learning environment used, which is outside the regular four-walled classroom, a "progressive" educational move, and inside an internal patio in the school, typical of colonial houses in Guatemala such as the one where the school is located. The classroom and (the transition to) the colonial patio as *actual* spaces offer a gesture for the *virtual* spaces available for planning and performing education.
11 Étienne Balibar and Immanuel Maurice Wallerstein, *Race, nation, classe: Les identités ambiguës* (Paris: La Découverte, 1988).
12 See Carol Smith, "Interpretaciones norteamericanas sobre la raza y el racismo en Guatemala: Una genealogía crítica," in *¿Racismo en Guatemala? Abriendo debate sobre un tema tabú*, eds. Clara Arenas Bianchi, Charles R Hale, and Gustavo Palma Murga (Guatemala: AVANCSO, 1999), 93–126; José Bengoa, *La emergencia indígena en América Latina* (Fondo de Cultura Económica, 2000); Laura Giraudo, Neither "Scientific" nor Colonialist": The Ambiguous Course of Inter-American Indigenismo in the 1940s," *Latin American Perspectives* 39, no. 5 (2012): 12–32.
13 On the differences between Guatemalan *indigenismo* and Mexican *indigenismo* see, for example, Giraudo, Neither "Scientific" nor "Colonialist": The Ambiguous Course of Inter-American Indigenismo in the 1940s"; Marta Casaús Arzú, "El papel de mediación de Antonio Goubaud en la antropología guatemalteca,"

accessed November 6, 2013, www.academia.edu/468240/El_papel_de_media cion_de_Antonio_Goubaud_en_la_antropologia_guatemalteca.

14 After an upbringing in a privileged "Ladino" family in Totonicapán, Guatemala, and his studies in pedagogic psychology from La Sorbonne in Paris, Arriola served as director of the Psychology Laboratory in the Ministry of Education. His first book, published in 1930, was entitled *Ensayos sobre la sicología indígena* (roughly: Essays on Indigenous Psychology). He was the director of the newly founded Faculty of Humanities at the Universidad de San Carlos. During Jorge Ubico's government, he worked as a teacher educator in prestigious schools and was a normal school director and *magisterio* leader with Edelberto Torres and Normalist leader Mardoqueo García; see Mardoqueo García Asturias, *100 años de normalismo, 1830–1930* (Guatemala: Serviprensa Centroamericana, 1988). Arriola was an active revolutionary and supporter of the 1944 revolution that overturned Ubico's military regime. In the same year, he served as Ministry of Education during the revolutionary government *junta*. This was the beginning of ten years of the so-called "Democratic Spring" in Guatemala. In 1955 he succeeded David Vela, who had in turn succeeded Antonio Goubaud Carrera, as director of the National Indigenist Institute and the Guatemalan Social Integration Seminary, a position he held until 1963. Significantly, he also served as the editor of journals and publications considered "the anthropological press of Guatemala." Carlos Salvador Ordóñez Marriegos, "Vida y obra de Jorge Luis Arriola Ligorría (1906–1995)" (Guatemala, n.d.).

15 Jorge Luis Arriola, "Presentación," *Guatemala Indígena* 1, no. 1 (1961): 5–6. For the Spanish original see Appendix 8, item 2.

16 Adams, Casaús Arzú, and Adams point to the diversity within indigenist thought and philosophies in Guatemala. Richard Newbold Adams, *Joaquín Noval como indigenista, antropólogo y revolucionario* (Guatemala: Editorial Universitaria, Universidad de San Carlos de Guatemala, 2000); Marta Casaús Arzú and Teresa García Giráldez, *Las redes intelectuales centroamericanas: Un siglo de imaginarios nacionales (1820–1920)* (F&G, 2005); Abigail E. Adams, "¿Diversidad cultural en la nacionalidad homogénea? Antonio Goubad Carrera y la fundación del Instituto Indigenista Nacional de Guatemala," *Mesoamérica: Revista del Centro de Investigaciones Regionales de Mesoamérica* 29, no. 50 (2008): 65–95.

17 Simona Violetta Yagenova, *Los maestros y la revolución de octubre (1944–1954): Una recuperación de la memoria histórica del sindicato de trabajadores de la educación de Guatemala (STEG)* (Guatemala: Editorial de Ciencias Sociales, 2006).

18 "In 1940 the ministry of education of Ubico declared that . . . Guatemala did not have 'indigenous problems.'" Adams, *Joaquín Noval como indigenista, antropólogo y revolucionario*, 12., cited in *Boletín del Instituto Indigenista Nacional* 1, no. 1 (1945): 8. Marta Casaús Arzú asserts that the inclusion and incorporation of the "Indian" to the nation was no longer a preoccupation during the first years of Ubico's dictatorship. The "Indian" was no longer a national but an academic concern. The growing "interest of anthropologists and archaeologists was purely *scientific* and taxonomic," Casaús Arzú and García Giráldez, *Las redes intelectuales centroamericanas*, 383 (emphasis added). The past history of the "Indian" (re-emerging from the discovery of the Quiriguá Stela 26, the translation of Morley's book about Quiriguá, Adrián Recinos's translation of the Popol Wuj, and the opening of the "Maya" Studies section at the Faculty of Anthropology, History and Ethnology) and his "degenerated" fate became the main subject of scientific study.

19 For instance, Antonio Goubaud Carrera (although debatable), Juan de Dios Rosales, David Vela, and Miguel Ángel Asturias. See, for example, Epaminondas

Quintana, *La generación de 1920* (Guatemala: Tip. Nacional, 1971); Ordóñez Marriegos, "Vida y obra de Jorge Luis Arriola Ligorría (1906–1995)"; Miguel Ángel Asturias, *Sociología guatemalteca: El problema social del indio*, ed. Julio César Pinto Soria (Guatemala: Editorial Universitaria, Universidad de San Carlos de Guatemala, 2007); Casaús Arzú and García Giráldez, *Las redes intelectuales centroamericanas*. Miguel Ángel Asturias et al., *Fragmentos de una correspondencia: Brañas-Asturias, 1929–1973* (Guatemala: Editorial Universitaria, Universidad de San Carlos de Guatemala, 2001), see esp. chaps. 4 and 5; and Edgar S. G. Mendoza, *Antropologistas y antropólogos: Una generación* (Guatemala City: Universidad de San Carlos de Guatemala, 2000).

20 According to Guillermo Bonfil, some indigenists maintained that "it was necessary to help the Indian die well, that is, it was important to implement a series of measures that made de-indianization less brutal. The situation of Indian culture (the hackneyed process of acculturation) needed to be oriented scientifically so that the transformation was the least painful possible." For the Spanish original see Appendix 8, item 3. Guillermo Bonfil, "Los pueblos indios, sus culturas y las poltíicas culturales," in *Cultura maya y políticas de desarrollo*, eds. Coordinadora Cakchiquel de Desarrollo Integral, Programa de Producción de Material Didáctico, and Departamento de Investigaciones Culturales (Chimaltenango, Guatemala, C.A.: Ediciones COCADI, 1989), 139.

21 Dennis Casey, in his PhD dissertation on the history of *indigenismo* in Guatemala, argues that, "[i]n 1946 few indeed were the studies that had attempted any *scientific* or at best an in-depth consideration of this sector of Guatemala's population. Very little was known of the customs, habits, traditions, religious believes and social organizations of the various Indian groups in Guatemala." Dennis F. Casey, "Indigenismo, the Guatemalan Experience" (Ph.D. Dissertation, History, University of Kansas, 1979), 274.

22 "Goubaud insists that the heart of the matter is a new form of knowledge, in the acquisition of new methodologies, and *new* scientific approaches *through* anthropology, history, ethnology, and archaeology; all the modern sciences that enable Guatemalans to have a better understanding of themselves and others." For the Spanish original see Appendix 8, item 4. Casaús Arzú, "El papel de mediación de Antonio Goubaud en la antropología guatemalteca," 13–14. With a French and Basque family background, Goubaud Carrera is considered Guatemala's first "professional" anthropologist. Jorge Ramón González, "Guatemala, la nación y las comunidades," *Culturas de Guatemala*, (April 1997): 297–321; Giraudo, "Neither Scientific" nor "Colonialist": The Ambiguous Course of Inter-American Indigenismo in the 1940s." Goubaud Carrera was educated between the German schools in Guatemala, the La Salle's St. Mary's College in Oakland, and the University of Chicago. In 1944 he was invited to create the National Indigenist Institute in Guatemala. His early interest for indigenous matters emerged while in the Bay Area, and while studying anthropology at Chicago he was directly influenced by anthropologists Solomon Tax and Robert Redfield. Robert Redfield, Sol Tax, and Robert A. Rubinstein, *Doing Fieldwork: The Correspondence of Robert Redfield and Sol Tax* (New Brunswick: Transaction Publishers, 2002).

23 Goubaud Carrera "Informe por Lic. Goubaud Carrera" (septiembre 26, 1946), 1. Cited in Casey, "Indigenismo, the Guatemalan Experience," 220.

24 Giraudo, "Neither Scientific" nor "Colonialist": The Ambiguous Course of Inter-American Indigenismo in the 1940s."

25 Antonio Goubaud Carrera, "El grupo étnico indígena: Criterios para su definición," *Boletín del Instituto Indigenista Nacional*. 1, no. 2–3 (1946): 9.

26 Ibid., 9. For the Spanish original see Appendix 8, item 5.

27 See, for example, Robert Redfield, *Tepoztlán, a Mexican Village: A Study of Folk Life* (Chicago: The University of Chicago Press, 1930); Robert Redfield, Sol Tax, and Robert A Rubinstein, *Doing Fieldwork: The Correspondence of Robert Redfield and Sol Tax* (New Brunswick: Transaction Publishers, 2002); Robert Redfield, "Culture and Education in the Highlands of Guatemala," *American Journal of Sociology* 48, no. 6 (May 1, 1943): 640–48; Robert Redfield, "Ethnic Groups and Nationality," *Boletín Indigenista* 5 (1945): 235–45; Robert Redfield, "Primitive Merchants of Guatemala," *Quarterly Journal of Inter-American Relations* 1, no. 4 (1938): 42–56.
28 George Stocking, "Ideas and Institutions in American Anthropology: Thoughts Toward a History of the Interwar Years," in *Selected Papers from the American Anthropologist 1921–1945*, ed. George Stocking (Washington: American Anthropological Association, 1976), 1–53.
29 Smith, "Interpretaciones norteamericanas sobre la raza y el racismo en Guatemala: Una genealogía crítica," 97–98.
30 On the influence of Robert Redfield on Guatemalan anthropological research see, for example, Ibid.; and Mendoza, *Antropologistas y antropólogos: Una generación*.
31 Principles of Western European enlightenment. Guatemala, *Constitución de la República de Guatemala: Decretada por la asamblea constituyente en 11 de marzo de 1945* (Guatemala: Tip. Nacional, 1946), 3.
32 Smith, "Interpretaciones norteamericanas sobre la raza y el racismo en Guatemala: Una genealogía crítica," 98. Through his continuous anthropological interest in describing "cultural change," Redfield described cultural change in the educational dynamics of the mid-Western highlands of Guatemala as follows: "The school makes more change for the Indian than for the 'Ladino,' because through association with 'Ladinos' in the school he learns Spanish and in not a few cases is disposed to put off Indian dress, to live in the manner of the 'Ladinos,' and so to become a 'Ladino.' There is here no obstacle of prejudice or law to prevent this not infrequent occurrence. The school is one important institution, therefore through which the Indian societies tend to lose members to the 'Ladino' society and so ultimately disappear." Redfield, "Culture and Education in the Midwestern Highlands of Guatemala," 641.
33 Goubaud Carrera, "El grupo étnico indígena: Criterios para su definición," 10.
34 For the Spanish original see Appendix 8, item 6. Ibid., 11. Thus the public opinion that was surveyed was not that of those already *conceived* as *indígenas*, contrary to what Marta Casaús-Arzú suggests. Casaús Arzú, "El papel de mediación de Antonio Goubaud en la antropología guatemalteca." Although Goubaud Carrera's initiative was innovative (in the Guatemalan context) in consulting the population on what criteria defined an "Indian," it retained the dynamic of defining the "Other" by the hegemonic forces in power, which were addressed in indigenous movements almost five decades later.
35 See, for example, Redfield, Tax, and Rubinstein, *Doing Fieldwork*.
36 Goubaud Carrera, "El grupo étnico indígena: Criterios para su definición," 11 (capital letters in original).
37 Ibid., 18 (emphasis added). For the Spanish original see in Appendix 8, item 7.
38 "Western" here refers to a specific location of engagement and participation, that, in relationship to the ocular, references what Martin Heidegger questioned as "the world picture," that is that *we are in the picture* when the world becomes the picture: the distinguishing marker of the modern age from the medieval era. Martin Heidegger, *The Question Concerning Technology and Other Essays* (New York: Garland Publishing, Inc., 1977), 128. And "society becomes 'modern,'" according to Susan Sontag, "when one of its chief activities is producing

126 *Anthropological Borders*

and consuming images." Susan Sontag, *On Photography* (New York: Picador, 1977/2001), 153. Clothing, body size and shape, skin color, hair, and eyes are markers in the production and consumption of the *image* of "Indigenous" people and the *people*.

39 Yet an historical-philosophical analysis is still possible and even necessary from the information he provided. Still such an analysis is beyond the purposes of this chapter.
40 Ibid., 14. For the Spanish original see Appendix 8, item 8.
41 Ibid., 14. For the Spanish original see Appendix 8, item 8.
42 Jaime Bucaro, Historial del IIN 1945–1956, (n.d.), "Instituto Indigenista de Guatemala: Informe de sus trabajos y actividades" #1559 in Listado del Archivo del Instituto Indigenista elaborado por la antropóloga Silvia Barreno Anleu. 64 folios mecanografiados. (Col. IIN, 1), CIRMA.
43 Goubaud Carrera, "El grupo étnico indígena: Criterios para su definición," 25. For the Spanish original see Appendix 8, item 8.
44 Ibid., 25. For the Spanish original see Appendix 8, item 8.
45 For a genealogical account of race and American anthropological ideas and their influence in Guatemala see Smith, "Interpretaciones norteamericanas sobre la raza y el racismo en Guatemala: Una genealogía crítica."
46 Goubaud Carrera, "El grupo étnico indígena: Criterios para su definición," 26. For the Spanish original see Appendix 8, item 9.
47 Adams, "¿Diversidad cultural en la nacionalidad homogénea? Antonio Goubad Carrera y la fundación del Instituto Indigenista Nacional de Guatemala," 74. For the Spanish original see Appendix 8, item 10.
48 Goubaud Carrera cited in Ibid., 91–92. For the Spanish original see Appendix 8, item 11.
49 Goubaud Carrera cited in Ibid., 92 (emphasis added). For the Spanish original see Appendix 8, item 12.
50 Ibid., 9. For the Spanish original see Appendix 8, item 13.
51 Giraudo, "Neither Scientific" nor "Colonialist": The Ambiguous Course of Inter-American Indigenismo in the 1940s."
52 Margarita Wendell, "En torno a un programa de afabetización bilingüe," *Guatemala Indígena* 2 (1962): 136. For the Spanish original see Appendix 8, item 14.
53 For more on the training for missionaries/linguist/anthropologists see, for example, David Stoll, *Fishers of Men or Founders of Empire? The Wycliffe Bible Translators in Latin America* (London: Zed Press, 1982); and William Cameron Townsend and Richard S. Pittman, *Remember All the Way* (Huntington Beach: Wycliffe Bible Translators, 1975).
54 Ibid., 130. For the Spanish original see Appendix 8, item 15.
55 Ibid., 137. For the Spanish original see Appendix 8, item 16.
56 Ibid., 138. For the Spanish original see Appendix 8, item 17.
57 About a decade earlier, the IIN, using Mark Watkins' linguistic anthropological production of alphabets for the Mam, Q'anjob'al, and Kaqchikel languages, employed the pedagogic strategy in designing the booklets, which according to Casey, was to separate the booklets "into two parts on a bilingual basis. The first part as designated to teach literacy in the Indian Language while the second part contained lessons to teach one to be literate in Spanish." Casey, "Indigenismo, the Guatemalan Experience," 282.
58 Jaime Bucaro, "Historial de IIN 1945–1956: Instituto Indigenista de Guatemala: Informe de sus trabajos y actividades" (Guatemala, n.d.); Ibid.
59 Ibid., 12. For the Spanish original see Appendix 8, item 18.
60 For the Spanish original see Appendix 8, item 18.
61 Ibid., 10. For the Spanish original see Appendix 8, item 18.

62 According to Casey, Watkins traveled throughout the Department of Alta Verapaz, Chimaltenango, and Sacatepéquez for two weeks with several others doing detailed "field work" in Patzún, Chimaltenango. "The investigation involved lengthy considerations of the *morphology, syntax* and *phonetics* of the language." The outcome was an alphabet using Spanish-language sounds for the Kaqchikel language. Later, at the request of the Maryknoll missionaries and during more field work in Huehuetenango, Watkins also developed alphabets in the Mam and Q'anjob'al languages based on *vowels* and *consonants*. These linguistic anthropological developments served as the basis for literacy training in public schools in 1948 and the fabrication of booklets or *cartillas*. These didactic materials would be "used later by staff members at the *Instituto Indigenista* for teaching Spanish speaking Guatemalans the native languages." Casey, "Indigenismo, the Guatemalan Experience," 281–82.
63 Bucaro, "Historial de IIN 1945–1956: Instituto Indigenista de Guatemala: Informe de sus trabajos y actividades.", 10–11. For the Spanish original see Appendix 8, item 19.
64 Ibid., 11. For the Spanish original see Appendix 8, item 19.
65 As reported by Bucaro. Ibid., 10–11.
66 Kay B. Warren, *Indigenous Movements and Their Critics: Pan-Maya Activism in Guatemala* (Princeton: Princeton University Press, 1998).
67 See, for example, Edward F. Fischer and R. McKenna Brown, eds., *Maya Cultural Activism in Guatemala* (Austin: University of Texas Press, 1997); Santiago Bastos and Aura Cumes, *Mayanización y vida cotidiana: La ideología multicultural en la sociedad Guatemalteca*, 3 vols. (Guatemala: Cholsamaj Fundación, 2007); Santiago Bastos et al., *Entre el mecapal y el cielo: Desarrollo del movimiento maya en Guatemala* (Guatemala: Facultad Latinoamericana de Ciencias Sociales (FLACSO), 2003); Santiago Bastos and Roderick Leslie Brett, *El movimiento maya en la década después de la paz (1997–2007)* (Guatemala: F&G Editores, 2010); Arturo Arias, "The Maya Movement, Postcolonialism and Cultural Agency," in *Coloniality at Large: Latin America and the Postcolonial Debate*, eds. Mabel Moraña, Enrique Dussel, and Carlos Jáuregui, 519–38 (Durham: Duke University Press, 2008).
68 Luis Enrique Sam Colop, "Derecho del hombre bicultural en Guatemala," in *Cultura maya y políticas de desarrollo*, eds. Coordinadora Cakchiquel de Desarrollo Integral, Programa de Producción de Material Didáctico, and Departamento de Investigaciones Culturales (Chimaltenango, Guatemala, C.A.: Ediciones COCADI, 1989), 107. For the Spanish original see Appendix 8, item 20.
69 Classroom observation (Bilingual Education Class), August 11, 2012. For the Spanish original see Appendix 8, item 21.
70 Santiago Bastos, "Multicultural Projects in Guatemala: Identity Tensions and Everyday Ideologies," *Latin American and Caribbean Ethnic Studies* 7, no. 2 (2012): 156.
71 Coordinadora Cakchiquel de Desarrollo Integral et al., *Cultura maya y políticas de desarrollo* (Chimaltenango, Guatemala, C.A.: Ediciones COCADI, 1989).

This logic to devise, use, and deploy a unit to articulate a particular struggle for progress is also noticeable in the emergence of ethnological practices in Guatemala in the 1930s. Sol Tax in his 1937 study of the "*Municipios of the Midwestern Highlands of Guatemala*," makes a case for the *municipio* to be "the primary (and possibly final) ethnic unit" of study for the progress of Guatemalan ethnology. Tax was defending the *municipio* against essential concepts such as language or (tribal) culture, which he argued were insufficient as units to allow a well-founded (functionalist) analysis. He contended that "the Indians today who speak dialects of one language (such as Quiche or Cakchiquel) are not in any sense organized as a social group . . . The linguistic terms cannot be used unquestioningly, therefore, to describe ethnic groups." Sol Tax, "The Municipios of the Midwestern Highlands of Guatemala," *American Anthropologist* 39, no. 3 (1937): 424–26. This is in sharp contrast to how the indigenous struggles define *pueblo* precisely along ethnic and linguistic lines, with a political dimension different from the politics described by Tax. *Municipios* are "territorial administrative divisions commonly recognized in all governmental matters . . . [and] the basic ethnic divisions and cultural groups into which the country is divided." Ibid., 425. *Municipios* are marked territorially: pueblos are marked beyond the territorial. Tax's is a response to the linguistic divisions taken from a precolonial past, operating from his loyalty to the present and the new "functionalist" ethnographic/scientific method. The indigenous movements' response employs linguistic divisions, with the sophistication allowed from anthropological knowledges produced later, while units such as *municipios* permeate historical and anthropological analytics within the movements. Employing a *unit* as an overarching indispensable logic remains intact.

72 This is, for obvious reasons, the case given that during the 1950s and 1960s human rights was not fully available as a discursive framework through which cultural and political claims could be justified. On the claims to difference through the rights framework, see, for example, Sam Colop, "Derecho del hombre bicultural en Guatemala."

73 In the teacher education classrooms I visited in Guatemala, traditional education is characterized by the students I interviewed as sitting and the teacher lecturing; if anyone dares to talk out of turn or moves without permission, the teacher can offer a spanking or physical or other forms of punishment. Traditional education primarily involves rote memorization and the repetition of classroom content driven by "objectives" instead of "competencies."

74 Charles R. Hale, *Más que un indio/More Than An Indian: Racial Ambivalence and Neoliberal Multiculturalism in Guatemala* (Santa Fe: School of American Research Press, 2006).

75 In educational and "indigenous" matters, Demetrio Cojtí Cuxil is an influential "Maya" intellectual. Originally from Chichicastenango, Cojtí Cuxil was the first "Maya" in Guatemala to receive a doctorate. Educated in the teacher preparation boarding school program in the *Instituto Indígena Santiago*, and later receiving a doctoral education in communication at the University of Louvain in Belgium, Cojtí Cuxil has served as deputy minister of education (2000–2004), and since 2004 has worked as a consultant for OAS, UNDP, and other international organizations. He has been a leading figure in multiculturalism, education in indigenous languages, and bilingualism. Since the early 1980s he has been speaking publicly about ethnic identities and a unified indigenous politics. Some of his most influential works that continue to generate discussions today are *La configuración del pensamiento político del pueblo maya* (Asociación de Escritores Mayances de Guatemala, 1991). See also Warren, *Indigenous Movements and Their Critics*.

76 Coordinadora Cakchiquel de Desarrollo Integral et al., *Cultura maya y políticas de desarrollo.*, 24. Importantly, the book is a response to the historical situation of domination and emerged in times of necropolitical violence, to use Achilles Mbembé's term, when "indigenous" peoples were experimented upon and is a direct response to assimilation, the dissolution of "Maya" culture into the "Ladina" culture, and the final cultural extermination of the "Maya" *pueblo*. Achille Mbembé, "Necropolitics," *Public Culture*, no. 15 (2003): 11–40. Ibid., 14. Along these same lines, almost two decades later, "Maya Kaqchikel" sociologist *Aura Cumes* states that "el racismo no nos ha dejado intactos, *ha dejado huellas profundas*, afectos a todo nivel que es básico revisar, si le apostamos a

la liberación de nuestros pueblos y a la construcción de un país diferente [racism has not left us intact, *it has left deep marks*, effects on every level that are necessary to revise, if we are to bet on the liberation of our peoples and the construction of a different country]. Aura Cumes, "El Racismo Como Ideología" (Guatemala, 2006), 5.
77 Ibid., 7. For the Spanish original see Appendix 8, item 22.
78 Ibid., 9–10. For the Spanish original see Appendix 8, item 23.
79 Classroom observation (Indigenous Language 2 and 3 class), April 1, 2013. For the Spanish original see Appendix 8, item 24.
80 See, for example, Coordinadora Cakchiquel de Desarrollo Integral et al., *Cultura maya y políticas de desarrollo*; Cojtí Cuxil, *La configuración del pensamiento político del pueblo maya*; Luis Enrique Sam Colop, "Hacia una propuesta de ley de educación bilingüe" (Thesis for the Licenciatura en Ciencias Jurídicas y Sociales, Universidad Rafael Landívar, 1983); Luis Enrique Sam Colop, *Jub'saqtun omay kuchum k'aslemal: Cinco siglos de encubrimiento*, Seminario Permanente de Estudios Mayas, no. 1 (Guatemala: Cholsamaj, 1990); Warren, *Indigenous Movements and Their Critics*.
81 Classroom observation (Introduction to Curricular Design class), March 21, 2013. For the Spanish original see Appendix 8, item 25.
82 Redfield, "Culture and Education in the Midwestern Highlands of Guatemala," 647.
83 Ibid., 647.
84 Smith, "Interpretaciones norteamericanas sobre la raza y el racismo en Guatemala: Una genealogía crítica," 103.
85 Arias Arturo, "The Maya Movement, Postcolonialism and Cultural Agency," *Journal of Latin America Cultural Studies: Travesia* 15, no. 2 (2006): 252.
86 Classroom observation (Guatemalan, Mesoamerican, and Universal History class), March 20, 2013. For the Spanish original see Appendix 8, item 26.
87 *Censo General de La República de Guatemala* (Guatemala, 1880), 10.
88 *Censo General de La Población de La República de Guatemala* (Guatemala: Dirección General de Estadística, 1893), 15.
89 *Censo de la población de la República de Guatemala* (Guatemala, 1921), 1.
90 *Quinto censo general de población* (Guatemala: Dirección General de Estadística, 1942), 31.
91 Ibid., 236.
92 Ibid., 292–93.
93 The Quiché group included Quiché, Cakchiquel, Tzutujil, Uspantca. Mam included Aguacateca, Jacalteca, Kanjobal, Chuj, and Ixil. Pocomam included Kekchí, Pocomchí, Central Pocomam, and Oriental Pocomam. Chol included Chortí, and Caribe. Spelling as in the original document. *Sexto Censo de Población 1950*, vol. 4 (Guatemala: Dirección General de Estadística, 1950).
94 Ibid.
95 Eats wheat bread habitually? Yes or no. Uses indigenous clothing habitually? Yes or no. If the person wears shoes, write "Z"; if he/she wears sandals "C"; if he/she is barefoot "D." For the Spanish original see Appendix 8, item 27.
96 "The research on people who use some kind of shoes is important because according to medical criteria many endemic or epidemic illnesses are related to whether people have their feet covered or uncovered when they walk." *VII Censo de población* (Guatemala: Dirección General de Estadística, 1964), 65. For the Spanish original see Appendix 8, item 28.
97 *Censo de población* (Guatemala: Dirección General de Estadística, 1973).
98 Ibid.; *Censos nacionales de 1981* (Guatemala: Dirección General de Estadística, 1985); *X Censo nacional de población y V de vivienda* (Guatemala: Instituto Nacional de Estadística, 1996); *Censos nacionales XI de población y VI de habitación 2002* (Guatemala: Instituto Nacional de Estadística, 2003).

130   Anthropological Borders

99   According to Cojtí Cuxil, this is a colonial definition of the *indígena*. "Traditionally, in the Population Censuses: Indigenous is that one who wears shoes, does not speak Castilian and does not wear European kinds of clothing" Cojtí Cuxil, *La configuración del pensamiento político del pueblo maya*, 95. For the Spanish original see Appendix 8, item 29.
100   *Características generales de población y habitación* (Guatemala: Instituto Nacional de Estadística, 1994), 140.
101   Ibid.
102   *Censos nacionales XI de población y VI de habitación 2002* (Guatemala: Instituto Nacional de Estadística, 2003), 255.
103   "Achi, akateko, Cho'ortí, Chuj, Itza, Ixil, Jakalteko (Poptí), Kaqcuikel, K'iche', Mam, Mopan, Poqomam, Poqomchi', Q'anjob'al, Q'eqchi', Sakapulteko, Sipakense, Tektiteko, Tz'utujil, Uspanteko, Xinka, garífuna, Ladino, Idioma español, Ninguno, Otro." Ibid., 255.
104   See, for example, Cojtí Cuxil, *La configuración del pensamiento político del pueblo maya*, esp. chap. 4; and John D. Early, "Revision of Ladino and Maya Census Populations of Guatemala, 1950 and 1964," *Demography* 11, no. 1 (1974): 105–17.
105   Hale, *Más que un Indio/More than an Indian*.
106   Julia Kristeva and Leon S. Roudiez, *Powers of Horror: An Essay on Abjection* (New York: Columbia University Press, 1982).
107   Coordinadora Cakchiquel de Desarrollo Integral et al., *Cultura maya y políticas de desarrollo*, 9–10.
108   Denis Cosgrove, *Apollo's Eye: A Cartographic Genealogy of the Earth in the Western Imagination* (Baltimore: The Johns Hopkins University Press, 2003), XI.
109   Perhaps with an implied reference to Spanish and other European travelers?
110   Coordinadora Cakchiquel de Desarrollo Integral et al., *Cultura maya y políticas de desarrollo.*, 7.
111   Ibid., 11. For the Spanish original see Appendix 8, item 30.
112   Ibid., 17.
113   Cumes, "El racismo como ideología."
114   Field notes July 1, 2012. For the Spanish original see Appendix 8, item 31.
115   Focus group discussion August 8, 2012. For the the Spanish original see Appendix 8, item 32.
116   Focus group discussion August 8, 2012. For the Spanish original see Appendix 8, item 33.
117   Coordinadora Cakchiquel de Desarrollo Integral et al., *Cultura maya y políticas de desarrollo.*
118   Fabian, *Time and the Other*, 24.
119   Ibid., 24.
120   Carlos Giménez, *Guía sobre interculturalidad, primera parte, fundamentos conceptuales* (Guatemala: PNUD-Guatemala, 1997); Carlos Giménez, *Guía sobre interculturalidad, segunda parte, el enfoque intercultural en las políticas públicas para el desarrollo sostenible* (Guatemala: PNUD-Guatemala, 2000). For more on interculturalism, it's tensions and applications, see, for example, Meike Heckt, *Interkulturelle bildung in einer ethnisch gespaltenen gesellschaft* (Berlin: Waxmann Verlag, 2000); Meike Heckt, *Educación intercultural liberadora para todos en Guatemala: Una posibilidad para el futuro de una sociedad multilingüe y pluriétnica: Texto para el debate* (Cobán: Ak' Kutan, Centro Bartolomé de las Casas, 2003); Saríah Acevedo, "La transición incompleta entre la homogeneidad y la multiculturalidad en el estado de Guatemala: El ministerio de cultura y deportes," in *Mayanización y vida cotidiana: La ideología multicultural en la sociedad guatemalteca*, eds. Santiago Bastos and Aura Cumes, vol. 2, 3 vols. (Guatemala: Cholsamaj Fundación, 2007), 9–44;

Rolando Castillo Quintana, "Multiculturalismo, interculturalidad o pluralismo cultural: Un debate no resuelto en la sociedad guatemalteca," in *El Lenguaje de los ismos: Algunos conceptos de la modernidad en América Latina*, ed. Marta Casaús Arzú (Guatemala: F&G Editores, 2010), 431–54; Bastos, "Multicultural Projects in Guatemala: Identity Tensions and Everyday Ideologies.," 155–72; Anabella Giracca, "Los retos educativos frente a la interculturalidad como modelo transformador," *Revista Guatemalteca de Educación* 1, no. 2 (2009): 15–26; Castillo Quintana, "Multiculturalismo, interculturalidad o pluralismo cultural: Un debate no resuelto en la sociedad guatemalteca."

121 *Módulos de aprendizaje: Segundo grado*, vol. 2, 2 vols. (Guatemala: Ministerio de Educación, 2005).

122 *Imágenes homogéneas en un país de rostros diversos: El sistema educativo formal y la conformación de referentes de identidad nacional entre jóvenes guatemaltecos* (Guatemala: Asociación para el Avance de las Ciencias Sociales en Guatemala, 2001).

References

Acevedo, Saríah. "La transición incompleta entre la homogeneidad y la multiculturalidad en el estado de Guatemala: El ministerio de cultura y deportes." In *Mayanización y vida cotidiana: La ideología multicultural en la sociedad guatemalteca*, edited by Santiago Bastos and Aura Cumes, 2: 9–44. Guatemala: Cholsamaj Fundación, 2007.

Adams, Abigail E. "¿Diversidad cultural en la nacionalidad homogénea? Antonio Goubad Carrera y la fundación del Instituto Indigenista Nacional de Guatemala." *Mesoamérica: Revista del Centro de Investigaciones Regionales de Mesoamérica* 29, no. 50 (2008): 65–95.

Adams, Richard Newbold. *Joaquín Noval como indigenista, antropólogo y revolucionario*. Guatemala: Editorial Universitaria, Universidad de San Carlos de Guatemala, 2000.

Arias, Arturo. "The Maya Movement, Postcolonialism and Cultural Agency." In *Coloniality at Large: Latin America and the Postcolonial Debate*, edited by Mabel Moraña, Enrique Dussel, and Carlos Jáuregui, 519–38. Durham: Duke University Press, 2008.

———. "The Maya Movement, Postcolonialism and Cultural Agency." *Journal of Latin America Cultural Studies: Travesia* 15, no. 2 (2006): 251–62.

Arriola, Jorge Luis. "Presentación." *Guatemala Indigena* 1, no. 1 (1961): 5–6.

Asturias, Miguel Ángel. "El problema social del indio." B.A. Theses Licenciatura en Derecho, Universidad de San Carlos de Guatemala, 1923.

———. *Sociología guatemalteca: El problema social del indio*. Edited by Julio César Pinto Soria. Guatemala: Editorial Universitaria, Universidad de San Carlos de Guatemala, 2007.

Asturias, Miguel Ángel, César Brañas, Julio César Pinto Soria, Arely Mendoza Deleón, and Arturo Taracena Arriola. *Fragmentos de una correspondencia: Brañas-Asturias, 1929–1973*. Guatemala: Editorial Universitaria, Universidad de San Carlos de Guatemala, 2001.

Balibar, Étienne, and Immanuel Maurice Wallerstein. *Race, nation, classe: Les identités ambiguës*. Paris: La Découverte, 1988.

Bastos, Santiago. "Multicultural Projects in Guatemala: Identity Tensions and Everyday Ideologies." *Latin American and Caribbean Ethnic Studies* 7, no. 2 (2012): 155–72.

Bastos, Santiago, and Aura Cumes. *Mayanización y vida cotidiana: La ideología multicultural en la sociedad Guatemalteca*. 3 vols. Guatemala: Cholsamaj Fundación, 2007.

Bastos, Santiago, Manuela Camus, FLACSO, and Centro Educativa y Cultural Maya. *Entre el mecapal y el cielo: Desarrollo del movimiento maya en Guatemala*. Guatemala: Facultad Latinoamericana de Ciencias Sociales (FLACSO), 2003.

Bastos, Santiago, and Roderick Leslie Brett. *El movimiento maya en la década después de la paz (1997–2007)*. Guatemala: F&G Editores, 2010.

Bengoa, José. *La emergencia indígena en América Latina*. Guatemala: Fondo de Cultura Económica, 2000.

Bonfil Batalla, Guillermo. "Los pueblos indios, sus culturas y las poltíicas culturales." In *Cultura maya y políticas de desarrollo*, edited by Coordinadora Cakchiquel de Desarrollo Integral, Programa de Producción de Material Didáctico, and Departamento de Investigaciones Culturales, 137–64. Chimaltenango, Guatemala, C.A.: Ediciones COCADI, 1989.

———. *México profundo: Una civilización negada*. México: Grijalbo, 1994.

Bucaro, Jaime. *Historial de IIN 1945–1956: Instituto Indigenista de Guatemala: Informe de sus trabajos y actividades*. Guatemala, n.d.

Características generales de población y habitación. Guatemala: Instituto Nacional de Estadística, 1994.

Butler, Judith. *Gender Trouble: Feminism and the Subversion of Identity*. New York: Routledge, 2006.

Casaús Arzú, Marta. "El papel de mediación de Antonio Goubaud en la antropología guatemalteca." Accessed November 6, 2013. www.academia.edu/468240/El_papel_de_mediacion_de_Antonio_Goubaud_en_la_antropologia_guatemalteca.

Casaús Arzú, Marta, and Teresa García Giráldez. *Las redes intelectuales centroamericanas: Un siglo de imaginarios nacionales (1820–1920)*. Guatemala: F&G, 2005.

Casey, Dennis F. "Indigenismo, the Guatemalan Experience." Ph.D. Dissertation, History, University of Kansas, 1979.

Censo de población. Guatemala: Dirección General de Estadística, 1973.

Censo de la población de la República de Guatemala. Guatemala, 1921.

Censo General de La Población de La República de Guatemala. Guatemala: Dirección General de Estadística, 1893.

Censo General de La República de Guatemala. Guatemala, 1880.

Censos nacionales de 1981. Guatemala: Dirección General de Estadística, 1985.

Censos nacionales XI de población y VI de habitación 2002. Guatemala: Instituto Nacional de Estadística, 2003.

Castillo Quintana, Rolando. "Multiculturalismo, interculturalidad o pluralismo cultural: Un debate no resuelto en la sociedad guatemalteca." In *El Lenguaje de los ismos: Algunos conceptos de la modernidad en América Latina*, edited by Marta Casaús Arzú, 431–54. Gutemala: F&G Editores, 2010.

Cojtí Cuxil, Demetrio. *La configuración del pensamiento político del pueblo maya*. Guatemala: Asociación de Escritores Mayances de Guatemala, 1991.

Coordinadora Cakchiquel de Desarrollo Integral, Programa de Producción de Material Didáctico, Coordinadora Cakchiquel de Desarrollo Integral, and Departamento de

Investigaciones Culturales. *Cultura maya y políticas de desarrollo.* Chimaltenango, Guatemala, C.A.: Ediciones COCADI, 1989.
Cortés, Fernando. *La presidenta municipal.* Mexico: Estados Unidos de America and Diana Film, 1975.
Cosgrove, Denis. *Apollo's Eye: A Cartographic Genealogy of the Earth in the Western Imagination.* Baltimore: The Johns Hopkins University Press, 2003.
Cumes, Aura. *El racismo como ideología,* 1–5. Guatemala, 2006.
Derrida, Jacques. *Aporias.* Stanford: Stanford University Press, 1993.
Early, John D. "Revision of Ladino and Maya Census Populations of Guatemala, 1950 and 1964." *Demography* 11, no. 1 (1974): 105–17.
Fabian, Johannes. *Time and the Other: How Anthropology Makes Its Object.* New York: Columbia University Press, 1983.
Fischer, Edward F., and R. McKenna Brown, eds. *Maya Cultural Activism in Guatemala.* Austin: University of Texas Press, 1997.
García Asturias, Mardoqueo. *100 años de normalismo, 1830–1930.* Guatemala: Serviprensa Centroamericana, 1988.
Giménez, Carlos. *Guía sobre interculturalidad, primera parte, fundamentos conceptuales.* Guatemala: PNUD-Guatemala, 1997.
———. *Guía sobre interculturalidad, segunda parte, el enfoque intercultural en las políticas públicas para el desarrollo sostenible.* Guatemala: PNUD-Guatemala, 2000.
Giracca, Anabella. "Los retos educativos frente a la interculturalidad como modelo transformador." *Revista Guatemalteca de Educación* 1, no. 2 (2009): 15–26.
Giraudo, Laura. "Neither 'Scientific' nor 'Colonialist': The Ambiguous Course of Inter-American Indigenismo in the 1940s." *Latin American Perspectives* 39, no. 5 (2012): 12–32.
González, Jorge Ramón. "Guatemala, la nación y las comunidades." *Culturas de Guatemala,* (April 1997): 297–321.
Goubaud Carrera, Antonio. "El grupo étnico indígena: Criterios para su definición." *Boletín del Instituto Indigenista Nacional* 1, no. 2–3 (1946): 9–26.
Guatemala. *Constitución de la República de Guatemala: Decretada por la asamblea constituyente en 11 de marzo de 1945.* Guatemala: Tip. Nacional, 1946.
Hacking, Ian. *Rewriting the Soul: Multiple Personality and the Sciences of Memory.* Princeton: Princeton University Press, 1998.
Hale, Charles R. *Más que un indio / More Than An Indian: Racial Ambivalence and Neoliberal Multiculturalism in Guatemala.* Santa Fe: School of American Research Press, 2006.
Heckt, Meike. *Educación intercultural liberadora para todos en Guatemala: Una posibilidad para el futuro de una sociedad multilingüe y pluriétnica: Texto para el debate.* Cobán: Ak' Kutan, Centro Bartolomé de las Casas, 2003.
———. *Interkulturelle bildung in einer ethnisch gespaltenen gesellschaft.* Berlin: Waxmann Verlag, 2000.
Heidegger, Martin. *The Question Concerning Technology and Other Essays.* New York: Garland Publishing, 1977.
Imágenes homogéneas en un país de rostros diversos: El sistema educativo formal y la conformación de referentes de identidad nacional entre jóvenes guatemaltecos. Guatemala: Asociación para el Avance de las Ciencias Sociales en Guatemala, 2001.

Kristeva, Julia, and Leon S. Roudiez. *Powers of Horror: An Essay on Abjection.* New York: Columbia University Press, 1982.
Mbembé, Achille. "Necropolitics." *Public Culture,* no. 15 (2003): 11–40.
Mendoza, Edgar S. G. *Antropologistas y antropólogos: Una generación.* Guatemala City: Universidad de San Carlos de Guatemala, 2000.
Módulos de aprendizaje: Segundo grado. Vol. 2. 2 vols. Guatemala: Ministerio de Educación, 2005.
Ordóñez Marriegos, Carlos Salvador. *Vida y obra de Jorge Luis Arriola Ligorría (1906–1995).* Guatemala, n.d.
Quintana, Epaminondas. *La generación de 1920.* Guatemala: Tip. Nacional, 1971.
Quinto censo general de poblacion. Guatemala: Dirección General de Estadística, 1942.
Redfield, Robert. "Culture and Education in the Midwestern Highlands of Guatemala." *American Journal of Sociology* 48, no. 6 (May 1, 1943): 640–48.
———. "Ethnic Groups and Nationality." *Boletín Indigenista* 5 (1945): 235–45.
———. "Primitive Merchants of Guatemala." *Quarterly Journal of Inter-American Relations* 1, no. 4 (1938): 42–56.
———. *Tepoztlán, a Mexican Village: A Study of Folk Life.* Chicago: The University of Chicago Press, 1930.
Redfield, Robert, Sol Tax, and Robert A. Rubinstein. *Doing Fieldwork: The Correspondence of Robert Redfield and Sol Tax.* New Brunswick: Transaction Publishers, 2002.
Sam Colop, Luis Enrique. "Derecho del hombre bicultural en Guatemala." In *Cultura maya y políticas de desarrollo,* edited by Coordinadora Cakchiquel de Desarrollo Integral, Programa de Producción de Material Didáctico, and Departamento de Investigaciones Culturales, 101–15. Chimaltenango, Guatemala, C.A.: Ediciones COCADI, 1989.
Sexto Censo de Población 1950. Vol. 4. Guatemala: Dirección General de Estadística, 1950.
Smith, Carol. "Interpretaciones norteamericanas sobre la raza y el racismo en Guatemala: Una genealogía crítica." In *¿Racismo en Guatemala? Abriendo debate sobre un tema tabú,* edited by Clara Arenas Bianchi, Charles R. Hale, and Gustavo Palma Murga, 93–126. Guatemala: AVANCSO, 1999.
Sontag, Susan. *On Photography.* New York: Picador, 2001.
Stocking, George. "Ideas and Institutions in American Anthropology: Thoughts Toward a History of the Interwar Years." In *Selected Papers from the American Anthropologist 1921–1945,* edited by George Stocking, 1–53. Washington: American Anthropological Association, 1976.
Stoll, David. *Fishers of Men or Founders of Empire? The Wycliffe Bible Translators in Latin America.* London: Zed Press, 1982.
Tax, Sol. "The Municipios of the Midwestern Highlands of Guatemala." *American Anthropologist* 39, no. 3 (1937): 423–44.
VII Censo de población. Guatemala: Dirección General de Estadística, 1964.
Townsend, William Cameron, and Richard S. Pittman. *Remember All the Way.* Hunting Beach: Wycliffe Bible Translators, 1975.
Warren, Kay B. *Indigenous Movements and Their Critics: Pan-Maya Activism in Guatemala.* Princeton: Princeton University Press, 1998.
Wendell, Margarita. "En torno a un programa de afabetización bilingüe." *Guatemala Indígena* 2 (1962): 129–40.

X *Censo nacional de población y V de vivienda*. Guatemala: Instituto Nacional de Estadística, 1996.

Yagenova, Simona Violetta. *Los maestros y la revolución de octubre (1944–1954): Una recuperación de la memoria histórica del sindicato de trabajadores de la educación de Guatemala (STEG)*. Guatemala: Editorial de Ciencias Sociales, 2006.

● ● ● ● 4 Authoritarian Regimes in Reform and Fractal Curricular Possibilities in Protests

Guatemala, as it continues to be fabricated, is "behind" in human and "development indicators."[1] Yet when it comes to "educational reform," the country is on par with other nations in talking about, planning, and implementing reform. The common argument to mobilize reforms is precisely to revert the dreaded human and development backwardness. A version of this can also be found in OECD countries after the release of PISA results that put most nations "behind." The commonsense of reform as educational "change," which is viral in both public and private sectors of the population in Guatemalan society, assumes that intervention is and will lead to progress.[2] Otto Perez Molina, the president at the time, authoritatively described the implementation of the *pre-service primary education teacher education* reform in 2013, usually referred to as the "professionalization of *magisterio*,"[3] as "an important leap towards quality that cannot be postponed,"[4] because quality leads to the country's insertion in global processes. The proposal, or imposition, to reform teacher education was met with resistance, which was violent at several moments. A sector of the population (among them some teachers, students, community members and leaders), which was not opposed to reform for progress, but read into the proposal the double gesture of inclusion and exclusion that was inscribed in it, took their disagreement to the streets. Criminalized youth, bloodshed, injuries, threats, and political repression, among other things, were the partial results of the confrontations.

This context marks yet another moment of intensity pertinent to this research concerned with "indigenous" making and teacher education. The focus at this point in the book may seem to have shifted from "indigenous" making to teacher preparation solely. Although "indigenous" concerns may not appear so obvious, they were a crucial aspect in the aspirations embedded in the proposed reform.[5]

The chapter takes the educational sciences to task for their fabrication of curriculum and its promise. This task is informed by the history of curriculum and history of science analysis in the previous chapters. The (data) statements that the chapter zooms in on are located in "public" discussions, the historiography of education, and archives, including the written curricula of two documents in particular: *Modelo de Formación Inicial Docente-Propuesta* (by the Guatemalan Ministry of Education [MinEduc]) and *Propuesta de Carrera Docente, Parte Académica, y Técnico-Administrativa* (sponsored by USAID).[6] The chapter addresses the expert knowledges operating in the reform and the kinds of people they aim to make. Instead of making an argument, this chapter aspires to create an impression that questions the historical present of reform.[7] Thus, the reading the chapter offers from archival fragments is not argumentative in the classical way. Part of this implies not just the conventional (con/textual) analysis of policies, but also necessitates devoting a considerable portion of the chapter to thinking about and thinking through the "object of inquiry" (the making-up of "*lo indígena*").

Authoritarian regimes, as is suggested in the title, are an analytical device. Rather than a metaphor to describe the moral and legal supremacy of particular curricular reasons, it is a metonym. As a metonym, authoritarian regimes create the impression that commonsensical essences and elements enjoy the right to make an ultimate decision and produce considerable power to influence action, belief, opinion, and conduct over others, with practical effects. Informed to a certain degree by Guatemala's dictatorial and/or authoritarian politics in the twentieth and twenty-first centuries, the questions to be raised in this chapter about the historical present of the *magisterio* reform point to the absolute ruling and autocratic control of commonsensical reasons, as well as their paradoxes, contradictions, and tensions.

The chapter is divided into five sections. The first section locates the authoritarian regimes in statements that emerged at the time the proposal for the reform was being introduced. The section also introduces fractals, which throughout the chapter serve as a temporal concept that drives the historical analysis. Drawing from a notion of time available in the Mayan Popol Wuj, fractals and fractal geometry offer an alternative and poignant style of tracing the educational heritages of curriculum possibilities and impossibilities. In an effort to create an understanding of the ways in which the reform was being defined and mobilized, the second section discusses salient arguments found in protests, the mass media, social media, and quotidian interactions. The third section traces from the late nineteenth century the authoritarian curricular lines noticeable in those public arguments. *Curricular lines* refer to the tracks that order educational aspirations, actions, beliefs, opinions, and the conduct of action over others. The chapter engages with three of the most salient ones: nation, quality, and development. This historical tracing is far from an exhaustive review and draws from the analysis in the previous chapters. The review is not linear, and therefore maintains the historical style developed elsewhere in the book. The fourth section is an analysis of two curricular proposals and the salient authoritative curricular lines. The textual analysis is in many ways a provocation to interrogate the "indispensable" foundations of curriculum. To conclude, the last section inserts

Authorritarian Regimes in Reform 139

manifestación in curriculum. This insertion is an action that seeks new becomings in education, forged in the dual stance of remaining suspicious about, and daring to suspend, authoritarian regimes in education.

Lo indígena, Time, and Fractals

Statement 1

Figure 4.1 Fractal art—Fulani textile.

Statement 2

The Necessary Reform . . .

From the MinEduc Proposal: **Guatemalan** women and men have the **right** to **quality** education. An education that ensures our integral formation as **human** beings, that allows us to reach the **competencies** that help us carry out our **citizenship** in a **conscious** manner, and that allows us to acquire the necessary **skills** to successfully perform in the world of **work**.[8]

Statement 3

. . . Not Possible

Jorge Mario Joloma, a student from the Rafael Aqueche Institute, reports that the student sector rejects the reforms to the teacher preparation study plan given that these do not include an improvement in the quality of education, but an extension of the study time from three to five years. Educational improvements will not be made just by increasing the years of study to five, there are other factors that are truly affecting it, . . . he commented.[9]

Statement 4

So That There is Better Life Development

Principal of Century Normal School: Here at the Institute we agree with curricular transformation [as defined in the reform], because it is necessary and vital to change our society in Guatemala. We have deficiencies and one of them is that we are being left in the last place in education, trapped already for more than one hundred years . . . we need that transformation. This is vital to change our society so that there is better life development.[10]

A common denominator in these statements (from a student, a principal, and a government document) is their reference to time. Their totality is the result of complication, and simplicity, and messiness, but with a degree of order. Out of the four fragments, the Fulani fractal art piece must perhaps be an oddity—an oddity, which, indeed, has a lot to say and do in any impression the chapter may ever make. In 2012 the two moments that were arguably receiving perhaps the most national attention in both the media and in quotidian experiences were the teacher education reform and the Oxlajuj B'ak'tun (or Oxlajuj B'aqtun).[11] These two moments are at the heart of this inquiry. Confrontations, violent encounters, occupied schools, and paralyzed major towns and cities often made the national headlines. Apocalyptic messages, jokes, and expert debates over "indigenous" and "non-indigenous" calendars, archaeology, and multiple notions of time took much of the national and international attention.

At the ninth Annual Mayan Congress in 2011, which was in fact dedicated to the Oxlajuj B'ak'tun, linguist and "Popol Wuj expert" Carlos López discussed one of the notions of time that he reads in the Popol Wuj.[12] López used *fractals* as a means to understand a notion of Mayan time, a notion that conceives that "time evolves and involves," "expands and contracts," "moves in different directions," and "is not fixed."[13] López is not alone in this conceptual predicament; numerous other Mayan leaders and intellectuals who are well versed in Mayan material histories share it. López is willing to contend that this notion of time defies the "Western monologic, linear, vectorial, or repetitive" use of time that we encounter, for instance, in the anthropological discourses discussed in Chapter 3 and that are also operating in the teacher preparation reform analyzed later.[14] If one were to take this contention as an invitation to study the reform historically—including the impulses found in the notion of reform itself—and also to continue with the book's style of troubling linear analytics, this notion of time would be more pertinent to Latin America sensibilities, as found in various ways of conceiving of time and simultaneities of time.[15] Understanding time as fractal would highlight the complications in the case of the reform, the historically approximate self-similarity of its aspirations, its invisible authoritarian simplicity, and the possibilities for creativity that can turn the rules and the historical commands inside out.

The image of the Fulani textile provided in this chapter is in conversation with Benoît Mandelbrot's fractal geometry. This notion of fractal may not be the same one that López and "Maya" leaders read in the Popol Wuj, but they are perhaps in conversation with one another. Mandelbrot is a "French-American" mathematician from a "Jewish-Polish" background, whose work developed outside of mainstream research and resulted in the development of equations to define objects indefinable by traditional Euclidean geometry. His emphasis was on geometric intuition; this intuition allowed him to theorize about fractals, a new class of mathematical shapes whose uneven contours could mimic the irregularities found in nature. Irregularity and roughness were the rule, where smoothness was the exception. For Mandelbrot, things typically considered to be "rough," a "mess," or "chaotic" like mountains, shorelines, lungs, blood vessels, and the clustering of galaxies—fractals—had a degree of order. As one looks at these objects at different scales, while zooming in on one part, or zooming out, one sees structures that are recognizably *similar—not equal, not the same.* This is a very important notion to keep in mind later in the analysis. Fractal patterns are not only available in nature, but also in art, music, poetry, literature, *and* in history. As the eye meets the rough and chaotic moment that has been the teacher education reform, a moment of multiple complications indeed, there is also a degree of order to it, determined by certain simple rules. Complication, simplicity, messiness, and a degree of order are indeed a curricular opportunity with exponential potential for creation and an escape for the imagination.

Before I engage with the reform itself, note that I have welcomed into the analytical conversation linguistic and mathematical activities, sciences whose knowledges have intervened, albeit from other perspectives, in the fabrication of *lo indígena*. In much the same way that I have done in previous chapters and at the outset of the book, these knowledges are invited into the conversation as a gesture to "talk back" to similar instruments, in the hope of productive outcomes. There is always immeasurable potential at the limits—"Guatemala" has taught me that. Another point to keep in mind in what follows is that the analysis brings together statements from the Ministry of Education, public officials, teachers, students, parents, and communities. If the text comes across as "the state" being placed in opposition to the "communities," this is to highlight the complicated production of aspirations launched in the reform and not to maintain a dichotomy that often disallows generative meditations. And finally, authoritative regimes must not be conflated with the state. This is not a case of the malevolent and authoritative state vs. the oppressed or resisting communities. Authoritative

142 *Authoritarian Regimes in Reform*

regimes, as I will thoroughly discuss, are notions, discourses, performances, aspirations, and desires that produce a particular order and are generated from multiple locations from within and beyond the state–communities binary.

Roughness and Simplicity of "the Nation in Need of Development": The 2012 Teacher Education Reform Moments of Intensity

Statements three and four earlier are caught between Kairos and Chronos: the timeliness of Guatemalans needing a quality education, that is "the right time" (Kairos) to reform, and the expansion of a time that tick-tocks (Chronos), marks the sequence, defers access, and defers educational opportunities. The statements were part of a complicated scenario with a cacophony of arguments, and with a certain degree of anguish, in which only some statements were intelligible. This section puts these statements together as a way to notice the circulation of ideas and specific terms with which re-form is being defined and mobilized.

In the public domain, justification for the *teacher education* reform was threaded with the needles of quality and the already familiar ones of betterment and development. An unfounded direct correlation was often drawn that better teachers = better education results, that having qualified teachers in the school guarantees quality education at the elementary and secondary levels. Moreover, that quality education is the secure access pass to successful civic engagement and economic development. The promise of the new curriculum is ordered through a vectorial logic, with a predetermined course of effects. The rationale continues: not only is Guatemala leading Latin American statistics in terms of poor teacher preparation beside Haiti,[16] according to human development indicators, Guatemala is still a backward society. The country is lagging behind its Latin American counterparts.[17] Additionally, Businessmen for Education (*Empresarios por la Educación*) reported that Guatemalan employees rank high in employer dissatisfaction. Basic education needs reform. Teachers need their capacities increased. Future teachers' aptitudes need to be bettered. The Socio Economic Committee, made up of businessmen, unions, and leaders of cooperatives, unanimously supported the strategy toward quality education. In how the reform is justified in these expressions, one begins to see how not only principles of the corporate world and production are operating in redirecting education, but also what counts as the reason for curriculum.

Quality is narrated as a direct result of increasing time spent in schools. The longer student teachers spend in classrooms—before it was three years and now is five—the better prepared they are assumed to be. Better preparation also means extending and migrating teacher preparation, perhaps partially but still determinately, from traditional Normal Schools and private institutes (that is, secondary school education) to institutions of higher education. The *bachillerato* certificate, granted upon completion of the *initial phase* of the teacher education program, became insufficient for a graduate to be hired to teach in or compete for a public post.[18] Completion of the "specialization phase" became a mandatory prerequisite for access to the market. Others, operating from within the same opportune moment (Kairos) and expansion of time framework, proposed that the program should be extended by increasing the academic input of the existing model in favor of more specialization and improvements to the learning process. Questions of quality were also asked of university education, which had not yet demonstrated quality in its own teacher education processes. University education has been criticized for being too distant from the concrete reality of the Guatemalan population and for allowing professional and personal interests to outweigh social and community interests. The university has already distanced its student teachers from the possibility of a teaching experience characterized by a quotidian devotion, vigor, and commitment to the education of boys and girls. This point in the argument arises from the modern construction of the expert and expert (in this case, pedagogical) knowledge, in addition to the anthropological principle of closeness to the community and their quotidian affairs and education's duty to social reconstruction.

The highest point in the reform has undoubtedly been the state's decision to partition the program into two stages and to hand over the second stage to the university to administer—something never before seen in Guatemalan mass pre-service elementary teacher preparation.[19] Guatemala only has one public university (as written in the constitution), which is overpopulated and has already exhausted its capacity to serve the qualified thousands that compete for access to higher education. Hosting the 17,000 student teachers who graduate each year is logistically implausible. That is, whatever percentage of these thousands who choose and have the means to attend college. Guatemala, however, has over a dozen private universities. A few of the arguments against these institutions are that it's the privatization of a public good and it is a neoliberal reform that prevents people from any chance they might have had to begin a teaching career, demanding they continue in school for three more years, and thus inflating the demand for higher education that can be supplied by the private sector.[20] This affects "indigenous" student teachers, both rural and urban, who work while studying in order to support themselves and their families. The struggle of social media and in the protest in the streets was for "the protection of public, bilingual, and intercultural education because first peoples [*pueblos originarios*] had the right to study in their own languages, the right to public, free, and quality education."[21]

Other intelligible voices in the complicated picture expressed that the number of high school graduates is too large, anyhow. The Ministry of Education pointed out that it is surprising that such a large number of students are looking at *magisterio* as the most favorable career path. Graduating from a Normal School, others said, does not, in any case, guarantee getting a job, but may be a route to bolstering the 80,000 already unemployed teachers in the country.[22] The reform was urgent, partly because, as specialists say, students did not even pass 2% of standardized tests at the end of the year, and not even two out of 100 students reached the minimum level. But accredited teachers with a university degree would eventually earn a higher salary. Some students expressed that the authoritarian proposal does not, however, even guarantee that students complete their education, thus denying them the same right to education that the proposal itself demands. This is also the case in terms of access to the labor market, which is the ultimate goal of the reform. Though images of students' and parents' resistance and their occupation of schools and the streets inundated the media, their perspectives were generally left unheard. When they were available, they were quickly dismissed for their lack of authenticity and for being the result of manipulation.[23]

In the midst of this rough image of teacher preparation, *teacher preparation* itself is peripheral. The arguments outlined earlier, despite their entangled tensions, do little to excavate the central curricular concepts, that is, quality, betterment, development, the teacher, and the nation, upon which the reform is mounted to mobilize the public. Yet teacher preparation is at the same moment *central* as a point of contestation over the administration of schooling and the sorting of people and desires, educational access, production, and standardization. This complicated contestation, to use Mandelbrot's language, is ordered by a simple equation that left intact the *nation-state* and the *performance of the citizen*, a formerly republican discipline, which in turn dictates the ultimate direction of curricular aspirations. Guatemalan women and men whose duty is *advancement* for the *economic prosperity* of the nation is another number left intact and unquestioned in this simple equation. I will return to the discussion of this equation later in the chapter.

With this backdrop, one can begin to zoom in and out of sections in the fractal history that are educational reforms in Guatemala in an effort to understand the foundations of the 2012 reform. The next section retraces these foundations and their becoming authoritarian with regard to how they seem to order what is possible and permissible in teacher preparation curricula.

Fractal History: Salient Authoritarian Regimes in Motion

Reform—"the mobilization of publics and with power relations in defining public space,"[24] not fixed, and moving in different directions—can be mapped in its repetition, *not as sameness*, throughout the history of "modern(izing)" education. The uneven contours of this particular "professionalization" reform can be traced to 1996. The Peace Accords, the Agreement on the Identity and Rights of Indigenous Peoples and the country's socioeconomic and agrarian situation all served as the platform for opening the professionalization reform workshop. The years 2003, 2006, and 2008 saw the roughest moments in attempting to modify the Normal Schools,[25] which always operated under the aegis of quality and development.[26] Elements of cultural pertinence and respect for multiplicity, as clearly visible in the National Base Curriculum (CNB), the largest curricular reform in recent history, were more prevalent at the beginning of the reform efforts when memories of the peace process were fresher.[27] To a certain degree, the teacher education reform makes connections to the themes of interculturalism, which, regardless of their actualizable potential in curriculum and classrooms, serve to calm some fervent critics of the homogenizing Guatemalan state.

In this vein, and zooming in on the 1944 revolution, the educational re-form inscribed in the "Seminar of Social Integration" and literacy campaigns set their gaze on the rural, the peasant, and the "indigenous," especially in terms of their integration to the nation, and their conversion to acceptable ontologies and advanced epistemologies (see Chapters 2 and 3). These revolutionary policies and actions, today remembered with nostalgia in critical spheres, retained *the nation*, already virtually formed at the time, as the horizon of enactment of what was possible in curriculum. Zooming out to the 1960s, the 1962 re-formed National Education Organic Law established a formal relationship between education and operations of the Indigenist Institute, which was conducting research on how to culturalize "indigenous" communities. The aspiration then was not educational quality per se, as was the case in the professionalization reform in 2012. However, today's quality-driven education reform promises to yield results that carry qualities of approximate self-similarity to those expected in the 1960s in terms of culturalizing "indigenous" "communities, modernizing education and the nation, and increasing competitiveness by the rules, not only of the global market, but also of what counts as existing, participating, and belonging within complex economies of affect. This tracing of historical developments fractally may feel like too fast a movement that is missing important nuances of these moments of intensity. Much historical work, however, has documented in multiple ways these historical unfoldings. The gesture here is to highlight a certain degree of order, following Mandelbrot, in times typically considered rough and complex in Guatemalan education history.

Zooming in between the revolutions of 1871 and 1944, we find a time of "educational crisis" for conservatives, whose plea it was to reform education in the name of quality instruction. "Lack of changes" during the liberal regimes before 1944 had conservatives campaigning to readjust education via private management, as was the "successful case" under the Catholic Church, which, before the 1871 revolution, employed religious principles established from the colonial era.[28] The educational reforms that emerged after 1871's liberal revolution took place within positive philosophy, "modernity," embracing principles of obligatory and free education with a civil character, and textbook selection based on modern theories of objective teaching, and positive education based on encyclopedic, gradual, and progressive instruction.[29] Not too far from those tensions is the friction in the public discourse about the professionalization reform. Modern theories of teaching, regardless of how they are understood in relation to modernizing education, are invoked throughout in the audible discussions on improving the *magisterio*. The reform reinscribes the conservative-liberal-progressive yearning of a modernity deferred and the illusion of a certainty of seizing reality, changing it, and reaching to *the* future, somehow objective, positive, inevitable, and predictable. As with the nation, an appellation to modernity and modernizing continues to circumscribe what is possible and impossible to imagine in curriculum.

Toward the end of the nineteenth century, science, research, and the pedagogical sciences become more noticeable in the preoccupation over the ends of education and educational reform. A number of pedagogical publications emerged in 1888, for example, *Popular Education*, *Journal of the Central American Pedagogic Congress*, *Public Instruction*, *Scientific Propaganda*, and *The Normal School*.[30] In the 1893 Central American Congress, teachers met to look for solutions to problems such as the teaching of manual work and the education of "indigenous" peoples.[31] The latter was indeed a priority of the congress[32] and of the continuous making up of "indigenous" (s)objects. Pedagogy and the preoccupation with the ends of education are repeated (but not as sameness) in the professionalization reforms, in the expressions of concern over the better preparation of teachers—teachers more competent to teach the practical competencies for the workforce of tomorrow. The ends of education are already overdetermined by the authority of terms such as deficiencies of origin,[33] numbers, figures, and ranking; the present and its accountability to the future, and nation-state centeredness.

Liberal and populist reformers of the first decades of the twentieth century planted educational reform on the land of the *patria* and watered it with science and knowledge, expecting to collect the fruit of progress, as was showcased in the feast of educational festivals such as Manuel Estrada Cabrera's Minerva festivals in the first two decades of the twentieth century (see Chapter 1). Slightly zooming out to the 1930s and into the early 1960s, science (or appeals to "in the name of science") dictated the way "indigenous" peoples were to be migrated to "modernity,"[34] and this was aided by pragmatist thought (i.e., the philosophy of John Dewey, William James, George Herbert Mead, etc.) and Protestant linguistics (see Chapter 2). The announcement of the "new type of school" referred to a *practical* and *functional* character. The advancement of literacy, the opening of rural Normal Schools, and the reform and expansion of early childhood education and elementary schools in rural areas were, among others things, the educational mobilizations at the time for the *advancement of the poor* and disenfranchised.[35] Approximate self-similarity in these mobilizations in terms of the focus on reading, the rural, and the training of teachers is noticeable in 1910s and 1920s with their fervent preoccupation with progress.[36] *Progress* continues to be iterative in this fractal history. From the mid-1940s onwards, the becoming-democratic Guatemalan nation-state did not abandon the liberal promise of progress in and through educational reform, even if for the benefit of those "in the waiting room of history."[37] The pragmatist elements, the practical, and the functional, are key in this fractal history equation. They are reproduced in the landscape of today's reform and in establishing the horizon of what education aspirations are possible: citizens trained in the necessary competencies for work and for competing in the labor market, for solving practical predetermined problems, competencies that are "real" and "relevant," and enable know-how in "all" aspects of life.[38]

Calling for the improvement of *pedagogy* and *didactics*, the professionalization reform relies on educational *psychology* for the increased development of *competencies*, towards *individual* success, and for the betterment of the *nation*. These series of effects have approximate self-similarity to the celebrated first Central American Pedagogic congress of December 1893, the National Congresses of Pedagogy in 1923 and 1929, the attempts at creating an experimental psychology laboratory in 1926,[39] and the rise of American-style pragmatism with the Active School, "teaching for action," and manual work in all subject areas, because, the *patria* wanted "workers, not useless drones of the social hive."[40]

This fractal tracing of reforms in recent history serves as the foundation, or to follow the fractal style, as the formula from which the teacher reform is generated. Notions of plurality, the nation, modernity and modernizing, preparing a workforce, progress and advancement, and the practical are traceable in the current teaching reform. In the next section, I discuss three of the authoritarian curricular lines available in the discourses about the reform, evidenced in two crucial documents. The nation, quality, and development were partially addressed in reform debates, but were left unproblematized in the larger national manifestations outside *and* within the educational sciences and institutions.

The Curricular Debates that Did and Did Not Take Place in the Remaking of Human Kinds

The Nation

Educational reforms in general have tended to treat the *patria*, and now the nation, as the core to the ordering of life and the self, and so references to "Guatemala" are usually of the authoritative type; the professionalization reform is no exception. To reintroduce one of the salient authoritarian curricular lines, let us return to statement 1 earlier: the *"Necessary reform . . ."* taken from the reform proposal by the MinEduc at the beginning of the chapter. The political and philosophical limits of the curriculum and the teacher have already been set under the appellation of the broader national frame and in the name of the humanistic narratives of democracy, citizenship, consciousness, competencies, skill, and the world of work. Consider, for instance, the following statement on the state of the art of educational research, teacher preparation, and policies by anthropologist Ricardo Lima Soto:

> [We] have been deprived of advancements and achievements, and we have been, amongst other countries, submerged with the least of achievements and the complete lack of teacher professionalism as well as the resulting didactic proposals. Thus the most affected ones are the citizens and the country . . . we are feeding underdevelopment, and backwardness worldwide, instead of providing and preparing ourselves as a nation for the very complex challenges of a globalized world, along with free trade agreements, and the urgency for productivity that is required to satisfy material and spiritual needs.[41]

This statement emerges from the periodic meeting of Educational Researchers of Guatemala sponsored by the Jesuit Universidad Rafael Landivar. Lima Soto is not alone in the educational plea launched via the nation. Multiple influential figures in these educational research meetings and other gatherings employ the nation as the orbit in which any curricular proposal circulates. Although the nation's roughness can be noticed in how it has been a point of contention from political, cultural, social, and even linguistic angles, it is a line of action with invisible authoritarian simplicity. It is so simple: education is for the service of the nation, so the nation can relate/compete with others globally. What is there to be asked about this configuration? The *Propuesta de carrera docente, parte académica, y técnico-administrativa* (from here on "Teaching Career proposal") states outright that the task is for Guatemala to gain a superior ranking according to educational measures in order to guarantee harmonious social relations of quality. In the document, the "principles of the teaching career" are oriented toward bettering the educational quality of the country,[42] because, as the *Modelo de formación inicial docente-propuesta* (from here on "MinEduc proposal") states, "the current model of teacher preparation in Guatemala has expired and needs to be renewed."[43] The actions of the new teacher need to be founded on the state vision.[44] The new teacher is to educate a student-citizen conscious of her ethnic and national being with self-esteem and a sense of national belonging.[45] To be that new teacher in the country, one needs to be ". . . a special person, with a special vocation, with a special mission in Guatemalan society, and [sic] a specific role in the construction of the nation we want."[46] Sustaining this assertion, the Teaching Career Proposal reiterates that "if as a country we aspire to develop ourselves . . . [we must] start with the teachers who, with their education, conduct, and performance, will ensure better results in the educational processes."[47]

Considering the rough educational and sociopolitical histories of Guatemala, what kinds of teacher conduct, growth, knowledges, and performance are desirable to address educational problems? Or should the question actually be, ought these be the totalizing terms in the mobilization of publics in defining the (public) space of education and teacher education? And how totalizing and authoritarian are they after all, beyond the effects they are already producing in creating the illusion of a defined plan for sorting out educational problems and social concerns? Although the MinEduc proposal and the ways it was socialized were not short on confrontation, and despite the fact that a few of the terms in the reform were indeed challenged, the "nation" continued and continues to enjoy a well-established and uninterrupted economy of affect. The "nation" continues to be the trustworthy organizer of educational aspirations from the so-called far left to the far right. Interestingly and paradoxically the nation necessitates those who define it, and those who are not in it, to draw its borders (see Chapter 1) in order to exist. These dynamics of marking differences between people inherently produce exclusion. Countering exclusion has been the goal of various social struggles; multiple uprisings throughout history have been motivated by the unequal dynamics of the state serving a few at the expense of others—other people, ontologies, epistemologies, cosmologies, or (non-) world views. However, the nation per se, and its authority, has remained unproblematized. Virtually all noticeable educational aspirations have been and continue to be drawn to it, extending the project of inclusion of peoples to the nation—a project that already defines how one needs to be, act, think, and behave in order to deserve to be included.

What else should education turn to if not toward the nation constituted by those who have historically been in and excluding those who have been out of it? To determine who is in, some need to be out. What else should teachers be loyal to if not to the "fragile" country, whose dream of competing with other global players can no longer be deferred? And yet what would a reform—as the mobilization of publics and sensitivities—be like if the authority of the nation would have faced protests? In other words, what if the protest had been against the nation-state as the curriculum organizer? What would the reform have looked like if the recent and not-so-recent violent histories in Guatemala, which shrank ways of being and knowing, had been invoked in the protests against the reform not from outside, but from *within* the curriculum being proposed? What would the effects of the reform have been, or what could they be, as the reform is being implemented today? Could the few marginal voices of suspicion, raised in schools every time "Guatemala" was invoked, have reverberated in the sealed rooms where reform negotiation talks took place? While perhaps leaving the walls of the room intact, could the voices have created a barely intelligible cacophony that would have confused the people present and sent them back to their educational duties *troubled*? Can the world of school reform rotate without the nation as its orbit? Perhaps politics and educational reform—where

150 *Authoritarian Regimes in Reform*

the nation *is* assumed as the inevitable organizer—employ a reason that is incommensurable with curriculum's historical and theoretical aspirations. Still, suspicious of such reason, and with a participatory stance that dares to point to limits of even the most absolutist rule such as that of the nation, I propose an uncharted exploration not post-nation but *beside* it. Nonetheless, why the preoccupation with the nation? A critical reading of its deployment as an ordering principle in violent and painful Guatemalan histories offers lessons about *the nation's unsustainability as an authoritarian curricular regime.*

Quality

The forty-page proposal by the MinEduc, from which statement 2 "*Necessary reform . . .*" is taken, goes to great lengths to justify the professionalization reform under the appellation of *quality*—and as part of a "quality tribunal" in the making.[48] **Quality** is another authoritarian curricular line and not a new euphemism. The reason for its current mobilization has fractal historical qualities as discussed in the previous section. The text is produced by *técnicos*, another word for experts, in collaboration, in the first stages of its production, with the United States Agency for International Development (USAID), and in the last stages with the *Deutsche Gesellschaft für Internationale Zusammenarbeit* (GIZ). Twelve of the members in the working team sought advice from specialists in El Salvador, Honduras, Mexico, and Peru. "The concern for quality 'authorizes the authority' of experts,"[49] from both "regional" (in Latin America) and "international" (the United States and Germany) contexts, in collecting or fabricating empirical data, itemizing the philosophical framework, determining the curricular structures, and prescribing the course design.

Through classroom observations, conversations with students, teachers, and Ministry of Education personnel, the team of experts found empirical evidence in Latin America to justify the urgency of transforming initial teacher education in Guatemala. The framework for transformation is authorized by the expert guidelines provided by UNESCO on educational quality. This description underscores the importance of the "South" consulting with the "North/West," but, most importantly, the "South" looking to the "South" for answers; a decololonizing gesture, perhaps, or the enactment of a global strategy of borrowing experience and expertise from other counterparts.[50] Paradoxically, the South consulted is indeed already ahead in terms of drawing from the international community (the "North/West") to inform "their own" educational and teacher preparation reforms.[51] In any case, consulting with the experts in the West as well as the practices of the rest abjects Guatemala—once again away from the rest to which it does not yet belong. Guatemala's "backward" position, being cast as lacking progress, and lagging far behind the modernity of industrialized nations, is maintained through international and Latin American rankings on teacher preparation assigned by calculative and inscription devices hardly ever rigorously questioned in Guatemala or much of Latin America.[52] I wonder if the act of ranking and the making-up of Guatemala's delay in catching up with Latin America and the world follows the reason of fabricating difference and Guatemala as "the Other," which is indispensible for fabricating the self, an advanced self, modern and superior, as in the dynamics of Euroegocentrism and the logics that enable the "infinite task of Europe."[53]

As the standard that justifies the reform in this and other texts, quality appears multiple times: quality education, quality of education, quality of formation, better quality, betterment of quality, the right to quality, verification of quality, low quality, lack of quality, quality desire, quality of life, quality school, quality model, quality assurance, quality emphasis, teaching quality, academic quality, professional quality, scientific, pedagogic, and technological quality, and educational quality.[54] Quality, perhaps even more than the nation, is characterized by its invisible authority in which its establishment as a main line of curricular action is naturalized, making it virtually immune to be the subject of interrogation. Who would dare be against quality education, anyway?

Following the challenge posed by the Normal School student in the "... *not possible*" statement earlier, quality is, therefore, that which is desirable in its absence. Beyond that, if one is to hold the guidelines in the proposal to the same logic that produces them, then what quality is per se and how it is to be translated remains undefined and undetermined. Thus quality is a signifier that paradoxically contains everything and nothing at the same time. A standard that is not a standard. This could be a productive tension in curriculum. In the educational model proposed, sentence starters such as "quality ... is characterized by ..." and "the [necessary] conditions to achieve educational quality [are]: ..." unfold into a multiplicity of other slippery signifiers such as "rights," "education for all," "the human," "sustainability," "justice," "equity," "social context," "past, present, future," "skills for life," "values," "societal transformation," and the fact that quality is "measurable."[55] Quality seeks definition in other idioms that slip into other idioms, and so on, saying, in the end, everything and nothing.

The proposal includes the kinds of conditions that are necessary to achieve educational quality. These included "technical conditions to ensure quality" and "specific conditions established for the improvement of educational quality," that is to say, quality is achieved by ensuring quality. The structural conditions of this quality include a "system for quality assurance," "standards and curriculum," and "assessment."[56] These three conditions are less a suggestion for understanding what it is that quality wants and more expressions of the reduction of educational aspirations to an instrumentalism that meets the demands of audit culture. The more specific conditions are not much different in this regard: "school management," "instructional leadership"—which means "supervision and school leadership"—and "pedagogic projects to improve learning."[57] "Resources" and "support services ...

152 *Authoritarian Regimes in Reform*

infrastructure, textbooks, libraries, technology, school food, others" are the final condition for quality included in the document.[58] This last point meets the challenge raised by Jorge Mario Joloma, the Normal School student, and the larger resisting body. The working assumption here, however, is that the materiality of education is reducible to these elements and that there is a certain stability, neutrality, and peacefulness attached to their availability. Guatemalan histories, and not only educational histories, have important and often unexplored lessons vis-à-vis what kinds of textbooks are to be/being used. What kinds of images and stories should they include? To access what kinds of cosmologies? And which philosophies? What kinds of school food should they reference? Which agriculture and diets do they therefore privilege and for whom? What kinds of technologies are given preeminence? And to access what kinds of knowledges? What kinds of infrastructures? Which bodies are included, excluded, and made abject? Which kinds of schools? With what kinds of requirements? Uniforms? A fractal exploration of, for example, regimes of appearance would remind us of rough and simple histories of the politics of the *corte* and *güipil*, the making of the "Indian" woman via her dress (see Chapter 3), and the coercive demand she rid herself of it and assimilate in order to participate in the nation.

Development

Here I discuss one last authoritarian curricular line, which drives from statement four: **development.** Century Normal School principal's desire *"that there is better life development"* (in statement four earlier) is the message conveyed to student teachers in an effort to inform them about the position the school is adopting. It was intended to discourage any potential revolt by students and parents, who had indeed occupied other normal schools. After 100 years of being entrapped in the "last place in education," who would not agree that development is *the* way out, especially after over 100 years of self-similar messages in the educational sciences that development is the answer to an ailing nation? Development, without which the projects of most of the educational sciences would be inconceivable, is also employed to advance the reform agenda in a second reform proposal document.

While I was sitting in the teachers' lounge at Rural Bilingual Normal School (RBNS) waiting to observe a *bachillerato* class in early 2013, one of the community members, a teacher who identifies as "Maya," approached me with a copy of a thin book and asserted that the teachers had never agreed with the Ministry of Education's proposal. Handing the thin book to me he said, "but this is *our* Proposal": The Teaching Career Proposal. The cover reads "San Carlos University's teacher education school." At the very top is the USAID logo and a line that reads "From the Peoples of the United States of America, Educational Reform in the Classroom." As indicated on the cover, this proposal was sponsored by USAID's educational reform efforts through an agreement with San Carlos University. The document was published in September 2011 and defined the terms of the "teaching career." These terms, in a fractal history, not only appeared connected with the *escalafón docente*,[59] whose heritage dates back to 1927,[60] but reproduced the foundations of categories and levels inserted in a hierarchy of advancement. This hierarchy was made intelligible through classifications of those prepared or fit for the task and those excluded as unfit.

The invisible authoritarian simplicity of development is reinscribed when justifying the proposal for "human development," and "societal development," of "education for life and development."[61] In defining the "objectives of the teaching career," falling under the *national* frame and the authority of educational *quality* improvement, there is a call for "suitable people," with more "merits," "qualities," "development and professional growth," "higher . . . merits, knowledge, and experiences," "better qualified," and "better prepared," with "good education, and . . . better performance."[62] *Good, more, better,* and *higher* are terms that authorize the demand for reform. These terms, including quality, as in the MinEduc proposal, determine every impulse in the reform and paradoxically nothing at the same time. If the document is a curricular directive that is expected to be enacted, what exactly are the educational community and the *magisterio* to make of such terms? The question here is not to ask "what is quality?" or "what is good?" or "what is better?" in an effort to know what these terms should be about, which, as Maarten Simons and Jan Masschelein warn us, are an indication of the presence of an entrepreneurial gaze.[63] Instead, the questions are meant to hold these terms in abeyance to highlight their apophatic rendering of being present by being said (as announced in the document) and being absent by being left unsaid (the hollowness in their semantic instructiveness) at the same time and in a text/proposal that seems to demand that the terms be performed as the educational *solution*.[64] The apparent tension here could be a productive one, which I will discuss in the following section.

With the history of education maintaining a strong relationship with the church (regardless of denomination) and continuing to be enabled by language related to God, one should consider whether the reform terms retained a religious connection. "Suitable teachers" are indeed commonly described by many in the general public, educationists, and officials, as those with a "vocation to teach." They have been "chosen" and "called to teach," and in a pastoral fashion, are expected to lead young souls on the "right" path. The reform is directing an ascending struggle as if moving closer to the heavenly father, searching for higher knowledge and growth in a forward and upward movement. Doing good, being good, and becoming better all resonate with the preparation for the salvation of the soul and the second coming of Christ. Explicit religious language was, obviously, not evident in the documents under examination here, just as it is also obvious that the terms of the reform being interrogated here (nation, quality, development) are not natural. The terms employed are in fact available via particular histories along the tracks of a railroad that connected Guatemala with the "North," not only for the export of bananas, but also for the import of aid to a land ready and arable after centuries of cross-Atlantic Christian/colonial labor.

Although the liberal-conservative quarrel over church-managed versus secular education may be over, particular educational aspirations continue to be informed by and written with Christian ideals. It could be argued that on the surface there is nothing wrong with religion as manifested in the particular gestures noted earlier; however, some of its inscribed notions, selectively accompanied by a social Darwinian style, have the potential for foreclosing curricular possibilities, through an obligatory educational reform that robs particular kinds of people of their possibilities for participation in education.

In the MinEduc's proposal, the "profile of the new teacher"[65] described a type of teacher who is first and foremost "conscious of the self" in both professional and personal contexts. A self that, according to the Teaching Career Proposal, is ordered through the teaching service process, a living organism that is sorted by admission categories, ranked, determined by general principles of suitability (by merit, determining the best teachers), whose existence in the system depends on their aptness to survive in the assigned environment, with the training, experiences, and knowledge that allows them to ascend in the hierarchy. Lima Soto stressed that an agreement must be reached on the profile of the admission and graduation of applicants, as well as the kind of education that will be offered according to quality controls.[66] The Teaching Career Proposal defines processes of admission, steps to ascend to the various levels, and how to descend and perish just as living organisms do in "Western" biological understandings. The career quality tribunal is also defined in order "to eliminate opportunism, . . . incompetence, . . . inexperience, . . . traffic of influences," or any conditions that threaten improvement.[67] As a "Latin American" I can recognize the effort being made to eliminate what the United States and Europe have been rehearsing with us over the years as "corruption." Therefore, increased regulation of teacher preparation would be practiced at the "university level" to achieve "a superior level," and the process for both pre- and in-service teachers would be "obligatory." The document asserted that the basic reform would not be possible without this mechanism. The survival, ascension, and advancement of the teacher will be guided by "the advancement of science and technology to face the reality of teaching in the classroom and the school."[68]

To conclude this section, let us return to the history of reform and the debated, yet still unshaken, century-old preoccupation with *lo indígena* and the making up of people. Both the Teaching Career document and the MinEduc proposal were framed by the principle that teachers and teaching are to be in support of the "cultural development of the state" and the "development of the four *pueblos*." Both documents, as well as the public debates, are peppered with language that indicates diversity. Although the languages of culturalizing, improving, and assimilating the "Indian" that were prevalent in earlier decades have disappeared more recently, complex and sophisticated semantics retain their gaze over *lo indígena* as the site on which the national project is to continue unfolding. The documents call for the "development of identities . . . [and] the knowledge and respect of other cultures and languages,"[69] and in the context of dismantling "the curriculum of poverty in teacher professional development," a process of selection with "inclusive character for cultural diversity" is proposed.[70] Images appear on a stair-like graphic in the teaching career document and include silhouettes depicting not only men and women in what is conventionally understood in "Western" worlds as professional attire (i.e., suit for men, skirts and heels for women), but also "Maya" men and women wearing *corte* and *güipil*. The process of visual insertion gestures to processes of inclusion in the ascension of the teaching, technical, and administrative personnel ladder and participation in spaces historically reserved for a few and not for "indigenous" peoples. These gestures are not only inserted in the fractal history of the teaching ladder (*Escalafón Docente*) from the late 1920s. The gestures also emerge within classificatory and hierarchical reasoning noticeable at various salient historical moments in the making of *lo indígena*.

Manifestación and Triggering the Emergence of New Becomings

The fractal analysis offered earlier is a *manifestación*, along with 1) the discontent with the teacher education reform that took students, parents, teachers, and leaders to the streets; 2) reformers', educationists', and members of government's preoccupation with education; and 3) the historical spirit of mobilization in Latin America. Generally a *manifestación* is a public gathering of people intended to express disagreement, to object, or enact what Jacques Rancière calls dissensus.[71] The act of *manifestación* in this analysis is not in putting forth an argument but an expression of dissensus in order to make a curricular impression. To recapitulate, the histories of educational reform in Guatemala have been characterized neither by continuities nor by discontinuities. They have been rough, and irregular, with a certain degree of order attained by an equation of social and educational facts based on seeking quality for the development of the nation; an equation that virtually (not always actually) determines what is to be imagined and done. Education reform in Guatemala has been messy to a certain degree, but, as demonstrated earlier, has maintained a recognizably similar template according to which educational aspirations have been ordered. Similar is not to say the same or equal. Creating the impression that things have not changed, that (teacher) education today is the same as ten, fifty, or one hundred years ago, or that things have changed (that curriculum nowadays is an equal platform of participation) would be to deny that education and teacher education are constant becomings.[72] Becomings are a movement not in extension, but rather in intensity. The arguments of both change and lack of change populate the public discourse in education. At times the arguments are in contiguous sentences uttered by the same interlocutor.

Zooming in on the irregularities of the history, and more specifically on one particular part—be it the nation, quality, or development, which, with self-similarities to other points in the fractal, may appear as the same— could reveal the unresolved *and* irresolvable paradoxes and tensions inherent in education and the educational sciences. I am willing to contend that embracing and operating from within these paradoxes and tensions is critical for becomings that turn the rules and historical commands, especially if they enjoy unrecognizable authority, inside out. This process is, in fact, key for the constant becoming of teacher education and what is possible, but yet unimaginable in new becomings, in the creation of curricula whose inscribed desire is not the subject becoming another prefigured subject, another person to be made according to the educational equation already available, an education that does not know its destiny. A new becoming cannot be achieved by imitation while looking at the projection screen of industrialized nations, "cultured" societies whether out there (in Europe or the United States) or right here (in other Latin and Central American nations or Guatemala) and successful educational systems as legislated by international standardized comparisons.

New becomings require judicious study of the fractal histories in which current educational configurations have been made possible, revealing the inner tensions in the configurations. This educational reform and the impulses to revise education are indeed netted in many paradoxes, tensions, and contradictory directions. New becomings are triggered precisely within such tensions. An example of these are those inherent to the nation that includes and excludes at the same moment and the historical *social mobilizations* that have strived to challenge these dynamics by countering social exclusion despite failing to suspend the matters of fact that produce them and turn them into matters of concern.[73] Turning them into matters of concern means to shift one's attention to zooming out of them, to hold them to interrogation, "to put them to the test, to overflow their boundaries, to reveal the fragile envelopes in which they are contained" and delivered for our consumption, to include new actors, or see actors anew at the eruption of new curricular becomings.[74]

Here I propose a dual stance that is historically informed and is also required in curricular performance: to remain *suspicious* and to dare *suspend*. Suspecting and suspending are acts inspired by pre-existing struggles and social movements such as the *manifestaciones* against the professionalization reform by student teachers and parents, the *manifestaciones* of parents and children for more teachers in rural communities, or "indigenous" communities' *manifestaciones* against transnational development projects throughout the country. Here I am referring to the amplification and multiplication of the acts of suspicion that are engaged when one perceives the tensions and paradoxes at the center of what authorizes and orders education, or vice versa, when one perceives the authoritarian regimes and strives to unpack the tensions in them. Perception is informed by an historical sense of distrust of the trustworthy: in this case not of the "foreign," but of the most familiar, the common, and the obvious. The nation, quality, and development are only a few of these authoritarian regimes. When under suspicion, the ruling curricular lines that are available have no other alternative than to be suspended, stopped in their tracks, opened, and interrogated based on the effects, often good-willed, that they ostensibly desire and promise to produce.

Suspicion and gestures toward acts of suspension have already taken place, albeit in tensions and paradoxes, within the curriculum enacted at Rural Bilingual Intercultural Normal School. Mariela, one of the Indigenous Language teachers, moves with caution when bringing up notions of "development" in classroom discussions. Her cautionary stance is rooted in her long history as a combatant for "indigenous" peoples' right to a dignified existence. Ixcán, where the school is located, was the site of multiple massacres during the war. This is a fact that permeates the lives of student teachers, teacher educators, and community members more broadly. Mariela's curriculum actively emphasizes that hundreds of "indigenous" peoples were killed and disappeared in the name of national development and combating communism, while they were themselves fighting for the redistribution of land and for their multiple ways of being. In regions such as Ixcán, leaders and educators such as Mariela are profoundly suspicious of newer iterations of development projects carried out by mega and/or transnational corporations. Still, despite being suspicious, Mariela paradoxically refers to Guatemala's development as the task to be achieved. She reiterates that "indigenous" peoples are at the center of the country's development and denies that "Mayas" lack development, or oppose development. "Mayas are not the cause of backwardness in Guatemala."[75] Perhaps there are multiple notions of development operating in Mariela's curricular enactment. Perhaps development is both disabling and enabling in curriculum. Perhaps development is at the participatory limits of curriculum, the last kick before its long overdue death sentence, or perhaps its renaissance is the ultimate educational desire. This tantalizing messiness is a curricular opportunity to exploit the fractal history of development, as well as what it has to say about the current state of educational affairs and the recapitulation of colonialism in the constant remaking of particular kinds of people through curriculum. I suspect that paradoxical encounters via acts of suspicion in curriculum can forge new becomings of what education cannot expect and does not yet know.

A second and final instance of a gesture toward suspension is the policy assignment Nicanor gave to his fifth-year *magisterio* students in the Indigenous Language and Learning Class. At the Rural Bilingual Intercultural Normal School there is a very present sense of suspicion toward the state borne out of Ixcán's and the village's intense history of war and the state's repressive measures. Despite that, and because of that, the assignment invites the students' gaze onto the "foundations, the laws of indigenous languages in Guatemala"[76] in an attempt at suspension. The students research, select, and read laws such as the Protection and Production of Indigenous Textiles, Crafts Development and Protection, Creation of the Mayan Languages Academy, and the Peace Accords. A common argument and source of frustration in critical sectors of Guatemalan society is that written policies and agreements are not put into practice. The class assignment seeks to intervene in this argument. The Indigenous Language and Learning Class focuses on pedagogy from an applied linguistics perspective, drawing from the country's Protestant linguistic foundations of language and language pedagogy, along with anthropological knowledges. Nicanor's approach adds a critical and political dimension to the course. Attempts to read and analyze policies related to the country's "indigenous" matters are not common events in teacher education classes. Yet despite the palpable sense of suspicion that attempts to suspend the state, and tangentially the nation, the latter is left almost untouched, even when celebrated and criticized for not delivering the promise announced in its written policies. This curricular event is another opportunity to exploit the fractal history of the nation and its failure as a curriculum organizer to deliver a profoundly altered state of ontological and epistemological affairs. Extensions of this moment of suspension, and these extensions as an extension of the "indigenous" event, can be generative for new curricular becomings.

The invitation to take a second look, or multiple looks, at educational reform and what authorizes them has been inspired precisely by classroom events such as the two described earlier. Policy analysis in Nicanor's class takes us back to the shores that this book departed from in Chapter 1, and specifically to where the invitation to take a second look at *lo indígena* and diversity was launched.

Notes

1 Mesa Técnica de Formación Inicial Docente, *Modelo del subsistema de formación inicial docente* (Guatemala: March, 2012).
2 Thomas S. Popkewitz, *A Political Sociology of Educational Reform: Power/Knowledge in Teaching, Teacher Education, and Research* (New York: Teachers College Press, 1991).
3 *Magisterio*, a word we will encounter throughout the chapter, refers to teaching, teachers, the body of teachers in a nation, the teaching profession, teacher training, and teacher education. It denotes mastership with authority and has meant and could also mean the academic degree or title of master. I will use the term in Spanish in the interest of brevity and to respect these multiple connotations. Additionally, it is the elementary education *magisterio* that is the target of this reform. According to the practice of teacher preparation in Guatemala, as was and is still the case in other contexts in the Americas and Europe, teachers were and are being prepared in normal schools for three years. In the case of Guatemala that is fourth to sixth grade, which are the last three years of secondary education. After graduation with a *magisterio* (teaching) degree, the

Authoritarian Regimes in Reform 159

students were able to teach in preschools or elementary schools depending on the program they had entered. In the "professionalization reform" analyzed in this chapter, these three years become the "initial phase." After the initial phase, the students are expected to enter higher education to complete the "specialization phase" to be eligible to teach.

4 Bernie Morales, "Ilumina FM. Nueva Reforma Magisterial Inicial En 2013," accessed March 4, 2014, http://ilumina.fm/noticias/nueva-reforma-magisterial-inicia-en-2013/. For the Spanish original see Appendix 10, item 1.

5 The reform proposal presented by the Ministry of Education stated: "Initial teacher education emerges as a response to the educational policies that include, among others, the push for development of each *Pueblo* and linguistic community, privileging intercultural relations, as well as the development of science and technology. . . ." For the Spanish original see Appendix 10, item 2. Mesa Técnica de Formación Inicial Docente, *Modelo del subsistema de formación inicial docente, propuesta*, 21.

6 *Modelo de formación inicial docente-propuesta*. (Roughly "Model for Initial Teacher Preparation-Proposal"). *Propuesta de Carrera Docente, Parte Académica, y Técnico-Administrativa*. (Roughly "Proposal for the Teaching Career, Academic, and Technical-Administrative Sections").

Access to negotiations about the reform, to policy officials, and to students and parents directly involved in the protests was a challenge given the delicate nature of the situation. There were serious concerns about safety; some students had been taken to the hospital with serious injuries, and the minister of education herself suffered a fractured arm. The negotiation meetings were inaccessible due to heightened security. Leaders of the reform team from the Ministry of Education, as well as others in the organization, were highly apprehensive about giving interviews.

7 William F. Pinar, *What Is Curriculum Theory?*, Studies in Curriculum Theory (Mahwah: Lawrence Erlbaum, 2004).

8 Mesa Técnica de Formación Inicial Docente, *Modelo del subsistema de formación inicial docente*, 2. For the Spanish original see Appendix 10, item 3.

9 "La reforma educativa detrás de la discordia," *La Hora—Tribuna, No Mostrador*, accessed March 1, 2014, www.lahora.com.gt/index.php/nacional/guatemala/reportajes-y-entrevistas/159681-la-reforma-educativa-detras-de-la-discordia. For the Spanish original see Appendix 10, item 4. Students' perspectives were rarely available through the media, and when they were, they were often dismissed for being inauthentic and manipulated by particular political views.

10 Field notes July 26, 2012. For the Spanish original see Appendix 10, item 5.

11 The Oxlajuj B'ak'tun referred to "an important date in the Mayan count" or as some narrated it, "the end of the world according to the Maya."

12 Popol Wuj are a set of "texts" whose "origins" are located in the Maya K'iche' "culture." Carlos M. López, *Los Popol Wuj y sus epistemologías: Las diferencias, el conocimiento y los ciclos del infinito* (Quito: Abya-Yala, 1999). The texts are about K'iche' mythology and history prior to the arrival of the Spaniards in the sixteenth century. The transition between mythology and history is an interesting literary regression that Maya intellectual Sam Colop engages with in his last book. Luis Enrique Sam Colop, *Popol Wuj/Popol Vuh* (Guatemala: F&G Editores, 2011). Many dilemmas are associated with the translation of the Popol Wuj and how they have come to be available to us. Sam Colop, among others, addresses some of those tensions from a linguistics perspective.

13 Carlos M. López, "Tiempo y fractales" (conference paper, Oxlajuj B'aqtun: Cambio de Ciclo y Sus Desafíos K'exk'exal Majkixhtaj K'al Jelanilehal, Guatemala City, 2011). For the Spanish original see Appendix 10, item 6.

160   Authoritarian Regimes in Reform

14. Ibid. For the Spanish original see Appendix 10, item 7. See also, López, *Los Popol Wuj y sus epistemologías.*
15. Boaventura de Sousa Santos, "Public Sphere and Epistemologies of the South," *African Development* 37, no. 1 (2012): 43–67; and Boaventura de Sousa Santos, *Epistemologies of the South: Justice Against Epistemicide* (Boulder: Paradigm Publishers, 2014).
16. Beatrice Avalos-Bevan, "Critical Issues and Policy Directions Affecting Teacher Education in Seven Latin American Countries" (Comparative and International Education Conference, San Juan, Puerto Rico, 2012). See also, Denise Vaillant, *Formación de docentes en América Latina: re-inventando el modelo tradicional* (Barcelona: Octaedro, 2005). For more on teacher preparation in Latin America and the Caribbean see, for example, Isabel Flores Arévalo and Luis Miguel Saravia, eds., *La formación docente en América Latina y el Caribe* (Lima: Ministerio de Educación, GTZ, UNESCO, 2004); Ramón Ulises Salgado Peña, ed., *La formación de docentes en América Latina* (Tegucigalpa: Fondo Editorial Universidad Pedagógica Nacional Francisco Morazán, 2006); Isabel Flores Arévalo, ed., *¿Cómo estamos formando a los maestros en América Latina?* (Lima: Ministerio de Educación, GTZ, UNESCO, 2004); UNESCO et al., *Formación pedagógica de docentes de educación superior en América Latina y el Caribe: REDESLAC, perspectivas y relaciones* (Caracas: CRESALC: La División, 1988).
17. Relying on a particular set of unstated and unquestioned quality indicators that explain (presumably) that other nations are performing better than Guatemala, the proposed reform states that "different from most Latin American countries, initial teacher preparation [in Guatemala] is not carried out in teachers' colleges or at the university." Mesa Técnica de Formación Inicial Docente, *Modelo del subsistema de formación inicial docente*, March 2012, 9. For the Spanish original see Appendix 10, item 8. On the limits of quality as a particular regime of government and self-government see Maarten Simons and Jan Masschelein, "The Permanent Quality Tribunal in Education and the Limits of Education Policy," *Policy Futures in Education* 4, no. 3 (2006): 292–305.
18. The complete title of the degree in Spanish is *Bachillerato en Ciencias y Letras con Orientación en Educación* (Baccalaureate in Letters and Sciences with Educational Orientation).
19. *Secondary education* was offered in 1945 (with the opening of the Faculty of Humanities at Universidad de San Carlos (USAC) and was expanded in 1968 (after the opening of the School of Teacher Education for *Enseñanza Media*—roughly middle school). In 2003, through Ministry Accord No. 923, normal schools preparing *pre-primary and primary education* teachers were given university accreditation. In the same year the government attempted a professionalization of *magisterio* and the preparation of *school administrators* at the university level. After a semester in operation and with 50,000 teachers enrolled at three universities, the program was closed. And in 2008 the Academic Program for Teachers' Professional Development (PADEP) was created at USAC. In 2009 the program was offered in ninety-five municipalities and graduated 2,543 *in-service* pre-primary and primary education teachers. Oscar Hugo López Rivas, *Carrera docente, parte académica y técnico-administrativa: USAID reforma educativa en el aula and Universidad de San Carlos de Guatemala escuela de formación de profesores de enseñanza media* (Guatemala, 2011). For a descriptive account of the types of teacher preparation programs offered at the university level, see, for example, Luis Alfredo Revol Piril, "La formación de docentes en Guatemala," in *La formación de docentes en América Latina* (Tegucigalpa: Fondo Editorial Universidad Pedagógica Nacional Francisco Morazán, 2006), 181–93.
20. Perhaps the most characteristic feature of neoliberalism is the systematic application of state authority, in a variety of antidemocratic policies and practices, to impose market imperatives on public policy development?

Authoritarian Regimes in Reform 161

21 "Marcha por la defense de la carrera de magisterio" (community page), *facebook*, accessed August 30, 2012, www.facebook.com/pages/Marcha-Por-La-Defensa-De-La-Carrera-De-Magisterio/597399613619824.
Given that the perspectives of those directly involved in the resistance were often absent from mainstream media, social networks have been key in providing a platform for those perspectives.

22 For an account of the sociocultural conditions of teacher preparation schools mainly told from the perspective of the students in the case of Mexico, see Margarita Teresa Rodríguez Ortega and Teresa de Jesús Negrete Arteaga, *Condiciones socioculturales en la formación de docentes para educación básica* (México: Universidad Pedagogica Nacional, 2010).

23 For an account, in the social networks, of how the events unfolded see, for example, "Marcha por la defense de la carrera de magisterio," www.facebook.com/pages/Marcha-Por-La-Defensa-De-La-Carrera-De-Magisterio/597399613619824

24 Popkewitz, *A Political Sociology of Educational Reform*, 1.

25 López Rivas, *Carrera docente, parte académica y técnico-administrativa*.

26 Educational quality improvement was part of the broader renovation impulses found throughout Latin America in the 1990s. Such reforms promoted certain defined political aims derived from international agreements and recommendations on "priorities and strategies to modernize education and teaching," with an emphasis on principles of educational quality and equity, and teacher improvement, educational capacity, information and evaluation systems for rigorous decision making in educational policies. Vaillant, *Formación de docentes en América Latina*, 13.

27 The claim that resonates in dissident circles is that the intercultural and bilingual components of the initial reform efforts were subtracted in the reformation of the *magisterio* in 2012.

28 Josefina Antillón Milla, "Educación, época contemporánea: 1898-1944," in *Historia general de Guatemala*, ed. F. Rojas Lima, vol. 5 (Guatemala: Asociación de Amigos del País, Fundación para la Cultura y el Desarrollo, 1996), 559-74. See also Bienvenido Argueta Hernández, "Ethnic Constitution in the Guatemalan Educational System: Toward a Phenomenological Analysis of the Birth of Racism in Pedagogical Discourses (1890-1930)" (Ph.D. Dissertation Education, Ohio University, 1998). See also Arnoldo Escobar, "Introducción al area de educación, época contemporánea: 1898-1944," in *Historia General de Guatemala*, ed. F. Rojas Lima, vol. 5 (Guatemala: Asociación de Amigos del País, Fundación para la Cultura y el Desarrollo, 1996), 557-58.

29 Benjamín Moscoso Palencia, "De la historía de la filosofia de la educación en Guatemala," in *Historia de la educación en Guatemala: Memoria XI encuentro nacional de investigadores educativos de Guatemala 2006; educación y equidad social: memoria XII encuentro nacional de investigadores educativos de Guatemala 2007*. (Guatemala de la Asunción: Universidad Rafael Landivar, 2008), 29-39; and Escobar, "Introducción al area de educación, época contemporánea: 1898-1944."

30 Bienvenido Argueta Hernández, "El discurso moderno de 1771-1895: Presentación durante el XI encuentro nacional de investigación educativa: Historia de la educación en Guatemala," in *Historia de la educación en Guatemala: Memoria XI encuentro nacional de investigadores educativos de Guatemala 2006; Educación y equidad social: memoria XII encuentro nacional de Investigadores educativos de Guatemala 2007* (Guatemala de la Asunción: Universidad Rafael Landivar, 2008), 161-67.

31 Antillón Milla, "Educación, época contemporánea: 1898-1944."

32 Ibid.

33 López Rivas, *Carrera docente, parte académica y técnico-administrativa: USAID reforma educativa en el aula and Universidad de San Carlos de Guatemala escuela de formación de profesores de enseñanza media*.

34 Castilianization and culturization efforts were in place before castilianization and culturization became the educational reform of progressives and revolutionaries of the democratic spring between 1944 and 1954.
35 Argueta Hernández, "El discurso moderno de 1771–1895: Presentación durante el XI encuentro nacional de investigación educativa: Historia de la educación en Guatemala."
36 From an article published in 1927 in the first year of the Journal *La Educación Rural* whose primary readership was meant to be rural teachers: "A very true statement is that those cultures or peoples who don't read are dead. . . . Poor people, they are blind because they live in darkness . . . What would a teacher be? Teachers read, it is necessary to renew the spirit, in the same way that nature does it with matter. Teachers read, make an effort, as you do when you buy candy, a ticket to a show, or a beer, and buy good books if you want to go, as Marden said: 'always ahead,' or if you want to live as the poet D'Anunzzio said: 'always awake.'" For the Spanish original see Appendix 10, item 9. "Renovarse es vivir," *La Educación Rural* 1, no. 4 (1927): 47.
37 Dipesh Chakrabarty, *Provincializing Europe: Postcolonial Thought and Historical Difference* (Princeton: Princeton University Press, 2000).
38 Federico Roncal Martínez, "Educación basada en competencias: Posibilidades y desilusiones," *Revista Guatemalteca de Educación* 1, no. 2 (2009): 35–63.
39 Alfredo Carrillo Ramírez, *Evolución histórica de la educación secundaria en Guatemala, desde el año 1831 hasta el año 1969*, 2 vols. (Guatemala: Editorial José de Pineda Ibarra, 1972).
40 La secretaría de educación pública, "Los Beneficios de La Lectura," *La Educación Rural* 1, no. 8 (1927), 111. For the Spanish original see Appendix 10, item 10. In an earlier issue of the same journal, a list of books that a teacher should read was published. Some in the list were *School and Society*, John Dewey; *Schools of Tomorrow*, John Dewey; *Experimental Pedagogy and the Psychology of The Child*, Édouard Claparède; *A New School in Belgium*, A. Faria de Vasconcellos. Publicaciones de la Secretaría de Educación Pública, *La Educación Rural* 1, no. 4 (1927).
41 Ricardo E. Lima Soto, *Memoria X encuentro nacional de investigadores educativos de Guatemala: Legislación e investigación educativa* (Guatemala: Universidad Rafael Landivar, February 2006), 129. For the Spanish original see Appendix 10, item 11.
42 López Rivas, *Carrera docente, parte académica y técnico-administrativa: USAID reforma educativa en el aula and Universidad de San Carlos de Guatemala escuela de formación de profesores de enseñanza media*, 20. For the Spanish original see Appendix 10, item 12.
43 Mesa Técnica de Formación Inicial Docente, *Modelo del subsistema de formación inicial docente*, 8. For the Spanish original see Appendix 10, item 13.
44 Ibid.
45 Ibid.
46 Ibid., 36. For the Spanish original see Appendix 10, item 14.
47 Ibid., 9. For the Spanish original see Appendix 10, item 15.
48 See Marteen Simons and Jan Masschelein, "The Permanent Quality Tribunal in Education and the Limits of Education Policy." *Policy Futures in Education* 4, no. 3 (2006): 292–305.
49 Ibid., 299.
50 Gita Steiner-Khamsi, ed., *The Global Politics of Educational Borrowing and Lending* (New York: Teachers College Press, 2004).
51 Vaillant, *Formación de docentes en América Latina*.
52 On inscription devices, see Simons and Masschelein, "The Permanent Quality Tribunal in Education and the Limits of Education Policy."

53 Rodolphe Gasché, *Europe, or The Infinite Task: A Study of a Philosophical Concept* (Stanford: Stanford University Press, 2009). Europe here denotes the non-South, following Boaventura de Sousa Santos, "the South is not a geographical location," although it can be and indeed is made geography, generating particular dynamics often of power. The South, for de Sousa Santos, is a metaphor of human suffering and of resistance to overcome or minimize that suffering, it is an anticolonial, anti-imperialist South, which exists in the "global North in the form of excluded, silenced, and marginalized populations, such as undocumented immigrants, the unemployed, ethnic or religious minorities, and victims of sexism, homophobia and racism." de Sousa Santos, "Public Sphere and Epistemologies of the South," 51. See also de Sousa Santos, *Epistemologies of the South*.

54 Mesa Técnica de Formación Inicial Docente, *Modelo del subsistema de formación inicial docente*.

55 Ibid., 12–13. For the Spanish original see Appendix 10, item 16.

56 Mesa Técnica de Formación Inicial Docente, *Modelo del subsistema de formación inicial docente*, 13–14. For the Spanish original see Appendix 10, item 17.

57 Ibid., 13. For the Spanish original see Appendix 10, item 18.

58 Ibid. For the Spanish original see Appendix 10, item 18.

59 *Decreto 1485 del congreso de la Republica de Guatemala. Escalafón docente* is a system to hierarchically classify teachers according to their education, teaching experience, and merits. According to these particular established norms, teachers can "climb up the ladder" or "ascend" in the system.

60 *1927 Ley orgánica y reglamentaria del personal docente de la república*.

61 López Rivas, *Carrera docente, parte académica y técnico-administrativa: USAID reforma educativa en el aula* and *Universidad de San Carlos de Guatemala escuela de formación de profesores de enseñanza media.*, 5, 9. For the Spanish original see Appendix 10, item 19.

62 Ibid., 18–19. For the Spanish original see Appendix 10, item 20.

63 Simons and Masschelein, "The Permanent Quality Tribunal in Education and the Limits of Education Policy."

64 Michael A. Sells, *Mystical Languages of Unsaying* (Chicago: University of Chicago Press, 1994).

65 Mesa Técnica de Formación Inicial Docente, *Modelo del subsistema de formación inicial docente, propuesta*, 14.

66 Lima Soto, "Memoria X encuentro nacional de investigadores educativos de Guatemala: Legislación e investigación educativa."

67 Ricardo E. Lima Soto, *Memoria X encuentro nacional de investigadores educativos de Guatemala*. For the Spanish original see Appendix 10, item 21.

68 Ibid., 21, 12, 22, 8, 12. For the Spanish original see Appendix 10, item 21.

69 Mesa Técnica de Formación Inicial Docente, *Modelo del subsistema de formación inicial docente, propuesta*, March 2012, 11. For the Spanish original see Appendix 10, item 22.

70 López Rivas, *Carrera docente, parte académica y técnico-administrativa*. For the Spanish original see Appendix 10, item 23.

71 Jacques Rancière. *Dissensus: On Politics and Aesthetics* (London: Continuum International Publishing Group, 2010).

72 Gilles Deleuze and Claire Parnet, *Dialogues II* (New York: Columbia University Press, 2007); Gilles Deleuze and Felix Guattari, *A Thousand Plateaus: Capitalism and Schizophrenia*, trans. Brian Massumi (Minneapolis: University of Minnesota Press, 1987); Gilles Deleuze and Felix Guattari, *Kafka: Toward a Minor Literature* (Minneapolis: University of Minnesota Press, 1986).

73 Bruno Latour, *What Is the Style of Matters of Concern?* (Amsterdam: Uitgeverij Van Gorcum, 2005).

74 Ibid., 39.
75 Classroom observation (Language and Literature in L1), April 19, 2013.
76 Classroom observation (Indigenous Language and Learning Class), March 21, 2013.

References

Antillón Milla, Josefina. "Educación, época contemporánea: 1898–1944." In *Historia general de Guatemala*, edited by F. Rojas Lima, vol. 5, 559–74 Guatemala: Asociación de Amigos del País, Fundación para la Cultura y el Desarrollo, 1996.
Arévalo, Isabel Flores, ed. *¿Cómo estamos formando a los maestros en América Latina?* Lima: Ministerio de Educación, GTZ, UNESCO, 2004.
Arévalo, Isabel Flores, and Luis Miguel Saravia, eds. *La formación docente en América Latina y el Caribe*. Lima: Ministerio de Educación, GTZ, UNESCO, 2004.
Argueta Hernández, Bienvenido. "El discurso moderno de 1771–1895: Presentación durante el XI encuentro nacional de investigación educativa: Historia de la educación en Guatemala." In *Historia de la educación en Guatemala: Memoria XI encuentro nacional de investigadores educativos de Guatemala 2006; Educación y equidad social: memoria XII encuentro nacional de Investigadores educativos de Guatemala 2007*, 161–67. Guatemala de la Asunción: Universidad Rafael Landivar, 2008.
―――. "Ethnic Constitution in the Guatemalan Educational System: Toward a Phenomenological Analysis of the Birth of Racism in Pedagogical Discourses (1890–1930)." Ph.D. Dissertation, Education, Ohio University, 1998.
Avalos-Bevan, Beatrice. "Critical Issues and Policy Directions Affecting Teacher Education in Seven Latin American Countries." Paper presented at the annual meeting of the 56th Annual Conference of the Comparative and International Education Society, San Juan, Puerto Rico, April 2012.
Carrillo Ramírez, Alfredo. *Evolución histórica de la educación secundaria en Guatemala, desde el año 1831 hasta el año 1969*. 2 vols. Guatemala: Editorial José de Pineda Ibarra, 1972.
Chakrabarty, Dipesh. *Provincializing Europe: Postcolonial Thought and Historical Difference*. Princeton: Princeton University Press, 2000.
Deleuze, Gilles, and Felix Guattari. *Kafka: Toward a Minor Literature*. Minneapolis: University of Minnesota Press, 1986.
―――. *A Thousand Plateaus: Capitalism and Schizophrenia*. Translated by Brian Massumi. Minneapolis: University of Minnesota Press, 1987.
Derrida, Jacques. *Aporias*. Stanford: Stanford University Press, 1993.
Escobar, Arnoldo. "Introducción al area de educación, época contemporánea: 1898–1944." In *Historia General de Guatemala*, edited by F. Rojas Lima, vol. 5, 557–58. Guatemala: Asociación de Amigos del País, Fundación para la Cultura y el Desarrollo, 1996.
Gasché, Rodolphe. *Europe, or The Infinite Task: A Study of a Philosophical Concept*. Stanford: Stanford University Press, 2009.
"La reforma educativa detrás de la discordia." *La Hora—Tribuna, No Mostrador*. Accessed March 1, 2014. www.lahora.com.gt/index.php/nacional/guatemala/reportajes-y-entrevistas/159681-la-reforma-educativa-detras-de-la-discordia.
La secretaría de educación pública. "Los Beneficios de La Lectura." *La Educación Rural* 1, no. 8 (1927): 111.

Authoritarian Regimes in Reform   165

Latour, Bruno. *What Is the Style of Matters of Concern?* Amsterdam: Uitgeverij Van Gorcum, 2005.

Lima Soto, Ricardo E. *Memoria X encuentro nacional de investigadores educativos de Guatemala: Legislación e investigación educativa.* Guatemala: Universidad Rafael Landivar, February 2006.

López, Carlos M. *Los Popol Wuj y sus epistemologías: Las diferencias, el conocimiento y los ciclos del infinito.* Quito: Abya-Yala, 1999.

———. "Tiempo y fractales." Paper presented at Oxlajuj B'aqtun: Cambio de Ciclo y Sus Desafíos K'exk'exal Majkixhtaj K'al Jelanilehal, Guatemala City, 2011.

López Rivas, Oscar Hugo. *Carrera docente, parte académica y técnico-administrativa: USAID reforma educativa en el aula and Universidad de San Carlos de Guatemala escuela de formación de profesores de enseñanza media.* Guatemala, 2011.

"Marcha por la defense de la carrera de magisterio" (community page). *facebook.* Accessed August 30, 2012. www.facebook.com/pages/Marcha-Por-La-Defensa-De-La-Carrera-De-Magisterio/597399613619824.

Mesa Técnica de Formación Inicial Docente. "Modelo del subsistema de formación inicial docente." Guatemala, March 2012.

Morales, Bernie. "Ilumina FM: Nueva Reforma Magisterial Inicial En 2013."Accessed March 4, 2014. http://ilumina.fm/noticias/nueva-reforma-magisterial-inicia-en-2013/.

Moscoso Palencia, Benjamín. "De la historia de la filosofia de la educación en Guatemala." In *Historia de la educación en Guatemala: Memoria XI encuentro nacional de investigadores educativos de Guatemala 2006; educación y equidad social: memoria XII encuentro nacional de investigadores educativos de Guatemala 2007,* 29–39. Guatemala de la Asunción: Universidad Rafael Landivar, 2008.

Pinar, William F. *What Is Curriculum Theory? Studies in Curriculum Theory.* Mahwah: Lawrence Erlbaum, 2004.

Popkewitz, Thomas S. *A Political Sociology of Educational Reform: Power/Knowledge in Teaching, Teacher Education, and Research.* New York: Teachers College Press, 1991.

Rancière, Jacques. *Dissensus: On Politics and Aesthetics.* London: Continuum International Publishing Group, 2010.

"Renovarse es vivir." *La Educación Rural* 1, no. 4 (1927): 47.

Revol Piril, Luis Alfredo. "La formación de docentes en Guatemala." In *La formación de docentes en América Latina,* edited by Ramón Ulises Salgado, 181–93. Tegucigalpa: Fondo Editorial Universidad Pedagógica Nacional Francisco Morazán, 2006.

Rodríguez Ortega, Margarita Teresa, and Teresa de Jesús Negrete Arteaga. *Condiciones socioculturales en la formación de docentes para educación básica.* México: Universidad Pedagogica Nacional, 2010.

Roncal Martínez, Federico. "Educación basada en competencias: Posibilidades y desilusiones." *Revista Guatemalteca de Educación* 1, no. 2 (2009): 35–63.

Salgado Peña, Ramón Ulises, ed. *La formación de docentes en América Latina.* Tegucigalpa: Fondo Editorial Universidad Pedagógica Nacional Francisco Morazán, 2006.

Sam Colop, Luis Enrique. *Popol Wuj / Popol Vuh.* Guatemala: F&G Editores, 2011.

Sells, Michael A. *Mystical Languages of Unsaying.* Chicago: University of Chicago Press, 1994.

Simons, Maarten, and Jan Masschelein. "The Permanent Quality Tribunal in Education and the Limits of Education Policy." *Policy Futures in Education* 4, no. 3 (2006): 292–305.

Sousa Santos, Boaventura de. *Epistemologies of the South: Justice Against Epistemicide*. Boulder: Paradigm Publishers, 2014.

———. "Public Sphere and Epistemologies of the South." *African Development* 37, no. 1 (2012): 43–67.

Steiner-Khamsi, Gita, ed. *The Global Politics of Educational Borrowing and Lending*. New York: Teachers College Press, 2004.

Unesco., Regional Center for Higher Education in Latin America and the Caribbean., Unesco., and División de Educación Superior y Formación del Personal de Educación. *Formación pedagógica de docentes de educación superior en América Latina y el Caribe: REDESLAC, perspectivas y relaciones*. Caracas: CRESALC: La División, 1988.

Vaillant, Denise. *Formación de docentes en América Latina: re-inventando el modelo tradicional*. Barcelona: Octaedro, 2005.

5   No Closure

Beginning One

So

    I know your academic deals far too well
    I know you hold her hostage
    Chained to your supremacy
    And as I speak
    You whip her
    So she never attempts to run away
    You punch her
    In the stomach
    So she spits the words out
    The question that shouldn't need to be asked
    Because your method shoulda been self-explanatory
    The fifth or sixth step of your method couldn't be clearer
    Findings
    Results
    Answers
    So you punch her again
    Harder
    'Til she can no longer . . .
    'Til her last breath screams
    "So?"
    But you aren't satisfied
    Till you suck the last bit of suspicion and rejection out of her
    Till she masters your mastery
    You grab her so tight
    Force yourself into her
    Till she and you fuse
    You believe you have succeeded
    As she asks
    So?

    So?
    You repeat

168 *No Closure*

Standing tall over the plantation
You ask
So what?
You ask me
Now that you've done all that historical work
Now that you've done all that intellectual work
Now that you've done all that theoretical work
What are you going to *do*?
What is the result?
What is the answer?
What is the solution?
You come for me
to hold me hostage too
To assimilate me into you
To tame my untamable wild and rebel soul

I refuse
Like the Indians rejecting Columbus at the encounter
I refuse
Like the Haitians rejecting slavery
I refuse
Like Jake Roper rejecting Don Dale
I refuse
Like Berta Cáceres rejecting you
I refuse

My inquiry refuses too
For it can't be domesticated
Converted
Subjected
To the extractive practices
That threaten me to protect you

There is no "so?"
Deal with it.
My inquiry does not produce
Results of experiments
Like syphilis in women's bodies
Black bodies in massive prisons
Or ethnic wars
It produces agitation
Screams desire to escape
Demands and builds
The impossible

There is no "so?"
Or "I understand what you are against
But what are you for?"
What I am for is against you!

And your violence upon that which opposes you
And your ruthless dictatorship
Over what counts as being
Thinking
And
Doing

So what I've got is a message for that sister
you believe you took
She no longer needs you
She never needed you
She is invention
She is marroonage
She is everything you can't keep

Dear reader,

Thank you for conversing with me as we walked together through the pages in this book. I do not have a conclusion that summarizes the book, ties it neatly, and packages it away. This is not that kind of book. There is no conclusion here but a call for invention, marroonage, and what can't be kept. At a time when that which is outside the norm/al is suppressed (#EmergingUs), when what does not fit is removed and displaced (#NoDAPL), when what fails to comply is incarcerated and exterminated (#BLM), there cannot be conclusions or closures. In this particular political moment new kinds of people are being made up, others are being re-made, and others are simply being exterminated. These last few pages are not closure. The times call for more than that. The four monologues that follow suggest the consequential, demand the impossible, and call for invention. I apologize for the linear order in which I present these three beginnings. Sometimes language triumphs in retaining the status quo.

Beginning Two

Monologues

Science

"That was a good presentation.
The statistics,
the charts,
the facts,
and figures the presenter provided . . .
they show how it *really* is."

Declarations like these are common. You hear them emerge as audiences discuss research findings, results, answers, and solutions to problems in conferences, meetings, and gatherings of human scientists and scholars in the humanities. They are often expressed in response to presentations addressing matters of public concern (often educational, sociological, political, or related to human rights). Do you ever consider how the charts, facts, statistics, and figures have been fabricated to deliver a sense of certainty about reality? Do you question the visual fabrication of facts reasoned numerically, and enabled by positivistic histories of meaning making via "science," allegedly indisputable, limitless, natural, and given? How, in the name of science and through particular interpretations of science, are realities charted? And how are these interpretations used to order perception, determine what is real, what is to be acted upon, and how? This work has attempted to expose the historically contingent process of making an object of scientific inquiry, to understand the shifting articulations in the process, and at the same moment to suspend these scientific orientations to consider the effects they produce. This inquiry was produced at the limits of thinking in the educational sciences. It embraced the invitation to cross disciplinary boundaries and think through the histories of science, philosophies of difference, and postfoundational approaches. They were only instrumental collectives to inquire in less conventional and reductive ways about the educational horizons of enactment set for important matters including diversity, difference, and indigeneity. However, these collectives are far from being solutions and answers. In fact they insist on informed, thoughtful, deconstructive, and consequential critiques of themselves. My critique of the collective comes in the subtle curatorial process of selecting, from a rather large body of work, specific notions that are consequential to the political commitments in this inquiry. These notions are consequential in that they seek to inspire meditations and inform debates about curriculum and education that are seriously invested in plurality and diversity. Returning to "science," the inquiry in this work calls for a re-evaluation of the scientific and of science-like approximations that order perception, in order to stop and interrogate the immunity that these approximations enjoy. Let us question how, via claims to the "scientific," statistics, figures, and facts delay, distract, inhibit, and order our capacity to notice what is at stake in education, thereby taming the possible impossibilities in the question of diversity.

Eventalizing

> "If Mrs. Rigoberta Menchú is so Maya
> why doesn't she sleep on a *petate*[1]
> and why does she wear deodorant?"
> "Indigenous people are illiterate,"
> "the Mayan students do not know how
> to speak in *their own* language, and
> they don't want to wear *their own* indigenous clothes."
> "The Mayas of today are not like the Mayas from the past."
> "These are not Mayas"

Does it surprise you that these statements emerged from contemporary educational contexts in Guatemala? Indigenous peoples, like other peoples made different, are often turned into fixities in the making of policies, in curriculum planning, for educational reforms, and in political discussions within the academia, on the streets, and by the state. What statements emerge within the contexts you know best? How are "Aboriginals," "Pacific Islanders," "Native Americans," "Latinas," "Blacks," "First Nations," "Roma," "Moroccans," "Turks," "Syrian," "scheduled castes," "migrants," "tribal," "asylum seekers," "displaced people," and "refugees" talked about in education, policies, and research? Eventalizing is a style of inquiry that historicizes how differences become salient and move, and insists on the study of differences in motion as contested, varying, and unstable. *Lo indígena* is an event that is perceptible through moments of intensity, marked at times of historical contestation. Eventalizing is a political proposal to continue setting in motion that which runs the risk of becoming set within containable borders. When addressing curriculum issues, we should pay serious consideration to the permanent contestation over difference and its boundaries, as much as the mechanics of its constitution, and to how these boundaries participate in defining curriculum. Curricular activities—including design, planning, implementation, history, theory—can no longer ignore twentieth-century legacies of indigenous making if they aspire to address the question of diversity or issues of participation and access in educational spaces.

Guatemala

"How could you ask educational questions
decentering such an important thing as the nation?"
"The state does not do anything."

Why do we in education find it so hard to think of education and research outside of the nation? What are we losing when complex educational matters get bounded by geopolitical borders? What if, instead of being the first and most determinant entity for examining and planning education, the nation-state is considered just one of many elements in the nexus from which multiple educational dynamics emerge? And two more questions. When raising indigenous concerns one must remember that the nation-state signifies invasion, imposition, and extraction. Why must we expect the nation-state to *deliver* when what we have learned from critical histories is that the nation-state has often *taken*? Why continue to recenter the nation-state even when the efforts are to challenge, interrogate, and oppose its supremacy? The locale of this inquiry—which raises questions about the making-up of difference and the limits of diversity—is Guatemala. A crossroads of migratory ideas, aspirations, and tactics originating in multiple locations (which are also determined by the geopolitical borders) in "Europe" and the "Americas" is Guatemala. "Guate no existe."[2] Guatemala is not the alpha and the omega. A meeting of aspirations, struggles for clean water, clean air, natural resources, and land is Guatemala. Land of struggle for existence for that which cannot be translated into Guatemala as the nation-state is Guatemala. "Indigenous" is an event in Guatemala, on Guatemala, and through Guatemala. Guatemala is an event. The making-up of "indigenous" and difference has occured in Guatemala and has also made Guatemala. Inquiring into the making up of kinds of people and diversity could have been comparative between Guatemala and Peru, or Mexico, Bolivia, Australia, Kenya, Norway, the United States, etc. Notice the prominence of the nation-state. I have inquired into the making-up of kinds of people and diversity through a transnational approach. Notice still the presence of the nation-state. Though this approach is aware of the nation-state, it does not take Guatemala for granted and understands its eventual production through the exchange of knowledges, experts, and expert institutions from places such as Germany, France, the United States, and Mexico, which have come together historically in the indigenous event. "Indigenous" and its making is a singularity not just of Guatemala, but one that repeats itself fractally; not as sameness, as native, tribal, aboriginal, and many other "others" in other places and spaces. If you were to suspend the nation-state, what inquiry and interrogations would emerge, and how would you go about investigating diversity in the contexts that puzzle and trouble you? If you are in the field of education, how are "teachers," "teacher educators," "curriculum scholars," and "policy makers" complicit in the making-up of kinds of people and diversity in those very contexts that fall within the nation as the orbit?

Teaching

> Teachers matter again.
> There have been multiple waves of who is to blame for school's inability to fix society
> The curriculum what
> The curriculum how
> The policies
> The pupils
> The teachers
> society itself

How have teachers mattered in schooling? What are and have been teachers' roles in the making up of human kinds and the fabrication of difference in schools? How have teachers been made-up and then how have they been making history? Teachers certainly are a contested site: I am on the side of rebellion. Rebellion, not primarily against the easily recognized hegemonic forces of the state, the oligarchy, imperialism, supremacy, etc., although that too, but rebellion against that which has become familiar. Rebellion against the search for who or what we are. We are teachers. We are experts. We are this identity. We are that identity. That is the familiar. That is what we have produced as sacred and protected, and the work of those who dare question must be dismissed. That line of reasoning takes us back to the very colonial practices that are rejected in the first place. That is the familiar that this rebellion refuses. I am on the side of rebellion that refuses education—education as the recapitulation of colonial practices that are so incisive that we fail to notice because we fear to question. Rebellion is the still-possible space invented in the interaction between those historically made up as teachers, as somebody other than the missionary, expert, or state functionary, and those historically made up as learners, as something other than the object of conversion, salvation, migration, and revitalization. Rebellion is knowing that under the mandated state curricula, which presumably suppress nonmandated curricula, lie infinite fractal possibilities. Technologies to control teachers and teaching, regardless of the nation-state, have not yet outsmarted the resilience, resourcefulness, and agility generated among "teachers" and/as "students" within a classroom. Rebellion is taking the mandated curricula and their standards and subjecting them to interrogation, rearticulation, debate, and dispute when no one is watching. The familiar are a very limited version of the curriculum. They have been instructed to pretend they aren't limited by the totality. They need to pretend so that the curriculum maker feels trapped and lost. Pretend back. Pretend you are trapped and lost. You may already be doing a good job at pretending. Let's share, while we pretend, how we are interrogating, rearticulating, debating, and disputing curricula. Please allow me to have a go.

Beginning Three

Mira. History Not Yet History

A Rough Draft

Mira. is an encounter that is difficult to qualify as a "work in progress" because "progress" is one of the normalizing orders that the book and *Mira.* insist must be interrogated. "In the making" comes too close to "making" in making up people, which is also another order troubled in both the book and *Mira. Mira.* is becoming. *Mira.* is not a project. It is not protection and projection of that which cannot be unavowable. I learned, from the young people in Guatemala that are producing *Mira.*, that *Mira.* seeks to expose the avowable. "*La historia que aun no es historia.*" "History which isn't yet history." That is the subtitle of the show given by the curators. *Mira.* is an exposition and a show. *Mira.* means "look" and is accentuated desire to focus, literally, one's view on issues that matter.

The curators, Daniel, Yenifer, Rafael, and Higinio Marcelo, are from Patzún, Parramos, Ixcán, and Guineales in Guatemala. In December 2016 they made their way to Antigua, Guatemala, and the photo archive to "look."[3] With public funding from the New Arts Venture Challenge from the Arts Institute at the University of Wisconsin-Madison, these four young people and teachers interrupted the photo archive and its familiarity with

Figure 5.1 Untitled

experts. This was Daniel, Yenifer, Rafael, and Higinio Marcelo's first time in a photo archive like the one in CIRMA. What the archive knew about these young people was in boxes, in a temperature-controlled room that chills. Archivists, historians, anthropologists, sociologists, and legal scholars, among other experts, have been there many times, through the boxes, through the images, making stories, and making-up people. I invited Daniel, Yenifer, Rafael, and Marcelo to come to the photo archive to interrupt, unmake, and invent collaboration, teacher preparation, and interconnectivity within contexts of shared and ambivalent histories. I will return to this later.

I met Daniel, Yenifer, Rafael, and Higinio Marcelo four years ago in teacher preparation classrooms and Mayan family homes. Back then they were some of the student teachers and youth whom you have met throughout the book; now three of them are teachers. They met each other for the first time through *Mira*. Daniel grew up speaking "Kaqchikel" and "Spanish," Yenifer grew up speaking "Spanish," Rafael grew up speaking "Popti" and "Spanish," and Higinio Marcelo "K'iche'" and "Spanish." Although some of them had heard each other's *pueblos'* names before, they knew very little about them and their histories. *Mira.* began to foster an interregional exchange for these "Guatemalan" youth. Over a period of six intense days they collaborated in putting together a provocative and compelling show of thirty-three archival images. The two images in this section are part of that show.

When I proposed to Dani, Yeni, Rafa, and Marcelo (the names they use for each other) that they join *Mira.*, I told them that Guatemala's photographic archives tell untold stories about "indigenous" lives, "diversity," education, history, and the imagination, and that *Mira.* has a double intention. First it draws from the young people's innovations and aspirations in order to challenge the colonial history of exhibits, by piercing academic and non-academic spaces with images that relate to "indigenous" matters from their own experiences (some of the curators identify as "Maya"). The second intention of *Mira.* is to invite viewers to learn, meditate, inquire, reflect, and attempt to understand one of Latin America's most violent historical contexts: the experiences of "Maya" people. In the "Americas," where the United States is a crucial entity, Latin American histories, and "indigenous Guatemalan" histories in particular, are a fertile space to join efforts in rethinking, for instance, schools, social and racial relations, politics and families, history and geography, "indigenous ways of being," migration, and how we make the "Other."

Gender, activism, peace, war, death, what is real, what does indigenous look like, and what is a photograph were the most prominent discussions and emergent curriculum in the curatorial unraveling. As they opened boxes full of photographic positives and clicked on images in electronic files, the young people told stories of disappeared family members, relatives who were combatants in the war, and neighbors who witnessed tactics of war and torture. The discussions were expansive. Each narrative led to multiple others and those lead to others as if they had been waiting for far too long to be released. The presentation of "human" subjects in the images produced multiple silences and close examination of the visualities of bodies, accessories, clothing, hair, smile, strength, and the historical conditions that queer the norms of what a woman or a man can, is, and ought to *(fill in the blank)*. The images asked the curators to meditate on how they see gender. The curators asked the images to say more, to show more. Dani, Yeni, Rafa, and Marcelo were fully aware that *Mira.* would meet viewers in other parts of the world and that it would go on asking others questions. As the images were emerging from the archive, sometimes the curators praised them for delivering truth, for showing "how things really were"; other times they dismissed the poor image for failing to deliver clarity and impact. They knew *Mira.* would find other young people in the United States, Australia, and Guatemala who would "talk back." The curators worried about how others would see Guatemala. They sought acceptance. They also sought concern for the history the images can tell and which is not yet history.

Before *Mira.* is shown in the United States, Australia, and Guatemala, its thirty-three images will meet secondary and high school students in these countries with shared and ambivalent histories like those being made and told by *Mira.*: indigenous stories, stories of aboriginality, genocide, multiculturalism, "undocumented" immigration, resistance, invasion, incarceration, removal, but more importantly the multitude of other stories that can only emerge when art meets young people with important cultural legacies that must invent ways to communicate at the limits of the depleted languages currently in existence. Through a process of visual transformation, transfiguration, and transcoloration (adding color, extracting color, disorienting objects, stretching, expanding, shrinking the image, and manipulating its multiple elements), the young people will respond to *Mira.* They will talk back at those who made the images, the images' objects, the histories that produce the image; anything and everything their encounter with the images provokes. When the thirty-three images in *Mira.* are hung in a gallery, a library, or a hall, they will be accompanied by the talk back, that is thirty-three additional images no longer *Mira.*, but new creations, with new meanings, provoking other meditations, interrogating, demanding another look. The talk back is a complex nexus—of interconnections between young people in Guatemala and other contexts, and back to Guatemala—in which ages, stages, and ranking collapse, as does the conservative wall that borders the historically made-up teacher and the historically made-up student.

I think *Mira.* and the talk back are on to something, something that involves the collapse of more walls, collaborations to co-create unmaking, generating means of communicating the unavowable. Might these be possibilities for curriculum otherwise?

Figure 5.2 "Juego de Niños"

Notes

1 A mat that serves as a bed made of woven dry fibers of a palm tree. Etymologically the word comes from the Náhuatl word *petlatl*. Many friends and family in Guatemala and the Caribbean coast of Colombia slept on these when they were children. Those who sleep on *petates* are understood to be lacking resources to sleep on a "proper" bed with a mattress, are often from the villages as opposed to the cities, and are not yet modern.
2 Francisco Goldman, *The Long Night of White Chickens* (New York: Grove Press, 1992).
3 The photo archive of the *Centro de Investigaciones Regionales de Mesoamerica* (CIRMA).

Reference

Goldman, Francisco. *The Long Night of White Chickens*. New York: Grove Press, 1992.

Appendix 1
Linguistics Program Guatemalan University

Guatemalan University (GU) was founded in Guatemala City in the 1960s. There are over a dozen universities in Guatemala and a few other institutes, schools, and centers of higher education, most of which are private. GU is one of them. Similar to many other universities, GU has several branches throughout the country, especially in more urbanized areas. These areas serve as centers of convergence where students from all strata participate in higher education programs—from the social and health sciences to engineering and the humanities. The humanities is composed of two schools: the School of Languages and the School of Linguistics. GU is considered a pioneer in offering linguistics and sociolonguistics programs in the country.

In the mid-1980s the newly constituted Applied Linguistics Program in Secondary Education[1] and the Sociolinguistics Program[2] opened up "new fields of study" in the country. The two programs emerged as a response to deal with the "problems derived from multilingualism,"[3] to build "solid foundations [for] bilingual-bicultural education,"[4] and to "address the problems that the educational system faces."[5] The Applied Linguistics Program in secondary education is a three-year degree. Graduates of this program receive the equivalent of a teaching certification with an emphasis on bilingual and intercultural education. At the time of this research, the students attending the program aspired to become secondary education teachers. The majority of them were planning on continuing the Sociolinguistic Program, which is a higher degree that lasts two years. The courses offered in each of the programs have had a practical orientation so that the students can work within public and private institutions in the nation. The content of the courses has focused on the "ethnic groups of the country." In 2002 the School of Linguistics began offering the Master's in Sociolinguistics program.

The program holds classes during the weekend as most of the students work full time. The students commute from Guatemala City, nearby towns, and towns as far away as nine hours' travel. Most of the students are self-paying, whereas indigenous students from rural areas are funded through scholarships so that they "have the opportunity to get a higher education degree." "According to the statistics," said the director of the school, "there is a lack of indigenous professionals compared to other sectors."

180 *Appendix 1*

The three programs have prepared linguists and sociolinguists who have become leaders in shaping language matters in the country. Several of them have worked within the Ministry of Education engineering the institutionalization of linguistics in the country. These linguists and sociolinguists have worked in making (language education and multicultural) policies and curriculum and preparing other sociolinguists and teachers in secondary schools and higher education. They have also worked directly or indirectly in the production of textbooks and educational materials and have worked as consultants for international organizations for cooperation and NGOs.

The classes I observed in the Applied Linguistics Program in Secondary Education and the MA in sociolinguistics were teaching of languages, bilingual education, general didactics, morphology, pedagogy, and indigenous language.

Notes

1 *Carrera de Profesorado en Enseñanza Media*
2 *Licenciatura en Lingüística*
3 See the Spanish original in Appendix 11, item 1.
4 See the Spanish original in Appendix 11, item 2.
5 See the Spanish original in Appendix 11, item 3.

Appendix 2
Century Normal School

Figure 6.1 Century Normal School
Photo courtesy of the *Fotografía Japonesa* Collection, CIRMA.

Located in Antigua Guatemala, a colonial and highly touristic city in the Panchoy Valley—*Pangán* for the Kaqchikeles,—Century Normal School (CNS) serves both local female students and many more traveling kilometers to receive an education as elementary school teachers. The school sits in the Kaqchikel region (as defined by the linguistic map of Guatemala and the religious/linguistic work of the Summer Institute of Linguistics in the country). Kaqchikel is classified as one of the officially recognized twenty-two Mayan languages in the Guatemalan state. As a majority Mayan language, and because of its predominance in this region, Kaqchikel is taught in CNS during the Indigenous Language class[1] (in 2012 when I was conducting observations in the school).

Antigua Guatemala (formerly *Santiago de los Caballeros de Guatemala*) was founded in 1543 by Spanish conquistadors. Antigua is the third capital of the Goathemalan Kingdom (today Chiapas, Belize, Guatemala, Honduras, Nicaragua, and Costa Rica). The first two capital cities were Iximche' and the Almolonga Valley. Archaeologically, Iximche' is narrated as the pre-Columbian capital of the Maya Kaqchikel kingdom in the late post-Classical Period. Iximche' was a location of battle and alliance where Spanish military Pedro de Alvarado figures as the founder. After its partial destruction in the Santa Maria earthquake in 1773, the capital city moved from Antigua to *Guatemala de la Asunción*, or Guatemala City, thirty-eight kilometers away from Antigua Guatemala. The architect Juan Bautista Antonelli (from what is now known as Italy) designed Antigua in 1543, and in 1979 it became a UNESCO World Heritage. Established as the Real Audiencia de Guatemala in 1549, Antigua was an important center for the Spanish Crown in colonial times. By 2012 it has grown as a tourist hub, a leisure escape for many, a high business center for the small local elite and for many international business "men" and "women." Many older Mayan men, women, and children street vendors from nearby villages converge here to offer their goods to mostly European, American, Canadian, and wealthy Latin American tourists but also to local *capitalinos* from Guatemala City who visit the town on weekends. Antigua is the preferred location for academic events and other gatherings of various kinds.

In this privileged location of the urban or semi-urban setting, and its prestige built through almost 100 years of educating girls, CNS enjoys a reputation of which students, teachers, and parents are very proud. CNS opened its doors in 1915 during the administration of Manuel Estrada Cabrera. At the time of its opening, there was an absence in the region of "a center of teaching for women to broaden their knowledges."[2] Ever since its opening, CNS has prepared female teachers in Primary Instruction," "Urban Primary Education," or "Primary Education." After graduation, some of the students entered university, and many others started their teaching careers (this is at the time this research was being conducted and prior to the teacher education reform (see Chapter 4)). Since 1915 many of the graduates have become educators, leading politicians, mothers, and businesswomen. As a Normal School, CNS has always been and continues to be publicly funded.

The longer history of Normal Schools in the Guatemalan context dates back in some historical accounts to 1835 and in others to 1871 in the Cádiz Cortes when schools were instituted both in Spain and overseas.[3] In Guatemala, teacher education had a "false" start with the establishment of the Lancaster School in the early to mid-1830s. The Portuguese Antonio C. Coello was the first instructor. The early 1830s, much like the 1870s, the mid-to-late 1920s, and the mid-1940s were times of emergence for Normal Schools which charted a path in and through military governments, repressive governments, "democratic" governments, and neoliberal governments. During the 1870s several Normal Schools for males were opened throughout the nation (Quetzaltenango, Antigua, Chiquimila, etc.). Normal Schools for girls emerged from the mid-to-late 1890s. By 2011 there were 417 Normal Schools in the nation.

In 2012 CNS had a population of approximately 1,800 students. Over a hundred parents (many of whom wore *corte* and *güipil*) queued outside the school for hours aspiring for a placement for their daughters for the 2013 academic year. The principal noted the school has capacity for 1,200 students, most of whom came primarily from the Sacatepéquez department, where the school is located, and from various rural towns in the Chimaltenango department. Several students have commutes that range from 15 minutes to 1.5 hours. Others rent a room in the city and visit their families in their hometowns at the weekend or during school breaks. A Kaqchikel teacher in the school noted that the majority of the students in the school do not speak Kaqchikel and several are ashamed of wearing "their" *corte* and *güipil*.

The classes in the teacher education curriculum I observed were indigenous language, pedagogy, philosophy, curricular design, and social science. Some of the classes were taught by alumni of the school who had either become experienced teachers or who had earned a university degree in an education-related field.

From 2013 CNS began implementing the *pre-service primary education teacher education* reform[4] (see Chapter 4). The year 2015, which is the year of its centennial celebration, will be the first time that CNS will not graduate teachers, but students [*bachilleres*] who, after three school years (fourth to sixth) with an emphasis in education, will have to attend university two more years in order to be eligible to teach in public schools.

Notes

1 *Idioma Indígena*
2 Stated in a diary kept in the school library.
3 For more descriptive accounts of the histories of education in Guatemala, including teacher education see Carlos González Orellana, *Historia de la educación en Guatemala* (Guatemala: José de Pineda Ibarra, 1970). Alfredo Carrillo Ramírez, *Evolución histórica de la educación secundaria en Guatemala, desde el año 1831 hasta el año 1969*, 2 vols. (Guatemala: Editorial José de Pineda Ibarra, 1972). Enrique Estrada Sandoval, *Historia de la educación* (Guatemala: Editorial Oscar de León Palacios, 1993); Josefina Antillón Milla, "Educación, época contemporánea: 1898–1944," in *Historia general de Guatemala*, ed. F. Rojas Lima, vol. 5 (Guatemala: Asociación de Amigos del País, Fundación para la Cultura y el Desarrollo, 1996), 559–74. For a critical analysis of some of this historiography see Bienvenido Argueta Hernández, "Análisis de las perspectivas étnicas en la historiografía de la educación en Guatemala," *Istmo* 14 (2007): 1–33. For more on the history of Normal schools see for example, Mardoqueo García Asturias,

100 años de normalismo, 1830–1930 (Guatemala: Serviprensa Centroamericana, 1988). René Arturo Vilegas Lara, *La escuela normal que yo conocí* (Guatemala: Serviprensa Centroamericana, 1984). For more recent accounts of teacher education see for example, Samuel Fadul, "La formación de maestros en Guatemala," in *Reforma educativa en Guatemala* (Guatemala: ASIES, Asociación de Investigación y Estudios Sociales, 1997); Bienvenido Argueta Hernández, *Censo de escuelas normales en Guatemala 2004* (Guatemala: Universidad Rafael Landivar, 2005); María de los Ángeles Akú Ramírez, "Entre la panificación y la improvisación: Políticas de formación de maestros de primaria en Guatemala y el Salvador" (M.A., FLACSO Guatemala, 2011).

4 *Profesionalización del magisterio de educación primaria*

Appendix 3
Jóvenes Institute

Figure 7.1 Jóvenes Institute
Photo courtesy of PRODESSA.

Jóvenes means youth. In this school in particular it means male youth. "Many of them are from the highlands," the school's academic coordinator said when introducing me to the students in 2011. With that she also implied that they were *indígenas*. *Jóvenes* Institute is a boarding school exclusively for indigenous boys, who, although living up to 450 kilometers away, come to "receive," as some students described it, a "better education" than they would have received in their villages of origin. In 1949 the founder of the school explained that

> to the Institute are brought, from those towns and villages, the best equipped by nature and divine grace to be carefully formed in the

human and the divine so that tomorrow, graduated as teachers, doctors, businessmen, and hopefully also as priests, the conquest of Indians by Indians can begin.[1]

Similar to Century Normal School, *Jóvenes* Institute contributed to the education of leaders, educators, politicians, and Maya intellectuals who have been the linchpin in indigenous and Mayan movements.

Although receiving some funding from the state, *Jóvenes* is primarily a private institution. At the time of this research, parents and sponsors paid about 500 *Quetzales* (65USD) a month, which is a considerable amount by village standards. As is often the case, the socioeconomic status of the students in the school varies. However, virtually all the students and their families believe that investing in the students' education will lead to a better future. This is regardless of them entering or continuing a teaching career.

Located in the outskirts of Guatemala City, *Jóvenes* is a calm, walled, and guarded space that most of the students appreciate. The school has plenty of green areas and space for sports and agricultural activities and access to shopping malls and all the buzz and chaos of Guatemala's capital. The curriculum includes both academic and agricultural activities. Although some students explained they were unhappy about having to engage in early morning duties such as agriculture, pig breeding, stockbreeding, and aviculture, they agreed it was worth being at the school because of its urban location, which allowed them to enjoy city activities on Sundays. For a few hours they are granted permission to leave the school grounds. Some of the rewards after a week of hard work include wandering about in Antigua, going to the movies, going to the 6th Avenue in Guatemala's city center, shopping in the malls near the school, or simply staying in the school and relaxing. As a Catholic school founded and led by a brotherhood, Mass and prayer are an important part of the weekly curriculum.[2] Some classes taught by brothers begin with prayers, as does every school meal. Mass is held on Wednesdays and Sundays.

In 1949, to commemorate the new premises of the school, the founder explained the mission of the school. The school "is a deed [. . .] by the Archbishopric of Guatemala in representation of the Church which continues the tradition of the first Bishop."[3] Francisco Marroquin "founded schools in indigenous languages to go to the Indian to civilize him in his own language."[4] "The church was the defender of the aboriginal race before the outrage of the conquerors who only wanted wealth and bounty from them."[5] The school's commitment was to continue "that millennial sense of civilizing the aborigine,"[6] "making possible his intellectual and moral improvement,"[7] "his only ambition is drunkenness,"[8] and has a "profound poverty of body."[9] That "[the] Indian that is degenerating is the one the institute wants to regenerate."[10] Therefore it was necessary to "uproot his ancestral vices, and sow a new mode of life,"[11] and importantly make him "free from the oppressive and criminal chains of communism."[12] They are "two millions of beings without school, without culture, without being an active part of the national richness, who do not produce or consume, and who do not know why they are Guatemalans."[13]

In 2012 *Jóvenes* had six *magisterio* classrooms, two for each teacher preparation grade level (fourth to sixth). At the time this project was being carried out, the National Base Curriculum (CNB) was being implemented, and the school was offering teacher preparation in bilingual intercultural elementary education. Some of the classes taught in the double shift included religion, biology, Spanish and comprehension, physics, English, computing, psychology, pedagogy, teaching strategies, curriculum design, Maya cosmogony and math, indigenous language, educational history, and Help a Child *lectura*. I observed the last six classes listed here. Several of the teachers and teacher educators would be considered "Ladinos," some of whom were also brothers. Some of the teachers were from Guatemala, and some were from other countries in Central America. Some were enrolled in the teacher preparation programs at the university as part-time students, and a few of them had a long teaching trajectory. Finally, considering the background of the school, and the fact that Jesuit activities vis-à-vis education in Guatemala continue to be highly productive, *Jóvenes* employs many of the textbooks and reference books produced by primarily Jesuit publishers and related publishing houses. These books make a significant portion of the school's library, and other books have been donated by American NGOs and by the educational international cooperation with the United States, Germany, and other European countries. A large part of the library consists of classics of Western literature and Guatemalan authors such as Miguel Ángel Asturias and his *"Hombres de Maíz"* and *"Mulata de Tal"* and Adrian Recinos and his edition in Spanish of the *"Popol Vuh."*

Notes

1 See the Spanish original in Appendix 11, item 1.
2 For an account of a similar boarding school for women, see Emma Delfina Chirix García, *Cuerpos, Poderes Y Políticas : Mujeres Mayas En Un Internado Católico = Ch'akulal, Chuq'aib'il Chuqa B'anobäl : Mayab' Ixoqi' Chi Ru Pam Jun Kaxlan Tz'apatäl Tijonïk.* (Guatemala: Ediciones Maya' Na'jo, 2013).
3 See the Spanish original in Appendix 11, item 2.
4 See the Spanish original in Appendix 11, item 3.
5 See the Spanish original in Appendix 11, item 4.
6 See the Spanish original in Appendix 11, item 5.
7 See the Spanish original in Appendix 11, item 6.
8 See the Spanish original in Appendix 11, item 7.
9 See the Spanish original in Appendix 11, item 8.
10 See the Spanish original in Appendix 11, item 9.
11 See the Spanish original in Appendix 11, item 10.
12 See the Spanish original in Appendix 11, item 11.
13 See the Spanish original in Appendix 11, item 12.

Appendix 4
Rural Bilingual Intercultural Normal School

Figure 8.1 Rural Bilingual Intercultural Normal School

Located in the northern part of the Quiché department, in a small village of the Ixcán region bordering Mexico, Rural Bilingual Intercultural Normal School (RBINS) is a co-ed public institution. Quiché is one of the departments historically made-up indigenous, and thus narrated as having a majority indigenous population. The school sits on one of the sixteen *parcelamientos*[1] of micro-region seven of Ixcán in the North West of Guatemala. Ixcán is designated in recent geolinguistic maps of Guatemala as a multilingual region. Various migratory processes are commonly understood to have created the conditions for multilingualism, including internal migration in the late 1960s and transnational migration after the signing of the Peace Accords in 1996. Classes are composed of students with Mam, Q'anjob'al, Q'eqchi', Chuj, K'iche', Popti', Akateka, and Ixil heritages. RBINS serves students from the locality of the school and nearby villages. Before 1966 "the region was a jungle."[2] Part of the history of the villages in Ixcán is told along the lines of migration and the armed conflict.

Ixcán has plenty of natural resources. The region's fertile land was distributed to land-starved "indigenous" groups in 1966. Entire families left mainly the Cuchumatanes Mountains to resettle in their newly acquired plots of land. Local imagery and narratives from students and parents tell how the region was founded by William Woods.[3] In 1969 Woods replaced Father Edward Doheny, who had arrived in Ixcán in 1966 to take possession of the lands, accompanied by those who were to become the first settlers and the National Institute for Agrarian Transformation.[4] Father Guillermo Woods, as he is known locally, allocated more land to more people. Today many of these multilingual pioneers and their families rely on the produce of their plots of land for their sustenance while powerful transnational corporations with megaprojects (agro, mining, etc.) threaten their subsistence.

Ixcán and the Quiché Department at large was "one of the areas of greatest conflict in Guatemala"[5] during the thirty-six years of repression. Examples and stories narrated in the elementary teacher education classes at RBINS often relate to times of war. Some of the teachers and parents were themselves former members of the Guerrilla Army of the Poor (EGP), the Self-Defense Civil Patrols (PAC), and the Communities of Population in Resistance (CPR). Some of the student teachers in the school were born prior to the Peace Accords. Though the complexity of the conflict cannot be addressed here, it is crucial to highlight the particular conditions in which curriculum is produced.

RBINS emerged out of the struggle for "intercultural," "pertinent," and "indigenous languages education" that was articulated with the languages inscribed in the Accord on the Identity of Indigenous Peoples and the Accords for a Firm and Durable Peace (discussed in Chapter 1). As an intercultural teacher education school, RBINS was one of the approximately seventy-seven Bilingual Intercultural Normal Schools in the country in 2012. Intercultural teacher preparation was an educational possibility that, according to several teachers, was unimaginable before the war and the Peace Accords. In 2003, under decree 011-2003, RBINS opened its doors to sixteen future teachers of early childhood and primary education. With land donated by the community in collaboration with the school associates, in 2006 the first section of the school (four classrooms) was built with state funds through FONAPAZ (National Funds for Peace). The expansion of the school (four more rooms) was financed through the "international cooperation" with the Spanish government and the Organization of Iberoamerican States.

This particular village was selected to be the location for RBINS because it is centrally located affording easy access to students in other subregions of Ixcán. Today, students do not only come from the 400 *parcelas* in the village, but also as near as one hour by foot and as far as seven hours by bus. Most of the students spend the week in the village and may go home on weekends. At the time of this research, the school had one section of fifth and sixth grade students of primary teacher education[6] with a total of fifty-three students and fourth to sixth grade of early childhood education[7] with eleven students. There was also a fourth-grade academic program in letters with a focus on elementary education.[8] This program is the "initial" training of teachers who, after finishing two years of studies and graduating from the Normal schools, are expected to complete two more years at the university in order to be eligible to teach. The implementation of this change is part of the *pre-service primary education teacher education*[9] (see Chapter 4), which started taking place in 2013 despite large public resistance.

Some of the classes in the teacher education curriculum that I observed were social studies and citizenship formation, indigenous language, language and literature L1, indigenous language and learning, Guatemalan and Mesoamerican history, teaching and pedagogy, bilingual and intercultural education, statistics, and introduction to curricular design. In the academic program in letters, I observed pedagogical foundations and language and literature L1.

Notes

1 A *parcela* in the Ixcán context is a plot of land of 400 *cuerdas*, or 8.000 square meters, that were distributed to "landless" peoples in the 1960s. A *parcelamiento*, thus, is a collection of *parcelas*. These are commonly called *aldeas*, or *pueblos*.
2 As it is commonly referred to by *ixcanecos* (people from Ixcán).
3 He was a North American Maryknoll priest. Catholic Church and Diocese of Santa Cruz del Quiché, *Padre Guillermo Woods*. (Guatemala: Diócesis del Quiché, 2000).
4 Ricardo Falla, *Masacres de la selva: Ixcán, Guatemala, 1975–1982* (Guatemala: Editorial Universitaria, 1992).
5 Ibid, 3. For more on the armed conflict and Ixcán in particular see, for example, Santiago Otero Diez et al., *Testigos del morral sagrado: En homenaje a los catequistas sobrevivientes que han trabajado con dedicación, aun arriesgando la propia vida, por la construccion del reino de dios* (Guatemala: ODHAG, 2011); Pilar Yoldi, Carlos Amézquita, and Proyecto Interdiocesano Recuperación de la Memoria Histórica (Guatemala), *Tierra, guerra y esperanza: Memoria del Ixcán (1966–1992): Informe REMHI* (Ixcán: Diócesis del Quiché, Proyecto Interdiocesano Recuperación de la Memoria Histórica, REHMI, 2000). And Ricardo Falla's latest book Ricardo Falla, *Ixcán. El campesino indígena se levanta. 1966–1982*, vol. 3, Al atardecer de la vida. . . : Escritos de Ricardo Falla, sj. (Guatemala: Instituto de Investigaciones del Hecho Religioso, Universidad Rafael Landívar, AVANCSO, Editorial Universitaria, Universidad de San Carlos de Guatemala, 2015).
6 *Magisterio de Educación Primaria Bilingüe Intercultural*
7 *Magisterio de Educación Infantil Bilingüe Intercultural*
8 *Bachillerato en Educación Elemental*
9 *profesionalización del magisterio de educación primaria*

Appendix 5
Introduction
Spanish Excerpts

English	Spanish
1. Individual ladinization involves a process of social mobilization and the learning of new personal habits by the individual in question. That means that an individual has come out of a cast or social class and that, through a change of habits and other associations, has entered another one. Group ladinization, in which an entire community abandons gradually indigenous customs, does not imply social mobility, but is in essence a transcultural process, though which a social group gradually becomes more Ladino and less indigenous; that means it is a process though which norms and social organization change.	1. La ladinización individual involucra el proceso de la movilidad social y el aprendizaje de nuevos hábitos personales por el individuo en cuestión. Ello significa que un individuo ha salido de una casta o clase social y que, a través de un cambio de hábitos y de asociados, ha entrado en otra. La ladinización de grupo, en la cual una comunidad entera abandona gradualmente las costumbres indígenas, no implica movilidad social, sino que es en esencia un proceso transculturativo, por medio del cual un grupo social gradualmente va pareciendo mas ladino y menos indígena; es decir es un proceso por medio del cual cambian las normas y la organización sociales
2. [T]hree quarters of the people that completed the survey consider that customs are the essential characteristic [to differentiate what is indigenous]. This criterion is based, like we said, on the persistence of cultural patterns (house, dress, tongue [/language], bilingualism, with indigenous phonetics predominance, kind of food, furniture, technological limitations in various professional activities, belief in magic, civic-religious organization, etcetera).	2. Mas de las tres cuartas partes de las personas que respondieron en el cuestionario consideran la costumbre como característica esencial [entre los patrones de diferenciación de lo indígena]. Tal criterio se basa, como dijimos, en a persistencia de patrones culturales (vivienda, traje, lengua, bilingüismo, con predominio de la fonética indígena, genero de alimentación, moblaje, limitaciones tecnológicas en las diversas actividades profesionales, pensamiento mágico, organización cívico-religiosa, etcétera).

(Continued)

Appendix 5 (Continued)

English	*Spanish*
"The cultural characteristic referred to by the term 'custom',"_ says Goubaud Carrera, who died too soon for anthropology and continental indigenism, and who initiated this kind of work in Guatemala _ "received 86% votes in the entire country, followed by speaking an indigenous language in the home, 84%; ethnic group (physical appearance) is of least importance amongst them, with 67% votes."	"El rasgo cultural señalado con el termino de 'costumbre'," _dice Goubaud Carrera, muerto prematuramente para la antropología y el indigenismo continental, iniciador de estos trabajos en Guatemala _"aparece para todo el país con un 86% de respuestas afirmativas; le sigue el hablar un idioma indígena en el hogar, con 84%; el grupo étnico (apariencia física) es el de menor importancia entre todos ellos, con un 67% de respuestas afirmativas."
This survey proves what almost all of us know in relation to the possibilities that the indigenous person has to change *status*, passing into the non indigenous group through the social mobility process, which could be faster if the attitude towards him was more appropriate in terms of creating the possibilities for integration in the various scenarios of his life, so that individual and group *ladinización* can be accelerated, which would lead to important benefits for the country	Esta encuesta viene a comprobar lo que casi todos sabemos en relación a las posibilidades que tiene el indígena de cambiar su status, pasando al grupo no indígena por el proceso de movilidad social, el cual podría ser mas rápido si la actitud hacia el fuese mas propicia, en cuanto a favorecer las posibilidades de integración en los diversos ordenes de su vida, a fin de acelerar la ladinización individual y la de grupo, lo que conllevaría beneficios muy importantes para el país
3. The pedagogic experience at Instituto Indígena Santiago is framed in the question of how to educate within cultures. To achieve this, it was necessary to strengthen the cultural foundations through teaching native languages, studying the Mayan alphabet, recuperating historical memory and research as a means for students to acquire instruments of analysis of their own identity, revaluing their habits and traditional beliefs and feeling proud of being indigenous.	3. La experiencia pedagógica del Instituto Indígena Santiago, está enmarcada en la pregunta de cómo educar dentro de las culturas. Para lograrlo, fue necesario fortalecer las bases culturales mediante la enseñanza de las lenguas nativas, el estudio del alfabeto maya, la recuperación de la memoria histórica y la investigación, como medios para que los estudiantes lograran adquirir instrumentos de análisis de su propia identidad, revalorando sus hábitos y creencias tradicionales y sintiéndose orgullosos de ser indígenas.
4. Given the conditions of exploitation of the life and conscience of the Indian, . . . [it is necessary] to form seeds of apostles of the *indígena* race . . . so that from childhood, formed integrally, which means Christianly, tomorrow he would	4. Ante esa realidad de explotación de la vida y de la conciencia del indio, . . . [se hace necesario] formar un semillero de apóstoles de la raza indígena . . . para que formado integralmente, que es tanto como decir cristianamente, fuera el día de

English	Spanish
be the new essence of the exploited race of yesterday and abandoned today, so that he would be the free race of tomorrow, free of fear, free of ancestral holes, free from racial humiliations, free from ignorance	mañana el fermento nuevo de la raza explotada de ayer y abandonada de hoy a fin de que llegara a ser la raza libre de mañana, libre de temor, libre de vacíos ancestrales, libre de humillaciones raciales, libre de la ignorancia
5. The highest intellectual levels [the Indian] can reach are difficult to score; but it is known that he has slow comprehension and is stubborn.	5. Los niveles intelectuales máximos a que llega [el indio] son difíciles de marcar; pero si se sabe que tiene la comprensión muy lenta y es terco.
[He] speaks Spanish phonetically disrupting the vocabulary, repeating the same words with a regretful syntax.	Habla español, perturbando fonéticamente el vocabulario, repitiendo las mismas palabras y con una sintaxis lamentable.
Psychologically [he] has attitudes to be a lawyer, politician, military and farmer. His ability to imitate is also notable (which is a quality of inferior races) thanks to this ability, [he] is skilled to work in architecture and drawing, but is incapable of creating	Psicológicamente tiene aptitudes para abogado, político, militar y agricultor. También es notable su facilidad para imitar (cualidad de las razas inferiores) gracias a esta facilidad es hábil para la arquitectura y el dibujo; pero es incapaz de crear
The Indian should be educated with the goal of changing him from slave to a free man; from selfish man into a useful man to his fellow man; from being coarse in life to a man apt and intelligent. To transform the Indian social environment based on education is what common sense recommends. Make him think. Make him feel. Make him act.	Al indio debe educársele con el propósito de cambiarlo de esclavo en hombre libre; de egoísta en hombre útil a sus semejante; de rudo para la vida en hombre apto e inteligente. Transformar el medio social indígena a base de educación es lo que aconseja el sentido común. Hacerlo pensar. Hacerlo sentir. Hacerlo accionar
6. We are talking about one or various processes that take shape in a new phenomenon, the introduction in the life of Maya people of *a discourse that did not exist before*: of considering oneself "Mayan" and through that reclaim equality with pride and rights	6. Estamos hablando de uno o varios procesos que toman forma en un fenómeno nuevo, la introducción en la vida de los Mayas de un discurso que antes no existía: el de considerarse "maya" y por ello reclamar igualdad con orgullo y derechos

Appendix 6
Chapter 1
Spanish Excerpts

English	Spanish
1. How far does this difference go? The Indian represents a past civilization and the mestizo, or *ladino* as we call him, a civilization that is to come. The Indian comprises the majority of our population, lost his strength in the time of slavery to which he was subjected, he is not interested in anything, . . . he represents the mental, moral, and material poverty of the country: he is humble, dirty, dresses differently and suffers without batting an eye. The ladino makes up the third part, lives in a distinct historical moment, with desires of ambition and romanticism, aspires, wishes, and is, in the end, the living part of the Guatemalan nation. What a brave nation that has two-thirds of its population dead to intelligent life!	1. ¿Hasta cuando esta diferencia? El indio representa una civilización pasada y el mestizo, o ladino que le llamamos, una civilización que viene. El indio forma la mayoría de nuestra población, perdió su vigor en el tiempo de esclavitud a la que se le sometió, no se interesa por nada, . . . representa la penuria mental, moral y material del país: es humilde, es sucio, viste de distinta manera y padece sin pestañear. El ladino forma una tercera parte, vive un momento histórico distinto, con arranques de ambición y romanticismo, aspira, anhela y es, en ultimo resultado, la parte viva de la nación guatemalteca. ¡Valiente nación que tiene dos terceras partes muertas para la vida inteligente!
2. The Catholic church and its separation from the Mexican State dwells on the loss of privileges during the colonial period: the tithe, civil control over the population through the 'sacred sacraments' and it's censuses, mainly baptisms, communions, and anointing of the sick/dead. They provide a spectrum by ages, and current civil condition. There is also education which is exclusive to the Catholic church	2. La Iglesia católica y su separación del Estado mexicano reside en la pérdida de privilegios de los que viene gozando durante todo el periodo colonial: el diezmo, control civil de la población mediante los 'sagrados sacramentos' y sus censos, donde destacan los bautizos, las comuniones, la confirmación, los matrimonios y las defunciones. Que dan un espectro por edades y condición civil de

(*Continued*)

Appendix 6 (Continued)

English	Spanish
during the same period. [The Church] even controls the immigration of foreigners into the country, prohibiting permanent residence in the national territory to foreigners whose country of origin is not Catholic	demografía del momento. También está la educación, que es durante el mismo periodo una exclusividad de esta Iglesia. Esta controla incluso la inmigración de extranjeros al país, prohibiendo la residencia definitiva en territorio nacional de extranjeros cuyo origen es de países no católicos
3. In September 1797, [the Economic Society of Friends of the Country] offer[ed] a gold medal and meritorious membership to whoever wrote the best essay on the following subject: "Demonstrate solidly and clearly the advantages that would result for the State if all Indians and ladinos of this kingdom put on shoes and dressed in Spanish styles, and they experienced for themselves the physical, moral and political benefits; proposing the most smooth, simple and practicable means to reduce them to the use of these things, without violence, coercion or mandate. . . . one of the most important social problems was about, as you can see, no other than to propose the means to make the aboriginal class and the other large portion of the less privileged social class, to enter civil life and partake of its benefits. Let's just say it straight. Primary and educational practical instruction is what we need for those masses of struggling Indians, that constitute a real hindrance for the development of the country	3. En Septiembre1795, [la Sociedad Económica de Amigos del País] ofreci[o] una medalla de oro y el diploma de Socio de Merito, al que escribiera la mejor memoria sobre el tema siguiente: "Demostrar con solidez y claridad las ventajas que resultaran al Estado de que todos los indios y ladinos de este reino se calcen y vistan a la española, y las utilidades físicas, morales y políticas, que experimentaran ellos mismos; proponiendo los medios mas suaves, sencillos y practicables para reducirlos al uso de estas cosas, sin violencia, coacción ni mandato. . . . uno de los mas importantes problemas sociales [t]ratábase, como se ve, nada menos que de proponer los medios de hacer entrar en la vida civil y participar de sus beneficios a la clase aborigen, y otra porción numerosa de la clase menos acomodada de la sociedad. Digámoslo de una vez. Instrucción primaria practica y educativa, es la que se necesita para esas masa de indios rezagados, que constituyen una verdadera rémora para el adelanto del país
4. Try to persuade the utility and means so that the Indians and Ladinos dress and use footwear the Spanish way	4. Persuadir la utilidad y medios de que los indios y ladinos vistan y calcen a la española
5. When we speak of the multilingual, multiethnic, we are talking about a concrete matter, if we say that Guatemala is multilingual, why? Because there are 25 languages, right? It is not an ideological	5. Cuando hablamos de multilingüe, multiétnico estamos hablando de una cuestión concreta, si decimos que Guatemala es multilingüe, ¿por que? Por que hay 25 idiomas, ¿si? No es cuestión ideológica, es una

English	Spanish
matter, it is a reality, we can go and count, we can survey, we can keep an account of how many people there are by language	realidad, podemos llegar a contar, podemos encuestar, podemos registrar cuanta gente hay por cada idioma
6. It is known that the first civilized men that came to these regions were captained by Votán, the mysterious and extraordinary character that disembarked in Tabasco, Mexico, from the northern regions. To establish his civilizing system, he had to submit the salvage Mexicans and later fund a powerful empire named Xibalba or Xibalbay, whose capital was Nachan or Na-Chan	6. Sábese que los primeros hombres civilizados que á estas regiones llegaron, fueron los capitaneados por Votán, personaje misterioso y extraordinario, que desembarco en Tabasco, México, procedente de las regiones septentrionales. Para establecer sus civilizadores sistemas, hubo de someter a los salvajes mejicanos, y fundar despues, un poderoso imperio con el nombre de Xibalba ó Xibalbay, cuya capital fue Nachan ó Na-Chan
7. According to Juarros is *Sinca; xorti*, according to the small ethnographic map that was published in Paris, with the "Letter from the Republic of Guatemala," compiled by Juan Gavarrete. The 17th of October 1884, Daniel G. Briton presented before the American Philosophical Society the following, translated into English: "The name is said in different ways *Xinca, Xinka* and *Sinca*. The first one is correct, in which the initial x is the same as the soft English *sh*, as in *show*"	7. Según Juarros es *Sinca; xorti*, según el pequeño mapa etnográfico que se publico en Paris, con la "Carta de la Republica de Guatemala," compilada por Juan Gavarrete. El 17 de octubre de 1884, Daniel G. Briton expuso ante la Sociedad Filosófica Americana lo siguiente, traducido del ingles: "Su nombre se dice de diferentes formas: *Xinca, Xinka y Sinca*. El primero es el correcto, el que la *x* inicial tiene el valor de la *sh* suave inglesa, como el *show*"
8. The state and organized sectors of society should join forces for the solution of the *agrarian problem and rural development* which are fundamental to respond to *the situation of the majority of the population* that lives in rural environments, and which is the most affected by poverty, inequity and the weakness of state institutions	8. El Estado y los sectores organizados de la sociedad deben aunar esfuerzos para la resolución de la problemática agraria y el desarrollo rural, que son fundamentales para dar respuesta a la situación de la mayoría de la población que vive en el medio rural, y que es la más afectada por la pobreza, las iniquidades y la debilidad de las instituciones estatales
9. Firm and durable peace should be cemented in socioeconomic participatory development oriented towards *common good*, which should respond to the necessities of the *entire population*. Such development requires social justice as one of the pillars of *national*	9. La paz firme y duradera debe cimentarse sobre un desarrollo socioeconómico participativo orientado al bien común, que responda a las necesidades de toda la población. Dicho desarrollo requiere de justicia social como uno de los pilares de la unidad y

(Continued)

Appendix 6 (Continued)

English	Spanish
unity and solidarity, and of sustainable *economic growth* as condition to respond to the social demands of the population	solidaridad nacional, y de crecimiento económico con sostenibilidad, como condición para atender las demandas sociales de la población
10. Oh! Sublime Minerva Temple . . . always remain as eternal/enduring as the science of which you are an emblem. And you, oh noble Guatemalan nation, venerate in your Minerva Temple the love for study and progress	10. ¡Oh! Templo sublime de Minerva . . . consérvate siempre imperecedero como la ciencia de la que eres emblema. Y tu, oh noble nación guatemalteca, venera en tu templo de Minerva el amor al estudio y al progress
11. Yes, Gentleman, the civilizations of the Old world and the vigor of the far Orient already in our two seas and via the railroad that joins us, converge to the heart of Guatemala to cure it of the anemia of more than three centuries of atavism, and the intake of oxygenated and new blood make it throb with the heartbeat of interculturalism and the modern sentiment	11. Si, Señores, las civilizaciones del Viejo mundo y el vigor del lejano Oriente tocan ya en nuestros dos mares y, por el ferrocarril que los une, convergen hacia el corazón de Guatemala, para curarla de la anemia de tres siglos de atavismo y con la infiltración de oxigenada y nueva sangre, hacerla palpitar con las palpitaciones del interculturalismo y el sentimiento moderno
12. The identity of the *Mayan* peoples is recognized as well as the *identities* of the *Garífuna* and *Xinca* peoples within the *unity of the Guatemalan nation*, and the government is committed to promoting a reform to the Political Constitution to this end before the Congress of the Republic	12. Se reconoce la identidad del pueblo *maya* así como las *identidades* de los pueblos *garífuna* y *xinca*, dentro de la unidad de la nación guatemalteca, y el Gobierno se compromete en promover ante el Congreso de la República una reforma de la Constitución Política de la República en este sentido
13. The philosophy of Bilingual and Intercultural Education is based on *the coexistence of various cultures and languages* in the country, oriented towards strengthening *unity in diversity* of the Guatemalan nation. Develop a stable social bilingualism for the Maya-speaking student population and a harmonious coexistence amongst peoples and cultures	13. La Filosofía de la Educación Bilingüe Intercultural se sustenta en *la coexistencia de varias culturas e idiomas* en el país, orientado a fortalecer la *unidad en la diversidad* cultural de la nación guatemalteca. Desarrollar un bilingüismo social estable para la población estudiantil mayahablante y una convivencia armónica entre pueblos y culturas
14. The official language in Guatemala is Spanish. The state recognizes, promotes and respects the languages of the Mayas, Garífuna and Xinka peoples	14. El idioma oficial de Guatemala es el español. El Estado reconoce, promueve y respeta los idiomas de los pueblos Mayas, Garífuna y Xinka

English	Spanish
15. *Identity.* The Mayas, Garífuna and Xinka languages are essential elements in national identity; their acknowledgment, respect, advancement, development and usage in the public and private spheres is oriented towards national unity in diversity and are meant to strengthen interculturalism between co-nationals	15. *Identidad.* Los idiomas Mayas, Garífuna y Xinka son elementos esenciales de la identidad nacional; su reconocimiento, respeto, promoción, desarrollo y utilización en las esferas públicas y privadas se orientan a la unidad nacional en la diversidad y propenden a fortalecer la interculturalidad entre los connacionales
16. *Usage.* In the Guatemalan territory Mayas, Garífuna and Xinka languages can be used in the *languages communities in which they correspond*, in all their forms, without restrictions in the public or private space, in educational, academic, social, economic, political and cultural activities	16. *Utilización.* En el territorio guatemalteco los idiomas Mayas, Garífuna y Xinka podrán utilizarse en las comunidades lingüísticas que correspondan, en todas sus formas, sin restricciones en el ámbito público y privado, en actividades educativas, académicas, sociales, económicas, políticas y culturales

Appendix 7
Chapter 2
Spanish Excerpts

English	Spanish
1. I have more a vision of village, more of conviction, more of support for the boys and girls, because I understand the struggle. I lived their discrimination in school. Just recently when I was in a small school in Huehuetenango on Thursday, I was telling the teachers that I lived their painful life in school. In one of the most painful punishments that I have engraved in my life, my third grade teacher put me on a shelf, like on a bookshelf because I did not speak Castilian. It was punishment for not saying "good morning." She left me there in front of all the Castilian speaking kids, *Ladinos*, *Mestizos*. That puts a mark on you. But it is not about vengeance, it is about willingness to work for kids not to suffer	1. [Y]o tengo una visión mas de pueblo, mas de convicción. [. . .] Mas de apoyo a los niños, las niñas por que entiendo la lucha. Yo viví esa discriminación en la escuela. Justamente cuando estaba en una escuelita en Huehuetenango el jueves, le comentaba a los maestros yo viví esa vida dolorosa en la escuela. Por no hablar el idioma castellano mi maestra de 3er grado en uno de los castigos mas dolorosos que tengo marcado en mi vida es que me puso como en una cómoda o librera. Me puso ahí como castigo por no decir buenos días, verdad, y allí me dejo como castigo ante todos los niños, que eran niños castellano hablantes, ladinos, mestizos. Eso lo marca a uno. Pero tampoco es una venganza, sino es un querer hacer eso para que los niños no sufran
2. Please girls, I am asking you, write in your notebooks . . . [so that] when the supervising teacher [during student teaching] asks you, can you teach the kids Kaqchikel?	2. Por favor niñas, les pido que escriban en sus cuadernos . . . [para que] cuando la maestra les pregunte, ¿pueden enseñarle Kaqchikel a los niños?
3. How come? Yes! That's why I need you to keep your notebooks, you have material there. You can teach them the numbers, the parts of the body in Kaqchikel, the songs that we know. . . . Don't make me look bad. And not only me, also the	3. ¿Cómo asi? Por eso es que necesito que guarden sus cuadernos, ustedes tienen material allí. Les pueden enseñar los números, las partes del cuerpo en Kaqchikel, las canciones que sabemos. . . . No me hagan quedar mal. Y no solamente a mi

(*Continued*)

Appendix 7 (Continued)

English	Spanish
school, because "in Century Normal School they are not teaching them well." . . . Let me anticipate that I need for us to work a lot on didactic materials. You will have to make an album with drawings or whatever as teachers you consider you can teach the kids in Kaqchikel. . . . You are being educated to be teachers and you are creative. You are going to invent games on how to teach the kids the Kaqchikel vocabulary, so in this unit, please, I am going to need lots of creativity. . . . The Kaqchikel vocabulary is infinite. I have a booklet. . . . In this unit, I can give you more vocabulary so you can copy it, make your own binders, and choose from there."	sino también a la escuela, porque "en la Normal de Ciclo no les enseñan bien." . . . Les anticipo que lo que necesito es que trabajemos mucho en material didáctico. Van a hacer un álbum con dibujitos o lo que ustedes consideren como maestras que le pueden enseñar a los niños. . . . Se les esta preparando para ser maestras y son creativas. Van a inventar juegos de cómo ensenarle a los niños el vocabulario en Kaqchikel, entonces esta unidad les voy a dar mas vocabulario. . . . El vocabularion en Kaqchikel es infinito. Tengo una cartilla. . . . En esta unidad les puedo dar mas vocabulario para que anoten, hagan sus propias carpetas, y saquen de allí.
4. A drawing related to Kaqchikel. You can choose a *nahual*. You already have the chart with the *nahuales*	4. Un dibujo relacionado con el Kaqchikel. Pueden elegir un nahual. Ya tienen un cuadro con los nahuales
5. People in the communities who mastered the language of each of them foreigners could not do all of that work without the tight collaboration [with people in the communities]	5. Gente de las comunidades que dominaba el idioma de cada una de ellas personas extranjeras no podían hacer todo este trabajo sin la estrecha colaboración de la [gente de las comunidades]
6. The indigenous person that speaks Castilian, that dresses like the Europeans, we will not call him Indian, we will not differentiate him from the mixed race	6. Al indígena que habla el castellano, que viste a la europea, ya no le llamamos indio, ya no lo distinguimos de la raza mixtada
7. 1) Research linguistically and culturally the autochthonous groups in the country and publish the findings. 2) Translate sections of the Holy Scriptures to support the development of written literature. 3) Collaborate with public and private literacy and bilingual education programs. 4) Serve the basic necessities of communities where members [of the SIL] are based.	7. 1) Investigar lingüística y culturalmente a los grupos autóctonos del país y publicar los hallazgos. 2) Traducir porciones de las Sagradas Escrituras y apoyar el desarrollo de una literatura escrita. 3) Colaborar con programas de alfabetización y de educación bilingüe, tanto públicos como privados. 4) Atender necesidades básicas de las comunidades donde se encuentran los miembros.

English	Spanish
5) Train suitable people, both beginning readers and advanced students, on linguistic concepts, anthropology, bilingual education, and translation	5) Capacitar a la gente idónea, tanto nuevos lectores como estudiantes avanzados, en conceptos de lingüística, antropología, educación bilingüe, y traducción
8. Language that the Spanish brought and which we kept The negative part [of the Spanish Conquest] is that many lost their lives [the Spanish] changed all the modernity that the Mayas had, and the organization they had."	8. El idioma que traían ellos nos lo quedamos Y lo negativo es que muchos perdieron la vida [Los españoles] cambiaron toda la modernidad que los mayas tenían y la organización que ellos tenían
9. The Spanish brought us a magnificent present: The language, a pure language, abundant, expressive, better than the existing [indigenous] languages; a language that is constantly elevated by poets and those of us [Spanish users] who enjoy its beauty and harmony	9. Los españoles nos trajeron un presente magnifico: el idioma, un lenguaje puro, abundante, expresivo, como el mejor entre los [indígenas] actuales, que es exalto constantemente por los poetas y cuantos gozamos de su belleza y armonía
10. For the first time in Guatemala, from February 1986, the University [Mariano Gálvez] will begin the professional training of national linguists that can contribute to the *solution of linguistic-educational problems* in the country and additionally carry out the necessary sociolinguistic research for the profound knowledge of autochthonous tongues and cultures of Guatemala [emphasis added]	10. Por primera vez en Guatemala, desde febrero de 1986, la Universidad [Mariano Gálvez] iniciara la formación profesional de Lingüistas nacionales que puedan contribuir a la solución de problemas lingüístico-educativos en el país y, además, llevar a cabo las investigaciones sociolingüísticas necesarias para un conocimiento profundo de las lenguas y culturas autóctonas de Guatemala
11. Go to the [Mayan] languages and find the [morphological] rule . . . because it's there, find it!	11. Váyanse a los idiomas [mayas] y encuentren la regla [morfológica] . . . porque allí esta, encuéntrenla!
12. There was only one language. The ancient language was the proto-Maya. Nab'ee Maya Tzij, . . . the grandmother, or the grandfather of the languages, the proto-Maya There was only one language for the Mayans but little by little it was dividing itself, and from that proto-Maya other languages derived, Mam, the Q'anjobal language, the Ixil language, the K'iche' language	12. Solo existía un idioma. El antiguo idioma era el idioma el protomaya. Nab'ee Maya Tzij [. . .] el abuelo o la abuela de los idiomas, el protomaya Solo existía un idioma para los Mayas, pero poco a poco se fue dividiendo, y de eso pues, de este protomaya se derivaron los otros, el idioma Mam, el idioma Q'anjob'al, el idioma Ixil, el idioma K'iche'

(*Continued*)

Appendix 7 (Continued)

English	Spanish
13. According to what Mayan writers have left written, . . . the ancestors, . . . what comes up in the Popol Wuj, also in the Chilam Balam, and the Annals of the Kaqchiqueles, . . . all of that explains the origins of the Maya people	13. Según lo que escritores Mayas han dejado escrito, . . . los señores antiguos, . . . lo que aparece en el libro del Popol Wuj también en el Chilam Balam, en los Anales de los Kaqchiqueles . . . todo se explica pues de esta manera el origen del pueblo Maya
14. The Mayas are not the cause of backwardness and lack of development in Guatemala. [It's not true that] they oppose development. . . . No, because if one were to study this topic well, one can realize that the Mayas knew what Europeans and other peoples had not discovered	14. Los mayas no son la causa del atraso en Guatemala, sin desarrollo. [No es verdad que] se oponen al desarrollo. . . . No, porque estudiándolo bien, los Mayas ya sabían [. . .] lo que los europeos y otros pueblos del mundo no habían descubierto
15. Incomplete and over-abundant with vivid imaginations, purely tropical in character. Like the Bible of the Hebrews, the *Popol Vuh* also tells the creation of the world and mentions a supreme creator who produces and makes the beings . . . As a whole, this book gives proof of some intelligence and culture, at least if one considers the age of barbarism and prejudice in which they lived (original English translation)	15. Libro de una exuberancia imaginativa desordenada, y puramente tropical. Como la biblia de los hebreos, comienza el Popol-Vuh relatando el génesis del mundo, en el cual relato hace mención de un "Creador y Formador Supremo, que engendra, que da el ser," . . . En general el libro manifiesta alguna cultura intelectual al menos hasta donde puede imaginarse en aquella época de prejuicios y de salvajismo (Spanish original)
16. Concentrated in the northwestern region of the country . . . and more often affects the "indigenous" Guatemalan than the non- "indigenous," more women than men, more the rural that the urban population	16. Se concentra en la región nor-occidental del país . . . afecta mas a los guatemaltecos indígenas que a los no indígenas, mas a las mujeres que a los hombres, mas a la población rural que a población urbana
17. Those missionaries . . . taught writing, reading and a little more to very many indigenes using mostly the Spanish alphabet. These teachings produced good results one of which is the *kiché* author of the POPOL VUY. This *kiché* author's name is unknown; the good results were also the authors of the MEMORIAL KAKCHIKEL written here in Sololá by the	17. Aquellos señores misioneros . . . enseñaron la escritura, la lectura y algo mas a muchísimos indígenas, empleando el alfabeto español en gran parte, de cuya enseñanza se cosecharon frutos buenos en los que figuro el autor *kiché*, del POPOL VUY, cuyo autor *kiché* es de nombre desconocido; así también figuraron los autores del MEMORIAL KAKCHIKEL escrito

English	Spanish
gentlemen Sir. Francisco Hernández Arana SHAJILA and Sir. Francisco Díaz SHEBUTA (ej-lease "quej")	aquí en Sololá por los señores don Francisco Hernández Arana SHAJILA y don Francisco Díaz SHEBUTA (ej-lease "quej")
18. The teacher should try to teach more Castilian in a progressive manner and in a very elementary way in order to castilianize the indigenous students . . . and continue these exercises until having formed LADINO CHILDREN that can interpret the true meaning of words they hear in the course of the upcoming classes	18. El maestro debiera de procurar enseñar mas Castellano, de manera progresiva y muy elemental para castellanizar a los alumnos indígenas . . . y terminar estos ejercicios hasta haber formado NIÑOS LADINOS, que pudiera interpretar la *verdadera significación de las palabras* que oyeran en el transcurso de las clases posteriores
19. It depends on what you are reading because if I am reading an informational book that is teaching me the process of cultivating rice, would I enjoy it?	19. Depende lo que se este leyendo. Por que si estoy leyendo yo un libro informativo que me esta enseñando cual es el proceso para cultivar el arroz, ¿será que lo voy a disfrutar?
20. No. I am informing myself. Because I do not enjoy it does not mean I am not a good reader. A good reader is that one who reads to inform her/himself, to learn	20. No. Me estoy informando. No por que no disfrute no voy a ser un buen lector. Un buen lector va a ser aquel que esta leyendo para informarse, para aprender

Appendix 8
Chapter 3
Spanish Excerpts

English	Spanish
1. We as future teachers should teach children new knowledge that we learn here so that they change the mentality that they have in the communities, mostly in rural communities where the mentality of children is not well developed. Therefore, when one receives new knowledge . . . one should apply it and teach it to the children so that they turn out intelligent and creative and well developed.	1. Nosotros como futuros docentes debemos de ensenar a los niños nuevos conocimientos que nosotros aprendemos aquí para que ellos cambien la mentalidad de eso que tienen de las comunidades, mas se da en las comunidades rurales donde no se desarrolla la mentalidad del niño. Entonces uno cuando recibe nuevos conocimientos . . . uno debe aplicar con los niños para que los niños salgan inteligentes y creativos y desarrollados.
2. That [the *Guatemala Indígena* journal] would embody the living educational space of indigenism to improve the knowledge of the world vision of the Indian, their civic-religious, social, and economic organization, their folkloric art, etcetera, analyzed with scientific rigor, far from halting or sentimental outbreaks, and for the planning of new and reasonable solutions to the Indian problem, not always understood by governments.	2. Que [Guatemala Indígena] sea una cátedra viva del Indigenismo, para el mejor conocimiento de la visión del mundo del indio, de su organización cívico-religiosa, social, económica, de su arte folklórico, etcétera, analizados con rigor científico, lejos de explosiones sentimentales o claudicantes, y para el planeamiento de nuevas y razonables soluciones al problema indígena, no siempre entendido por los gobiernos.
3. It was necessary to help the Indian die well, that is, it was important to implement a series of measures that made de-indianization less brutal. The situation of Indian culture (the hackneyed process of acculturation) needed to be oriented scientifically so that the transformation was the least painful possible.	3. Había que ayudar a bien morir al indio, es decir, había que poner en practica una serie de medidas que hicieran menos brutal la desindianización. La situación de la cultura india (el tan manido proceso de aculturación) debía orientarse científicamente, a fin de que el transito resultara lo menos doloroso posible.

(*Continued*)

Appendix 8 (Continued)

English	Spanish
4. Goubaud insists that the heart of the matter is a new form of knowledge, in the acquisition of new methodologies, and *new* scientific approaches *through* anthropology, history, ethnology, and archaeology; all the modern sciences that enable Guatemalan to have a better understanding of themselves and others.	4. Goubaud insiste tanto en que el quid de la cuestión está en una nueva forma de conocimiento, en la adquisición de nuevas metodologías y nuevas aproximaciones científicas, a través de la antropología, la historia, la etnología y arqueología; todas ellas ciencias de la modernidad que posibilitan a los guatemaltecos un mejor conocimiento de sí mismos y de los otros.
5. The indigenous population in American countries is in *transition* since it came into direct and indirect contact with other populations in the world.	5. La población indígena en los países de America esta en transición desde que hubo de entrar en contacto directo e indirectos con las otras poblaciones del mundo.
6. An indigenous population. The great majority of the people who were surveyed, belong to the Ladina population (non indigenous).	6. Una población indígena. La gran mayoría de las personas a quienes se les envió la encuesta pertenecen a la población ladina (no indígena).
7. If we try to study the sociological characteristics that determine a human group, we realize that there are sufficient bases of support to conduct an analysis of such characteristics. When a person or a group of people enter into a social relationship with another person or group of people, there are *palpable characteristics* that influence both of them in their treatment of one another. Some of these outstanding differences are: (1) clothing; (2) the language; (3) the habits, customs or conduct; and of course, perhaps more importantly (4) the person's physical appearance: the size and body shape, the skin color, the hair and the eyes, and any other detail of the physical aspect [emphasis added].	7. Si tratamos de estudiar las características sociológicas que determinan a un grupo humano, encontramos que ya existen suficientes bases de apoyo para llegar al análisis de estas características. Cuando una persona, o un grupo de personas, entra en relaciones sociales con otra persona o grupo de ellas existen *características palpables* que influencian a ambos en su trato mutuo. Algunas de estas características mas sobresalientes son: (1) la indumentaria; (2) el idioma; (3) los hábitos, costumbres o formas de conducta; y desde luego, quizá en primera línea (4) la apariencia física de la persona: la talla y forma somática, el color de la piel, del cabello y de los ojos, y los demás detalles del aspecto físico.

8. In this municipality there are no indigenous peoples.
    Without meaning for this study.
    There are no uniform or general criteria in the country.
    The criteria differ in the various departments of the Republic.
	8. En este municipio no hay indígenas.
	    Sin significado para este estudio.
	    No existe en el país un criterio uniforme y general.
	    Los criterios difieren en los diversos departamentos de la República.

English	Spanish
the most generalized criteria are the habits and customs of the *indígena* population [86%]. speaking the autochthonous language in the home [84%].	el criterio mas generalizado se refiere [sic] a los hábitos y las costumbres de la población indígena [86%]. hablar un idioma indígena en el hogar [84%].
9. Skin or hair color have no relationship either man's intelligence or to his humanity, and therefore this makes it much quicker to achieve social solidarity among the ethnic groups in the country.	9. El color de la piel o del pelo no tienen ninguna relación con la inteligencia ni la humanidad del hombre, y que por lo tanto puede llegarse a una solidaridad social mucho mas rápida entre los grupos étnicos de todo el país.
10. with the goal of developing a curriculum for this language.	10. con el objetivo de desarrollar un currículo para este idioma.
11. Concrete or *scientific* about the world vision according to the indigenous peoples of the country, [there is] nothing yet to prepare Guatemalan teachers [to work with] the indigenous population of the country.	11. Concreto ni científico acerca de la visión del mundo según los indígenas del país, nada aún para preparar a los maestros Guatemaltecos para la población indígena del país.
12. When we know the factors that make up their mentality, the springs that activate their emotions, then perhaps we would be able to *convert* indigenous peoples to be part of our Western culture, once research has informed us of the right way [emphasis added].	12. Cuando conozcamos los factores que forman su mentalidad, los resortes que mueven sus emociones, entonces tal vez podamos convertir a los indígenas en parte de nuestra cultura occidental, una vez que la investigación haya indicado el camino adecuado.
13. the illiterate peasant in colorful costumes that was delaying the progress of the nation. The potential citizen.	13. el campesino iletrado de colorido traje que estaba atrasando el ritmo de la nación a la nación. El ciudadano potencial.
14. Tactic's Integral Improvement Plan to lead children to a real comprehension of Spanish, with an ability to read.	14. Plan de Mejoramiento Integral de Tactic llevar a los niños a una comprensión real del español, con habilidad de la lectura.
15. Booklets in the *pocomchí* dialect were to demonstrate that an indigenous child could learn to read faster and actually comprehend what he read if the learning process was to start in his own language and to later orient him to Spanish.	15. Las cartillas en el dialecto pocomchí era para demostrar que un niño indígena podría aprender a leer mas rápidamente y con verdadera comprensión de lo que lee, si el proceso de aprendizaje era comenzado en su propio idioma, para luego conducirlo al español.
16. These kinds of materials because they created an understanding for indigenous children.	16. [m]ateriales de este tipo, puesto que creaban entendimiento a los niños indígenas.

(Continued)

Appendix 8 (Continued)

English	Spanish
17. The teacher said: 'this method is the only one that should be taught in schools like this where all the people only speak the dialect. But it came too late. It should have been used for years.'	17. Dijo el: 'Este método es el único que debiera enseñarse en escuelas como esta donde toda la gente solo habla el dialecto. Pero ha venido muy tarde. Debiera haber sido usado hace años.'
18. Offers a good service in the future. Studied, analyzed, and corrected the pedagogical technique. To establish a generalized dialect for each tongue.	18. Ofrezca un buen servicio en el futuro Estudió, analizó y corrigió la técnica pedagógica. Establecer el dialecto generalizado de cada lengua.
19. The fundamental phonemes of Quiche, Kekchi, Kanjobal, Tzutujil, and Xinca. Provide the fundamental phonemes and the linguistic unity of the region.	19. Los *fonemas fundamentales* del Quiche, Kekchi, Kanjobal, Tzutujil, y Xinca, proporcionar los fenómenos fundamentales y la unidad lingüística de la región.
20. The right to cultural pluralism.	20. El derecho a la pluralidad cultural.
21. To understand that we are a very diverse country.	21. Para entender que somos un país muy diverso.
22. The necessity to improve the standard of living of rural communities in Guatemala, especially the Mayan communities, poses challenges to our creativity and spirit of service. The Non Governmental Organizations for Development, NGOs, have been making various efforts to cooperate for the development of these communities; however, each day we observe that we need to better define the orientation and the kind of development that we would like to make happen, so that our programs are concrete contributions to the development of the country. Above all, we need to consider, in our activities, the multicultural characteristics of Guatemala.	22. La necesidad de mejorar el nivel de vida de las comunidades rurales de Guatemala, especialmente las comunidades mayas, *plantea desafíos a nuestra creatividad y a nuestro espíritu de servicio.* Las organizaciones no Gubernamentales de Desarrollo, ONGs, hemos venido realizando diversos esfuerzos en la cooperación con el desarrollo de estas comunidades; sin embargo, cada día observamos que necesitamos definir mejor la orientación del tipo de desarrollo que queremos realizar, para que nuestros programas sean aportes concretos al desarrollo del país. Ante todo, debemos considerar, en nuestras actividades, las características multiculturales de Guatemala.
23. We understand that it is the culture that the Maya people started developing more than 10 thousand years ago in the south of what is the Mexican republic today, throughout Belize and Guatemala, in part of Honduras and el Salvador. The	23. Entendemos que es la cultura que el pueblo maya empezó a desarrollar hace mas de 10 mil años, en el sur de la actual republica de México, en todo Belice y Guatemala, y en parte de Honduras y el Salvador. La civilización maya tiene sus raíces en

English	Spanish
Mayan civilization has its roots in humanity's pre-history. The Mayan culture for several millennia has been developing in what is today Guatemala, in some epochs with great splendor . . . We are Maya, the ones that carry the culture of our forefathers—more than 4 million Guatemalan that speak a Mayan language. We protect our Mother Nature, we maintain, to a certain extent, our own technology; and additionally, we identify as Mayas (roj, qawinaq; qawinaquil qi').	la prehistoria de la humanidad. La cultura maya, desde hace muchos milenios se ha venido desarrollando en la actual Guatemala, en algunas épocas con gran resplandor . . . [S]omos mayas los portadores de la cultura de nuestros antepasados los mas de 4 millones de Guatemaltecos que hablamos un idioma maya; que conservamos nuestra Madre Naturaleza; conservamos, en cierta medida, tecnología propia; y además, nos identificamos como mayas (roj, qawinaq; qawinaquil qi').
24. The numbers express the quantity or the order of things. In the Mayan languages, counting has a basis of 20 numbers, that is why it is said that it uses a *vigesimal* system. . . . The use of the system by the population has generally decreased. The elders still maintain and use part of the counting system. There are also books written in the past where one can research this system.	24. Los números expresan la cantidad o el orden de las cosas. En los idiomas Mayas la numeración tiene una base de 20 números, por eso se dice que se utiliza un sistema vigesimal. . . . El uso del sistema ha decaído de manera general en la población. Los ancianos todavía conservan parte del conteo. También hay libros escritos antiguamente donde se puede investigar sobre este sistema.
25. In books it is said that it was a conquest, and that is a traditionalist approach, but they never managed to reflect on the fact that it was an invasion.	25. En los libros dice que fue la conquista, y ese es un enfoque tradicionalista pero nunca llegaron a reflexionar que fue una invasión.
26. 80% of the Guatemalan population belong to Mayan descendants . . . even if we use current technology . . . biologically [referring to DNA] and anthropologically as well, even we do not know how to speak our languages.	26. El 80% de la población guatemalteca pertenece a la descendencia maya . . . Por mas que utilicemos la tecnología actual . . . biológicamente [refiriéndose al ADN] y antropológicamente también aunque no sepamos hablar nuestros idiomas.

27. Eats wheat bread habitually? Yes or no.
    Uses indigenous clothing habitually? Yes or no.
    If the person wears shoes, write "Z"; if he/she wears sandals "C"; if he/she is barefoot "D."
	27. ¿Come habitualmente pan de trigo? Si o No.
	    ¿Usa habitualmente traje indígena? Si o no.
	    Si la persona usa zapatos, anote "Z"; si usa caites "C"; si es descalzo "D."

28. The research on people who use some kind of shoes is important	28. La investigación de la población que usa alguna forma de calzado

(*Continued*)

Appendix 8 (Continued)

English	Spanish
because according to medical criteria many endemic or epidemic illnesses are related to whether people have their feet covered or uncovered when they walk.	tiene importancia pues existe el criterio medico que muchas enfermedades endémicas o epidémicas de la población guardan relación con el hecho de que la persona tenga o no cubiertos los pies para caminar.
29. Traditionally, in the Population Censuses: Indigenous is that one who does not wear shoes, does not speak Castilian Spanish and does not wear European kinds of clothing.	29. Tradicionalmente, en los Censos de Población: Indígena es aquel que no utiliza calzado, no habla castellano y no usa traje de corte europeo.
30. where there are two kids of people distinctly different in history, language, and culture	30. donde existen dos pueblos marcadamente diferentes en historia, idioma y cultura
31. We who are training to be teachers, . . . we should become that image of fishers, fishers of knowledge, fishers in evangelizing many children [living] in ignorance, to take that bread of knowledge to the students.	31. Nosotros que nos estamos convirtiendo para ser maestros . . . debemos convertirnos en esa imagen de ser pescadores, pescadores de saber, pescadores de evangelizar a muchos niños que en ignorancia, de llevarles ese pan de saber a cada uno de los estudiantes.
32. Well my goal after finishing 6th grade *magisterio*, is first of all to change the education that teachers are practicing, the traditional model, and then apply the new models I learned here in the new institute and apply them there in my community to improve the development of my community and the society.	32. Bueno mi meta es cuando cursar 6to magisterio, en primer lugar cambiar la educación que los maestros hoy están poniendo en practica, el modelo pedagógico tradicional, entonces aplicar los nuevos modelos que yo capte aquí en el Nuevo instituto y aplicarlo allá a mi comunidad para mejorar el desarrollo tanto de mi comunidad como de la sociedad.
33. Our parents did not take advantage of many things, and there are many communities that continue to not take advantage, so my purpose in teaching the kids is to change their mindset, and in some ways change their imagination, change their ways of reasoning so they become more sociable, so that they change from having that mentality of being lazy, of not doing anything to work or get something economic.	33. Nuestros padres desaprovecharon muchas cosas y hay muchas comunidades que lo siguen desaprovechando, entonces mi razón para llegar a enseñar a los niños es que cambiarles la mente, y de alguna forma abrirles la imaginación, la razón para que sean mas sociables y que cambien de que no tengamos esa mente de perezosos, de no hacer nada para trabajar o para conseguir algo de economía.

Appendix 9
Survey to Classify the *Indígena*

ENCUESTA A DEVOLVER

Clasificación DEPARTAMENTO DE Encuesta No. 1.
del indígena.

Municipio de .... Aldea ....
Nombre (y cargo) de quien llena esta encuesta ....
.... Fecha ....

EN ESTE MUNICIPIO UNA PERSONA ES INDIGENA:

1.—¿ Porque usa solo ropa indígena? Sí o no (subraye sí o no)

   a) Que prenda (s) de ropa al usarla (s), se pondría solamente una persona indígena: ....
....
....

1.—¿ Porque usa solo ropa indígena? Sí o no (subraye sí o no)

   a) Que prenda (s) de ropa al usarla (s), se pondría solamente una persona indígena: ....
....
....

2.—¿Porque habla lengua indígena? Sí o no (subraye sí o no)

   a) ¿Porque habla lengua indígena en su hogar? Sí o no (subraye sí o no)
   b) ¿Porque habla lengua todo el tiempo que puede? Sí o no (subraye sí o no)
   c) ¿Porque habla el castellano con diferencia de pronunciación Sí o no (subraye sí o no)

3.—¿Porque las costumbres de la persona son costumbres indígenas?   Sí o no (subraye sí o no)

   a) Sirvase poner a continuación cuales son esas costumbres *meramente* indígenas que sirven para decir que una persona es *indígena*:

COSTUMBRES INDIGENAS ....
....
....
....

4.—¿Es indígena una persona por la apariencia física? (Color de la piel, clase de pelo, etc.)   Sí o no (subraye sí o no)

   a) Si se usan estas razones de apariencia física, ¿cuáles son estos rasgos físicos que denotan a una persona como indígena en ese municipio?

RASGOS FISICOS ....
....
....
....

5.—Si una persona tiene apellido indígena, ¿se le considera como tal?   Sí o no (subraye sí o no)

   a) Si se tiene a una persona como indígena por su apellido, sirvase dar a continuación algunos de los apellidos indígenas más usuales en ese municipio.

APELLIDOS INDIGENAS ....
....
....

Observaciones adicionales: ....
....
....

Appendix 10
Chapter 4
Spanish Excerpts

English	Spanish
1. an important leap of quality that cannot be postponed	1. un salto de calidad importante que no se puede seguir postergando
2. Initial teacher education emerges as a response to the educational policies that include, among others, the push for development of each *Pueblo* and linguistic community, privileging intercultural relations, as well as the development of science and technology	2. La formación inicial docente se instituye como respuesta a las políticas educativas que incluyen, entre otras, el impulso de cada Pueblo y comunidad lingüística, privilegiando las relaciones interculturales, así como el desarrollo de la ciencia y la tecnología
3. Guatemalan women and men have the right to quality education. An education that ensures our integral formation as human beings, that allows us to reach the competencies that help us carry out our citizenship in a conscious manner, and that allows us to acquire the necessary skills to successfully perform in the world of work	3. Los guatemaltecos y las guatemaltecas tenemos derecho a una educación de calidad. Una educación que asegure nuestra formación integral como seres humanos, que nos permita alcanzar las competencias que nos ayuden a ejercer de manera consciente nuestra ciudadanía y nos permita adquirir las habilidades necesarias para desenvolvernos con éxito en el mundo de trabajo
4. Jorge Mario Joloma, a student from the Rafael Aqueche institute, reports that the student sector rejects the reforms to the teacher preparation study plan given that these do not include an improvement in the quality of education, but an extension of the study time from three to five years. Educational improvements will not be made just by increasing the	4. Jorge Mario Joloma, estudiante del Instituto Rafael Aqueche, indica que el sector estudiantil rechaza las reformas al plan de estudios magisterial debido a que éstas no contemplan una mejora en la calidad de la educación, sino solo una ampliación en el tiempo de estudio, de tres a cinco años. No se puede mejorar la calidad educativa aumentando los estudios a cinco

(*Continued*)

Appendix 10 (Continued)

English	Spanish
years of study to five., there are other factors that are truly affecting it, . . . he commented	años; existen otros factores que de verdad afectan, . . . comentó.
5. Here at Century we agree with curricular transformation [with the reform] because it is necessary and vital to change our society in Guatemala. We have deficiencies and one of them is that we are in last place in education, trapped already more than one hundred years . . . we need that transformation. This is vital to change our society so that there is better life development	5. Aquí en el instituto estamos de acuerdo con la transformación curricular por la razón de que es necesario y vital para cambiar nuestra sociedad en Guatemala. Tenemos deficiencias y una de ellas es que nos estamos quedando en el ultimo lugar de educación, atrapados ya hace mas de cien años . . . necesitamos esa transformación. Esto es vital para cambiar nuestra sociedad para que tenga un mejor desarrollo de vida.
6. Time evolves and involves It expands and contracts Moves in different directions Is not fixed	6. tiempo *evoluciona e involuciona* se expande y se contrae Se mueve en direcciones distintas No es fijo
7. Western monologic, linear, vectorial, or repetitive	7. Monológico occidental, lineal, vectorial, o repetitivo
8. Different from most Latin American countries, initial teacher preparation [in Guatemala] is not carried out in teachers' colleges or at the university	8. A diferencia de la mayoría de países latinoamericanos, la formación inicial docente en Guatemala no se realiza a nivel superior o universitario
9. A very true statement is that those cultures or peoples who don't read are dead. . . . Poor people, they are blind because they live in darkness . . . What would a teacher be? Teachers read, it is necessary to renew the spirit, in the same way that nature does it with matter. Teachers read, make an effort, as you do when you buy candy, a ticket to the movies, or a beer, and buy good books if you want to go, as Marden said, "always ahead," or if you want to live as the poet D'Anunzzio said: "always awake."	9. Los pueblos y los hombres que no leen son muertos, dice una sentencia muy cierta . . . Pobres gentes, son ciegos del alma porque viven en la oscuridad. . . ¿que será un maestro? Maestros leed, es necesario renovarse el espíritu tal como lo hace la naturaleza con la materia. Maestros leed, haced un esfuerzo, como lo hacéis para comprar una golosina, una luneta o un vaso de cerveza, y comprad buenos libros si queréis ir como digo Marden: "Siempre adelante" o si quieres vivir como digo el poeta D'Anunzzio: "Siempre despiertos"
10. [Wanted] workers, not useless drones of the social hive	10. [Quería] obreros y no zánganos de la colmena social
11. [we] have been deprived of advancements and achievements, and we have been, amongst other countries, submerged with the least	11. privarnos de avances y logros y nos han sumido entre los países con menos logros y falta total de calidad tanto en la formación de

English	Spanish
of achievements and the complete lack of teacher professionalism as well as the resulting didactic proposals. Thus the most affected ones are the citizens and the country . . . we are feeding underdevelopment, and backwardness worldwide, instead of providing and preparing ourselves as a nation for the very complex challenges of a globalized world, along with free trade agreements, and the urgency for productivity that is required to satisfy material and spiritual needs	maestros como en sus consecuentes propuestas didácticas. El mas afectado así, es el ciudadano y el país. . . . Estamos alimentando el subdesarrollo y el retraso a nivel mundial, en lugar de proporcionar y preprararnos como nación para los retos complejísimos del mundo globalizado, de los tratados de libre comercio, y de la emergencia de una productividad que pueda competir y satisfacer sus necesidades materiales y espirituales
12. Principles of the teaching career	12. Principios de la carrera docente
13. [t]he current model of initial teacher preparation in Guatemala has expired and needs to be renewed	13. El modelo de formación inicial docente de Guatemala se ha agotado y necesita renovarse
14. a special person, with a special vocation, with a special mission in Guatemalan society, and [sic] a specific role in the construction of the nation we want and [sic] a specific role in the construction of the nation we want	14. una persona especial, con una vocación especial, con una misión especial en la sociedad guatemalteca y un rol especifico en una construcción de la Nación que queremos y un rol especifico en la construcción de la Nación que queremos
15. If as a country we aspire to develop ourselves . . . [we must] start with the teachers who, with their education, conduct, and performance, will ensure better results in the educational processes	15. Si, como país, aspiramos a desarrollarnos . . . [debemos] empezar por los maestros, quienes con su formación, su conducta y su desempeño aseguran mejores resultados en los procesos educativos
16. Quality . . . is characterized by The [necessary] conditions to achieve educational quality [are]: . . . Rights Education for all The human," Sustainability Justice Equity Social context Past, present, future Skills for life Values Societal transformation	16. La calidad . . . se caracteriza por que Las condiciones [necesarias] para alcanzar la calidad educativa [son]: . . . Derechos Educación para todos Humanos Sostenibilidad Justicia Equidad Contexto social Pasado, presente, futuro Valores Transformar sociedades

(*Continued*)

Appendix 10 (Continued)

English	Spanish

17. Technical conditions to ensure quality
    Specific conditions established for the improvement of educational quality
    System for quality assurance
    Standards and curriculum
    Assessment
	17. Las condiciones técnicas para asegurar la calidad
	    Las condiciones especificas se establecen para el mejoramiento de la calidad
	    Sistema de aseguramiento de la calidad
	    Estándares y currículo
	    Evaluación

18. School management
    Instructional leadership
    Supervision and school leadership
    Pedagogic projects to improve learning
    Resources
    Support services . . . infrastructure, textbooks, libraries, technology, school food, others.
	18. Dirección escolar
	    Liderazgo pedagógico
	    Supervisión y dirección escolar
	    Proyectos pedagógicos enfocados en mejorar el aprendizaje
	    Recursos
	    Los recursos . . . infraestructura física, libros de texto, bibliotecas, tecnología, alimentación escolar y otros.

19. Human development
    Societal development
    . . . education for life and development
	19. Desarrollo humano
	    desarrollo . . . de la sociedad
	    . . . educación para la vida y para el desarrollo.

20. Objectives of the teaching career.
    suitable people
    Merits
    Qualities
    Development and professional growth
    Higher . . . merits, knowledge, and experiences
    Better qualified
    Better prepared
    Good education, and . . . better performance
	20. Objetivos de la carrera docente.
	    Personas idóneas
	    Méritos
	    Cualidades
	    Desarrollo y crecimiento profesional
	    Mayores . . . meritos, conocimientos y experiencias
	    Mas cualificados
	    Mejor desempeño
	    Buena formación, y . . . un buen desempeño.

21. to eliminate opportunism . . . incompetence, . . . inexperience, . . . traffic of influences . . .
    University level
    A superior level
    Obligatory
    . . . the advancement of science and technology to face the reality of teaching in the classroom and the school.
	21. eliminar el oportunismo, . . . la incompetencia, . . . la inexperiencia, . . . el trafico de influencias . . .
	    Nivel universitario
	    Nivel superior
	    Obligatorio
	    . . . los avances de la ciencia y la tecnología, para enfrentar la realidad de la practica docente en el aula y en la escuela.

22. [the] development of identities . . . [and] the knowledge and respect of other cultures and languages	22. [el] desarrollo de las identidades, . . . [y] el conocimiento y respeto de las demás culturas y los otros idiomas

English	Spanish

23. [dismantling] the curriculum of poverty in teacher professional development
    inclusive character for cultural diversity
	23. [desarmando] el currícula de pobreza del desarrollo profesional docente
	    carácter inclusivo por diversidad cultural

Appendix 11
Linguistics Program Guatemalan University and *Jóvenes* Institute Spanish Excerpts

Linguistics Program Guatemalan University

English	Spanish
1. the problems derived from multilingualism	1. the problemas derivados del multilingüismo
2. solid foundations [for] bilingual-bicultural education	2. bases sólidas [para] la educación bilingüe
3. address the problems that the educational system faces	3. los problemas que afronta el sistema educativo

Jóvenes Institute

English	Spanish
1. To the Institute are brought, from those towns and villages, the best equipped by nature and divine grace to be carefully formed in the human and the divine so that tomorrow, graduated as teachers, doctors, businessmen, hopefully also as priests, the conquest of Indians by Indians can begin	1. Se trae a este instituto de esos pueblos y aldeas, a lo mejor dotados por la naturaleza y la gracia divina, para cuidadosamente formarlos en lo divino y en lo humano a fin de que el día de mañana graduados de Maestros y Médicos, Industriales y ojala también de sacerdotes se inicie la conquista del indio por el mismo indio
2. Is a deed . . . by the Archbishopric of Guatemala in representation of the Church which continues the tradition of the first Bishop	2. Es obra . . . del arzobispo de Guatemala en representación de la Iglesia, que continua así la gloriosa tradición del Obispo Primero
3. founded schools in indigenous languages to go to the Indian to civilize him in his own language	3. fundado escuelas de lenguas indígenas para ir al indio y civilizarlo en su propia lengua
4. The church was the defender of the aboriginal race before the outrage of the conquerors who only wanted wealth and bounty from them	4. La iglesia fuéla [sic] defensora de la raza aborigen ante los desmanes conquistadores de quienes no querían sino riqueza y botín

(*Continued*)

Appendix 11 (Continued)

English	Spanish
5. The millennial sense of civilizing the aborigine	5. ese milenario sentido de civilizar al aborigen [sic]
6. making possible his intellectual and moral improvement	6. haciendo posible así su mejora intelectual o moral
7. His only ambition is drunkenness	7. Su única ambición es la embriaguez
8. Profound poverty of body	8. honduras de us [sic] pobreza de cuerpo
9. [The] Indian that is degenerating is the one the institute wants to regenerate	9. [el] indio que se degenera, quiere regenerar este instituto
10. Uproot his ancestral vices, and sow a new mode of life	10. arrancar vicios ancestrales y sembrar nueva modalidad de vida
11. Free from the oppressive and criminal chains of communism	11. Libre del yugo fanático y criminal del comunismo
12. Two millions of beings without school, without culture, without being an active part of the national richness, who does not produce or consume, and who do not know why they are Guatemalans	12. Dos millones de seres sin escuelas, sin cultura, sin ser parte activa en la riqueza nacional, sin producir y sin consumir, sin saber que son guatemaltecos

Index

academia 59, 171
Accord of the Identity and Rights of Indigenous Peoples (AIRIP, 1995) 44, 45, 52n31, 107
Accords for a Firm and Durable Peace (1996) 17, 41–2, 58, 190, 199; *see also* Guatemalan Armed Conflict, the (1960-1996)
Acevedo, Blanca Estela 69, 87n56, 90
Active School, the 147
Adams, Richard xxx, 21n8, 21n9, 23n15, 27, 108–9, 123n16, 123n18
Agreement on the Identity and Rights of Indigenous Peoples, the 144
AIRIP *see* Accord of the Identity and Rights of Indigenous Peoples
alphabetization 66, 69, 75, 85n41, 103–5
alphabets 3, 14, 38, 74, 77, 81, 79, 86n47, 89n85, 89n86, 100, 126n57, 127n62, 194, 206
anthropology 3, 5, 18, 24n21, 36, 41, 44, 66, 73, 95, 96, 100, 101, 109, 111, 115, 120, 121n2, 122n5, 124n22, 125n28, 195, 205
Annual Mayan Congress (2011) 140
Árbenz, Jacobo 66
archaeology 73, 115, 124n22, 140, 210
archives 6, 14, 15–16; *see also* Center for Mesoamerican Research; *Mira.*
Arévalo, Juan José 64, 66
Arriola, Jorge Luis 2, 21n8, 21n10, 27, 99–100, 123n14, 123n15, 123–4n19, 131
Asturias, Miguel Angel vii, xiii, xvii, 3–4, 7, 10, 22n13, 22n14, 27, 35–6, 42, 50n7, 50n9, 53n40, 54, 87n56, 90, 96, 122n6, 123n19, 123–4n19, 131, 187; *see also Universidad Popular*
authoritarian regimes 137–66

Balibar, Étienne 98, 122n11, 131
Bastos, Santiago 7, 10, 22n11, 25n28, 25n35, 28, 108, 113, 127n67, 127n70, 130–1n120, 131, 132
Batres Jáuregui, Antonio 35, 38, 42, 51n17, 51n18, 53n39, 54, 69, 87n56, 90
Bible, the 67, 71, 74, 88n75; *see also* Christianity; missionaries; religion; Wycliffe Bible Translators
Bilingual Intercultural Vice-Ministry *see Vicedespacho Bilingüe Intercultural*
bilingualism xxvii, 3, 8, 16, 46, 128n75, 193, 200
binary oppositions 72, 74, 112, 113, 142
biology 111, 154, 187, 213
Bonfil Batalla, Guillermo 99, 109, 122n7, 124n20, 132
borders: anthropological xvii, 5, 45, 46, 48, 65, 95–135, 176; containable 171; cultural 46; linguistic 62; national 35, 44, 45, 149, 171; open and closed 17, 46; *see also* linguistic territorialization; nation state, the
Britzman, Deborah 82, 90n105, 91
Bucaro, Jaime 86n45, 86n48, 91, 104, 126n42, 126n58, 127n63, 127n65, 132

campesinos xv, 19n1, 211
Caribbean xxv, 106–8, 160n16, 177n1
cartography 1, 52n21, 77; *see also* borders; nation state, the
Castellanización (Castilianization) 43,

66, 67, 75, 79, 85n41, 105, 162n34, 207; and the "illiteracy problem" 80
Castilian (language) 57, 67, 70, 79, 85n40, 100, 130n99, 203, 204, 207, 214; *see also* Spanish (language)
Castilianization *see Castellanización*
Catholic Church 22n12, 37, 50–1n13, 63–4, 70, 88n72, 88n74, 91, 145, 186, 191n3, 197–8
censuses, Guatemalan 50n13, 77–8, 80, 89n89, 90n91, 101, 111–12, 117, 130n99, 130n104, 197, 214; *see also* demography; statistics
Center for Mesoamerican Research (CIRMA) 2, 20n1, 23n15, 25n29, 27n59, 35–9, 51n15, 53n45, 64, 68, 70, 71, 113, 126n42, 175, 177, 181; *see also* archives; *Mira*.
Central American Pedagogic Congress 70, 85n40, 146, 147
Centro de Investigaciones Regionales de Mesoamerica *see* Center for Mesoamerican Research
Century Normal School (CNS) 16, 59, 98, 110, 140, 152, 181–4, 186, 204
children xxvi, 2, 36, 67, 68, 103, 108, 114, 117, 156, 177n1, 182, 207, 209, 211, 214
Chol 19n*, 112, 129n93
Christianity 37, 38, 66; and discourses of liberation 70, 88n72; *see also* missionaries; religion; religion-science tactics
Chronos 142; *see also* Kairos
CIRMA *see* Center for Mesoamerican Research
citizenship xxvi, 21, 139, 148, 191, 217; *see also* nation state, the
classroom xix, xxv, 9, 11, 13, 15–18, 34, 40, 45, 49–50n3, 52n28, 57, 59–64, 72, 82n3, 82n4, 82n5, 82n6, 87n57, 87n65, 88n70, 88n73, 89n76, 89n77, 90n100, 90n103, 90n104, 95–135, 142, 145, 150, 152, 154, 157–8, 164n75, 164n76, 173–5, 187, 190, 220; *see also* curriculum; educational research; National Base Curriculum; teacher education; textbooks
clothing 82n12, 101, 102, 112, 125–6n38, 129n95, 130n99, 176, 242, 245, 246; *see also* shoes; Spanish customs and styles

CNB *see* National Base Curriculum
CNS *see* Century Normal School
COCADI *see Coordinadora Cakchiquel de Desarrollo Integral*
Cojtí Cuxil, Demetrio 109, 110, 128n75, 129n80, 130n99, 130n104, 132
Collins, Wesley 71, 88n67, 91
colonialism 5, 20n157, 69
communism 66, 85, 157, 187, 224
Coordinadora Cakchiquel de Desarrollo Integral (COCADI) 109–11, 116, 124n20, 127n68, 127n71, 128n76, 129n80, 130n107, 130n110, 130n117, 132
Cortés, Fernando 98, 122n9, 133; *see also La presidenta municipal* (film, 1975)
cosmologies, indigenous 8, 24n26, 27n55, 84n23, 149, 152
cosmopolitanism 39
cultural pluralism 63, 95, 105, 107–19, 130–1n120, 212
Cumes, Aura 7, 10, 22n11, 25n28, 25n35, 28, 82, 113, 127n67, 128–9n76, 130n113, 130n120, 132, 133
curriculum 4–6, 9, 15–18, 23n17, 43, 58–61, 69, 70, 77, 82, 95, 99–100, 103, 104, 107, 110, 117–20, 122n10, 137–66, 170–80, 183, 186–7, 190–1, 211, 220–1; *see also* classroom; education; educational research; National Base Curriculum; teacher education; textbooks
customs 3, 5, 21, 101, 102, 108, 124, 193, 194, 210–11

Darwinism, social 37, 38, 69, 154
Dary, Claudia 42, 53n42, 55
de-Indian-ization 99
Deleuze, Gilles 13–14, 20–1n7, 25n37, 25n40, 25n41, 25n42, 26n45, 26n47, 26n49, 26n52, 26n53, 28, 54n49, 55, 72, 74, 88n71, 91, 163n72, 164
demography 11, 77, 100, 102, 111, 112, 115; *see also* censuses, Guatemalan; statistics
Derrida, Jacques 2, 20n6, 28, 34, 40, 47, 48, 51n19, 53n34, 54n51, 55, 75, 89n82, 91, 96, 122n4, 133, 164; *see also problēma*

development xviii, xxvi, 5, 14, 18, 22–3n15, 35, 37–8, 40–8, 51n20, 52, 66, 70–1, 73, 81, 86n47, 87n66, 88n72, 95–7, 105, 108–19, 127n62, 137–8, 140–50, 152–8, 159n5, 160n19, 160n20, 198–201, 204–6, 212–14, 217–21; *see also* progress; quality
Didi-Huberman, Georges 26n54, 28
difference xxvii, 4–5, 11, 15, 22n15, 39, 45, 46, 59, 77, 96, 100–1, 105, 108, 111–21, 149, 151, 170–2; *see also* diversity; making up kinds of people; Othering
Direction of Bilingual and Intercultural Education (DIGEBI) 46–7, 54n48; *see also Vicedespacho Bilingüe Intercultural*
dissensus *see* Rancière, Jacques
diversity xix, xx, xxv–xxviii, 1, 8, 15, 19n*, 33–56, 59, 62, 63, 72, 73, 74, 82n3, 86n43, 95–135, 154, 155, 158, 170–5, 200–1, 221; and education 1, 8, 95–135; and language 73, 74, 82n3, 86n51
Dussel, Inés 26–7n54, 28, 49n3, 55

education *see* classroom; curriculum; Educational Advancement Against Discrimination Law; educational research; National Base Curriculum; Normal Schools; teacher education; textbooks
Educational Advancement Against Discrimination Law (EAADL) (2002) 43
educational research 19n*, 148; *see also* classroom; curriculum; teacher education
England, Nora 71, 73, 84n28, 88–9n75, 91
Enlightenment, the 96, 125n31; and secularization of Judeo-Christian time 96
epistemologic death 2
Errington, Joseph 62, 83n11, 83n14, 84n21, 84n23, 84n24, 86n51, 87n53, 91
Estrada Cabrera, Manuel 43, 44, 52n29, 53n44, 55, 74, 78, 86n49, 89n78, 91, 146, 182; *see also Minervalias*
Estrada Paniagua, Felipe 44, 53n45

Europe xxv, 5, 36, 38, 44, 51n20, 60, 61, 62, 67, 68, 72, 73, 85n40, 86n51, 88n75, 99, 125n31, 130n99, 130n109, 151, 154, 156, 158, 163n53, 171, 182, 187, 204, 206, 214; *see also* modernity; Spain; Spanish (identity); West, the
event 1, 2, 11, 13–15, 17–18, 20n7, 25n39, 25n40, 26n45, 26n46, 37, 43, 57, 59, 63, 95, 97–100, 115–16, 119, 122n10, 158, 161n23, 171–2, 182; *see also* eventalizing
eventalizing 5, 11, 13, 16, 17, 25n39, 63, 170–2; *see also* event; moments of intensity
evolution 18, 35, 42, 43, 71, 86n51, 96, 107, 115, 116, 119; *see also* development
expert knowledge 11, 14, 17, 59, 96, 138

Fabian, Johannes 50n6, 96, 115, 120, 122n8, 130n118, 133
Facultad Latinoamericana de Ciencias Sociales (FLACSO) *see* Latin American Faculty of Social Sciences
FLACSO *see* Latin American Faculty of Social Sciences
flexia see von Schlegel, Friedrich
Foucault, Michel 14, 25n38, 26n51, 27n58, 29, 83n19, 91; and statements 14
fractals xx, 138–41; *see also* Fulani textiles; Mandelbrot, Benoît; mathematics
Francisco Marroquín Linguistic Project 71
Fulani textiles 139–41; *see also* fractals

"Garífuna" (identity) 22–3n15, 44–8, 97, 98, 106, 108, 118, 130n103, 200–1
Garífuna (language) 48
generacion de 1920 123–4n19
glyphs 7, 19n*, 110
Goubaud Carrera, Antonio 2, 3, 21n8, 25n36, 64, 100–5, 108, 112, 116, 122–3n13, 123n14, 123n19, 124n22, 124n23, 124n25, 125n33, 125n34, 125n36, 126n43, 126n46, 126n48, 126n49, 133, 194, 210; and 1946 social survey 100, 124n23, 124n25, 133

228 Index

Guatemala City 1, 14, 16, 36, 46, 48, 65, 179, 182, 186
Guatemalan Armed Conflict, the (1960–1996) 2, 19n1; *see also* Accords for a Firm and Durable Peace (1996)
Guatemalan Ministry of Education *see* Ministry of Education
Guatemalan University 16, 40, 63, 179, 223–4

Hacking, Ian 6, 9–10, 24n19, 24n23, 25n32, 29, 65, 85n37, 92, 121n2, 122n5, 133; and five-aspect dynamic framework 9
Hale, Charles R. 22n11, 24n20, 24n22, 25n29, 27, 29, 109, 122n12, 128n74, 130n105, 133
Help a Child 80, 90n100, 90n101, 90n103, 90n104, 187
Herbruger, Emil 35
history *see* memory
humor xxvi, 98, 114
hygiene 100

images xvii, xix, 14–16, 19–20n1, 26n54, 26–7n54, 33, 35–7, 44, 49, 49–50n3, 115, 118–19, 125–6n38, 144, 152, 155, 175–6; *see also* photography; visuality
immigration *see* migration
India María, la 97–8, 105–7, 113–18; *see also La presidenta municipal* (film, 1975)
indígena, lo xiii, xiv, xvii, xviii, xxviii, 4–31, 35, 39, 45, 49, 57–9, 65–7, 70, 95, 100–5, 110–11, 114–15, 138–9, 141, 154–8, 171, 193
"Indian problem," the 3, 4, 17, 21–2n10, 33–56, 69, 99, 108, 209; and Batres Jáuregui, Antonio 35, 38, 42, 51n17, 51n18, 53n39, 54, 69, 87n56, 90
"Indians" 2, 10, 36, 38, 51n18, 67, 69, 75, 77, 85n35, 100, 111, 127n71, 168, 186, 198, 223
Indigeneity xvii, 4, 7, 8, 43, 170; *see also* diversity; "Garífuna" (identity); "Indians"; *indígena, lo*; Ixil; *ladinización*; Xinca
indigenismo (indigenism) xiv, xviii, 3, 21n8, 86n47, 95, 98, 99–101, 105, 108, 109, 113, 115, 119, 122n12, 122n13, 124n21, 124n22, 124n23, 124n24, 126n51, 126n57, 127n62, 194, 209
Indigenous Languages Law 63
Instituto Indígena Santiago 3, 11, 22n12, 128n75, 194
Instituto Indigenista Nacional 21n8, 21n10, 25n36, 41, 123n16, 126n47
Interculturalism (*interculturalismo*) xiv, xv, xviii, xix, 14, 44, 48, 117, 118, 130n120, 145, 200–1; *see also* diversity
International Monetary Fund, the 77
integration; see *Ladinización*
Ixcán xxv, 1, 19n1, 46, 52–3n32, 63, 73, 88n74, 157, 173, 189–91
Ixil 1, 47, 54, 67, 72–4, 104, 110, 129n93, 130n103, 189, 205

Jóvenes Institute 16, 36, 63, 80, 185–7, 223–4

Kairos 142–3; *see also* Chronos
Kaqchikel (language) 40, 47, 54n54, 58–62, 72, 75, 81–2, 82n3, 86n47, 103, 105, 112, 126n57, 127n62, 175, 181–3, 203–4; *see also* Mayan (languages)
Kaqchikel (identity) 65, 105, 109, 128n76, 181–2
K'iche' 13, 36, 43, 73, 109, 112, 130n103, 175, 189, 205; *see also* Totonicapán

Ladino 5, 20n2, 21n9, 22–3n15, 36, 38–9, 42, 50n12, 51n18, 57, 65, 74, 79, 85n41, 97–8, 100–5, 108–16, 121n2, 123n14, 125n32, 130n103, 130n104, 187, 193, 197–8, 203, 207
ladinización 3, 21n9, 193–4
language *see* bilingualism; Castilian (language); Garífuna (language); Indigenous Languages Law; Kaqchikel (language); K'iche'; language heritages; linguistics; linguistic-oriented curriculum; linguistic territorialization; Mam (language); Mayan (languages); National Languages Law; *Pocomchí*; Spanish (language)
language heritages 57–94; arboreal 60, 72–5; and colonial practices 57, 60–2, 69, 75, 79, 82; and making up

kinds of people 59–81; performative effects of 60, 67; *see also* language
La presidenta municipal (film, 1975) 98, 122n9, 122n10; *see also* Cortés, Fernando
las Casas, Bartolomé de 100
Latin American Faculty of Social Sciences (FLACSO) 53n47, 55, 113, 127n67, 132
Latour, Bruno xxvii–xxviii, 25n27, 30, 61, 83n18, 92, 163n73, 165
law, the xvii–xviii, xxxi, 5, 33, 40–1, 43, 47–8, 53n37, 59, 63, 72, 107, 121n2, 125n32, 145, 158; and making up kinds of people xviii, 33, 121n2
liberalism 76
Lima Soto, Ricardo 148, 154, 162n41, 163n66, 163n67, 165
linguistic-oriented curriculum 16; *see also* bilingualism; logocentrism
linguistics xxxi, 17, 18, 43, 59–94 223–4; *see also* bilingualism; linguistic-oriented curriculum; Summer Institute of Linguistics
Linguistics School (Mariano Gálvez University) xxxi, 70
linguistic territorialization 61–3, 84n26; *see also* borders; logocentrism; nation state, the
literacy xxvi, xxvii, 13, 17, 36–39, 66–7, 71, 75–80, 83n10, 85n41, 86n47, 89n85 126n57, 127n62, 146, 204; *see also* logocentrism
lo indígena see *indígena, lo*
logocentrism 51n19, 75; *see also* Derrida, Jacques; linguistic-oriented curriculum; linguistic territorialization
López, Carlos 24–5n26, 30, 88n75, 92, 140–1, 159n12, 159n13, 160n14, 165

magisterio 117, 123n14, 137, 138, 143, 146, 153, 157, 158n3, 160n19, 161n21, 161n23, 161n27, 184n4, 187, 191n6, 191n7, 191n9, 214; *see also* teacher training
making up kinds of people xviii, 6–11, 15–18, 20n2, 33, 38, 67, 75, 77, 95–6, 99–100, 121n2, 138, 146, 151, 154, 172–5
Mam (language) 54n54, 57, 61, 64, 73, 81–2, 86n47, 87n66, 104, 105, 112, 126n57, 127n62, 129n93, 130n103, 189, 205; *see also* Mayan (languages)
Mandelbrot, Benoît 141, 144, 145; *see also* fractals
manifestación (protest) 1, 139, 143, 149, 155–6
maps 1, 12, 13, 52n21, 52n30, 65, 74, 77, 78, 82–3n8, 84n26, 181, 189, 199
Mariano Gálvez University *see* Linguistics School
marronage 169
Marroquín, Francisco 71, 79, 186
mathematics 38, 39, 51–2n20, 52n21, 141; *see also* fractals; science; statistics
Maxwell, Judith 71
Mayan calendar 24n26, 82n6, 140, 159n11
Mayan (identity) xxvi–xxvii, 8, 20n4, 22–3n15, 26n48, 35–6, 40, 44, 45, 50n12, 52n31, 65, 72–3, 106–7, 109–10, 140, 170, 175, 182, 186, 195, 200, 212–13; history of 35, 73, 107, 110, 115; and Popol Wuj 73–4, 115, 138, 140, 206; *see also* Mayan archaeological sites; Mayan efflorescence; *mayanización*
Mayan (languages) xxvi, 8, 14, 46–8, 54n54, 61, 62–3, 70–3, 107, 110, 138, 140, 182, 194, 205, 213; Mayan Languages Academy 72, 158; *see also* alphabets; glyphs
Mayan archaeological sites 14; and Mayan identity 10, 110–11; and periodization 35, 182
Mayan efflorescence 3, 22n11; *see also* Mayan (identity)
mayanización xxvii, 3, 7, 22n11, 25n28, 25n35, 112, 113, 115, 117, 127n67, 130n120
Mbembé, Achille 54n50, 56, 89n81, 93, 128n76, 134
McQuown, Norman 67, 71, 82n8, 93, 104
memory xxvii, 1, 3, 14, 26n50, 57, 194
Menchú Tum, Rigoberta 13, 19n1, 26n44, 30, 36, 170
Mesoamerica 5, 6, 10, 73, 90n91, 191
mestizos 13, 36, 57, 100, 111, 116, 197, 203

230 Index

Mexico 21n8, 22–3n15, 36, 52, 98, 103, 150, 161n22, 172, 189, 199, 212
migration 14, 50–1n13, 73, 84n23, 95, 103, 105, 113, 114, 119, 173–6, 189, 198
MinEduc *see* Ministry of Education
Minervalias ("festivals of instruction") 43, 53n44, 86n49; *see also* Estrada Cabrera, Manuel
Ministry of Education (MinEduc) (Guatemalan) xxvi, 8, 41, 42, 46, 53n33, 77, 84n28, 87n66, 97, 123n14, 123n18, 138, 139, 141, 143, 147–54, 159n5, 159n6, 180
Mira. 18–19, 51n15, 173–7; *see also* archives; Center for Mesoamerican Research
missionaries 57–94, 97, 126n53, 127n62, 206
modernity 37, 44, 50n12, 69, 101, 121, 146–7, 150, 205
modernization 38, 51n14, 70
Moller, Jonathan ("Jonás") 1, 2, 19–20n1, 30
moments of intensity 2, 5, 14, 17, 18, 20n7, 33, 57, 60, 63–4, 66, 71, 76–8, 80–1, 95, 98, 105, 107, 109, 119, 137, 142, 145, 171; *see also* eventalizing
Morley, Sylvanus 107, 109, 123n18
morphology 71, 86n47, 87n65, 127n62, 180
multiculturalism xiv–xix, xxvii, 18, 22n11, 41, 105, 107–9, 112–13, 117–18, 128n74, 128n75, 130–1n120, 176; *see also* pluralism

National Academy of Teachers, the 79
National Base Curriculum (CNB) 43, 58, 60, 107, 145, 187
National Congresses of Pedagogy 147
National Education Organic Law (1962) 41, 145
national identity 48, 51n16, 201
National Languages Law (2003) 43, 47–48, 107
nation state, the xxvi, 22–3n15, 76, 144, 146–7, 149, 171–3; *see also* borders; citizenship; linguistic territorialization
Nebaj 1, 2, 104
necropolitics *see* Mbembé, Achille
Netherlands, The 113

neoliberalism 160n20
NGOs (Non-Government Organizations) 72, 109, 118, 121n2, 180, 187, 212
Normal Schools xxv, 16, 59, 98, 108, 110, 123n14, 140–6, 151–2, 157, 158n3, 160n19, 181–4, 186, 189–91, 204
Norway 113, 172

OECD *see* Organisation for Economic Co-operation and Development
Organisation for Economic Co-operation and Development (OECD) 51–2n20, 137
Othering 45; *see also* Indigeneity; Orientalism
Orientalism 52n22, 52n26, 84n20; *see also* Said, Edward
Oxlajuj B'ak'tun 140, 159n11

periodization 24n18; *see also*: stagist logic
petate 170, 177n1
philosophy 45, 51n19, 145, 146, 183, 200
photography 17, 35–7, 43, 50n11, 125–6n38; *see also* images; visuality
PISA *see* Program for International Student Assessment
platicas (informal interviews) 16
pluralism 63, 87n52, 95, 105–31, 212; *see also* multiculturalism
Pocomchí 103, 112, 129n93, 211
de Pontelle, Leon 35
Poole, Deborah 33, 49n2, 56
Popol Wuj 24–5n26, 73–4, 79, 88–9n75, 123n18, 138, 140–1, 159n12, 160n14, 187, 206
Poqomam 47, 54n54, 130n103
Perez Molina, Otto 137
pragmatism 147
prehension 14
problēma 17, 34, 40, 45; *see also* Derrida, Jacques; "Indian problem", the
Program for International Student Assessment (PISA) 51–2n20, 137
progress xviii, 35, 43–4, 49, 78, 103, 108, 115, 119, 129n2, 127n71, 137, 146–7, 150, 173, 200, 211; *see also* development; liberalism; modernity; quality

Index 231

protest see *manifestación*
Propuesta de Carrera Docente, Parte Académica, y Técnico-Administrativa (Teaching Career proposal) 138, 148, 159n6; see also *magisterio*; teacher training
pueblos 98, 108–12, 117, 127–8n71, 128n76, 159n5, 200, 203, 206, 212, 217; see also "Garífuna;" Ladino; Mayan (identity); Xinka

Q'anjobal 73, 205
Q'eqchi' 104–5; see also Mayan (languages)
quality 4, 108, 137–48, 150–7, 160n17, 161n26, 162n48, 162n52, 163n63, 195, 217–20; see also development; progress
Quetzaltenango 36, 64, 77, 88n75, 183
Quiriguá 7, 35, 123n18

Rabinal 1, 19n1, 68
race 22n12, 49n2, 69, 70, 85n40, 102, 111, 122n11, 126n45, 186, 194–5, 204, 223; see also *mestizos*
Rafael Landivar University 70, 71, 87n63, 88–9n75
Redfield, Robert 101, 111, 124n22, 125n27, 125n30, 125n32, 125n35, 129n82, 134
Rancière, Jacques 155, 163n71, 165
reality 13–14, 24–5n26, 40, 46, 65, 72, 85n41, 88n72, 102, 143, 146, 154, 170, 199, 220
regime xiv, xvii, 49n3, 123n14, 137–66
religion xv, xix, 38, 59–60, 63–7, 72–3, 85n35, 154, 187; see also Christianity; missionaries; religion-science tactics
religion-science tactics 63–7, 73; see also religion; science
Rural Bilingual Intercultural Normal School see Normal Schools

Sacatepéquez (San Juan) 1, 61, 86n47, 105, 127n62, 183; protest (2012) *12*, 13, *34*
Said, Edward 40, 52n22, 52n26, 56, 62, 84n20, 93; see also Orientalism
Sam Colop, Luis Enrique 24–5n26, 31, 88–9n75, 93, 109–10, 127n68, 128n72, 129n80, 134, 159n12, 165

science xvii, xix, 4, 5, 6, 10, 15, 17, 19n*, 24n20, 27n55, 38–9, 43–4, 47, 51–2n20, 52n22, 63–7, 72–3, 78, 86n51, 97, 116, 137, 146, 154, 159n5, 169–70, 200, 217, 220; see also religion-science tactics; social science, statistics
Scott, Rubi 103–4
self definition 110, 112
Seminar of Social Integration, the 145
shoes 35, 38, 90n91, 100, 111–12, 115, 129n95, 129n96, 130n99, 198, 213, 214
SIL see Summer Institute of Linguistics
Sinca see Xinka
skits 97–98, 107, 110, 114, 118, 122n10
slavery 36, 168, 197
social Darwinism see Darwinism, social
social mobility 3, 21n9, 105, 193–4
social science xvii, xix, xxvii, xxviii, 6, 8, 19n*, 24, 70, 100, 113, 183
Socio Economic Committee, the 142
Spain 113, 182; see also West, the
Spanish (language) 4, 10, 22–3n15, 43–8, 52n32, 59, 61–2, 65, 67–8, 70–1, 79, 81–2, 82n3, 86n47, 86n51, 103, 112, 125n32, 126n57, 127n62, 158n3, 175, 187, 195, 200, 205–6, 211, 214 ; see also bilingualism; Castilian (language); National Languages Law
Spanish (identity) 10, 38, 51n18, 61, 62, 69, 83n13, 84n22, 86n51, 88n75, 110, 130n109, 182, 190, 198, 205
stagist logic 42, 47–8, 116
statistics 5, 89n89, 142, 169, 170, 179, 191; see also censuses, Guatemalan; demography; science
Stavenhagen, Rodolfo 109
subject formation 72–3
Summer Institute of Linguistics (SIL) 64–73, 84n28, 84n29, 85n33, 85n35, 85n41, 87n65, 103–5, 181, 204; see also missionaries; Townsend, William Cameron; Wycliffe Bible Translators
surveys 2–3, 21n9, 40, 62, 71, 84, 87n65, 100–2, 105, 116, 125n34, 193–4, 199, 210, 215–16

232 Index

Tax, Solomon (Sol) 21n8, 108, 124n22, 125n27, 125n35, 127–8n71, 134
teacher education 2, 5–6, 8, 13–18, 53n33, 59–60, 64, 69, 76, 95, 104, 110, 122n10, 128n73, 137, 140–158, 158n3, 159n5, 160n16, 160n19, 182–183, 183–184n3, 190–191, 217 see also classroom; curriculum; educational research; missionaries; textbooks
teachers see teacher education
Tedlock, Barbara and Dennis 88–9n75, 107
territorialization see linguistic territorialization
textbooks 14, 65, 84n28, 115, 118–21, 146, 152, 180, 187, 220; see also classroom; curriculum; teacher education
Thomson, Eric S. 107
Totonicapán 77, 123n14; massacre (2012) 13, 26n43
Townsend, William Cameron 65–6, 69, 79, 85n32, 87n56, 94, 126n53, 134; see also missionaries; Summer Institute of Linguistics; Wycliffe Bible Translators
Tzul Tzul, Gladys 121
Tz'utujil 47, 54n54, 130n103

Ubico, Jorge 1, 9, 99, 123n18
Universidad Popular 36; see also Asturias, Miguel Ángel
United Nations, the 77
United States, the xx, xxv, 44, 49n3, 66, 84n28, 87n66, 89n89, 99, 101, 103, 109, 113, 150, 152, 154, 156, 172, 175–6, 187; see also West, the

Valdeavellano, Alberto G. vii, xiii, xvii, 34, 35–6, 38, 50n4, 51n15
Valdés, J. Refugio 79, 90n93, 90n99, 94

Van Akkeren, Ruud 107
Vicedespacho Bilingüe Intercultural (Bilingual Intercultural Vice-Ministry) xxv, 8, 16, 40, 43, 52n28, 110, 157, 187, 189–90; see also bilingualism; Direction of Bilingual and Intercultural Education (DIGEBI); intercuturalism
Visuality 33, 49–50n3; see also images, photography
von Schlegel, Friedrich 86n51; and flexia 68

Watkins, Mark Hanna 67, 86n47, 104, 126n57, 127n62
Wendell, Margarita 103–4, 126n52, 134
West, the 14, 27n55, 38, 44, 50n12, 86, 100, 102–3, 107, 115–16, 125n31, 125n32, 125n38, 130n108, 140, 150, 154–5, 187, 211, 218; see also Europe; modernity; Spain; Spanish (identity); United States, the
Winak 52n30, 70–1, 83n16, 85n36, 87n61, 87n62, 87n63, 87n64, 87n65, 87n66, 88n67
World Bank, the 77
Wycliffe Bible Translators (WBT) 65–6, 84n28, 85n33, 126n53; see also missionaries; Summer Institute of Linguistics; Townsend, William Cameron

Xinca see Xinka
Xinka (Xinca, Sinca) 23, 40, 44–8, 52n30, 61, 97–8, 104–6, 108, 118, 130n103, 199, 200–1, 212; see also Indigeneity; pueblos
Xon, Maria Jacinta 121

Zanotti, Tomás 35–9, 43; Portrait of a First Communion 37